IMMORTAL LONGINGS

From a Photograph by Mrs F.W.H.Myers .   Photogravure by Annan & Sons, Glasgow

Frederic WH Myers
Photograph taken by Eveleen Myers *circa* 1890

IMMORTAL LONGINGS

FWH MYERS AND THE VICTORIAN
SEARCH FOR LIFE AFTER DEATH

Trevor Hamilton

imprint-academic.com

Published in the UK by Imprint Academic
PO Box 200, Exeter EX5 5YX, UK

Published in the USA by Imprint Academic
Philosophy Documentation Center
PO Box 7147, Charlottesville, VA 22906-7147, USA

ISBN 9 781845 401238 hardback
ISBN 9 781845 402488 paperback

A CIP catalogue record for this book is available from the
British Library and US Library of Congress

FOR

ANNE, DAN AND RALPH

Contents

Plate Sections between pages 110–111 and 198–199

Illustrations

Acknowledgements

I would like to thank the following institutions for permission to reproduce material: The Master and Fellows of Trinity College, Cambridge; the Syndics of the Cambridge University Library with regard to the Society for Psychical Research archive; the University of Liverpool Library (Josephine Butler papers); the University of St Andrews Library (special Collections); the West Glamorgan Archive Service (Tennant papers); the Royal Museum of Central Africa (Stanley papers); the Council of the Society for Psychical Research; the College of Psychic Studies; the University Press of Virginia (Correspondence of William James); the Mary Evans Picture Library (plate 18); the Tate Gallery, London (plate 1) and the National Portrait Gallery, London (plates 5 and 17).

Other quotations are of short passages, within the accepted guidelines, for the purpose of criticism and discussion and are fully attributed. Any errors in accuracy or non or incorrect attribution are apologised for and will be corrected in any future edition.

I wish to acknowledge, with gratitude, some financial support for this research from the Perrott-Warrick Trust.

My thanks to members of the Myers and other families who contributed background information.

A study like this which cuts across many topics and disciplines runs a high risk of making multiple errors. I would like to thank most warmly Bernard Carr, Alan Gauld, Emily Kelly, Leslie Price, Richard Tillett, Andreas Sommer and Rupert Sheldrake for reading part or all of the text and saving me from many mistakes. For those that remain I take full responsibility.

My deepest debt is to my wife Anne. She has provided me with considerable moral, emotional and intellectual support during the writing of this book and I dedicate it to her, and to our sons, Daniel and Ralph.

Trevor Hamilton
March 2009

MYERS FAMILY TREE

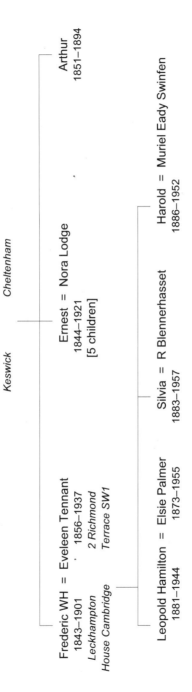

Frederic Myers = Susan Marshall
1811–1851   1811–1896
Keswick   *Cheltenham*

Frederic WH = Eveleen Tennant
1843–1901   1856–1937
Leckhampton *2 Richmond*
House Cambridge *Terrace SW1*

Ernest = Nora Lodge
1844–1921
[5 children]

Arthur
1851–1894

Leopold Hamilton = Elsie Palmer
1881–1944   1873–1955

Silvia = R Blennerhasset
1883–1957

Harold = Muriel Eady Swinfen
1886–1952

MARSHALL FAMILY TREE (SELECTIVE)

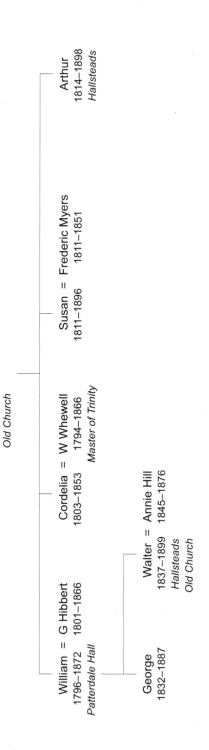

John Marshall = Jane Pollard
1765–1845   1770–1847
Hallsteads
Old Church

William = G Hibbert
1796–1872 1801–1866
Patterdale Hall

Cordelia = W Whewell
1803–1853   1794–1866
Master of Trinity

Susan = Frederic Myers
1811–1896   1811–1851

Arthur
1814–1898
Hallsteads

Walter = Annie Hill
1837–1899 1845–1876
Hallsteads
Old Church

George
1832–1887

John and Jane Marshall had 5 boys and 7 girls in all.
The full Marshall family tree is in *Marshalls of Leeds*, WG Rimmer, 1960, Cambridge U.P.

TENNANT FAMILY TREE (SELECTIVE)

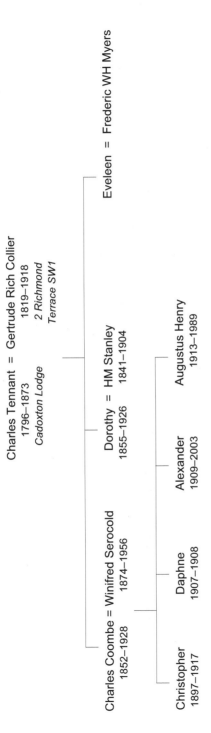

Charles Tennant = Gertrude Rich Collier
1796–1873   1819–1918
Cadoxton Lodge   2 Richmond
                 Terrace SW1

Charles Coombe = Winifred Serocold
1852–1928   1874–1956

Dorothy = HM Stanley
1855–1926 1841–1904

Eveleen = Frederic WH Myers

Christopher
1897–1917

Daphne
1907–1908

Alexander
1909–2003

Augustus Henry
1913–1989

Charles and Gertrude Tennant had four girls and one boy in all.
The full Tennant family tree is in the catalogue of Tennant papers (D/DT Vol 3), West Glamorgan Archive Service Swansea.

Introduction

When he [Myers] encountered someone whose aims and outlook were not unlike his own, he would cleave to him with a profound sense of comradeship in the Endless Voyage and would give him the most unbounded sympathy and support (Gauld 1968: 331).

Myers is a good looking fellow ... and a very intense and energetic character, suggesting despotism, meanness and all sorts of things lurking in the background which I didn't altogether like (Skrupskelis *et al.* 1998: 513)

As the above quotations indicate, Frederic William Henry Myers was a complex and original personality who provoked a range of contradictory responses from both contemporaries and later scholars who studied his life and work. The problem of understanding and assessing him and his achievements is further complicated by the fact that he was working in the hugely complex, novel and contested field of psychical research. This is an area which has often laid its participants open to charges of fraud, sexual indiscretion, financial gain, or just plain mischief making, as researchers struggle to get to the fundamental explanations for apparently anomalous phenomena. Nor does the marginal nature of the subject matter help. Both lack of interest and lack of knowledge by academics and other writers have allowed, more easily and frequently than in mainstream disciplines, the circulation of untested assertions and inaccurate facts. Finally, the situation has become even more entangled in recent years, as cultural historians, in varying degrees under the influence of postmodernist theoretical perspectives, have seen the records of late-Victorian psychical research as rich sources of evidence for their varied inter-textual readings of the *fin de siècle*. Much of this material is imaginative, enriching and insightful. But it is sometimes at the expense of fairness and accuracy, and the reputations of Myers and his close colleagues have, to some extent, suffered because of the sheer variety of the perspectives from which their work has been approached.

Evidence of the marginality of the subject, and therefore of the tendency to errors of both fact and interpretation to creep in, can be demonstrated by the way it is sometimes treated in general histories. It is interesting to speculate that there may be a greater unconscious bias towards error in such works, whenever psychical research is touched on, because the author, no doubt an admirable scholar in other respects, feels the subject beneath him or somehow dubious, even bogus. For example, both the references to Myers in Searle's volume in the New Oxford History of England (Searle 2004: 640–41) are wrong. Myers was not an Oxford-trained philosopher. He was a Cambridge-trained classicist. His classic book *Human Personality and Its Survival of Bodily Death* was published in 1903 and not in 1886–87.

Neither have more specialist writers, who have used the files of the SPR (Society for Psychical Research) for cultural, social or intellectual history purposes, necessarily been more accurate. They have avoided the obvious howlers and have often shown considerable ingenuity and depth of reading in their work, but have sometimes relied too exclusively in interpretation on one or two standard anti spiritualistic or psychical research sources (Hall 1980a, Brandon 1983). For example, Roger Luckhurst (Luckhurst 2002: 74–75), while acknowledging Hall's persuasive mix of character assassination and careful archival work, has indicated no awareness of the criticisms of that work by Alan Gauld (Gauld 1964) and Fraser Nicol (Nicol 1966). And both Luckhurst and Pamela Thurschwell seem to think that the case for telepathy, put forward by Myers and the SPR, was almost solely based on the work of the Creerys (experiments initially in the family of a clergyman) and the Blackburn/Smith (two young men from Brighton; one a journalist the other a stage mesmerist) experiments. Therefore, to cast doubt on both these was taken to mean that there was little evidence at all for it (Thurschwell 2004: 504). This ignores considerable other material tending (in some eyes) to support the existence of telepathy and which is listed as an appendix of Gauld's classic history of psychical research (Gauld 1968: 356–60). There are also subtler criticisms and as these impinge on Myers' character and achievements, they will be dealt with at the appropriate places in the main text.

However, these inaccuracies are minor fare compared to the convoluted and circumstantial thesis developed by Trevor H Hall to account for the death in 1888 of Edmund Gurney, Myers' co-worker in the SPR and closest friend. Hall (Hall 1980a: ix–xv) argued that Gurney committed suicide, having discovered that Smith and Blackburn had duped him. He further asserted that Myers, other senior members of the SPR, and his brother AT Myers, a medical doctor, covered this up and used their social status to persuade the jury to return a verdict of accidental death. More generally, Myers emerges as the villain of Hall's book, self-seeking, sloppy in research, untrustworthy, and a philanderer. In his introduction, which is warmly supportive of Hall's thesis, psychologist Elliot Slater even labels Myers 'psychopathological' (Hall 1980a: xxix). As we have seen, Hall's work and theses have been strongly challenged. But some of the mud has stuck and entered general academic discourse when writing about this period.

Why does any of this matter? There are several reasons. Firstly, Myers was a very distinguished figure in his own time. He had contacts of varying degrees of intensity and warmth with many leading late-Victorian figures: Browning, Tennyson, Swinburne, George Eliot, Stevenson, Ruskin, Balfour, HM Stanley, and the James brothers. He was also an outstanding classicist and his essays and correspondence provide insights into the changing attitudes towards the classics as the nineteenth century progressed. In addition, Robert Stein (Stein 1968: iii) has argued that Myers' theoretical and practical contribution to Victorian Letters illustrates, more effectively than that of any other significant individual, the impact of psychical research on the culture of the time. He was also a very popular poet and his intense and sensuous religious poem *St Paul* went through sixteen editions by 1900 (Stein 1968: 114).

Secondly, his life provides considerable insights into the social and cultural history of the period. He was something of a snob, was very close to Prince Leopold (Queen Victoria's youngest son) and wrote a widely (though not universally) praised memoir of him after his death (Myers 1884a: 611–24). Myers was on the outer fringes of the late-Victorian country house week-end circuit and his letters to his wife Eveleen provide revealing glimpses of that leisurely and vanished form of socialising. Eveleen herself showed considerable creative gifts as a photographer, and demonstrated that even then, given social position and income, it was quite possible for a woman to have a substantial independent identity and set of interests. Myers also pursued a long professional career as one of Her Majesty's Inspectors of Schools, a creature far more gilded and terrifying than today's functionary, and he played a substantial part, too, in the early movement for the higher education of women. On a more intimate level, Myers has been cited (Grosskurth 1964: 114–15) as an example, along with the Sidgwick brothers, Roden Noel (a minor poet), and JA Symonds, of the closet Victorian homosexual assailed with guilt and leading a double life.

Thirdly and most importantly, Myers, through his work with the Society for Psychical Research, made huge contributions to the study of hypnosis and abnormal psychology (along with Henry Sidgwick and the SPR, he supported and made significant inputs to the first four international congresses of psychology from 1889 to 1900) and towards the general development of psychodynamic approaches to the mind. That contribution was recognised in some quarters at the time of his death, but through most of the twentieth century his reputation dipped, his insights and researches were ignored, and it is only in the last twenty years (and particularly in the last decade) that there has been a substantial re-evaluation of his status. In fact, Myers' ideas continue to have resonance both with regard to the early history of psychology and to our current debates about the nature of consciousness (Kelly *et al.* 2007).

Myers raised, in the context of psychical research, the fundamental issues of the nature of consciousness and mind/body/brain relationships that are as relevant as ever in the age of neuroscience. In articles in the SPR's *Journal* and *Proceedings* and in his book, he undertook a massive survey of the unusual but not necessarily abnormal spread of human talents and capacities. His ultimate aim was to arrange this material in such a way that it would lead to, even if it could not actually prove, the conclusion that humankind had an inner transcendental core or individuality that would survive bodily death. Regardless of whether he achieved that objective, his work was extremely valuable, both as source material and as the expression of a developing theoretical perspective, which had some considerable influence on the work of major figures like Flournoy, Freud, Jung and James.

It was an ambitious attempt to move the SPR on beyond the heavily descriptive and anecdotal work of its early years. He was trying to use Darwinian classification methods to show that normal, abnormal and paranormal phenomena were related manifestations of the same core processes. William James, in 1901, recognised this comparative methodological approach as a significant contribution to the young science of psychology, just as he also acknowledged the explanatory, optimistic and creative potential of Myers' concept of the 'Subliminal Self' (James 1960: 223, 225). Myers, in contrast to some, though by no means all, contemporary intellectuals, believed that humanity was not degenerating, but in an evolutionary and progressive state. As more and more psychological processes became mastered, automatic, unconscious, the evolving human being would bring further latent capacities, like telepathy, clairvoyance, and telekinesis, out of the subliminal self and under the active control of the supraliminal self of normal, daily consciousness. So much so, he argued, that the human species had no idea what it might ultimately become.

Modern researchers rightly categorise much of his work as anecdotal and descriptive, his generalisations as sometimes too windy and unsubstantiated, and his prose style as strained and archly poetic. Yet, it is difficult to find anything in the later literature that approaches the breadth, depth and impact of *Human Personality and Its Survival of Bodily Death*. Henri Ellenberger's verdict was that he was 'not only a parapsychologist but also one of the great systematizers of the notion of the unconscious mind' (Ellenberger 1994: 314). His posthumous book should not be seen as the literary equivalent of a museum of Victorian curiosities.

In addition, his life is also interesting and moving in its own right. He fell in love with a cousin's wife and she with him. The husband was erratic, careless in his finances, manic depressive, syphilitic, and was eventually confined, for a while, to a mental asylum. Myers and the woman, Annie Marshall (who had five children), vowed that their relationship would be platonic, as expressed in one of Myers' poems: 'And the darkness of death is upon her, the light of his eyes is dim, But Honour has spoken, Honour, enough for her and for him' (Myers 1961: 19). She, however, went into severe depression after the removal of her husband to the asylum (caused by deep guilt at her part in his confinement and possible awareness of his syphilitic condition) and drowned herself in Ullswater, after having first attempted to cut her throat with scissors.[1] Myers remained devoted to her memory, and her apparent return through the mediums Mrs Piper and Mrs Thompson was a significant contribution to his final belief in life after death. However, even though he told his wife about the relationship, which had ended long before his marriage, and, according to most commentators, was spiritual and supportive and not physical, the episode coloured both his later life and his post mortem reputation (Beer 1998: 117–88).

His wife, Eveleen, probably did not realise the full intensity and depth of his feeling for Annie Marshall, even though he had told her about it at the time of their marriage. On his death, she tried to get, into her possession, all the copies of Myers' privately printed autobiography (Myers 1961), in which the relationship was described, and which Myers had sent out to a small number of intimate friends. She was also hugely critical of soi-disant post-mortem messages coming from mediums which hinted tangentially at this past love and the environments in which it flowered. These communications were interpreted by some at the SPR as, apparently, part of 'Myers'' efforts to provide evidence of his continued existence. This attitude of Eveleen Myers both hampered psychical research at the time and had an unintended and damaging effect on Myers' reputation years later. In the interests of science, Sir Oliver Lodge (a prominent physicist, a believer in life after death and leading member of the SPR), refused to return his copy to her. Nor was the copy belonging to Henry

---

1   See further pp. 39–47 below.

Sidgwick (Cambridge philosopher and several times President of the SPR) sent back. Mrs Myers published a highly expurgated version in 1904 but, in spite of several attempts by Lodge and others over the years, a full version was not printed till 1961, and that by the SPR itself (Myers 1904, Myers 1961). This prompted a hostile review by Archie Jarman in the magazine *Tomorrow*, a counter-riposte by Alan Gauld in the pages of the SPR journal, then a privately circulated pamphlet by Jarman in which he accused Myers of being both a philanderer and a homosexual. He threw in cheat and plagiarist for good measure. There was then a final rejoinder by Gauld to these charges (Jarman 1964, Gauld 1964, Jarman 1964, Gauld 1966).

The substance of these accusations will be examined at the appropriate place in the text, but putting the detail aside for the moment, Myers reputation appears to have been caught up in a battle between different groupings and factions within the SPR. Jarman was a lively and independent journalist, and he particularly drew attention to the serialisation in the *Sunday Times* in 1964 of Grosskurth's biography of JA Symonds, which revealed the homosexuality of Symonds, the Sidgwicks, and Myers. He argued that 'such types' then and now were unfit to be researchers or public servants. Whether or not this was tongue in cheek and intended to flutter and agitate any closet homosexuals in the SPR (for homosexuality was still illegal in the early 1960s in the UK) cannot, at this stage, be ascertained. What is clear, however, is that his pamphlet was part of a wider onslaught on the SPR founders and their methods, which was launched by Trevor H Hall and supported to some extent by Eric J Dingwall (veteran psychical researcher of pronounced independent and sceptical cast of mind), who was a thorn in the flesh of those in the SPR whom he thought insufficiently acute in research and judgement (Blackmore 1996: 209).

There appears to have been a desire, in the climate of the 1960s, amongst the younger members of the SPR, in alliance with an iconoclast like Dingwall, to dent the image of the founders, which may to younger members have had the fusty, dreary respectability that Lytton Strachey reacted against in his classic study *Eminent Victorians*. A flavour of this desire to peek beneath the surface is found in a letter of Fraser Nicol to Mostyn Gilbert (though both had a respect for Myers and no love for Hall): 'Incidentally many of the old SPR people were sexually interesting. Gerald Balfour, it is said, used to get into bed with Mrs Willett. Arthur Balfour is reported to have made a practice of tumbling in the hay with his boss's wife, Lady Mary Elcho ... several SPR members were gaoled for sexual offences' (SPR 76: 16.6.1970).

Most of the main figures in the early SPR have had their biographers: the Sidgwicks, Gurney, Lodge, Hodgson, Crookes, and James. Only Myers has not. (Podmore and Barrett have not had full biographies either, but in the former case there is inadequate material and the latter has had partial biographical treatment in one PhD thesis: Noakes1998.) Myers has suffered both the trivial indignity of the frequent misspelling of his name — Frederick, Meyers, etc — and other inaccurate references to his life and work, and also, much more importantly, damage to his reputation by assertions like the above. He was not always an easy man, and he had an unattractive side to his character. But, to his friends, and to his wife, he was seen as a hugely gifted and supportive individual who had high personal and scientific standards. Their view of him was at significant variance with that of his detractors. In the process of finding some middle ground, I hope to provide insights into aspects of the intellectual and social life of late nineteenth-century England as well as into the contested world of psychical research past and present.

The last chapter of this book discusses the legacy of Myers in terms of the enduring impact of his ideas, but it also interprets legacy in another, stranger sense, in its attempt to deal with one of the oddest phenomena in psychical research history, the cross-correspondences. These are contained in a vast body of automatic writing (writing without the conscious direction of the mind), stored in the WH Salter archive at Trinity and elsewhere, and analysed in detail in the pages of the SPR. They purport to be post-mortem communications from the leading Cambridge figures of the early SPR, and their lovers, friends and relatives. The communications are in the form of allusions, puzzles, cryptic clues, transmitted by a number of mediums (two of whom were in other continents), generally without knowledge of or contact with each other. They were delivered in an allusive fashion, the communicating intelligences stated, in order to counter the common objection of the sceptic, that messages coming from mediums could be fully accounted for by fishing (the asking of leading questions), cold reading (picking up clues from the sitter's body language and appearance), and, perhaps, telepathy between the living.

The cross-correspondences were once seen by many as providing some of the best evidence for post-mortem survival and eventually convinced so cool and balanced a researcher as Henry Sidgwick's wife, Eleanor (Sidgwick 1932: 26). Even so eminently sensible an historian of psychical research as Janet Oppenheim, has acknowledged their extraordinary and impressive nature, while not necessarily fully accepting the claims others have made for them (Oppenheim 1985: 133–34). However, in recent years, with a few exceptions (Fontana 2005: 175–85, Roy 1996: 100–25) they have tended to be interpreted as the product of a combination of chance verbal

repetitions and the nostalgic over-reading of an incestuous and unheal-
thily narrow elite (Moreman 2003, 2004). Or, ignoring the historical context, one could also read them in a post-modernist way, as a strange
psychic parody and prefiguring of surrealist practices, and the verbal
labyrinths and collages of T S Eliot or James Joyce.

There is an attempt, therefore, in the last chapter, without prejudice for
or against their ontological status, to provide a clear description of what
they were and what they were not. In a sense, just as the bulk of the book is
an attempt to provide a fair and balanced portrait of Myers in life, part of
the final chapter could be read, for those who are of the disposition to see
it as such, as an effort to do the same for him in death.

Note 1: A note on terminology: the words paranormal, supernormal,
anomalous have all been used in the text to indicate phenomena that are
puzzling, difficult to capture and replicate and which are inexplicable in
terms of our current scientific knowledge. No conclusion as to their ultimate status is intended by the use of these terms. The word alleged is
sometimes used and sometimes, no doubt, not used when it should have
been. No conclusion is meant to be drawn from this either.

Note 2: The main biographical and cultural aspects of Myers' life have
been covered in the earliest chapters. Those readers whose main interest
is in his work in psychical research can therefore concentrate on the later
sections, if they so wish.

Note 3: Documents have been cited in their original form. In many cases,
Eveleen Myers' letters for example, the style of punctuation etc gives a
useful insight into the personality of the writer.

Chapter One

Keswick to Cambridge

Marshalls and Myers at Keswick

St John's Church, Keswick, was built in the 1830s, of soft pinkish sand-stone, on a fine site recommended by the poet William Wordsworth. The first incumbent was Frederic Myers, the father and namesake of one of the most interesting — and now almost forgotten — explorers of the human mind in the Victorian period. He was Frederic William Henry Myers whose remains are buried, in a large family tomb, at the end of the church-yard which leads to the parsonage where he was born in 1843.

The Reverend Frederic Myers had been specifically invited by the Mar-shall family to be the first incumbent of the new church. The Marshalls, their wealth based on flax spinning, dominated the Lake District. It was said there was a Marshall on every lake and, as the leading Anglican land-owners, they saw their new church as part of the strategy to expand church building in the nineteenth century, as the Established Church and its rivals fought for the souls of the English working class. Myers was offered the living at £150 a year plus the parsonage. One of the Marshalls wrote to him hoping, 'to find that not withstanding the smallness of income, you are disposed to undertake the post' (Myers 16/108: 5.3.1838). Frederic Myers was a popular incumbent and there is, in the church, a tab-let to his memory donated by the members of the parish. His second wife (and FWH Myers' mother), Susan, also commemorated him by installing a stained glass window which illustrated three of Christ's parables. There are other memorials to members of the Myers family inside the church. However, one Myers is missing. Leopold Hamilton Myers, FWH Myers' eldest son and a novelist of some reputation in the 1930s, committed sui-cide in 1944, and he was cremated elsewhere.

Frederic Myers senior was born in 1811 and died in July 1851 at the age of thirty-nine. He was a highly educated man and the son of Thomas Myers, a mathematician and geographer, who was on the staff of the Royal Military Academy, Woolwich. Frederic went to Cambridge as a scholar of Clare College in 1829, becoming a fellow there in the early 1830s. He achieved a number of honours, the Hulsean essay prize in 1830, a Crosse scholarship and a BA in 1833, and in 1836 he took the Tyrwhitt Hebrew scholarship. His widow doggedly put together materials for his life, which was never published, but she successfully supported efforts to get his ecumenically focused work *Catholic Thoughts* through the press. It had, at first, only been published privately, as he was afraid too wide a distribution might unsettle his less sophisticated readers (Armstrong 2002: 12, 58). The book had two central themes: the rejection of the dominance of a small, select priesthood, and the need to interpret the Bible in a non-literal fashion. The text of the Bible was flawed, argued Frederic Myers, and did not accurately reflect God's intentions. The book was made widely available through general publication in 1873 and was re-issued in 1883 with a filial introduction by his son (Myers F 1883). Frederic Myers also had a strong interest in education and instigated a monthly series of lectures at the parochial meetings in the school room at St John's Church. He was not, however, strongly didactic and forceful. He was a tolerant and sensitive man and in private conversation could reject the concept of eternal punishment and the reality of the devil (doctrines which were already beginning to be challenged by the educated classes). In fact, one of his friends (Joseph William Blakesley, Fellow of Trinity and Dean of Lincoln) commented rather tartly on this. Mrs Myers had asked him if he had any letters she might use in a projected life of her husband. He replied, 'His comprehensiveness of feeling enabled him to hold simultaneously views which perhaps a severer intellect would have discovered to be incompatible with one another' (Myers 17/26: 11.2.1861).

Frederic Myers was taken ill in the spring of 1851 and died at Clifton, Cumberland on 20th July 1851. The marriage, though short, had been strong and full of mutual affection. He was buried in Keswick churchyard on 26th July. Susan Myers wrote a touching description of his last days, and on it, Eveleen Myers, FWH Myers' widow, later wrote, 'Last days so like his sons. Keep this always for children to read and live up to'(Myers, 17/70: n.d.). Before his death, the father managed to inspire his eldest son with a love of Virgil and gave him a good grounding in the classics at a very early age, writing to him on one occasion, 'I have looked over your six exercises. They are pretty well done, but not quite so well as you might have done them' (Myers 11/18: n.d.).

However, the most important early influence on Myers was his mother and they had a long, close relationship till her death in 1896. She had three children: Frederic 6.2.1843, Ernest 13.10.1844, Arthur 3.3.1845. As he described in his autobiography, she 'made our welfare the absorbing interest of her life. Her character was such as in each age in turn is attributed to "the old school"; — a character of strong but controlled affections, of clear intelligence, unflinching uprightness, profound religious conviction. Our debt to her is as great as that of sons to a mother can be' (Myers 1961: 8). Susan Myers kept a journal from February 1844 to September 1851, with the young Myers and his mother's concern that he develop in the right way figuring strongly. She seems to have been aware of the natural bounce and optimism of his personality (she said that there was too much 'prosperity' in his character) and she was concerned to develop in him a reflective approach to matters of this world and the next (Gauld 1968: 41). She was accused by one friend of the family of being rather too chilly and forbidding in her upbringing of the children: 'Mrs Myers she told me was a cold, hard, woman, and she beleived She was a Unitarian. She has not seen her for years and so she may be by this time softened. She said the children that is Frederick Myers and his brothers were brought up very carefully if anything too carefully. they were almost <u>prigishly</u> brought up' (D/DT 2579: n.d.). The same friend contrasted her unfavourably with Frederic Myers' first wife. Susan Myers, it was true, had a certain initial severity of manner, but she was obviously a shrewd and competent woman, with a good intellect and helpful and supportive to family and friends. Henry Stanley, the explorer, who later became Myers' brother-in-law, commented how alike she and Myers were, in both appearance and in character. He noted that, 'Fred has her eyes — her face — her intellect and deliberation' (Myers 4/97: 2.6.1891).

Susan Myers made sure that all her children had a strong Christian foundation to their upbringing. In her journal she noted that she was considering religious instruction for the young Myers. He was then two years and nine months (Gauld 1968: 38). As part of that process he was introduced to the primal concepts of death, extinction and punishment. The idea of extinction particularly terrified him. He described in his autobiography the impact that the sight of a dead mole, squashed by a cart, made on him as 'the first horror of a death without resurrection rose in my bursting heart'. He was also devastated by his mother's suggestion that totally evil people could be annihilated by God, rather than spend eternity in hell: 'The idea that such a fate should be possible for any man seemed to me appalling. I remember where I stood at the moment, and how my brain reeled under the shock'(Myers 1961: 7–8). He was obviously a highly imaginative child: 'I can remember my own feelings at four years old, when a respected elderly friend, 'stated that he was a bear, and simulated to some slight extent the movements of that quadruped. I knew all the time that it was Mr S; but the idea of bears, pre-existing in my mind, was so strongly stimulated that I was paralyzed with terror' (Myers 1886d: 158).

His mother's teaching was solid Evangelical, concerned with improving oneself now in preparation for the life to come, since the summons to the beyond could occur at any moment. However, there were hints in the journal that her efforts to induce a reflective humility in her son were not always successful. He expressed great delight in simple pleasures, but, 'along with this delight is a proportionate pain when he is disappointed in anything he has set his heart upon – or when his will is crossed, or his fancy, in anything' (Gauld 1968: 41). He was an inquisitive child, eager to learn and in love with natural beauty. In fact, Myers demonstrated elements of both a Wordsworthian and a Keatsian feel for nature as a child ; a sense of both mysticism and of sensuality. Writing of his family garden he stated, 'The thought of Paradise is interwoven for me with that garden's glory; – with the fresh brightness of a great clump and tangle of blush-roses, which hung above my head like a fairy forest, and made magical with their fragrance the sunny inlets of the lawn' (Myers 1961: 7).

In his account of the founders of the Society for Psychical Research, Fraser Nicol (Nicol 1972: 346–47) speculated, with reference to Myers, that, 'one cannot avoid the suspicion that the seeds of his future troubles at Cambridge (recounted by Gauld) were unwittingly planted by the love of a too-doting mother for her brilliant child'. In the light of other comments on the character of Mrs Myers, this is probably a superficial Freudian speculation. Myers grew up in a very supportive environment, had considerable natural gifts, a strong physique, an optimistic temperament, and huge energy. These gifts, in his cradle, were more than enough to encourage arrogance, without postulating a soft and 'too doting' mother. She, in fact, spotted the bumptious side to his character and tried to tone it down. Because of this, she tended, if anything, to underestimate his intellectual precocity. As she wrote in her journal, 'I do not see anything remarkable in his intellect so far – good sense and a *very* good memory seem to be his gifts' (Gauld 1968: 41). Certainly, his early letters to his mother, written on ruled paper, show little evidence of outstanding ability. Yet, his questions to her (which she recorded) about the nature of Heaven and Hell were, for a child of five, really quite perceptive:

> 'But can you tell Mamma, why God made only 2 places – one so very good as heaven, & the other so very bad as hell – & why not another, not *quite* so bad, for those who are a *little* good?' I said 'God gives us all our choice here on earth whether we will choose good or evil & tells us

this is one only time.' 'Then Mamma where do you think that little baby of Aunt C.'s who died before it had any name will go? — won't it go to heaven, for you know it had no time to choose?' (Gauld 1968: 42).

In order to harness Myers' natural bounce and to encourage spiritual development, mother and child wrote down their religious wishes for each other: eight hopes for each of them. The document makes quite grim reading now. Some of Susan Myers' aspirations for young Freddy were:

Fred's Mother for Fred: That he may be taught of God's Holy Spirit & led into all truth

Fred's Mother for Fred: That he may taste of the peace which is given to those who surrender their whole hearts to Christ

Fred's Mother for Fred: That in God's good time he may do him some notable service in the world with the great and good gifts which He has bestowed on him (Myers 3/111: n.d.).

There was also the dour series of resolutions set down at birthday times and to be lived up to throughout the year. The resolution, 'To remember always that GOD sees me and that I shall have to render an account of all my works to HIM' haunted Myers through his life (Gauld 1968: 42). He had a very powerful sense, long after the fading of Christian belief, that he was working *sub specie aeternitatis*, and this encouraged honesty when writing his brief, confessional autobiography, 'I hold that all things thought and felt, as well as all things done, are somehow photographed imperishably upon the Universe, and that my whole past will probably lie open to those with whom I have to do' (Myers 1961: 5). So, he substituted one watcher for another: the possibly impersonal and comprehensive Cosmic record for the unsleeping judgemental eye of the Christian God.

Myers, as a child, believed in Christianity with great literal intensity, as many children brought up in such an environment did. It is difficult for most of us to recapture the direct relationship which, in the 1840s and 1850s, even educated people had to the Bible. Arthur Stanley, a friend of the family who later, as Dean of Westminster, conducted Myers' wedding, once asked the young Myers what he would like him to bring back from the East. He replied that he would like a lily from Palestine. Stanley returned with one for him along with a delightful and carefully crafted letter in which he told the story of that lily. He gave the boy a vivid description of part of the Holy Land, made more concrete and personal by a reference to the topography of the Lake District: ' I cannot say how old this lily may be — but its parents must have grown in the springs for ages. They must have seen the wild buffaloes passing to and fro along the valley before Canaanite or Israelite had set foot on the banks of the Jordan; they must have caught the eyes of the two great hosts which met to fight on the shores of the little lake which lies below like one of the tarns of Cumberland, when Joshua came from the south and smote Jabin King of Hazor in the great battle beside "the waters of Merom"' (Myers 1904b: 9–13).

This unquestioning literal belief in the Bible, allied to his naturally optimistic personality, allowed him to be a particular comfort to his mother after his father's death. She confided to her diary, 'I cd. not have believed that a child of 8 yrs old could have given such sympathy <u>and</u> such comfort in deep sorrow as I have had from Freddy. He has been so very dear and tender, watching my countenance; and if he saw me very sad, stealing up to me with a loving kiss' (Myers 1904b: 8). Even allowing for a mother's hyperbole, Myers seems to have had a special capacity to support and encourage others throughout his life, and there are many examples in his correspondence of his sympathy with people in times of trouble and his willingness to help out. This characteristic was, of course, reinforced after his psychical researches broadly disposed him to believe in the human survival of death. However, this quality was just the positive side of his innate tendency to enthusiastically embrace a position with his whole emotional being. At times it led him into great despair, as the evidence for his particular position at the time waxed in quality; and also into making silly and premature judgements and gestures, which later caused embarrassment and pain. As his mother so perceptively stated in her journal, 'I see great danger in trusting to mere excitement of feeling in him' (Gauld 1968: 43).

Susan Myers, however, was no simple fundamentalist. She was intellectually curious and had a strong appreciation of the value of education and learning. She read widely through her life and often discussed the investigations of the Society for Psychical Research with both FWH Myers and with his brother Arthur. There are some examples of mesmeric phenomena in the Myers' archive which were most probably read by her, 'These mesmeric exploits, silly as they sound, come from private houses unconcerned with public exhibitions and so are all the more credible' (Myers 29/22: n.d.). One story related how three young ladies lost their way in the countryside and mesmerised each other in order to find their way back. It is worth commenting that the writer was prepared to give greater credence to the stories because they occurred in private houses, and because of the social position of the teller: 'This story rests on the authority of Mrs Acres who is a cousin of Sir Charles Styles.' These were two potential sources of error in the weighing of evidence that the later SPR, it might be argued, did not always avoid.

Myers' early life was secure financially as well as religiously. John Marshall, Susan's father, had built his fortune on the application of machinery to the spinning of flax (Rimmer 1960: 69). He had been a draper's assistant, but the death of his father Jeremiah in 1787 left him with a comfortable inheritance and surplus annual income to invest. It was not all that long before he became the leading flax spinner in the United Kingdom (Rimmer 1960: 69). By 1804 he had made about £40,000 from flax spinning and, at the end of the Napoleonic Wars, he had amassed almost £400,000. He was, however, a reasonable employer by the standards of the time and from the mid 1820s encouraged those children in his factories, who were prepared to behave properly and to benefit from it, to attend school (Rimmer 1960: 105, 112). He also contributed to funds for the establishment of the University of London, helped to found the Mechanics' Institute in Leeds, and campaigned for a university there. Towards the end of his business career he became briefly one of the MPs for Yorkshire (1826–30), but found Parliament and London life confusing and distasteful.

In his autobiography, Myers made little acknowledgement of his maternal grandfather's achievements, rather taking great pains to stress his worthy Yorkshire yeoman and squire origins on his father's side, and pointing out that his name was 'old-established in the West Riding of Yorkshire; and there is no reason to suppose that it indicates Jewish descent' (Myers 1961: 6–7). He also stated that he did not think he closely resembled in body or in mind any ancestor 'of whom account remains'. Yet, possibly for snobbish reasons, he may have failed to have seen that certain aspects of his character were not unlike those of his maternal grandfather, who built up a huge fortune on the basis of judgement, insight, dedicated hard work and unremitting energy. He was a man, who, like Myers, was reserved with outsiders, had huge drive and energy, and who also strongly believed in the power of education and self-improvement. Certainly, Myers was the only member of the Marshall clan with that kind of formidable self-motivating power. John Marshall's sons and grandsons became leisured country gentlemen, tinkering with the mills, and not really getting to grips with the fundamental economic issues (Rimmer 1960: *passim*). Their lives and careers epitomise the decline of English manufacturing in the nineteenth century as narrated on a broader canvas by Martin Wiener (Wiener 1981: 12–16). Myers quite often made references to mills and looms in his writing, but only as metaphors for the working of the human mind. Had he not been so fascinated by the inner world, had he been given the opportunity (for he was on the outer circles of Marshall influence and power), and, crucially, had he the disposition and interest (which he had not), he could have made a very effective business man.

Yet, whether they liked it or not, the industrial and commercial success of John Marshall laid the foundation for the Marshalls (and their spouses and relatives, including the Myers) to enjoy comfortable and privileged lifestyles through the nineteenth century (Rimmer 1960: 69). There were indeed an enormous number of Marshalls, spouses and relatives to support. The marriages of John Marshall's children between them produced thirty-eight Marshalls, Elliots, Temples and Myers, and by the 1870s a hundred and eleven male Marshalls were living in the Lake District (Rimmer 1960: 224–27). There were strong family bonds between the members. They moved freely between the family houses and the children of the various marriages spent much of their youth together. One son, William (the eldest of John Marshall's children), had a son Walter James Marshall, who married Annie Eliza Hill (a vicar's daughter); it was this Annie who was Myers' spiritual and platonic love and who, he eventually believed, sent messages from beyond the grave to comfort him.

Two Lake District properties that John Marshall acquired were to be of particular significance for Myers throughout his life. By the end of the Napoleonic War John Marshall had bought a summer residence Hallsteads (now an outdoor activity centre) on the west bank of Ullswater and a short distance away he acquired and improved Old Church—later an hotel and now a private house again—(Rimmer 1960: 99). His wife Jane, who was a very close friend of Dorothy Wordsworth, often received the poet and his sister at both properties. After Jane's unmarried Pollard sisters died (they had moved to Old Church to be near her), Annie Marshall with her husband Walter and their children lived there for part of the year (they also had a London house). Myers visited her frequently there and also at Hallsteads.

Myers was also born into an environment of powerful cultural, social and political connections. The link with Wordsworth has already been mentioned and John Ruskin too had contact with the Marshall family, though Myers was not to gain his friendship till much later in life. Thomas Spring-Rice, Lord Monteagle (his uncle by marriage to Myers' aunt Mary Anne Marshall) was a rather ineffectual and self-important politician— so lacking in dignity that one fellow lord once leap frogged over him. Ernest Myers, in a letter to Myers at Cambridge, noted that ineffectual pomposity: 'Uncle S is not only intensely superior but condescends to men of low estate & is very amusing'(Myers 3/106: n.d.). But he was a Lord even so, and had at one time been Chancellor of the Exchequer. William Whewell, the Master of Trinity College, was married to Cordelia, John Marshall's sixth child. The milieu was positive, supportive, stimulating and hierarchical, and, in conjunction with his outstanding natural gifts, fostered in the young Myers a considerable, possibly even overweening, sense of his own worth and status.

John Marshall was a generous father to all his children and settled funds on them at regular intervals. The eldest boy William became a landed gentleman inheriting property, income and estates and going into Parliament (Rimmer 1960: 118). The four younger sons went, with varying degrees of enthusiasm and commitment, into the flax business. Substantial settlements went to his married daughters and gifts to the unmarried ones, and at his death £110,000 was distributed between them (Rimmer 1960: 114, 118). Susan Myers moved to a small house in Blackheath after her husband's death. There was some concern in the Marshall family about her decline in fortune and that she was not able to send her boys to major public schools with the other young Marshall males (Rimmer 1960: 298). But it is clear from Myers' autobiography what the main motive was. She moved to Blackheath because of the excellence of the preparatory day schools and she clearly wished to have her sons at day schools rather than boarding schools. For a widow of her reflective and sensitive nature, the brutalising tales of public school life would have been difficult to take. Myers himself explicitly emphasized this point: 'She wished to keep her sons with her, and in 1856 went to live at Cheltenham, that we might attend Cheltenham College, at that time almost the only public school at which day-boys were not despised'(Myers 1961: 8).

At Cheltenham she was able to purchase Brandon House. It is obvious from the estate agent's catalogue that the house had real substance, and though not a 'country house', was a very superior bourgeois establishment. It was approached by a large driveway, had ample stabling for horses and carriage, and rooms for the servants. It was sold as a most desirable Cheltenham residence after her death in 1896. The house was in Painswick Road and was advertised as,'A Commodious Stone-Built Family Residence, of Noble Architectural Design' (Myers 17/79: 1.10.1896). It is clear that if Aunt Susan and her children were descending into poverty, it was only poverty as assessed by the highly rarified standards of the Marshalls.

Cheltenham College and Cambridge

Myers had first begun to display real intellectual precocity when he went to preparatory school at Blackheath. There he entered into a lifelong friendship with one of the teachers, the Reverend R Cowley Powles. Powles wrote appreciatively to him both at the time and later—how Myers was his favourite pupil and how he vividly remembered the quickness and sharpness with which Myers followed Powles' rendering of

Shakespeare into Greek: 'I shall never forget your first introduction to Greek Iambics. I can see now your quick eager looks as you followed the rendering of Shakespeare line by line into almost literal Greek' (Myers 1904b: 15). Hardly a teaching device that would recommend itself to the progressive preparatory school today!

Then Myers went to Cheltenham where he sparkled. Alan Gauld has commented (Gauld 1968: 89) that some of his teachers were critical about his accuracy with regard to the classics but he does not point out that Myers was much younger than the boys in the class he was placed in – no doubt many of them very able in themselves – and that he had caught up and was near the top or top by the time he left. Eveleen Myers, after Myers' death, lovingly copied out glowing references to him in the memoirs of Old Cheltonians. Douglas Sladen wrote:

> at thirteen on Entering Cheltenham School he was so advanced that he was placed with young men of seventeen and eighteen so precocious was his scholarship. I doubt if their ever has lived another English boy who learned for his own pure delight the whole of Virgil by heart before he passed the school age. He won the senior classical scholarship in his first year (at thirteen) – besides gaining the 1st prize for latin lyrics – he sent in two English Poems in different metres and both came out at the top and successful (Myers 27/7 n.d.).

There is an equally laudatory extract from another contemporary's reminiscences (Robert Edward Francillon, a writer of light fiction). This particularly stressed his emerging reputation as a poet: 'He was our poet; & while still a boy was a Tennysonian enthusiast who could show reason for his faith at the time when quite intelligent men and women scoffed at "Maud" & found "In Memoriam" obscure' (Myers 27/7 n.d.). In addition, his poetry was beginning to attract attention from informed adults. The poet, Aubrey Thomas de Vere, told Susan Myers that he was very much struck with the poems of Myers that Lady Monteagle (Mary Marshall) had shown him. He thought them superior to any poetry he had seen written at that age with regard to imagination, vigour of diction and artistic instinct. True, they had echoes of Tennyson. But that was quite natural, given Myers' age (Myers 2/38: 22.11.1859). A letter also survives from the aged Leigh Hunt, 'The verses of young Myers … appear to me to contain genuine poetical promise' (Myers 2/123: n.d.).

Cheltenham College in the 1850s was a business. It was a thriving enterprise in a growing market. Shares in the College rocketed through the 1850s and 1860s. For example, in 1856, shares (which included the right to nominate a pupil for entry) were worth six times their nominal value of £20 (Morgan 1968: 31). The Reverend William Dobson, who was Principal in Myers' time, was warmly remembered as the man largely responsible for this and who stimulated Cheltenham boys to achieve an unprecedented number of Balliol scholarships. When he left in the summer of 1859, the grateful Directors of the College gave him a phaeton and horses. Myers appreciated his qualities and stayed in touch with him. But his younger brother Ernest later wrote tartly to Myers at Cambridge that Dobson's successor as Principal, the Reverend Henry Highton, was not in the same league as a scholar, 'Highton has already made two terrific false quantities, recognised as such, I believe, by no one but myself! Pretty well for a Chel-Coll Principal, hay?'(Myers 3/102: n.d.).

Myers was likely to be an outstanding product and advertisement for that system. But, in order to ensure the almost inevitable scholarship, he was sent for coaching mainly in mathematics (always one of his weaker areas) to a clergyman in Surrey who formed a favourable impression of him. His wife wrote to Susan Myers that they rarely had any pupils, 'who seemed at once so talented and industrious as your son' (Myers 17/39: 16.5.1860). There was also a comment on the boy's fondness for walking and physical exercise, which was a salient characteristic of Myers almost to the end of his life. Myers went up to Cambridge on a minor scholarship in October 1860 with a reputation which had already travelled beyond his school. He had obviously imbibed the developing tradition at Cheltenham that it was a school that was not for the idle rich but for the middle ranking members of the community who by hard work and effort would gain successful careers in the services, in academic life, in business and in the Empire beyond. However, success appeared to come so easily to him, that the effect on his character was likely to be detrimental. For example, while still at school, he was *proxime accessit* for a national competition, the Burns poetry prize. This led to a heady letter from the Court Circular Office, asking him (at the age of 16) to become an occasional contributor of poems to it, 'I should be glad of any that bear on the upper classes of society, on the Queen, the Court, the poetry of old castles, old Halls, & generally on "Auld Lang syne"' (Myers 29/15: 5.2.1859). Myers, for much of his life, needed no encouragement to focus 'on the upper classes of society'.

Myers was not long in establishing an early reputation at Cambridge. He won the Chancellor's English Medal for poetry with his *The Prince of Wales at the Tomb of Washington*. He had to recite this publicly, in the Cambridge Senate House, to a not totally appreciative undergraduate audience. Whewell, the Master of Trinity, wrote to his sister-in-law, Mrs Myers, celebrating her son's performance: 'my thoughts came to congratulate you when Fred had the English Poem Prize adjudged to him, and on Tuesday last, when he recited the poem in public' (Myers 17/27: 24.5.1861). A contemporary of Myers, EM Oakeley, provided a little more detail. It appears that the early verses, which Myers recited 'in the uncom-promising sing-song which poets use', were greeted with 'laughs, groans, cat-calls, and hisses'. Yet by the end the audience had appreciated the poem and he received applause and an ovation. Oakeley further stated that he was popularly regarded in the University, 'as a rara avis in terris, certainly eccentric, probably negligible' (Myers 1921: 83). There was a developing side to his character that was too theatrical, intense, and self-absorbed for many people, and he may have recognised this in himself. There is some evidence that after this Myers, at least in public, played down his intellectual interests, and tended to associate with the heartier, more aristocratic crowd, though the arrogant exhibitionist in him re-emerged late in his undergraduate career, with almost disastrous results. Gauld has suggested (Gauld 1968: 92) that associating with the rowing set meant that he did not get the intellectual cut and thrust from his peers that might have given him greater balance.

We get a good sense of his activities at university and beyond, albeit in teasingly laconic form, through a daily record he kept of his life: one line entries for each day of the year, with volume 1 taking him from 1859 to 1884 (Myers 14/1) and volume 2 (Myers 14/2) covering the rest of his life. Myers referred to this practice in a lecture he gave to the young ladies of Dublin, after graduation, in which he described his method of recording his reading and the main experiences of life, 'and I would keep a chrono-logical list of books read and a skeleton diary with a single line for the events of each day, merely for reference and to give a backbone to mem-ory. A fuller diary tends to morbid egotism, though some record of moments of strong emotion may fitly be kept' (Myers 1868: 20). It is an example of the self-control and discipline of the man that he did in fact keep this diary scrupulously to the end. To our ears, perhaps, there is a rather over-manly and pompous dismissal of emotional wallowing in the last sentence. But one must remember his age and the fact that the lecture was to the young ladies of Dublin.

The early diary has frequent references to skating, rackets, croquet, boxing, rowing, walking and cricket, from the moment he went up to Cambridge. He was obviously a very physical man as well as hugely gifted intellectually. Occasionally, young men and their intense relation-ships vibrate beneath the hand-written one-liners, as in, 'Sidgwick is false!', the entry for 13th March 1861. This entry referred to Arthur Sidgwick, the schoolmaster and later Oxford fellow, rather than his older brother Henry, the philosopher. He also had an intense relationship with Cyril Flower (who became a politician and was made Lord Battersea) and there are periods of the diary when his name is on virtually every page. Another friend was the historian, Sir George Otto Trevelyan who, in visits to Myers' wife in later years, gave vivid insights into Myers' place and position amongst his small circle of intimate friends at university. She devotedly reported back the comments to Myers, stating that Trevelyan said he was jealous of Myers because he was so clever and because Arthur Sidgwick preferred Myers to him (Myers 6/114: 23.6.1887). She also told Myers that Trevelyan and his friends managed to classify their contemporaries as broadly intellectual, or sporty, or religious. Myers excelled in every category so he became known as 'the superb' (Myers 6/270: n.d.).

We can gather from first-hand accounts of the period (Taine 1957, Heitland 1926, Stuart 1911), some sense of what Cambridge, and particularly Trinity, was like at this stage in its history. It was probably the most prestigious college, and was gradually beginning to use a substantial bequest from earlier in the century to improve its efficiency and effectiveness as an institution (Lubenow 1998: 110). Myers, therefore, went up at a time of positive reform, but there were still considerable vestiges of the past in evidence. As a scholar he had free rooms, free dinner in hall, two loaves of bread and four inches of butter a day, £30 a year, plus a small annual stipend. Yet, there were duties in return. Scholars had to attend chapel eight times a week, read the lessons in chapel and read the grace in hall. Stuart has described the irritation the scholars felt particularly at the last duty, 'For some reason or other the scholars much more resented reading the grace than reading the lessons in chapel, particularly, I think, because we had to return thanks for the dinner which "we" had just eaten, the "we" being the fellows, for we, the scholars hadn't eaten it.' In addition, the scholars had to stay in the cold outside the hall, especially cold and draughty in winter, while waiting to be called in (Stuart 1911: 142–44).

Taine recounted the experience of a friend of his dining in Trinity at around the time Myers would have gone up: 'S recently dined in hall, at Trinity College, Cambridge. There were three hundred people present and the meal was served on silver plate. There was a small, separate table for undergraduates who are noblemen, and they wore a distinctive uniform' (Taine 1957: 195). He went on to state that these noblemen had flatterers who were called 'tuft-hunters'. In other words, they were people who toadied to the aristocrats in hopes of future preferment. Heitland painted a similar picture: 'Social distinctions created by wealth and poverty, or by family position and traditions, were still recognised with some frankness … Noblemen and Fellow-Commoners, though few, were a class in being, with distinctive Academic dress … In Trinity they wore blue and silver, and you might see a group of them if you happened to go into the great court in the morning' (Heitland 1926: 106–107). Arthur Balfour was of this class when he went up to Trinity College a few years later and particularly relished the right to dine at High Table with the dons (Adams 2007: 16). Myers was attracted to this group and remained for many years impressed by wealth and breeding, though he was quick to recognise intellectual and creative genius in others, of whatever background. One doubts whether Myers would have been a toady, since he had far too great an appreciation of his own abilities. But, nevertheless, probably like Evelyn Waugh in a later generation, he had a tendency to be beguiled by high breeding, particularly if it was associated with physical attractiveness and some intellectual spark. He obviously had yearnings, since there are two pedigrees in his papers — including a coat of arms — and a wistful red exclamation mark beside a newspaper account of his maternal grandfather's life and the rumour that he was in the running for a title had his political friends remained in power (Myers 14/7). However, of aristocratic rank *per se*, without other qualities, he had less respect, and he certainly showed great reluctance, as a fellow, to get involved in teaching, no matter how well-born the student.

Myers, as we have seen, appeared at this stage to cultivate an anti-intellectual front, though as often in such cases, this hid a lot of private thought, reading and ambition. Writing to his sister Charlotte, John Addington Symonds, the poet and man of letters, described the initial impression Myers made on him, 'He is such a curious creature ... not at all to my mind ... such as an entire indifference — contempt for merely intellectual pursuits' (Grosskurth 1964: 147). And, in fact, Conington, the Virgil scholar at Oxford, was rather shocked by this superficial posturing when Myers came to Oxford for the weekend in June 1861 (Grosskurth 1964: 147). But this was a temporary phase and the letters from Conington to Myers show that he eventually took Myers seriously as a classical scholar (Myers 2/3–10). This anti-intellectual pose would have been understandable in an individual of modest ability but given that Myers was both good looking and strongly built and was picking up prize after prize, while affecting a disdain for academic pursuits, he must have been most cordially disliked in a number of circles. These irritating characteristics may have prevented his election to the Apostles (the celebrated semi-secret Cambridge discussion group for gifted undergraduates) for which Arthur Sidgwick pressed hard (Myers 13/22: 18.10.1873), and to which his abilities fully entitled him.

There were, too, rumours that he was homosexual and gossip about this swirled around in society for a number of years. There are two letters which suggest, from very different perspectives, that Myers had, at the least, a temporary homosexual phase. Firstly, there is the letter from Symonds to Dakyns in which he describes himself, Myers and Arthur Sidgwick as, 'three of not the least intellectually constituted members of our Universities assailed by the same disease,' and in the same letter he mentions the dangers of 'idealising the passions of the Phaedrus' (Grosskurth 1964: 114–15). He particularly emphasized the insidious dangers that this posed to highly educated and well-read young men like Sidgwick and Myers. The second letter is a more melodramatic one from Josephine Butler to her son at the time of the Wilde affair (Wilde was sentenced to two years hard labour in 1895 for homosexual practices):

> Yes, I have heard also as you have, that the Oscar Wilde madness is spread like a plague thro' London fashionable & artistic society. Stuart told me Wilde is likely to be let off easily on that account. I long ago heard a dreadful account of Lord Battersea [formerly Cyril Flower]. It was Frederic Myers who first led him astray & many others. I hope Myers has got a fright. He quite deserves Oscar Wilde's fate. I am sorry for sensitive youths with some principle like Edmund Gurney, who died by his own hand, in despair because of having been so corrupted. His mother, my cousin, was such a good Christian woman. A friend of Lady H Somerset came to see me (Lady H S's husband went that road). She told me that London upper society is simply <u>rotten</u> with this vice. What fools people are who worship art & beauty & perfumes & poetry & nonsense in place of God (JB/1/1: 24.4.1895).

The reference to Lord Battersea has a certain resonance. In Lady Battersea's reminiscences she quotes a letter from RC Jebb (a contemporary of Myers and a professor of Greek at Glasgow and later Cambridge) to his mother, which described Cyril Flower's irresistible charm and the way everyone wanted to pet him. He was obviously very good looking and his handwriting — on the basis of the letters in the Myers' archive — was exuberantly flowery, so the cynical modern mind might immediately wish to impute a certain narcissim and covert homosexuality. Yet Jebb also stated that, 'He is the only man I have ever met who has some of the qualities of a charming woman also, and that without a shade of effeminacy!' (Battersea 1922: 167–68). There are certainly frequent references to Flower in Myers' early diary, as has been already stated, and Myers described the impact he first made on him in, to our tastes, very extravagant language, 'In 1863, just before my degree, Flower came up, — Flower, wreathed as it were, with roses, and scattering joy: — from that moment I was wholly given up to him, I lived mainly with his set, men junior to myself.' But it was a different time, with different linguistic conventions, and allowances should probably be made for Josephine Butler's highly coloured imagination (Myers 13/22).

In additional support of the thesis that Myers went through a homosexual phase at Cambridge, one could cite his explicit mention of Plato as a profound influence on him (Myers 1961: 10). Plato's *Phaedrus*, particu-

larly, was a source of controversy and embarrassment for many educated
Victorians. It was quite clear that Myers was aware of the link between the
love of young men, in that text, and the study of philosophy — a link which
George Grote (the historian) made overt in his writings, but which others
like WH Thompson (Master of Trinity) and Benjamin Jowett (Master of
Balliol) skated over in their translations from Greek (Turner 1981:
369–446). Jowett, in fact, robustly stated that if Plato had been a Victorian
he would have located his discussion within the context of relationships
between men and women. But there were counter trends. The writings
and practice of, amongst others, the Eton schoolmaster, William Johnson
[Cory][1] (*They told me, Heraclites, they told me you were dead*), had opened up
a wider range of classical texts to his students than the limited,
bowdlerised fare that the average schoolboy studied. These were texts
that expressed a particular interpretation of Greek love and family life
and the exaltation of male physical and intellectual beauty. The beautiful
late adolescent male was seen as the ideal companion in the cultivation of
the higher life (see Lees-Milne 1986). However, it is important not to exag-
gerate this. Though marriage was regarded as essentially for the procre-
ation of children, there could be enduring affection between husband and
wife and the relationship with the young man need not necessarily be a
physical one.

A certain balance and caution is needed here. Myers, as is not unusual
in all-male communities, had, as a young man, a strong emotional and
aesthetic attraction to some of his own sex. But that did not necessarily
mean that it was expressed physically. For example, both he and
Conington had been reading Johnson's homoerotic poems, but they obviously found the tone of some of them distasteful. As Conington put it to
Myers, 'So you have been reading Ionica — I agree with you that the writer
is wanting in self-respect' (Myers 2/3: 16.2.1861). This would tend to
imply that their view was that such relationships should be of a controlled
and non physical nature. It should also be remembered that Myers had a
desire to posture and shock as a young man (and occasionally throughout
his life) and he may well have expressed himself a little unwisely on the
topic in order to provoke the orthodox. The melodramatic, almost
blood-curdling narrative of a latter-day sodomite, vividly sketched by
Josephine Butler, should not be taken too literally. There seems little
doubt that if there was a physical aspect to his male relationships at university (and there is no direct evidence that there was), it was a temporary
phase. Myers' later life was characterised by strong and intense friendships with a small number of very gifted men but these were not homo-

---

1   Born William Johnson, he added the name Cory after his time at Eton.

sexual. They were built on the basis of intellectual interests and comradeship in the pursuit of common challenging goals. What was true,
however, and a point that Myers acknowledged in his draft autobiography (Myers 26/63/15), was that Hellenism 'encouraged that indifference
to ordinary persons, & excessive interest in physical beauty, which have
greatly injured my efficiency in life'.

He also showed considerable enthusiasm for the company of attractive
young women, and in his autobiography lamented that the Greeks had
not spent enough time studying and writing about them (Myers 1961: 10).
There are also contextual reasons why the letters of Butler and Symonds
are perhaps more sensationally phrased than the actual situation warranted. Symonds was hugely preoccupied by the moral dangers of trans-
lating his feelings into physical action, and in that process looked round
for companions who were – the phrase implies great struggle – 'assailed
by the same disease'. In other words, he exaggerated the situation with
regard to Arthur Sidgwick and Myers, both of whom, later, found the
transition into married life neither threatening, nor too painful, nor without its rewards. Mrs Butler may well have over-emphasized the situation
for other reasons. She was writing at the height of the Wilde scandal, a
time of considerable and self-righteous moral panic amongst the English
upper middle classes. She had been very close to Myers and possibly
resented his move outside her circle and his rejection of her perfervid and
dramatic Christianity. She also had a capacity for self-dramatisation and
the melodramatic and for gossip. Her assertion that Gurney (Myers' most
intimate friend and colleague in psychical research work) committed suicide because of a homosexual relationship with Myers is totally without
supporting evidence and has been put forward by no historian of psychical research. As we shall see, when examining the death of Edmund
Gurney, there is simply not enough evidence as to possible motive and
the most likely conclusion, on the basis of what evidence does exist, is
accidental death. It is highly implausible, in fact almost unbelievable, that
Myers could have retained the affection and loyalty of men of the calibre
and moral integrity of Oliver Lodge, Henry Sidgwick, William James and
others, if a temporary phase of same-sex attraction at university, had
metamorphosed into permanent membership of the illegal late-Victorian
homosexual community (Cook M: 2003).[2]

The friendship with Henry Sidgwick, in fact, got off to rather a bad
start. Their first sustained encounter was when Myers was coached by
Sidgwick as a freshman. The coaching system in Cambridge was an integral part of undergraduate academic life. Every young man aiming at a

---

2   A homosexual act was a criminal offence until 1967, even between consenting adults in private.

high position in the tripos needed either a mathematical or a classical coach (Rothblatt 1968: 199–201). At this time the tutor and the College lecture system were not seen as key sources of intellectual support, stimulation and advice. The coach was everything. He was a one to one trainer and, exhausting work though it was, a considerable income could be gained from it. Myers was not alone in finding Sidgwick remote, slightly odd, and even frigid. In a note in his papers on his friendship with him, Myers described the rather unfavourable impression that Sidgwick, as a young man, tended to make on the new undergraduates:

> He was of course an admirable scholar, but he taught with great coldness & was generally accused of unwillingness to take trouble with his pupils, & selfish indifference to their success. He was rarely seen by undergraduates except in Chapel, where his distant & frigid air, and his habit of 'eating his beard', — shovelling it by handfuls into his mouth, while he gazed coldly thro' halfshut eyes at the Freshmen opposite him, — used to inspire the said Freshmen with a feeling of uneasy dislike rising in the most sensitive among them to actual hatred. 'That old goat was there eating his beard again, — I should like to punch his head', may be taken as a typical Freshman remark on the subject (Myers 13/22: 18.10.1873).

They had their last session in February 1861 and there was little to indicate at this stage, apart from an appreciation by Sidgwick of Myers' poetry, that they would develop a long, intimate and mutually supportive friendship. In fact, at this time Sidgwick stated he was glad that Myers failed to get the English verse prize in 1862, and that it 'will do Myers a great deal of good' (Add.Ms.c. 99/13: December 1862).

Paradoxically, and in many ways typical of his quixotic vehemence, Myers was driven on one occasion to defend Henry Sidgwick even though he could barely stand him: 'My extreme & rapid attachment to his brother Arthur, (then aged 20, & in the year above me,) used to make me defend H.S. in company, & I well recollect defending him, (of course in his absence,) on Feb. 26/61 in so offensive & insolent a manner that the other men at dinner apprehended actual violence, as my interlocutor was a ferocious boxer, much older than myself (Myers 13/22: 18.10.1873).

Though disliked by some and seen as suspect by others, Myers nevertheless reaped a full harvest of honours and prizes at Cambridge in four years between the ages of seventeen and twenty-one. His son Leo summed up the achievement thus: 'At the University few men have won more honours. The record is as follows: a college scholarship and declamation prize ; two university scholarships ; no less than six university prizes ; second classic in the spring of 1864 ; second in the first class of the Moral Sciences Tripos in December of the same year, and fellow of Trinity in 1865' (Myers 1992: XI). Douglas Sladen waxed lyrical about the impression he made on people: 'He was a wonderful personality — no one who ever saw his unforgettable eyes, and beautiful majestic head, and heard his marvellously eloquent voice, could ever forget him' (Sladen 1915: 105).

Success led to considerable intellectual arrogance and along with this arrogance went a rather critical and judgemental attitude towards others that was still in evidence when he became a fellow. On the 12th February 1866 Jebb wrote to his mother, 'Today Myers and I had a walk, and marked each other, with much mutual contumely. It is very good for one to know how exactly how highly one's friends rate one's manners, intellect, &c. I will not tell you my marks, for they would raise a storm of indignation in so partial a judge: suffice it to say that I am not in the first flight' (Stray C 2006: p.c.). On the following day Jebb went through the same process with Henry Sidgwick, marking a number of colleagues who fared well, since Sidgwick's 'standard is not quite as severe & exclusive as Myers'.' Myers must have been extremely irritating at times. Yet, in spite of the unflattering evaluation, Jebb was still capable of writing to Myers in 1873, 'what a refreshment it is to me to talk to you' (Myers 2/143: 21.10.1873).

Such qualities led, in his own words, to acts 'of swaggering folly'. The one that had the profoundest implications for his long-term reputation was what might be called the Camden Medal Affair. He had won the Camden (a prize for Latin composition) in 1862 and he won it again in 1863 with a poem on the subject of 'India pacificata'. Some time later local newspapers (and some farther afield) picked up a story that Myers had taken a substantial number of his lines from other sources. GG Coulton, the Cambridge historian, recounted the story in his memoirs (Coulton 1944: 106–108), basing his account on information from two Trinity academics, McTaggart and Jackson. There was a protest against the prize being awarded to Myers since he had incorporated a substantial number of lines from Oxford prize poems ; and the protests went so far as to object to Myers proceeding to a BA degree. There was a lively correspondence in the press and it is likely that Myers, under a pseudonym, attempted to defend himself. Myers himself summed up the incident and the result:

> Having won a Latin prize poem, I was fond of alluding to myself as a kind of Virgil among my young companions. Writing again a similar poem, I saw in my bookshelves a collection of Oxford prize poems, which I had picked up somewhere in order to gloat over their inferiority to my own. I laid this out on my table and forced into my own new poem such Oxford lines as I deemed worthy of preservation. When my friends came in, I would point to this book and say, 'Aurum colligo

e stercore Ennii' — 'I am collecting gold from Ennius' dung heap,' — a remark which Virgil used to make with more valid pretensions. My acquaintances laughed; but when my poem was adjudged the best, a disappointed competitor ferreted out these insertions; and the Master of Trinity, although he roundly asserted that I had done nothing illegitimate, advised me to resign the prize (Myers 1961: 9).

Myers had written an extremely clear-headed letter to his Uncle Whewell, Master of Trinity, providing a sophisticated rationale for his behaviour. It appears that Whewell had not approached him directly but went via his mother, 'My Mother tells me that you say you would be glad that I should write to you about the affair of my Camden' (Myers 12/222: 26.9.1863). Myers' letter was well-written and well-judged. He did not wallow in emotion (though he clearly admitted the shame he felt about causing distress to his mother and sullying his good name) or throw himself abjectly on the mercy of his superior. He logically dealt with the two key questions that any sensible observer would have asked — how could you steal the lines without feeling that you were doing wrong and secondly how could you fail to see what would be the obvious response of other people? In answer to the first question, he justified his actions on the grounds of Virgilian practice and his own developing theory of poetry. He argued that the best poems relied on overall aesthetic effect, blending rhyme, rhythm, allusion, metaphor, into one pleasing whole, and to the second he said that he made no secret of the fact that he had taken lines from others. Yet, though he had marked the lines and had shown a copy to a friend, this was not the copy submitted to the judges and this, rather than any high flown intellectual justification for the practice was what stuck. He had obviously been influenced by Conington and his views on poetry; namely that there was a distinguished classical tradition of imitation and allusion within which his poem belonged. Yet not many people saw it in that light. Eveleen Myers, ever loyal, scrawled in crayon on the letter to Whewell, 'This was a cruel punishment for a childish act a mistaken act. His geneous was so great He needed no promptings from others poems.' However, the affair indicated a kind of reckless arrogance in Myers that occasionally burst out and which in later life sometimes got him into hot water.

In essence, to expand the point made above, what Myers was trying to do was to create an example of poetic practice in the tradition of Virgil. The originality of the poem resided in its overall effect and polish and not in mere originality of idea or individual phrase. Myers was following Conington (Stein 1968: 72–76) who argued that Virgil's appeal lay in artistic qualities of making, shaping, and polish, 'the finished excellence of his workmanship'; and that a particular element of this could be 'remote intellectual association'. In other words, allusions/references/echoes were part of an artistic heritage and tradition. Myers, in fact, went beyond Conington's view of Virgil's practice and argued, as Conington re-stated it to him, 'You say it would have no detraction from a poem if not a word of it were by the author and the thefts were so thick together as to involve numberless contradictions'. Stein has persuasively argued that his defence of his practice in the prize poem was not 'the hasty excuses of a schoolboy caught in the act of cheating' but part of his considered approach to poetry and its assessment and that these ideas, with variations, were 'repeated again by Myers in the next forty years' (Stein 1968: 72–76).

Yet, to many of those who gossiped about the affair at Oxford or Cambridge, or read the accounts that percolated through to the wider regional press, he was just seen as a cheat and a plagiarist. The subtleties of Virgilian practice and his extension of it were not picked up. Years later, at the time Charles Coombe Tennant was making enquires about Myers' suitability as a husband for his sister, Eveleen Tennant, this matter was still being raised:

> I went to my man on Saturday and he is a Cambridge man. He told me he had heard of Myers who was Senior to him at Cambridge, and that there was a discussion when he first went up about a prize poem. Myers had won the prize poem, and the man who was next to him in order of merit exclaimed strongly against the poem being adjudged to Myers, putting his finger on several lines, and passages that had been taken out of other authors (D/DT 2579: n.d.).

There were half-hearted attempts to deprive Myers of his degree but nothing came of this and he was placed second in the first class of the classical tripos in 1864. Despite his posturing and his association with the pass rowing men, Myers was in earnest about his scholarly and intellectual activity and very well aware that a high performance in the tripos was the mark of future academic and often professional success (Rothblatt 1968: 181–83). The classes were published in the papers and particularly outstanding performances were talked about for years afterwards. Myers decided to sit for another tripos, this time in moral sciences. Such was the concern of able people re the need for high performance that John Grote, who was in charge of the moral science course, wrote to him in 1864 and advised against him taking that tripos unless he was prepared to settle for a second. The letter (Myers 2/80: n.d.) is worth quoting in full as it illustrates Grote's carefully balancing his concern for the status of his new qualification with a sense of the importance of the first in terms of Myers' personal and professional reputation:

My dear Mr Myers.

I heard from Mr Todhunter today that you had sent in your name for the Moral Sciences Tripos — I am rejoiced <u>for the sake of the Tripos</u> — but I just send this line ; (as you were good enough to ask my opinion whether you would be wise in going in) not at all to discourage you, but to advise you <u>to think about it</u> — what I have heard since I saw you makes me feel that you run <u>a risk,</u> with the amount of reading you mentioned to me, of not being in the first class — & so far as this is a great point with you, I should be very sorry if you come out in the Second & felt at all that I had misled you or had advised you to go in — I know your abilities, & should not consider your first class at all hopeless — but having said what I have said, I must ask you to consider the responsibility to be <u>with you</u> — I think you should be guided by your <u>degree</u> of horror of the second — if that is <u>very great,</u> I should advise you to abstain.

With best wishes for your success if you do go in, I remain

Yours sincerely,

J Grote.

Myers, however, triumphed, with a first. His reactions are contained in a letter to his mother (Myers 12/2) on 11th December 1864:

My dear Mother,

I heard the Tripos at about 6 yesterday & wrote at once but being hurried unhappily forgot to post my letter, therefore write now with apologies.

You will kindly rejoice in the result!!! much pleases me & is as follows:

1) Jardine Myers Macartney Payne Gibson
2) Wood Greene Whalley
3) No third class

They say it was a splendid examination (i.e. men did well) & I was put up wholly for Political Economy & Essays about which I am much pleased as it shows that the Examiners were really searching & were not deceived by my fictitious appearance of knowing Philosophy — they add that my P Economy was extremely good. Jardine is a man who has taken up the tripos in the business-like way.

I shall be glad to help Arthur.[3] I return on Tuesday & will bring back £20 or £30 to give you for debt.

Your affectionate & dutiful son,

FWHM

I have almost decided on Natural Sciences if I can get pace of Senate

3   Myers' youngest brother.

Myers was quite clear-eyed about himself. He knew his strengths and weaknesses and this is what gave him his confidence. He knew what he could pull off. He had a very vigorous and powerful intelligence, and was extremely good at absorbing and classifying material, and expressing it forcefully under pressure. He was less happy with philosophical and mathematical abstractions and seemed pleased that the examiners had spotted this, implying that their acumen in this respect validated their judgement in highly praising his political economy. Philosophy was certainly never a major strength and when he came to assert the existence of telepathy, it was on the basis of empirical investigation, and not on a carefully worked out metaphysical position.

His performance was all the more impressive in that he had spent some of the year travelling to Greece and the Aegean to visit for the first time the places that he had read and fantasised about as a schoolboy and an undergraduate. He was particularly keen to visit the Greek Islands where Sappho and Praxilla had sung the burning, romantic, passionate poetry that so appealed to him: 'Drink with me! ... be young along with me! Love with me! wear with me the garland crown! Mad be thou with my madness; be wise when I am wise!' (Myers 1961: 11). Yet the reality proved more powerful than the imaginary and he realised that looking backward was unnatural, the yearning could not be satisfied, that he had to embrace his time and his world.

On this trip he became friends with RH Collins, later the tutor of Prince Leopold, and Myers had close and interesting friendships with both individuals. Collins paints a characteristically romantic picture of the young Myers, 'I FIRST saw Frederic Myers in the early summer of 1864. He was ... leaning over the side of a steamer in the harbour of the Piraeus reciting poetry to a companion ... We became friends on the ship ... At his special desire, we bathed in the troubled waters between Scylla and Charbydis' (Lodge 1901: 12). It should be pointed out that he was travelling in parts of the world that were still rather dangerous for tourists. It was the age of the brigand (Jenkins 1961: 1–21). There is an amusing account by Oscar Browning (Eton schoolmaster and Cambridge don) of his adventures in Italy and Greece a little after this time. Just before Browning's visit to Greece with a number of young men, there had been the murder of two Englishmen, Vyner and Herbert, by brigands. This caused a huge outcry in England and the Greek government gave Browning and Gerald Balfour a troop of horse to protect them on their excursions around Attica. When they moved on to Rome, Gerald Balfour and the other young men took revolvers with them. Browning refused one in case he shot them by mistake (Browning 1910: 194, 216). So, Myers had shown both bravery and considerable endurance in undertaking such a journey, particularly as for a substantial part of it he travelled alone. In his diary Myers briefly recorded his itinerary — Munich, Vienna, Athens, Rome, Paris etc, etc. On 26th June he reached Hallsteads after 80 days of travel, having swum in Charbydis and rowed on the Bosphorus. In the self-dramatising language that came so naturally to him, he described the final impact of the tour upon him: 'I left Greece with such a sadness as I have known in some twilight sculpture gallery, when I have pressed my face for the last time to the unanswering marble, and turned to go with eyes tear- brimming, and a bitter-sweet passion of regret' (Myers 1961: 11).

Chapter Two

Life, Love and Letters

Myers and Mrs Butler

Myers had, by the age of 22, achieved two first classes at Cambridge, a clutch of other awards, and a burgeoning reputation as a scholar and a poet. Yet, he lacked direction and ballast. He had no clear idea of a future career, and no settled view of the nature and purpose of life. Most educated people then, probably, took a modest position with regard to the ultimate verities, ranging from low-key conviction to mild atheism. But Myers' temperament was such that he needed certainty, an emotional imperative that drew him into belief, but a belief that ultimately had to be strong enough to stand up to the facts of the situation. He was without intellectual and emotional security at this stage in his life; for the vivid Hellenism of his university years had not survived his tour of the sites of the ancient world, and he had lost the literal Christian faith of his childhood. He sought diversion in travel and took an extensive tour of the northern United States. The trip was notable for one outstanding piece of flamboyant athleticism and romantic exhibitionism. He visited Niagara and, being a very strong swimmer, decided to swim under the falls. He told the tale in his autobiography, contrasting the energy and vitality of the waters with the apathy in his heart:

> Visiting Niagara alone, I resolved to swim across the river immediately below the falls ; in the track where boats cross with ease, before the turmoil of the river collects itself for the rapids below. This was before any of the professional exploits in swimming Niagara, and my proposed swim, which would of course be thought nothing of now, had seldom been attempted, so far as I could learn, except by deserters from the Canadian shore, some of whom were said to have been swept down and drowned in the whirlpool. There was thus some

imaginative sense of danger; though it was plain that where a
rowing-boat with one oarsman could ply, an ordinary swimmer
ought to be able to make his way also. I started from the Canadian side
(August 28th, 1865) late at night, to avoid spectators, and alone,
except for a man following with my clothes in a boat. As I stood on a
rock, choosing my place to plunge into the boiling whiteness, I asked
myself with urgency, "What if I die?" For once the answer was blank
of emotion ... I plunged in ; the cliffs, the cataract, the moon herself,
were hidden in a tower of whirling spray ; in the foamy rush I struck at
air ; waves from all sides beat me to and fro ; I seemed immersed in
thundering chaos, alone amid the roar of doom (Myers 1961: 12).

Myers commented that the indifference with which he regarded his possible demise, gave him insight into the intellectual inertness, the apathy
that most of humanity seemed to display with regard to their ultimate
destiny. But Myers' nature abhorred a spiritual vacuum and he found,
within a year, flooding through his mind and heart, an intense and
vibrant Christian belief whose wellspring was the beautiful Mrs Josephine Butler. She sent him a set of extraordinarily passionate and frank
letters which give us some insight into the nature of her appeal for sensitive, educated young men. Their strange mixture of the quasi erotic and
the yearning for religious rapture and certainty would have stirred and
befuddled the young Myers' senses.

She wrote, 'You have been so wonderfully gentle and kind & dear to me
for some months past ... Try always to pray, please ... You will fling your
whole being into it, & then you will be <u>safe</u>. it will use up the fire in you ...'
She explained why she felt relaxed about taking such an intimate tone
with him: 'My dear, my beloved Frederic, I love you very much. You
know how I have given my human to God, & so you must understand
how I can in his very presence call you by kind and pitying and tender
names' (Myers 1/88: n.d.).

It had not always been so. At Cheltenham the two families had got to
know each other well when George Butler became Vice-Principal of
Cheltenham College late in 1857. Myers had some tuition with him and
also met Butler and his wife socially. He seems, very early on, to have
developed something of a crush on Mrs Butler since he requested, in 1860,
a cast of the sculptor Alex Munro's bust of Josephine. Her biographer (Jordan 2001: 41) has commented on this bust, which is in the possession of
Girton College, that the pose was a most incongruous one for Girton, or
indeed for Josephine, since the hair was unbound and she was wearing
nothing except a simple chemise, exposing one naked shoulder. As is
often the way with crushes, Myers was both adolescently provocative and
inhibited with her at the same time. Ernest wrote to his brother at Cam-

bridge (no doubt relishing the role of mischief-making, younger brother) that, 'Mrs Butler observed publicly that your letters were intensely stupid, you never had two things to say' (Myers 3/107: n.d.). He also asserted that she said that Myers had continually tried to provoke and shock her when at Cheltenham but that he had never succeeded (Myers 3/103: n.d.).

A tragedy brought them much closer together. Susan Myers had become a good friend of the Butlers. She stood as godmother to their daughter Eva and, in the summer of 1864, her brother James Marshall lent the Butlers his house in the Lake District for a holiday (Jordan 2001: 55). Shortly after their return to Cheltenham, little Eva died in a fall from the top of the hall stairs. Susan Myers strongly supported Josephine through her grieving and helped her to try to assuage her grief by throwing her energies into good and charitable works. They discussed, for example, the idea of a home or a hospital for the destitute. Mrs Butler sought for allies in these new causes amongst young and idealistic university men of the upper middle classes, using a method which one can only label as spiritual seduction. Symonds described how she exerted her charisma on him, 'She talked vehemently of how she suffered in her mind. As she lay there exquisitely slender and mobile, full length on the sofa, she did look torn by demons. She told me the torture of her thought, how religious, social, political doubt weighed on her. She never lost her feeling for God, but could not help thinking of Him as a tyrant. Sympathised with me, when I said such thoughts goaded one on to suicide as a means of finding out the truth' (Grosskurth 1964: 83). Often she would be on the sofa or on her knees, before the looking glass, when the young man called. One can see how her fervour, her beauty, her willingness to struggle and take action would have appealed to Myers. And she herself was acutely aware of her physical looks and the power of her personality. She enlisted them as battalions in the various campaigns she fought throughout her life. Indeed, she commented tartly that the woman's suffrage movement of the time, being fronted by Lydia Becker, who was not a beauty, therefore, 'has not the gift of winning' (Caine 1993: 152). She had a tendency to confuse the spiritual and worthwhile with the aesthetically pleasing, a weakness to which Myers himself was also prone. Yet, poor Miss Becker's physical imperfections did not inhibit Myers from standing beside her and making a speech at the Free Trade Hall, Manchester, during the first public meeting in support of the female franchise in 1868 (Fulford 1957: 73).

Myers, at this stage in his life, seems to have been very unstable and to have suffered great swings of emotion and intellectual position. Even though he described himself as in a state of nihilistic despair when he swam beneath Niagara, he had already written a letter to Arthur Sidgwick expressing a very positive attitude towards Christianity: 'the moral evidence in favour of Christianity becomes, immediately the will is thoroughly subjected, quite overwhelmingly strong.' It was true for him. It was true for Mrs Butler and would that it were true for Arthur. What a conversion that would be, what a superior freemasonry of spirits! (Myers 12/194: 5.5.1865). The letter is fascinating on several counts. The appeal was totally an emotional and moral one. Myers rejected, in arguing the case for Christianity, the historical and scientific methodology that he would later embrace so wholeheartedly when investigating the apparently supernatural. And there was, as well, his yearning for and appeal to the comradeship of elite spirits — another characteristic which remained with him and can clearly be seen in the later friendships he made in his work with the Society for Psychical Research.

In spite of this intellectual and emotional inconsistency, his reading around this time indicates an increasing draw towards Christianity. In a letter to his mother he commented very favourably on Browning's *Easter Day* (Stein 1968: 110–11), and he was greatly stirred by Seeley's *Ecce Homo* (as Henry Sidgwick noted, Add.Ms.c.99/63: 27.2.1866), with its emphasis on Christianity as love in action, rather than mere dogma and ritual. JP Williams (Williams 1984: 83), however, has argued that his Trinity friend, Frederick Armine Wodehouse, through his personal example, was a more significant influence than Mrs Butler's on Myers' move back to Christianity (Myers 13/22). Certainly there were frequent, clustered references to Wodehouse in his diary at this time (Myers 14/1).

In late 1866 after a 'great moral crisis' (Myers 13/22) and the long, dark night of the soul, his belief in Christianity grew even more intense and in 1867 he sent an extraordinary letter to Arthur Sidgwick (Myers 12/202: 14.7.1867) asserting that his previous faith, and his conviction of the power of Mrs Butler to work good (the two were never clearly separated in his mind), 'was an infidel apathy as compared with the passionate intensity of my belief in her now'. And as further proof of her influence he described her impact on his cousin Stephen Marshall since, 'God through her wrought such a change in him that from narrow selfish surly he has become one of the noble of the Earth'. Stephen Marshall was the son of Henry Marshall (John Marshall's fourth son), who had the great house on Derwent Island and it was from there that Myers' letter to Arthur was headed. It is interesting that Stephen's religious conversion did not apparently extend to sensitive negotiations with the Marshalls's workforce. He peremptorily closed the flax mills in August 1871 (Rimmer 1960: 281–85) after a protest strike by the women workers and suggested to the senior partners that the foreman and overlookers at one site be completely replaced, to show that the Marshalls would not be threatened. His attitude was seen as far too harsh and inflammatory and he was eventually overruled.

The perfervid, almost sensual spirituality of these years, culminated in his long poem *St Paul*, first published in 1867. It became enormously popular with a certain constituency (Stein 1968: 114) and it went through sixteen editions before the end of the century. It was dedicated to Josephine Butler (the Greek dedication revealed that he owed his soul to her) and she read it and enjoyed it though, like others, she did find it obscure in parts. Sidgwick commented that no one could have written it but Myers and it was, 'very fine poetical rhetoric — consummate except for excess of artifice, and occasional lapses into bad taste and into startling vulgarity' (Add.Ms.c.105/31: 28.12.1867). Its heady and hectic rhythm stirred, intoxicated and mesmerised the reader, but the words expressed little real clarity of thought or sustained meaning. However, the poem had a kind of whirlwind intensity which gave a certain sort of temperament comfort. Myers himself was capable of providing similar support. He wrote Josephine Butler a long and sensitive letter on her father's death in January 1868 (Myers 11/187: 23.1.68). One is reminded of the comfort he gave to his mother on her husband's death and he clearly had, because of his own positive and energetic disposition, a capacity throughout his life to support and comfort individuals in their loss, or when generally down. At this period it was based on an intense Christian faith. Later in life it was sustained by his scientific researches into life after death.

Josephine Butler's attitude to Myers was ultimately a mixture of admiration, disappointment and apprehension. She was disturbed by the tittle-tattle about his possible homosexuality, as we shall see later. But, as already noted, she warmly appreciated his early work with her, opposing the sexual mistreatment of women and supporting access to higher education and voting rights for them. One of her letters contains a vivid account of her taking him to a hospital to meet a dying prostitute and the powerful impact it had on him:

> Frederic Myers spent last Monday & Tuesday with us. he went with me to the large pauper Hospital, & I took him to the bedside of Ellen Lambert & she was a girl with a most beautiful smile, & white teeth ; often she had smiled at me so kindly, but that day her beautiful mouth twitched, it was a strange spasmodic smile,& her mind was wandering. She looked the most pitiful wreck. I was going away when a woman near her cried 'She is calling you' & when I bent over her again she said ' Must you go! Oh! dont go, oh! dont go. Come back soon. Oh! why must you go?' I said I would come back <u>early</u> tomorrow. Next day Frederic went down again with me, & on her bed we saw a straight white corpse, little marble hands laid across, white feet stuck against the footboard, & the spasmodic smile & beautiful lips <u>fixed</u>.

The eyes scarcely shut. She had been dead only two hours. I made him come & touch her cold hand, & said 'Look at this . Only 18 years old. only two weeks left the street, slain by sin, & after a terrible struggle with death, this is all.' he trembled all over. I think all he saw those two days will make a deep impression but there are others who need to see such things more than he. For he never was cruel about women (JB1/1/12: 8.3.1867).

It was remarkable how long Myers managed sustain his intense religiosity. Jebb recorded in his diary for 26th Feb 1866 that Myers devoted himself to self-discipline. 'He never goes anywhere. He gets up at 6.30 and goes to bed at 10.00. His days are spent in reading *Ecce Homo* and in thinking.' Jebb also perceptively remarked that he did not think him happy (Jebb 1907: 81). However, this rather exhibitionistic spirituality did not damp his competitive zeal or his capacity to shock or take the unconventional position. In autumn 1868 he visited Henry Taylor in Bournemouth. A poet and civil servant, Taylor had an extraordinary working-at-home arrangement with the Colonial Office, and he was visited there by many celebrities. In the hagiographic tones of his daughter, 'Strangers came … Men of mark came … all seeking intercourse and discussion with a mind clear, just and tolerant, wholly indifferent in its calm anchorage to the veering winds of popular opinion' (Taylor 1924: 19). And Myers, a celebrity through his *St Paul*, came too: 'Fred Myers was exceedingly agreeable, but there is a fiery vehemence half apparent in him which made one feel that he might not be so to all men and in all moods.' Taylor was looking at a wide range of criminal issues in the colonies at this time and Myers, the young man of twenty-five, later wrote to the philosopher of seventy on the problem of the treatment of the habitual criminal. He proposed what he called a manly solution to the problem — execute him. It was a fluent, cold and perversely original letter. It was the product of a young man who, at this stage in his life, appeared to be reserving his sympathies for an elite and who nowadays would probably be seen as putting fascist and authoritarian desires for order above justice. He did, however, in a rather perfunctory manner, acknowledge that the criminal should be given an opportunity for repentance and reform, before resorting to the 'manly solution' (Taylor 1924: 248–61).

In the New Year of 1869, his life was threatened by a severe bout of pneumonia and he suffered a similar disillusion to that experienced at the time of his swimming beneath Niagara. He collapsed while lecturing at Manchester and spent much of February in bed in some pain. His right lung was badly affected and leeches were applied. A wavy line beside this period in his diary (Myers 14/1: February/March) indicated, as on other occasions, a period of particular significance in his life. Without doubt, the combination of an artificial and overblown spiritual intensity, which was both too stressful and too ethereal to sustain, and the increasing evidence from history and science, chipped away at his faith. He continued to observe the forms for a while but, in the draft version of his autobiography (Myers 26/63/21), he concluded that the last Sunday in October 1871 was the final time he attended church with any 'hope of learning aught of "the chief concerns of man"'.

It is noticeable at this time that he really began to recognise and to respond to Henry Sidgwick. One of Myers' first detailed letters to him (Myers 12/94: 17.10.1869) was an expression of his delight in Sidgwick's essay on Clough—the great poet of doubt and loss of faith in the previous generation. The severance from Mrs Butler's Christianity was permanent. Yet he did not break with her social reform aspirations. He actively supported higher education for women, and resigned his lectureship in 1869 to work for it, and he retained an interest in broader social and political reforms for them. There is some doubt, however, whether his resignation was purely to find more time for these wider objectives. Myers did not like lecturing and found dealing with the average 'poll man' (those studying for only a pass degree, usually young aristocrats) stultifyingly boring. Henry Jackson, a reforming fellow of Trinity, commented on Myers' and Sidgwick's teaching in the late 1860s: 'In those days the lecturing of Classical Lecturers was perfunctory. H Sidgwick prepared his lecture at breakfast and gave the rest of the day to Arabic. Myers, when his lecture was done, gave himself to mesmerism' (Parry 1926: 18). Proposed changes to this rather undemanding system, which would involve the fellows more fully in teaching, did not appeal to Myers. He looked about for other occupation.

Myers and Annie Marshall

As we shall see in a later chapter, Myers found a congenial if functional profession in the inspection of primary education, and a lifetime's spiritual vocation in the exploration of the paranormal. There was, however, an emotional void in his personal life. He obviously longed for both a physical and spiritual relationship, yet too fastidiously high standards may have prevented him from settling on anyone. A number of shadowy female figures flit in and out of his diaries but few attain any individuality or wider record. He made a proposal of marriage to a Miss E in 1871 which was rejected (Myers 13/22: 18.10.1873) and he had a dalliance with a Miss Drew in 1872 which came to nothing. 'Enough of Miss Drew' was the diary entry (Myers 14/1). At around this time Sidgwick, spotting his restlessness, suggested that marriage would do him good (Add.Ms.c. 100/231: 1.5.1872). But, as he commented in a later letter to his mother, at the time of his engagement to Eveleen Tennant (Myers 12/15: 28.12.1879), it was almost as if he had been trying to make himself fall in love. Perhaps, one might add, in the same way that he tried, by an effort of will and imagination, to make himself believe in God and Christ? He was, however, shortly to experience a genuine and unselfish love in the most unfortunate and trying of circumstances.

As a member of the Marshall family, Myers met many of the extended Marshall clan at one or other of their great houses in the Lake District, particularly Patterdale or Hallsteads. The first recorded meeting in his diary, with Annie Marshall, his great love in the 1870s, is for June 1867 — a lunch at Patterdale — with a later annotation from Petrarch, 'Blessed be the day, the month and the year' (Myers 14/1). Annie had, by this time, been married for a year. She was the daughter of a clergyman, the Reverend JR Hill, and if the comments of Myers' mother to him are to be believed, she seems to have been a beautiful and gifted swan in a family of commonplace geese (Beer 1998: 178). Her marriage to Walter Marshall gave her considerable social and financial status. Yet it came at a price. For Walter Marshall was a manic depressive. He would veer from extreme depression to over-extravagant and excitable behaviour. His father William, as the eldest of the great John Marshall's children, was brought up as a country gentleman, was bought a seat in Parliament (cost 5,000 guineas) and eventually received £150,000 in stocks together with a considerable amount of property in the Lake District (Rimmer 1960: 114). In 1872 he died and Walter inherited a substantial part of the estate, but this destabilised him and encouraged him in vague and grandiose financial and political ambitions.

A letter to Sidgwick suggests that love really began to grow between Annie and Myers when he met her at Vevey in 1871, during a long European holiday he was having (Myers 12/144: 2.8.1877). A note has survived, describing the impact she made on him there as she tried to cope with her husband's increasingly erratic behaviour (Myers 13/22). Myers was with them at Chillon and Montreux and he walked with her by the lake on the 21st February. There he learnt, 'how divine a thing human courage can be' and that 'there is nothing which a spirit of such magnitude cannot overcome or undergo'. On the 22nd she fainted when out with Myers and Walter (Myers 14/1). No doubt this was under the strain of coping with his increasingly erratic and exuberant behaviour. And she had, at the same time, the pressure of Myers falling in love with her. Entered in his diary on the next page, broken up into several pieces as was sometimes his way with material that required discretion, was, '*Adgnosco Veteris Vestigia Flammae*: I recognise traces of the former passion', the anguished cry of Dido in book IV of the *Aeneid*. Is there, perhaps, a hint here that the initial stirrings of love went back even farther than 1871?

Myers did not meet Annie again till June 1872 in London (the Walter Marshalls had a house in Town as well as the Lake District) where his feelings deepened and intensified. They talked on the leads of her house in Onslow Gardens. He had not seen her for sixteen months and she must have been feeling isolated and without support. For example, she had written to Susan Myers in September 1871 of the value of conversations with her and how she longed to have them again (Beer 1998: 147). In this situation it was not surprising, as John Beer (Beer 1998: 148, 151) has pointed out, that Tennyson's *Idylls of the King* and the final part of *Middlemarch* particularly appealed to Myers, with their accounts of high-minded lovers prevented by societal rules and conventions from being together. Myers, in fact, expressed to Eliot (Myers 11/118: 7.12.1872) his appreciation of her treatment of the relationship between Ladislaw and Dorothea, the latter trapped in her marriage to Casaubon: 'Noble love-making—the surprised and pure contact of lofty souls—is hardly ever described truly.'

From 1873 onwards it is possible to pick out the development of his feelings for her, as reflected in his diary entries. It is clear that they met fairly regularly at Hallsteads and Old Church in the Lake District, and in London over the following three years. He suffered depression for three consecutive days early in the New Year of 1873 at Cheltenham (unusual for one of his normally sanguine temper), which was relieved first by a visit from Annie, then one from Edmund Gurney, and finally by his meeting with Walter and Annie at Scarborough later in the month. At the foot of the page recording the Scarborough excursion, and of the next three pages, were placed single-line quotes from a poem by William Morris. When these were combined they clearly indicated the way love had been creeping up on him: 'Love is enough;/while ye deemed he was sleeping/ There were signs of his coming/and sounds of his feet' (14/1). For those interested in the puzzle of apparent post-mortem communications from Myers, it may be worth noting that the same device appeared in one of 'his' scripts (Johnson 1907–1909: 178).

Annie figured in many entries over the next three years—the dress she wore, the walks, the visit to the Royal Academy with her, the trip to Madeira and the Canary Islands with Walter and her. They were obviously meeting more frequently because Walter's situation was deteriorating. In May 1874 he decided not to go to America with Gurney because of the state Walter was in and later in the year, as a diversion, she was even introduced by him to Mrs Fay, the medium (Myers 14/1: November 1874). He shared his growing concerns with Sidgwick and in a letter inviting Sidgwick to Old Church and Hallsteads, mentioned, in general terms, a range of problems she had: 'Worse again and many troubles of various kinds hang over that unhappy household' (Stein 1968: 131).

He kept up his running — on May 16th 1874 he did two miles in thirteen and a half minutes. Beside the record of his time he added 'Inextricable sadness'. Through his life, while he was fit enough, one hazards that these runs, at times virtually every day, coincided with periods of intense spiritual and emotional disturbance. But she gave him great joy as well as being the involuntary source of anguish. His spirits soared whenever he encountered her. One of his poems encapsulates his sudden delight at an unexpected meeting with her: 'Oh, when thro' all the crowd she came,/My child, my darling, glad and fair,/How seemed she like a flying flame,/That parts at eve the dusk of air!' (Myers 1961: 22). And another records the decision that their relationship should be honourably platonic: 'And the darkness of death is upon her, the light of his eyes is dim; But Honour has spoken, Honour, enough for her and for him' (Myers 1961: 19). He wrote of that poem that, 'Its tone is one of almost intolerable strain' (Myers 1961: 38). The pressures were enormous. On the one hand there was their obvious physical and mental compatibility, and the fact that neither, at that time, was a conventional Christian. On the other, quite simply, was the damage that an affair, an elopement or whatever, would do to them and to their immediate families, as it surged through the wider tributaries of the Marshall clan and beyond. The rather rousing late Victorian rhythms of his poem should not divert one from that central, agonising tension, 'Full-souled, and awake, and alone, with the whole world's love in their eyes,/With no faith in God to appal them, no fear of man in their breast,/With nothing but Honour to call them, could yet find Honour the best.' Henry Sidgwick, no doubt, would have commented that he would have preferred 'Duty' as the motive. Interestingly, Myers used the more romantic 'Honour' to describe the constraints on their relationship.

Matters came to a climax in 1876 when Walter went through a particularly hyper-manic phase and started to spend even more wildly (Beer 1998: 157). He became involved in a property investment in London (lending money without adequate security) and grew abusive when questioned by his wife. Annie asked Myers, her husband's brother George, and her father to help, and on the following day arrangements were made to have him certified — if only temporarily — as insane. When Walter left his house with the family doctor he was immediately seized by two men, bundled into a horse-drawn cab, and taken to a nearby asylum. Shortly afterwards he was moved to Ticehurst in Sussex, where his wealth enabled him to live in comfort although with restricted freedom. Walter protested strongly at his confinement, agreeing that he was an excitable and demonstrative personality but not that he was insane. However, when he stated on the 24th May that he had contracted syphilis at 21 (Beer 1998: 160), the doctors began to treat his symptoms as indicative of a move towards General Paralysis of the Insane. (Whether Annie knew this, and whether it and her consequent fear for its possible impact on the health of her children had an effect on her decision to end her life, can only be conjectured.) Walter's early release was therefore highly unlikely.

Annie's mood grew increasingly dark and guilt-ridden. She went first to stay with her clergyman father and then later asked for a family meeting to discuss the situation. Racked with shame and remorse, a common reaction amongst relatives of the confined in the nineteenth century (Mackenzie 1992: 101), she offered to look after Walter herself. However, it was decided that all communications with regard to Walter should go through Annie's father and that a small committee handle the practical affairs (Beer 1998: 163). Annie was to go to their house at Old Church, hard by Hallsteads and Ullswater lake, and live quietly with her children and a governess. Myers and his brother Arthur, meanwhile, had left on July 2nd for a tour of Norway.

From Susan Myers' later communication to Myers and from accounts in the local papers, it is quite clear what happened (Beer 1998: 164–65). Annie became increasingly withdrawn and appeared to lose her confidence in Susan Myers, who previously had been one of her greatest supports. She said, 'she saw she had been quite wrong in everything.' Certainly that statement referred to Walter's certification but whether it also expressed guilt at the relationship with Myers we cannot know. The sheer tiredness and strain consequent on looking after Walter and five children, plus the pressure of the events of the summer of 1876, must have completely worn her out, and in her exhausted and remorseful state she could see no way out except suicide. Susan Myers, who had been keeping her company, had left on the evening of the 28th August to travel to Edinburgh. Annie had crept out sometime that night and her body was found in deep water on the following morning, the 29th. A shawl had been left on the edge of the lake. The newspaper reports of the inquest revealed that she had first tried to stab herself with scissors and when that failed she had drowned herself.

Myers, in his grief, spent a considerable time haunting the grounds at Hallsteads, almost, as he said, like an earth-bound spirit: 'Some of the serenest of those mourning years were spent in that valley in the grounds of Hallsteads, on Ullswater, which has been the setting of much of my inward life—There for many a twilight hour I have paced alone, and shaken from the thick syringas their load of scent and rain' (Myers 1961: 28). Serene seems a strange word to use in connection with grief and loss, but Myers came to believe that this relationship with Annie had a deeply spiritual element. He concluded that through contact with her—admiration for her efforts to deal with a very difficult situation, growing enchantment with her character and personality—he himself had been purged of his grosser physical desires. He compared their relationship to that of Dante and Beatrice or Petrarch and Laura, the woman in each case helping the man grow and initiating him into a higher ethical and spiritual purity. According to WH Salter (Salter 1955a: 10d), this was the turning point in Myers' life. This relationship rescued him from a life of rakish sensuality. That may be an over dramatic interpretation of the situation, in the light of Myers' later life. He had a strong sensual streak in his character and had always an appreciation of female physical beauty, but that the relationship, and its tragic end, refined and restrained the more obvious elements of that sensuality, there can be little doubt.

There are, however, those who have contested this more charitable and benign interpretation of the relationship. A particularly virulent example of this was a review, by Archie Jarman (Jarman 1964: 17–29), of Myers' *Fragments of Inner Life* when it was published by the SPR in 1961. Jarman saw Myers as, 'the intruder into a formerly happy, if unromantic, marriage … one might easily believe that had not the handsome, ardent and sensual poet intervened, she would have continued her quiet, fruitful life with her husband and the five young children whom she idolized'. Jarman asserted that Myers demonstrated little pity for Annie in his autobiography, that the tone was hypocritical and sanctimonious, that he was not honest and that his account of the Camden Medal Affair was misleading. He further argued that Myers was infatuated with Annie, that he met her three times a week between 1873 and 1876 and that Annie in the summer of 1876 was pregnant not with Walter's but Myers' child. He cited lines in one of Myers' poems, *A Sister for Phyllis*, as indirect evidence: 'I spake; she listened; woman-wise Her self-surrendering answer came.' He speculated that Myers approached Walter for a divorce in May 1876 so that he could marry Annie, that Walter refused and this led to his breakdown and incarceration. He further stated that Myers, seeing the situation as hopeless, abandoned her to her problems and left heartlessly for his cruise to Norway. He pointed out that Myers' mourning did not last long, that as early as 1878 he was chasing women again and that he married in March 1880, hardly the action of a man who had lost his true and eternal love. Finally, he argued that Myers' quest to prove post-mortem survival, was motivated not by a desire for re-union with Annie, but by an attempt to seek her forgiveness for the wrong he had done her. A more muted version of this thesis, with some modification and qualifications, has appeared in the work of Trevor H Hall and subsequently been cited, without careful examination, by a number of scholars outside the psychical research community, who have not noted the severe criticisms that Jarman's speculative thesis has received.

It is instructive to contrast Hall's and Jarman's conclusions, based on deftly juxtaposed circumstantial evidence (Hall 1980a: Slater intro xxix–xxxiii, 51–52, 198–99), with Beer's sensitive and close reading of the situation, the product of detailed archival research:

> Myers still under the sway of George Eliot's portrayal of noble love-making [Ladislaw and Dorothea in *Middlemarch*] followed by her insistence on the absoluteness of Duty, had come to recognize the existence of a love which could combine passionate attraction with stringently moral behaviour ... Their love might never be consummated in anything more than an interchange of eyes and a touch of hands, yet that would be enough (Beer 1998: 151).

Alan Gauld has also produced, in the *Journal of the Society for Psychical Research*, a measured and well-argued rebuttal to the Jarman thesis (Gauld 1964: 316–23). He pointed out that Myers clearly stated that he wanted to write a frank autobiography; that if he had been a hypocrite he would not have retained the friendship of some of the sharpest minds of the age; that Jarman misinterpreted the Camden Medal Affair; that the relationship between Annie and Myers was not a sordid, physical infatuation; that the poem he quotes hinting of Annie's surrender does not in fact refer to her; that there was no evidence of a pregnancy, only an oral tradition to that effect in the SPR and — if she were pregnant — there was no evidence that the child was by Myers; that her suicide could be adequately explained by the huge pressures on her generally; and that Myers regularly travelled abroad. There was no special significance in the trip to Norway. Finally, Myers remained on friendly terms with Walter, with Annie's father, and took an interest in her children. This was hardly the behaviour of a seducer and a cad.

This last point was a particularly powerful argument in favour of the innocence of the relationship, for Walter had been quite naturally outraged by his treatment. As Myers wrote to Sidgwick (Myers 12/132: 3.6.1876), 'Gull has seen W. & expresses a very unfavourable opinion. Newington tells Mr Hill he thinks he will never leave Ticehurst. W is now angry & complaining of plots etc. wh. much distresses A'. Myers also wrote directly to Walter (a draft of the letter survives) tackling the question of conspiracy head on:

As the certificate will show you, my evidence was limited to two statements: (1) That your normal manner showed the well-bred ... of an English gentleman. (2) That your manner on the evening of May 2 was of an opposite character ... My only other action in the matter was to despatch two telegrams, at your Wife's desire & in her name, on the morning of May 3, to her Father & to your brother George, requesting their immediate presence in town ... I have no reason to believe that the steps which were taken were in any way suggested or modified by any opinion of mine' (Myers 11/185: 27.1.1877).

Walter seems to have been reassured by this and there is little doubt that Myers' behaviour generally was that of a very good and devoted family friend and relative. For example, in 1874 he wrote to his mother, 'It is a great comfort to think of Walter as so well—the summer has answered capitally this year for him and Annie—and I trust the winter will go better too. The friends whom you and Ernest have helped them to get at Old Church have been a great element in the success' (Gauld 1966: 281). This is hardly the letter of a self-interested seducer. It should also be pointed out that there was an element of insanity or instability in Annie's family, since two of her sisters died insane; and the extra pressure of Walter's anger over his confinement and Annie's guilt about her part in this would, without postulating a physical affair, be sufficient to explain the tragedy.

However, Beer, while accepting that Jarman's case was flimsy, points out that, interpreted in the light of Victorian convention, there were elements of transgression in the relationship. It was all very well for Myers to undertake, 'such a strenuous platonic love ; he after all, had no other commitments' (Beer 1998: 184). It could be argued that this pressure on her was an act of cruelty. A number of observers have testified to Myers' rather domineering presence at times, to the force of his personality. For him the relationship may well have been rationalised as a transcendent love which was the key to the spiritual world and for which he lined up Plato, Dante, Petrarch, George Sand and others as justification. But it still put an additional burden on her. The line between family supporter and comforter and that of platonic admirer, even lover, was a very fine one. By stepping over it, no matter how delicately and tenderly, it may well have made everything just too complex and confusing for her.

After her death he hoped for messages from her and occasionally he thought he caught glimpses of her presence in séances, glimpses that became more sustained and visible when he encountered the high quality mediumship of Mrs Piper[1] and then Mrs Thompson.[2] The first hints at some communication beyond the grave occurred on a visit to Paris in 1877

1   See p. 202 below.
2   See p. 221 below.

when in a session with Madame Rohart, through table tilting, he got some fragmentary one liners: *name and father's name Annie Hil; month in which I saw you last Jui; relation to me Co.* Myers described the medium as a repulsive old crone. He had a number of sessions with mediums in Paris at that time, but despite his growing experience of the field he still, like many other investigators, found it difficult to accept that evidence of the most profound spiritual importance should come through unattractive messengers (Gauld 1968: 131–33).

Love and Marriage

The year 1876 had been a tragic year for Myers with firstly the news of Gurney's awful loss at the end of 1875 (three of his sisters were drowned while on holiday in Egypt) and then the impact of Annie Marshall's death on him later in the year. Myers described the former appalling event in a letter to George Eliot, 'You will have heard what has happened to the Gurneys. Three sisters who had taken an invalid brother to Egypt have been drowned in the Nile … Edmund Gurney loses in the youngest the very darling of his heart … & in both of the younger ones the only unfailing and instinctive sympathy in music which he knew …' (Myers 11/119: 2.1.1876).

Photographs of Myers (Myers 26/2–26) in the late seventies sometimes show him as rather ragged, and as having lost his youthful good looks. This was hardly surprising given what had happened to him and to Gurney. He received, however, no sympathy from that sharp Cambridge observer, Caroline Jebb, the American wife of his friend RC Jebb (Bobbitt 1960: 153), who commented on what appeared to be his increasingly anxious search for love and marriage after the death of Annie Marshall. She described his desperate quest for a wife, when on holiday in America, and his failure to realise that the kind of young women he was attracted to would not be interested in a man who was showing signs (in Victorian terms) of middle-age. She criticised his habit of talking too much and expecting the woman to provide an adoring, but attentive, audience (Bobbit 1960: 136–37): and when he finally did marry, she labelled Eveleen merely as 'a bar-maid' beauty (Bobbit 1960: 159).

There was, indeed, a sense of emotional desperation about these bachelor years. Myers had moved to London in the early 1870s, eventually ending up at 3, Bolton Row, Mayfair. Sidgwick had married in 1876 and Gurney in 1877, so Myers alone amongst his most intimate male friends was single. Furthermore, it was as if the death of Annie released him to focus on more immediate physical and emotional needs and he probably had the feeling that time was running out for him. Once married and in a stable and secure emotional and physical environment, his looks improved and later photographs taken by his wife register the change. Apart from a tendency to heavy colds, he remained generally in excellent health for the rest of his life, until the collapse of the final two years.

Myers and Eveleen first met very briefly in 1876 but there is no evidence that the young Eveleen particularly registered on him at the time. Yet when they met again in late 1879 the mutual attraction was strong. Eveleen Myers (Myers 25/118) noted on a card inviting Myers to call on Hamilton Aïdé (her mother's relative) for a musical soirée on 12th November 1879, 'Our first Meeting but one'and 'My first was in 76 — My hair was down. We met at Mrs Lewies (George Elliot) on 6th Feb. 1876. Fred's birthday.'[3] Things moved very quickly. The relationship deepened rapidly and on Sunday 28th December he wrote from Paris — where he had gone with Eveleen, her sister Dorothy, and their mother Gertrude — to his mother back in Cheltenham, and announced his engagement to Eveleen. He stressed that she was not to be alarmed and how different this emotion was 'from the ponderings over possible attachments, & attempts to feel them, which we know so well' (Myers 12/15) and also how unlike Eveleen was from the last girl Myers had brought to stay at Brandon House. He said that Eveleen cared for the serious, the intellectual side of him, and that, 'she has said absolutely nothing that either bored me or jarred in me in any way'.

He was marrying into a family very unlike his own except for the fact that both households had lost their male head when the children were relatively young. The Tennant ménage was very feminine and society orientated. There was the mother Gertrude, one son, Charles, and four girls: Alice (Elsie), Blanche, Dorothy (Dolly) and Eveleen. The family was much wealthier than the Myers, with a large town house in London and a country house in Wales with, in addition, extensive rented-out properties and farms (Tucker 1994: 59–81, 215–28). The girls, Eveleen and Dorothy, had been painted by the society painters Millais[4] and Watts. Their cousin Hamilton Aïdé was a popular novelist, poet and playwright who knew everyone. He provided male support and advice to the female Tennants after the death of the father in 1873 until the young Charles, the only boy, was old enough to fill that role. Mrs Tennant herself had close links with the great and good — and some of the not so good — in English and French society and entertained them at her frequent soirées and lunches. There is

3   See note 3 at end of Introduction (p. 8 above) on leaving quotations uncorrected.
4   See Plate 1, facing p. 110 below, for Millais' portrait of Eveleen.

no doubt that Myers was marrying into a family whose social position, connections and sheer wealth was far greater than his own. Even after the decline in the value of shares at the end of the First World War, the value of securities held by Mrs Tennant at her death was in excess of £63,000 and the Tennant estate itself in terms of properties, land and rents was valued at more than £114,000 (D/DT: 2552/1–3). In today's terms, she was a multi-millionaire.

Gertrude Tennant, née Collier, was born on 4th November 1819 in Galway in Ireland. She was the eldest daughter of Vice Admiral Henry Collier, whose own father — also Vice Admiral — had distinguished himself in the War of American Independence, and her brothers were colonels in the army. On her mother's side she was descended from Oliver Cromwell. Her husband, Charles Tennant, was a noted businessman and philanthropist living at Cadoxton Lodge near Swansea. They also had a town house at 2, Richmond Terrace, Whitehall, from where she ran her artistic and cultural salon. The usually waspish writer, Vernon Lee, wrote quite a flattering description of her encounter with Mrs Tennant (Gunn 1964: 85). She pointed out that she was particularly interested in 'rank, beauty and genius', but not rank to the exclusion of the other two qualities. It would, therefore, be unfair to categorise Gertrude Tennant as a mere snobbish hunter of titles and names. For, as EF Benson has pointed out, the society hostess of the late-Victorian period had 'really little in common with the old crusted Victorian snob who rated merit by precedence and preferred the presence of any Duchess however dreary to that of any Marchioness however amusing' (Benson 1930: 283). Moreover, her recent biographer (Waller 2009) has stressed her range of abilities and the depth and breadth of her contacts in European cultural and intellectual life.

The Tennant family was naturally a little suspicious about Myers and his motives for marrying Eveleen. What sort of man was he? Was he a fortune hunter? What were his resources? As part of the gathering of evidence about Myers' character and prospects, Edmund Gurney was called on by Hamilton Aïdé. Gurney was out, so he later wrote Aïdé what one can only call a marriage testimonial. He invited Aïdé to bring Charles Coombe Tennant (the son, who added the name Coombe in 1866) to meet him, so that he could talk to him in person, and he stressed in the letter that:

> my only difficulty in giving him the kind of information he would desire will be in not knowing where to begin or how to speak with a becoming appearance of moderation. Myers has been so long my dearest friend, I have so long held him to be at once the best & the most gifted man that I have ever known, we have been so absolutely one in every thought and aspiration ... And perhaps even in saying this I give sufficient evidence of <u>my</u> assurance, whatever that is worth,

of the certainty of a life with which his is linked being in the highest
sense blest and enriched (D/DT 2595: n.d.).

Hamilton Aïdé, armed with this testimony and having already met Myers
at least once, wrote to Gertrude on the 29th December 1879: 'It gives me
great pleasure to find you like Myers so much. I took an immense liking to
him — Rarely has a man, on first acquaintance, given me so strong a desire
to know him intimately' (D/DT 2579). He went on to point out to Gertrude
'he may be a valuable friend through life' and 'you do not enough cultivate friendships for your children in my opinion'. He clearly recognised
the practical, business-like side of Myers' character and saw that these
qualities would be a welcome addition to the Tennant establishment. He
was also particularly fond of Eveleen who, as he wrote to Myers, 'I love as
my own child … what a treasure of steadfast tendencys — what a pure and
blithe spirit is hers' (Myers 1/2). There were many letters of congratulation to Myers on the engagement, praising Eveleen's character and
beauty. E Clifford stated that he spoke of her beauty from personal experience, that Burne Jones testified to her genius and that, 'I am very glad you
are going to possess her' (Myers 1/121: n.d.). Eveleen was obviously seen
in a number of circles as a very significant catch.

Arthur Sidgwick, with whom Myers had had a very intense friendship
at university, wrote to express his delight at the news of Myers' forthcom-
ing marriage, and added significantly, 'I can imagine few richer or fuller
lives for a woman than to be your wife: and my evidence on the subject is
better than many others', as I know the waste places as well as the flower
and fruitage of what lies behind you' (Myers 28/9: 9.1.1880). If they had
been part of a homosexual circle round Symonds, as Grosskurth suggested, the letter has a maturity and generosity about it which implies that
their relationship in that sense was a passing phase. It is quite clear that
genuine pleasure was his response, rather than jealousy. Arthur
Sidgwick's brother, Henry, wrote in typical vein that he was, of course,
delighted, but, 'No doubt if you had taken my advice I should have
endeavoured to moderate your impetuosity' (Myers 28/37: 1.1.1880).

Meanwhile, Charles Coombe Tennant was playing his part in the investigation of Myers. He wrote a detailed letter to his mother (D/DT: 2579:
n.d.) describing what he had found out. He had obviously done his home-
work and certainly seems to have garnered the essentials — that the Myers
were the poor branch of the Marshalls, that Myers had only his HMI pay
to live off, that there had been a scandal about Myers at Cambridge
passing off other people's poetry as his own (how that garbled account
haunted him in certain circles), that he and his brothers had been brought
up strictly by Mrs Myers, who was a cold, hard woman. He pointed out

that Myers said that he had £2,000 a year to live on and he was obviously keen for his mother to probe where this came from. He specifically urged her to identify, 'the exact, the separate source of each individual portion of his income' and 'what he will settle on Evy either by what accumulated or out of future income'.

One cannot help concluding that Myers exaggerated his resources in order not to lose his future wife, assuming that he did in fact state that he had £2,000 a year to live on. That figure does not square with the 1880 list of assets (Myers 19/20) that Myers drew up at the time of his marriage. He seemed to have £600 from the HMI salary plus £50 from literary work. The remaining money was from investments and projected rent of their Cambridge house when they were in London or elsewhere. Some of the investment income, however, came from stock, securities and bonds that Eveleen brought to the marriage. And even with all this added in, the total income was £1,400, well below the £2,000 mentioned above. It should be noted, however, that his diary (14/1) does provide a summary of investment income before 1880, so that he must have had some additional resource. Nevertheless, his assertion (if he did actually say this) that he had £2,000 a year coming in, was the—perhaps pardonable—exaggeration of a lover fearful of losing a beautiful (and wealthy) prize. For in addition to her looks, her youth, and her investments, Eveleen also had property worth £63,000 settled on her. However, not all of this would go to Myers in the event of her death. He would receive one third for himself and any children, and the remainder would stay within the Tennant family. Even before the Married Women's Property Acts of 1882–84, trusts could protect the property of the wife. Such legal protection was, however, only available to the wealthy.

Myers' lack of great expectations (though what he had would put him on the fringes of the upper-middle class: Perkin 1989: 78), so accurately probed by Charles Coombe Tennant, did not tell against him. Mrs Tennant liked him very much and did not press the financial aspect as hard as her son might have wished. The standard financial arrangement in marriages of their class was, as Taine put it, 'A gentleman … insists that the gentleman who marries his daughter make a "settlement"on her, two, three or four hundred pounds a year, an income entirely at her own disposal once she is married, and which will constitute her "pin-money"' (Taine 1957: 73). Myers never provided this for his wife and it was Mrs Tennant who gave Eveleen an allowance of £200 a year, paid in two half year instalments (which she sometimes had to remind her mother to keep up). Nevertheless, Eveleen was obviously deeply in love with him and the household rated intellectual and creative qualities highly. Her mother was no fool and saw that Myers could provide a stable and caring environment for her daughter. Gertrude herself was an intense and gifted woman with many contacts in the literary and political worlds of Britain and France. Given her personal history and temperament, therefore, she was unlikely to stand in the way of her daughter's love for Myers. And in one of her earliest letters, Eveleen assured him that 'my Mother says I need not shew anything you write but keep it sacred' (Myers 6/2: n.d.).

The wedding was a splendid and worldly affair as befitted the status of the bride's family. They were married in Westminster Abbey by Dean Stanley, Myers' old family friend. Prince Leopold was unable to attend but did invite Myers to dine with Disraeli as a consolation prize! The couple then, after a few months wait till it was furnished and finished, moved to Leckhampton House in Cambridge (the architect was his cousin WC Marshall) and all the joys, tribulations and adjustments of early married life. At the bottom of his diary for Saturday 10th January 1880, Myers had written, breaking the lines up as if for security, 'Let me never be so far wanting/to my own felicity/as to be less than ravished with thy love' (Myers 14/1). Was this an implicit recognition that though there was strong physical attraction between them, and a certain shared *joie de vivre* (even if this expressed itself in different interests), there was not that deep intellectual and spiritual bond that he had shared with Annie Marshall? Or it may just have been a rather convoluted way of reminding himself to count his blessings.

The relationship had a strong physical and emotional basis and they were both volatile personalities in private. She wrote on one occasion, 'I have taken All your night shirts away so that you Must come to my Room' (Myers 6/23: 30.12.1881). As Peter Gay has vividly demonstrated (Gay 1984:71–108), one should not be dismissive and superior concerning any supposed Victorian diffidence about private sexuality. Her letters frequently express a physical yearning for his presence and a gushing acknowledgement of his almost quasi-divinity! She wrote from Brandon House on 6th February 1882 what a perfect little baby Leo was in his bath and how she was longing to get Myers back again, 'to hold you, my King' (Myers 6/24). The letters are full of such endless endearments and refrains to come back to her and, 'I have been so irritating but you are so forgiving'. However, such an extravagant affection could sometimes metamorphose into irritating, and even public, displays of temper and tantrum. Their sometimes tempestuous relationship was satirised by JK Stephen, 'Lo! When a man, obscene and superstitious, /Lo! When a woman, brainless and absurd, / Join to idealise the meretricious, / Love one another like a beast or bird.' This was a fine parody of Myers' *St Paul* (also parodied in Stephen's *Lapsus Calami*) and rather a cruel view of their relationship. Stephen was actually said to have repeated these lines to

Myers at a party in his house and though gross, they do hint at the way in which they were seen through the sour and jealous prism of some sections of Cambridge academia (Stray, C 2007: p.c.).

Yet they managed to work out a *modus vivendi* that suited their different temperaments and tastes. They spent a fair amount of time apart because of his HMI inspections and psychical research activities. She gradually came to accept these absences and to believe that his eye for a pretty face was harmless; for Myers was quite open with her about his appreciation of female charm and beauty. She wrote to him while he was on a demanding research tour in France towards the end of 1886, that he'd been working so hard that she hoped he could find some time to enjoy himself and 'I wish some lovely being be there to make it delightful for you'(Myers 6: 31.12.1886). In addition to research, Myers was adamant that he would spend an adequate amount of time with his widowed mother and that he would holiday with his brother Arthur. Arthur, who suffered from *petit mal*, needed support, particularly if they were going swimming or doing some hard, remote walking. A small number of letters survive from Arthur Myers (Myers 3/87–101) to his eldest brother. They are friendly and affectionate and reveal his determination to try to keep his affliction under control.

Their frequent periods apart meant that Myers and his wife corresponded with each other in some detail, with great regularity, and with profuse expressions of love and affection. To our tastes some of the endearments between them seem excessive, but the Victorians exploited the postal service to stay in frequent daily and often more than daily contact, and the linguistic conventions were more generous emotionally than in our own day. Her letters, particularly, have an almost overwhelming breathlessness about them. She wrote, for example, on 9.1.1883 when he had just left home, 'My darling it is now 1.25. You have been gone about 8 minutes and I feel such a longing to tell you what a perfect creature you are.' There could be few men who would not want to lap up this kind of thing.

Yet, it soon emerged that the docile fiancée who sat so placidly admiring and listening to Myers' intellectual flow, and the young wife, who penned letters of passion and admiration, had other sides to her character. She could appreciate his friends' qualities and what they meant to him, but she personally had no deep attachment to them and, quite naturally, often wanted her husband to herself. As she wrote to her mother and Dolly, 'Then Mr and Mrs E Gurney have invited themselves for a Sunday, as it will only be for one day I make no objections — but it is rather trying as I am not strong enough yet to entertain people I do not care about' (D/DT 2581/2: n.d.). The same refrain continued throughout the early years, particularly with regard to Gurney. One the one hand she was half-placatory, 'Do not be angry about what I have said about the E Gurney' (Myers 6/43: 3.1.1883). On the other, she could be waspish and direct: 'Will you tell me when you next write, what day Mr Gurney will have left our nest. I should so much prefer coming home to find my own beloved one alone' (Myers 6/314: n.d.). And, ignoring the attractions of the combined, magisterial intellects of Henry Sidgwick and his wife Eleanor, 'I won't have the Sidgwicks ... So no more about Sidgwicks' (Myers 6/258: n.d.).

But there was a difference between the natural desire of a young bride to have as much of a very busy husband's time as she could, and not share it with comparative strangers, and the kind of almost competitive possessiveness that Eveleen Myers demonstrated in later years. This was certainly difficult for Myers during his life time and it is also led to considerable problems with regard to psychical research after his death, as will be shown later. CD Broad, a later incumbent of the same philosophy chair that Sidgwick held, was particularly scathing on the subject of Eveleen's character: 'The latter [Eveleen Myers], indeed, would seem, from all accounts that I have ever heard of her, to have been a singularly egotistic and rather unscrupulous person' (Cummins 1965: xix). However, some of his sources would have come from the inner circle of SPR people who, as we shall see, lost sympathy with Mrs Myers over her behaviour towards mediums after Myers' death, and who suspected (totally without hard evidence it must be stressed) that she had destroyed a copy of his will (Salter 1955a) containing a substantial bequest to the SPR.

She also felt a distinct sense of intellectual inferiority to her husband and was concerned that she had not enough knowledge to keep pace with him or adequately to educate their three young children. She assured him that, 'I am going to work so hard when I am up again, to get such a store of knowledge for our own little Rabbit & heather-bird' (Myers 6/55: 3.9.1883). The Myers eventually had three children—Leopold Hamilton 1881 (named after Prince Leopold his first godfather), Silvia 1883 and Harold 1886. Myers carefully noted in his diary the rising sign under which they were born (Aquarius, Leo and Saggitarius, respectively). He was probably influenced by his close friend CC Massey, who was an enthusiastic if rather inaccurate astrologer and, at this stage, Myers' adviser on all things occult (Williams 1984: 215–22).

One gets a sense, from the letters between Myers and his wife, that she tended to bind the children to her (displaying that possessiveness commented on by Broad) and that the father was seen as a slightly distant and authoritarian figure, only concerned with academic performance and proper moral behaviour. That is, perhaps, slightly uncharitable, as she did spot that Myers and his eldest son were of different temperaments. She explained in a letter to him, how to get the best out of Leo: 'I <u>know</u> that <u>Leo</u> is in nature very like myself. He is <u>sensative</u> to an <u>agony</u> ... He is not quick with his books ... He ought never to be overworked ... never frightened ... never Humiliated — for <u>Pride</u> will prevent his showing how <u>smally</u> He thinks of himself ... he is yearning for some admiring love' (Myers 6/97: 11.8.1886). Myers did have a tendency to go for Leo and he can occasionally be found in the correspondence apologising for some outburst: 'I have quite resolved never to speak harshly to him but to let him always explain himself' (Myers 7/259: 21.10.1886).

He also sensed, at times, that he was being cut out of the relationship. He wanted her to wait so that they could tell Leo together that Myers had managed to get the boy into AC Benson's house at Eton (Myers 9/14: 21.2.1892). On another occasion he wrote in anguish, and to our post-Freudian ears rather embarrassingly, that 'Leo must not turn me out of your burrow! to which I belonged before Leo did' (Myers 8/335: 11.8.1891). Yet he loved his son — all his children — very deeply, judging by the many expressions of love and affection in the letters. For example: 'Dear old Leo! hug him for me till he squeaks' (Myers 8/370: 30.12.1891). Yet there was a difference in their attitudes. Myers was more than thirteen years older than his wife and the more intensely Victorian of the two of them. He agreed with her that they were both totally united in their love for their children, but argued that she thought more of their happiness and he more about their immortal souls. This statement was noted by Eveleen Myers as one of her husband's most characteristic statements when she took over his diary after his death (Myers 14/2). There is a heartfelt letter from him to her about Leo, with the central part torn out: 'I do not blame him for not being clever', but it was their duty as parents to provide him with material and emotional support and his, 'to work as hard as he can or he will fall behind others' (Myers 9/281: 24.12.1893). Myers, outstandingly gifted, by constitution addicted to hard intellectual and physical exercise, never really understood his diffident, sceptical, but talented son. One gets the strong impression of Leo, physically and metaphorically, trying never to be alone in the same room as his father. In later years he described him to friends, perhaps a little unfairly, as 'Theodore Pontifex the Second' (Bantock 1956: 137).[5]

Even if Myers did not always demonstrate easy affection for his children, particularly his eldest, he certainly felt it. There is a moving brief reference to them in his autobiography:

---

5   The reference is to the bullying clergyman father in Samuel Butler's *The Way of All Flesh*.

> My wife is beloved and loving ; my three children are an unfailing joy.
> All that lies around me breathes beauty and repose. The evening sun
> gilds this fair garden; the children play like leverets on the lawn; from
> my window I see quiet tilth and pasture beyond a girdling belt of
> flowers. This cannot be *my* destiny which is fulfilling itself in earthly
> felicity; it is the destiny of these innocent spirits linked with mine; but
> for me it is something accidental and posthumous, and presently it
> must fade away (Myers 1961: 41).

Yet, and yet. Though there is affection there, there is also distance. There
cannot be many wives who would wish to see their marriage and their
children viewed *sub specie aeternitatis*. He did not love with the particular,
entwined domestic possessiveness that she did. And she must have
found, even though she knew the story of Annie Marshall, the looking
backwards to a past love and forward to a posthumous reunion, difficult
to take. It was not just a platonic love for another which ended in the death
of the beloved. Myers saw the relationship in cosmic terms.

Nevertheless, there is little if any evidence, in the huge correspondence
between them, that he ever compared her unfairly to Annie Marshall or
dwelt over long on the relationship. A letter to Sidgwick suggests otherwise and hints, perhaps not totally realistically, that there was a physical
and spiritual resemblance between the two women:

> I think you will see in her things which you saw long ago, looking
> through eyes still lovelier from a heart which, with all its passion and
> all its purity, could not be <u>more</u> passionately pure. I have told her
> about Annie: — at once she felt all I would have her feel, and only
> longed that the likeness which I see should grow more complete. I am
> able to feel, and thus alone could my being flow in one channel, — as if
> she was a gift to me from Annie, — a pure child chosen by her whom I
> worship to be my companion thro' this world, till we meet 'where no
> loves are mutually exclusive, but each intensifies all'. This is what I
> have said to Evie, and her look and answer are treasured deep in my
> heart. I twice took Annie to look at Eveleen's picture (by Millais) as a
> girl of 16 in 1875, — and she admired as I did the glowing innocence of
> those child-eyes. They would have loved each other; — and I believe
> they <u>will</u> (Myers 12/151: 1.1.1880).

There is also an entry in his diary for July 29th 1880 when he took her to
the Valley at Hallsteads where he and Annie had walked and he had
mourned her among the rain-washed syringas. He marked the entry as a
red letter day (all days that he would have wished to live again were indicated thus) and 'E in Valley' was ringed in red also.

It was obvious however that Eveleen, as she herself recognised, had not
the intellectual seriousness of Mrs Sidgwick nor the shrewdness and
moral insight of Myers' mother. She must often have wondered what he

would see in her after the initial intoxication of early married life evapo-
rated, and have become insecure whenever there were any differences of
opinion. This insecurity was compounded by Myers' sometimes irritable
and impatient nature, partly genetic but also intensified on occasions by
overwork. Dorothy Tennant wrote to her mother about one such incident,
'Fancy Fred using such language to Eveleen' (D/DT 2580/1: 13.9.1881).
And there is an exchange of letters between Myers and Eveleen even
before their marriage (Myers 7/7: 19.1.1880) in which she complained of
his pushing her impatiently and he replying that he had not meant to and
would not do so in the future. He had also had to make her realise, perhaps not with complete truthfulness, that it was not her physical beauty
that really attracted him, 'for your beauty is not yourself, my child, it is the
least part of you' (Myers 7/1: 31.12.79). He pointed out that she should
not put him on a pedestal and that his ideal of life was not one of quiet
domesticity with no challenge, but one which contained 'seasons of struggle and contest' (Myers 17/13: 25.1.80). Yet, he continually re-iterated that
she was what he wanted and that, 'you are all that my heart had conceived
in your exquisite and satisfying companionship' (Myers 7/26: 12.9.1880) .

Eveleen Myers may not have been a Cambridge intellectual, a Mrs
Sidgwick, but she had talents of a different sort. She had a strong personality, she was loyal, if possessive, and she would fight for her family. As
Deenagh Goold-Adams, her grand-daughter, stated, 'My grandmother
was not one to reason why and the introspection and self-criticism of the
Myers family was quite alien to her. She wanted fame, fortune and beauty
for herself and all her dear ones and would fight for that with any weapon
that came to hand' (Myers 29/70: n.d.). And she would blossom into a
very fine photographer. She first started by photographing her children,
having asked Myers (Myers 6/141: 7.9.1888) if she could borrow his
mother's camera. He then bought her a very expensive camera for Christmas and in 1888/89 she had a dark room built and set up a photographic
studio. She had local technical support — a little man with a club foot who,
she said, would do anything for her (D/DT 2587/1: n.d.). She then moved
on to photograph some of their friends, distinguished visitors, and also
some of the great figures of the day like Browning and Gladstone. She
seems to have taken a particular liking to JA Symonds, writing to her
mother that 'Mr Symonds is by far one of the most interesting people I
have seen for years. He is very sympathetic & emotional & brilliant but
oh! so delicate' (D/DT 2587/1: 23.10.1889).

She achieved recognition almost immediately, showing her work at the
Linked Ring Salon in the 1890s and four of her works were published in
1891 in the *Sun Artists Journal*. In fact Issue 8 was devoted to her with an
introductory essay by JA Symonds, who as we have seen was one of

Myers' friends that she found the most sensitive and intriguing (Hannavy 2008: 1358). Her letters capture aspects of this: 'A grand time with Mr Gladstone … I took infinite trouble. He would not <u>consent</u> to head-rest. I could <u>not</u> order him about as much as I should like but I have in some things. Leo was so nice. He showed Mr Gladstone his "black Rabit" & told Gladstone he must not wink. Leo fixed Mr Gladstone & said to him "You <u>did</u> wink you <u>never</u> ought to wink" Gladstone laughed' (Myers 6/155: 26.4.1890). She was also capable of independent opinions. Frederik van Eeden, a Dutch psychologist with a strong interest in spiritualism, wrote to her about an impending visit during the Boer War, mentioning the unjustness of the war and how Myers had told him that she was 'dangerously inclining' to his, van Eeden's, views (Myers 29/44: 30.11.1899). Myers was no chauvinist and disliked needless belligerence, but he does appear to have been a consistent, if moderate, imperialist.

Eveleen was also good in a crisis. She was involved once in a hansom cab crash coming back to Cambridge from London, and she gave her mother a lively account of how she rose to the occasion and prevented her luggage from being stolen, 'a frightful crowd of roughs … in an instant surrounded me in a thick mass … one seized my bag … I rushed after Him. and tore it from him' (D/DT 2585/2: late 1888). She showed similar resource when HM Stanley (who married Dorothy) suffered an accident in the Alps. She and Leo had gone with the Stanleys to Murren in July 1891 and one day Stanley, skylarking with Dorothy, broke his leg. Eveleen and Leo rushed back the several miles for help and, on horseback (she was thrown twice) she led a posse, that she had organised, of two doctors and eight stretcher bearers, back to the stricken and embarrassed explorer (Myers 6/184: n.d.). She was also quite capable of taking on her formidable mother over the question of Arthur Myers' medical fees. Mrs Tennant took the grand dame approach of not paying Arthur Myers for his treatment of one of her servants — either seeing him as little more than a high class tradesman or as a member of the family who should have done it for nothing. The daughter was having none of this: 'You requested that he attend your servant. He is not like Dr Carrier a medical practioner — he is a doctor of medicine. He has bad health and works very hard. Fred … no doubt pays him even though he is his brother. It is not money — though he has a limited income. It is the principle of the thing. He gives a lot of his money away' (D/DT 2585/2: 28.12.1887). This disagreement reflected the confused picture as to the status of the expanding professional classes in the late-Victorian period. And Mrs Tennant obviously had a thing about doctors! When her grandson Leo said he wanted to be a doctor, she replied that she could not understand why he wished to be 'an insignificant unknown poor Doctor' (Myers 6/102: 18.10.1886).

Myers was also often away on HMI visits and on psychical research activity. This latter was only partly attenuated during the early period of the marriage and intensified soon after with the forming of the SPR in January 1882. There is some evidence that Eveleen, at times, reacted badly to these investigations. Myers referred, in a letter to Gertrude Tennant (explaining why they couldn't go to Cadoxton Lodge), to the recurrence of a mysterious illness that Eveleen had had at the very time, early in their marriage, when he was in Liverpool with Oliver Lodge, the physicist, investigating thought-transference (D/DT 2581/2: 13.9.1883). These turns also occurred later on in connection with the research into the famous medium, Mrs Piper. This reminds one of the extended periods of illness suffered by Kate Gurney (the wife of Edmund Gurney, Myers' intimate collaborator in psychical research) during her marriage. It was almost the only weapon she had during periods of emotional isolation, perhaps. However, Eveleen Myers was made of tougher stuff and, generally adjusted to the situation (with just occasional flare ups and strategic illnesses), whilst claiming an adequate share of his attention. She also often went back with or without the children to London to enjoy the salon life with her mother and sister.

There were compensations at Cambridge as well. The Myers were a worldly and sociable couple (though she often complained of the pressures on her, particularly as she was bringing up young children through the 1880s). Interesting people were met at dinner, for the Myers established a reputation for bringing the wider world into Cambridge. As she wrote on one occasion to her mother: 'I got through my five dinners running, very comfortably, and am feeling well'. They entertained many of the leading literary personalities of the day, but one, Rider Haggard, particularly displeased her: 'so naively and outrageously conceited' who 'talked with contempt of Henry James and George Eliot'and who advised James 'to throw more plot and adventure into his novels, & make them worthy to be read by men' (D/DT 2585/2: 22.2.1888).

Yet it must have been difficult for Eveleen and the children. There were frequent visitors on psychical research matters as well as the visits of mediums themselves. There is some evidence that Leo and Silvia were at times disturbed by this (Bantock 1956: 137). In addition, Myers conducted frequent SPR experiments at home, as he regularly admonished the readers of the *Proceedings* and *Journal* to do. A letter to Dorothy Tennant from a friend, congratulating Dorothy on her marriage, gives something of the flavour of the psychic games/experiments that took place. The friend reminded her of an occasion when she was staying at Leckhampton with Dorothy (Dolly), the Myers, and Walter Leaf (Trinity graduate and SPR member) and they were all playing at table-tilting. The table was asked to provide a word to sum up each person. Dorothy very appropriately got the word 'gusto' but, alas, her friend, the correspondent, got 'soft' (RMCA 6861: 20.5.1890).

As a fashionable couple, the Myers had access to important social events that the average Cambridge academic did not. Their own wedding, of course, had been a major society occasion, and they received invitations to the marriage of Henry Asquith to Margot Tennant, which was probably the wedding of the year in 1894. As Margot's own diary demonstrates, it was a massive gathering, and an old nurse of the family was offered an exorbitant sum for her admission ticket—which she loyally refused (Asquith 1962: 198–99). Myers' comments did not reveal him in his best light: 'Margot Tennant's wedding today was a splendid affair! By a mere chance we got seats at the very front and saw everything ... The bridegroom looked resolute and common ... His red-haired boys belonged conspicuously to "the middle classes"' (Myers 19/19: 10.5.1894). This was rather a tiresome and unfair comment, given that he himself sprang from the less financially endowed branch of the Marshall family, that his father was a not particularly wealthy clergyman, and that both Asquith and his son were outstanding classical scholars, possibly in the same league as Myers himself.

One wonders if there was any rivalry between Mrs Myers and Margot Tennant—Eveleen Myers receiving her £200 a year allowance from her mother and, according to Wilfred Blunt, Margot Tennant receiving a £2000 a year allowance from her father (see Blunt 1921). Nevertheless, Eveleen was able, through her mother's resources, to entertain in considerable style at 2, Richmond Terrace and it was used by Myers for at least one grand occasion—the reception for the delegates to the 1892 International Congress of Experimental Psychology. A description by Mark Twain of the explorer, HM Stanley, at Richmond Terrace gives something of the flavour of the establishment:

> Stanley is magnificently housed in London, in a grand mansion in the midst of the official world right off Downing Street and Whitehall. He had an extravagant assemblage of brains and fame there to meet me —thirty or forty (both sexes) at dinner, and more than a hundred came in after dinner. Kept it up till after midnight. There were cabinet ministers, ambassadors, admirals, generals, canons, Oxford professors, novelists, playwrights, poets and a number of people equipped with rank and brains (McLynn 1991: 378).

Eveleen became increasingly feisty and *grande dame* as she got older, careful with money and suspicious of her servants. She did not have a good reputation for getting on with servants and cooks. She was always concerned lest they were getting above their station, becoming too settled and comfortable, and that they were learning family secrets about which they might gossip. And certainly there are a number of employer/servant skirmishes in the letters, with the hapless Myers often asked to dismiss old ones and find her new ones. She had an obsessive distrust of them, writing to him on one occasion to ask whether it was wise to have house-hold alterations done with neither of them there (the kitchen was being refurbished). She trusted the cook but not the two female servants — she even instructed Myers, at Cambridge, to burn the letter (Myers 6/138: 15.8.1888). She frequently gave her brother-in-law, Henry Stanley, advice about how to treat his servants. She lectured him about the need to keep on top of them and she also scolded him for paying them too much. Myers was better at handling the servants, but true to form, tended to judge them partially by their looks. He wrote to her from Ballechin (a house in Perthshire, Scotland, famed for its ghostly manifestations) where he had gone ghost hunting, that he was glad to hear she had dismissed one par-ticular servant: 'Her deaf stupid frightened look is painful to me' (Myers 10/69: 17.4.1897).

Eveleen Myers was not the only gifted and temperamental female Ten-nant. Her sister Dorothy had a strong father fixation, writing a daily diary to him long after his death, and often slept in the same bed as her mother (McLynn 1991: 120). There seems, in fact, to have been an intense and life-long rivalry between Eveleen and Dorothy for their mother's affec-tion, Eveleen constantly complaining that her mother preferred Dorothy and always gave in to her. Yet, on other occasions her letters were full of tender and embarrassingly fulsome endearments to them both. In 1890, after an on-off prickly courtship, Dorothy, who had a small but growing reputation as a painter, married the celebrated Henry Stanley. It was a strange relationship but it lasted and it brought Myers into contact with Stanley and a new friendship relatively late in life.

Stanley found it difficult to make friendships on an equal level. Yet he took to Myers and one feels that there was a touch of mutual admiration in their relationship. Myers was taller than Stanley at around 5' 10" or so to Stanley's 5' 5" and a half (the half inch being very important to the small man) which was not sufficient of a gap to make him so insufferably uncomfortable with Myers, as he could be with much taller people. Myers, immediately on hearing of their engagement, wrote Stanley a detailed letter warmly welcoming him into the family, sketching the nature of Dorothy's character and upbringing — which he obviously found a little lax — and giving Stanley sensible advice, from his perspec-tive, as to how to handle her (RMCA 442: 16.5.1890). Myers said that she would be a good companion but had been heavily indulged. He was later to perform the same service for Dorothy, when she was trying to prevent

Stanley from going on another expedition and get involved in English politics. He also helped Stanley with his writing and his speeches and — above all — in defending Stanley against the charges of brutality and corruption displayed during his time in Africa.

In particular, Myers supported him over the Emin Pasha Relief Expedition. This was a rather squalid and complex freebooting expedition across Africa from the West to the East up the Congo to Equatoria to rescue Emin Pasha (a European war lord) under threat from the Mahdi and then South and East across the great East African Plains to Zanzibar. The expedition took from 1887 to 1889 and had a range of motives: to gain ivory, to extend the influence of the British and, generally, to establish religious and commercial influence. Stanley, and several of his white staff, behaved with considerable brutality and at times Stanley appeared mad and unpredictably violent and vindictive. But he got through. He overcame many obstacles, plunging through great rain forests, and braving enormous wasp swarms, giant ants, and poisonous snakes (McLynn 1991: 186–208). On his return to England he faced a whole raft of charges (particularly that he had abandoned his second in command, Barttelot, left at base camp with the rear column, to their fate). Myers, in letters to Mackinnon (SOAS: Emin Pasha File 60, IBEA Co File 25), the chair of the committee which was investigating the accusations, stoutly supported his brother in law. In spite of this, Stanley's star declined. Yet he held Myers in high esteem and Myers even managed to get him along to one or two meetings of the SPR.

Myers saw the tempestuous and volcanic element in Stanley and gave him good advice both in the Barttelot affair and with regard to wide public relations issues. He wrote to Eveleen (to be passed on to Dolly and then to Stanley) that, 'As the Barttelot affair is the main drawback to Stanley's future (however unjustly so,) it is essential that he should show himself conspicuously gentle, fair-minded, considerate, modest, a really great man, as he is, & as far as possible from the truculent swaggerer which his enemies pretend that he is' (Myers 9/38: 21.6.1892). This was particularly in the context of Stanley's efforts to get elected to parliament, an enterprise in which Dorothy greatly encouraged him, for she dreaded his return to Africa. Myers tried to find speakers for him, suggesting that Ernest Myers might make an address. He also proposed that GA Smith (the SPR's factotum) might be released to organise some other people to support him publicly (Myers 9/42 : 25.6.1892). Stanley was defeated at his first attempt in 1892, but on the 15th July 1895 he was elected MP for North Lambeth with a majority of 405 (McLynn 1991: 375). And Myers had certainly helped. As Dorothy wrote on the 28.6.1895, 'I can never — never sufficiently thank you for writing that splendid address for Stanley' (Myers 4/99). He had also written the previous one for Stanley in 1892.

It is doubtful whether there was a sexual basis to Dorothy and Stanley's marriage (so McLynn 1991: 396; see Jeal 2007: 419 for a different perspective). However, they both loved children, and Myers' children were much cosseted by them. Stanley wrote to Eveleen that he was delighted to have her and Leo's company to Switzerland and, 'I will teach him how to explore ... worth months of school education' (Myers 24/23: 1.6.1891). This was hardly what Myers would want to hear—though he was in favour of robust physical exercise. Leo found Stanley much more to his taste than his rather stern and demanding father and the admiration was reciprocated. Stanley later told Eveleen (Myers 24/25: 12.8.1895), after spending some more time in Leo's company, how impressed he was with Leo's maturity and that he would become a grand man. All this was a tribute to the gentle discipline he had received and that she had, 'a son whose love for you is as large as his being'. This must have been sweet music to her ears and a justification for the softer approach she took with Leo.

Myers' frequent absences on psychical research and his acceptance of invitations to stay in great houses—often without his wife—may well have grated on her. The correspondence with Mrs BEC Dugdale and his visits to the Dugdale family at Merevale Hall, in Warwickshire, in the late 1880s and early 1890s furnish a particularly typical example of such experiences. Merevale Hall—which still exists—was a great Victorian Gothic house built in 1840. Myers wrote, 'Those delightfully harmonious days at Merevale live on in my memory' (Myers 11/97: 11.9.1891) and such events were often interspersed with ghost stories or table tipping or planchette or some other psychical explorations. On Jan 9th 1892 he responded to rumours from Merevale that the ghosts of Lord Nelson and Lady Hamilton had been spotted (!) by one of their guests with, 'but I must, please, know all names and dates precisely. What was this house? When were the figures seen? etc etc—a first hand account from each witness is the first and indispensable thing' (Myers 11/98). He was also frequently at Thorne's, near Wakefield, the country home of his friend Charles Milnes Gaskell, whom he had met at his Surrey tutor's house before going up to Cambridge. Thorne's, a very distinguished late eighteenth century house, with over 100 acres of ground, was perhaps for Myers a little too unsettlingly close to the grime of Wakefield (Gamble 2008). He also visited Battle Abbey. On the 9th April 1896 he wrote from there, 'I had a most hilarious dinner with the Duchess! who was really very good fun!—topping off her champagne & chaffing Lord Acton about having known everybody who was celebrated even before he was born! & telling him little anecdotes about the Duke of Wellington' (Myers 10/16).

When at home in Cambridge he was very discriminating as to whom he would or would not have to dinner and to stay: 'Don't rashly ask people to stay! ... If there is some very charming young female you may ask her, but no males, & no one who will need dinner parties!' (Myers 7/187: 19.2.1885). He also mentioned names that he felt deserved an invitation either to call or to dinner if appropriate — Olive Schreiner the novelist and Dr Mackail, the handsome and refined Balliol fellow and Virgil translator, were specifically singled out. He was quite happy to have Mrs Oscar Wilde to dinner, a poetess in her own right, who had written a warm letter of sympathy to Myers on hearing of the death of Gurney, saying that she knew that they were both 'bound together with a very near bond of affection, apart from the intellectual work ...' (Myers 4/142: 5.7.1888). But, Myers sternly told his wife, he was not prepared to invite Oscar Wilde himself (Myers 8/129: 20.11.1888). Was it Wilde's sexuality or his intellectual flamboyance that Myers objected to? One has a sense that he probably found Wilde too theatrical and ill-bred and too much the centre of attention for his tastes. In general, Eveleen Myers was prepared to accommodate him in these matters, provided she did not feel that he was being monopolised too much by old friends who talked of nothing but psychical research, and that she was not threatened in any way.

Myers certainly enjoyed the company of attractive, intelligent and sympathetic young women, but one doubts very much if he attempted to go further with the relationships. There are a couple of rather flirtatious letters in the archive from Laura Tennant (of the other even more famous and wealthy Tennant family and no relation), who appears to have been a particularly fascinating creature (4/100–102: Jan/Aug 1885). But such flirtatiousness was part of her game and can in no way be taken seriously. However, the letters give a flavour of that strange combination of the coquettish and the lofty which was part of the milieu of the Souls (a social grouping of upper and upper-middle class individuals, with Arthur Balfour at their heart, who rated intelligence and looks almost as much as breeding): whose very beginnings Laura witnessed before her death in childbirth — and on whose very outer fringes Myers occasionally hovered. She wrote to Myers from the Glenn, Innerleithen saying that she had read Zöllner's *Transcendental Physics* (translated by Myers' close friend Massey) and later, 'I agree with you as to what you say about Spiritualism. If only one could be turned from materialism to a belief in the unseen world through its power.' She also vividly described her situation and invited him to share it, 'I wish you were here — In a glorious sunshine with a golden mist over all things ... I lie on the grass and read all day ... or float on our loch — in a horrid little boat that will leak'. And she said, as he too would understand, how, when things were so beautiful, one longed for people like Shelley and Marcus Aurelius to share them with.

Regardless of the number of young ladies who came to dinner, or who wrote breathy invitations to Scotland, the intensity of Eveleen's endearments did not diminish over time, as a cynical, modern reader might anticipate. On 27.3.1891 she wrote, re-reading *St Paul*, 'how I love it and value it'. On 19.7.1891 came, 'My Heavenly Fluffy writing his unique and unsurpassed poems ...'. And, on 7.12.1893, 'How I love you more & more& more' (Myers 6/203). Myers, himself, particularly in the early years, was capable, though not as frequently, of writing back in similar vein but in his own orotund style, 'I am delighted to hear of your very pleasant parties and that my brilliant pink-blushed birdie has been flitting so gaily about' (Myers 7/193: 20.3.1885). He had his arena and appreciated her need to shine in hers. On another occasion, he wrote in equally florid tones: 'Nature has fitted you to flatter in the gilded saloon, and to command the admiring attention of the giddy votaries of pleasure' (Myers 7/198: 9.7.1885). Such high flown endearments on both sides continued until the end, providing a roseate glow round the domestic detail and petty irritations of life that, quite naturally, were also part of the content of their letters.

Prince Leopold and Ruskin

Myers owed his important friendships with Prince Leopold, Queen Victoria's youngest son, and with John Ruskin, to a third friend, RH Collins,whom, as we have seen, Myers met on his trip to Greece in 1864.[6] Myers visited Collins at Windsor in 1868 where he was tutor to the eighteen-year old Prince Leopold, whom Myers met for the first time. He liked the prince, finding him engaging and sensitive, and he sympathised with his predicament. The prince had haemophilia and he led a restricted and guarded life against which he fretted. Myers wrote to Collins at the end of 1870: 'I think there are very few men whom I know who would not in such a position do a boy as much harm as good, — but I don't think that of you ; and in fact I can only say that if I had a son myself, of the same sensitive and affectionate nature, the very first person to whom I would be willing to entrust him would be you' (Zeepvat 1998: 75).

Collins (and Myers, no doubt, supported him in this) worked hard to get the Queen to allow Leopold to go to Oxford in 1872. This eventually happened in spite of her comment that, 'the inconvenience ... in not having a grown up Child in the house in case of Visitors will be considerable'.

6   See above, p. 31.

Leopold quickly formed a rapport with both Myers and with Ruskin, the Slade Professor of Art, and sent the latter a copy of Myers' poems published in 1870 (Myers 1870). Ruskin, honest and frank in his likes and dislikes, replied that he preferred the shorter,lyrical poems, 'Wordsworth with a softer chime' (Myers 4/15: 21.12.1872). He found, as other critics did, *St Paul* florid and alliterative. He disliked artifice in poetry as he did in painting. Collins worked assiduously to bring Myers and Ruskin together, as the prince obviously wished him to. 'I am sure you would like to know each other', he wrote on 7th February 1871 (Myers 1/127) but it was not till the spring of 1874, at a dinner party at Wykeham House (the house the prince rented in Oxford), that Ruskin and Myers were able to build on their earlier brief acquaintanceship from the 1860s. Ruskin had been anticipating a lively discussion, but Myers, however, refused to engage in literary debate (Beer 1998: 291). Ruskin confided to his diary (Evans and Whitehouse 1959: 774) that he had found the evening trivial.

But when they met again in November 1874, after the other guests had left, they had a long and earnest discussion about the possibility of life after death. Myers told Collins some time later:

> That long conversation with him [Leopold] and Ruskin on the next world was the only occasion in my life when I have found thorough sympathy in my own intense interest in the existence which awaits us, and which must in reality so utterly overbalance this mere fragment of life wch we have here—and the sight of the Prince's look of brave patience & Ruskin's look of yearning melancholy made me feel as if they two typified to me all that the world contains of dignity, delicacy and sadness (Zeepvat 1998: 102).

Ruskin entered in his diary that he dined with the prince and 'heard from Mr Myers, things most wonderful and most precious' (Evans and Whitehouse 1959: 824). Eveleen Myers described that meeting, as she heard it from her husband, in a letter to Dorothy in the early 1880s, when she was trying to bring Dorothy and Ruskin together:

> He came into Fred's room just as Fred was getting into bed and asked Fred to tell him all about his views of the life after death he would not leave Fred for hour's and was so <u>very</u> <u>very</u> interesting. He told Mr Collins the next day, that Fred 'had "done him <u>so</u> much good he has lifted a load off my soul".' The next day he asked Fred to come into his bedroom and go on with the talk. so they did for a time till Mr Collins sent for Mr. Ruskin saying the Prince wanted Him. and Fred went to his room. in about 15. minutes there was a knock at Fred's door in came Ruskin and sat on Freds bed and began again He said that Religion and Art were the only things He could possibly care about or think of (D/DT: 2581/1: n.d.).

This interest in spiritualism was quite widely, though discreetly, spread through the upper and upper-middle classes in the 1870s. It was not just a vulgar enthusiasm of the mob. It was a strange and intimate current flowing through society. For example, after his degree Leopold travelled Europe with the Hon Alexander (Alick) Yorke, who also became a friend of Myers and who was an amateur medium in his own right. He was Equerry to Prince Leopold till the prince's death in 1884 and then became Groom in Waiting to the Queen from 1884–1901. He is described, rather unkindly, in Victor Mallet's (Mallet 1968) introduction to Marie Mallet's letters detailing life at Victoria's court, as an 'elderly pansy'. He was a genial man, short and round, and with a rich moustache. He used scent, wore buttonholes, jewelled rings and tiepins. He organised many of the Court theatricals and *tableaux vivants* and was himself a fine teller of tales and jokes. One of his less successful ones was supposed to have stimulated the Queen's infamous response, 'We are not amused'. It was Yorke who wrote to Eveleen Myers, after Myers' death, with some of the earliest alleged messages from him.

Collins' letters demonstrate how much genuine affection Leopold had for Myers and that the snobbishness in Myers, that the James brothers so disliked, had underneath it a genuine affection for the young prince and sympathy for the difficult situation he found himself in. Yet, there were limits to what Leopold was able to do for his friends – no matter how much mutual liking and sympathy there was. Collins, for example, wrote to Myers that the Princess Louise, Leopold's sister, couldn't receive Mrs Butler's documents on women's suffrage since it might commit her politically (Myers 1/124: 26.7.1871). The prince had sympathy for the social problems of women but was not as positive as Mrs Butler about votes for women and he found the Contagious Diseases Acts[7] and related issues and implications rather distasteful (Zeepvat 1998: 102–103). So Mrs Butler's attempt to influence matters using Myers as a go-between failed. The incident in no way spoiled the relationship between Myers and the young prince. Leopold continued to write him affectionate and friendly letters. He acknowledged the copy of Myers' recently published biography of Wordsworth, which Myers sent him, and the following year he agreed to be godfather to Leo – quite a coup for Myers – and sent the baby a beautiful gold, drinking cup as a christening present (D/DT: 2581/2: n.d.). The affection was genuine, on both sides, if gilded a little perhaps by social climbing on Myers' part. He wrote to Collins after the prince's death: 'You

7 Acts passed between 1864 and 1869 which allowed, within a certain number of miles of the main military and naval bases, the registration and examination of women who were suspected of being prostitutes.

know better than anyone how I loved him, who is gone'(Myers 11/173: 29.3.1884). Leopold had been holidaying in Nice. On Wednesday 26th March he went to a ball at Mont Fleuri, on the 27th he slipped and banged his right knee, and died early in the morning of the 28th (Zeepvat 1998: 188).

After Leopold's death Myers wrote a long, gushing essay on the prince: *Leopold, Duke of Albany: – In Memoriam*. It appeared first in the *Fortnightly Review* for May 1884 and was reprinted in his *Science and A Future Life* in 1893. Collins reported to him the Queen's reaction: 'The Queen was here Saturday and said to me "I like Mr Myers' article very much – but think he made a little too much of the Windsor life being so stately" – or words to that effect. This amused me, as it is well known the Queen hates the Ceremonial Court Etiquette of Windsor herself' (Myers 1/131 : May 13 n.y.). It is not difficult, however, to sympathise with William and Henry James' American dislike of Myers' snobbery, when one reads the essay. The grandiose language with regard to his childhood at Windsor: 'And indoors, too, were merry mockeries and bursts of boyish sportiveness' (Myers 1893: 211–43); and his look just after receiving the Garter: 'his look was as though his spirit were kindling within him and yearning to take rank with his forefathers and heroes of a bygone age', and, 'Still was Mr Ruskin the honoured teacher; still was it possible to watch, in fuller maturity, the contact of the elder and the younger man', and so on with a breathless flattering solemnity which rings hollow to our ears now and even then, perhaps, to some. Myers, as witness his later letters to Lord Bute, could lay the flattery on trowel-like with the best of them. But, even though he wrote like that, Myers did very genuinely feel for the young prince. And he appreciated his interest in the SPR and commented on it (though he did nothing so vulgar as name it in the memoir).

He stated that the prince thought that Russian Nihilism and German Socialism were encouraged by a disbelief in a future life: the implication being that successful work by the SPR would lead to a happier, more stable social order! This was a serious point, and it could be argued that one motivation for the SPR was the creation of a secular immortality for the masses, to provide them with the re-assurance that would ensure social stability for the privileged in this world. Myers, Gurney and Sidgwick, occasionally referred to this issue (Williams 1984: 107–109); and the argument that the psychical research of the upper-middle classes was motivated by the urgent need for social control of the unsettled working classes has some superficial plausibility. But, certainly for Myers, the ultimate imperative was an individual one; if annihilation was the end for one and all, what was the point, even for a well-developed and civilised race in the future: 'Nor much shall profit with their perfect powers/To have lived so much a sweeter life than ours,/When, at the last, with all their bliss gone by,/ Like us those glorious creatures come to die' (Williams 1984: 108).

The friendship with Ruskin was to last longer since Ruskin, though much older, died only shortly before Myers himself. When they became friends in the 1870s they were both in some romantic and spiritual distress. Ruskin was in the middle of his agonised, puzzling relationship with Rose La Touche (thirty years younger than he was) and Myers was locked in his platonic affair with Annie Marshall. After both women died their situation achieved an even greater symmetry and they explored the nature of their loss and possible future comfort in conversations with each other, though they only hinted at the actual details in their correspondence. They both believed that through their love they had been able to gain some experience of the spiritual, the transcendent, and they had both explored the possible consolations of spiritualism.

Ruskin had, in fact, earlier experience of spiritualism than Myers. As Akin van Burd points out (Burd 1982: 10–19), Ruskin met the leading aristocratic spiritualists, the Cowper-Temples, in December 1863 in Curzon Street and discussed spiritualism. In February 1864 he attended a séance with them, at about the time the young Myers was embarking on his tour of Greece and the Near East. Ruskin's attitude was sceptical but not inflexibly so. He later had several sittings with Home where marginal manifestations took place and he rather liked the medium as an individual. Therefore, in the 1860s, he seems to have had much more practical experience of these phenomena than the young Myers, whose focus seemed to be on the personal, highly seasoned spirituality of Josephine Butler. After a disastrous session with a medium in 1868 Ruskin lost interest. However, as Ruskin was withdrawing from investigations into spiritualism, Myers was increasingly becoming involved.

Myers and Ruskin talked over their experiences when they met again at Broadlands, the Cowper-Temples' Hampshire seat, in January 1876. Rose La Touche had died in May 1875 and this had re-stimulated Ruskin's interest. He had stayed in Broadlands the previous month (3 mediums were also there at the time; rather an overdose one might have thought). One, a Mrs Ackworth, claimed that Rose, 'fair, tall & very graceful', was bending over and whispering to him. One wonders what the later Myers and the sceptical SPR would have thought of all this as evidence. Certainly, in January 1876, Ruskin and Myers were at least united in sharing aspects of tragic and unfulfilled love. Their friendship deepened when Ruskin went to stay with Myers in Cambridge in March 1876, and he may have advised Ruskin to retain a balanced attitude given the complex and murky world of professional and semi-professional spiritualism. Ruskin was in uncertain mood since a friend had already suggested that Mrs Ackworth had been caught in fraud and that another medium, Mrs Wagstaff, was a mere professional, who took fees and who could not be trusted (Hilton 2002: 609–13).

Ruskin had clearly been told about Myers' relationship with Annie, for he stated later in the year, 'What you have written is for us both; and for us both in almost precisely alike states of mind, and trial' (Myers 4/11: 31.12.1876). But they were unalike in temperament and situation. Poor Ruskin had not Myers' intellectual buoyancy nor did he have, as Myers had through the 1880s, the support of gifted and like-minded colleagues to help him develop a considered perspective as to the validity and nature of spiritualistic phenomena. They both, however, shared the Platonic view that the highest form of love is transmuted into the spiritual and that love is more important than lust. Myers, however, more so than Ruskin, would have found the physical and sensual side of love particularly difficult to transcend.

It is worth further exploring the similarities and differences in their attitudes and relationships. Myers was in love with a mature woman who had had five children. Ruskin was in love with a young woman of intense religiosity struggling to establish some intellectual and emotional independence from her parents (Oppenheim 1991: 256–58). Interestingly, John Beer describes Ruskin's love for Rose as being romantically mediaeval rather than Platonic (Beer 1998: 259), and this suggests a genuine difference between them. Myers' relationship with both Annie and with Eveleen was (despite his initial use of the word 'child' in his letters to Eveleen) much more active and companionable. Woman was spiritual but she was not remote. She was flesh and blood. Ruskin had reacted violently against the physical. Moreover, Ruskin had a tangential but strangely logical fanaticism about him which made genuine intimacy difficult. Myers, though determined to plough his own furrow, was prepared to accommodate his wife's needs and adapt himself to other people's points of view. Ruskin's rather different attitude is highlighted in an incident noted by Myers in his obituary of his friend (Myers 1900c). When friends (as a birthday present) bought back for Ruskin one of his favourite Turner pictures, he said he would rather that they had joined the Guild of St George. The Guild was Ruskin's rather quixotic scheme to improve the lives of the rural poor by the effective management of uncultivated land.

Their friendship continued through the late 1870s and 1880s, surviving Ruskin's bouts of brain-fever. On the 10th July 1877 Ruskin met Myers with Mrs Cowper-Temple and the Gurneys (Edmund Gurney had married Kate Sibley on the 5th June that year). Myers also met Ruskin at the Cowper-Temples on 20.7.1878 and 26.10.1879 (Myers 14/1). After his marriage Myers naturally saw Ruskin less frequently, but his wife Eveleen and her mother Gertrude wished to revive the connection in order to further the artistic career of Dorothy, who was a painter of street urchins and gaining some popularity. Ruskin was happy to meet Dorothy but replied to Mrs Tennant that his forty years experience couldn't be condensed into one lunch over a mutton chop (Beer 1998: 304). He also suggested in a letter to Myers that Dorothy and Kate Greenaway (another painter Ruskin admired) would each improve if they had some of the other's qualities (Beer 1998: 303). And Myers and Ruskin still continued to communicate sporadically as the years went by. On one occasion Ruskin complained bitterly about the ugliness of the drawings in thought-transference experiments (Myers 4/14). Like others he tended to associate these activities with highly developed spirit, with the beautiful and the true. Yet, as Myers himself was coming to realise, evidences of psychical activity often took place in shabby corridors and below stairs, amongst unsavoury and unedifying types.

Man of Letters

Myers reputation was first made, as we have seen, as a poet and there were even occasional settings of his poems to music; Sir Walter Parrott, Master of the Queen's Music, invited him to Windsor to listen to a setting of his madrigal (Myers 3/130: n.d.), and later Elgar put to music his poem on Queen Victoria. However, not all contemporaries were admiring. Edmund Gosse, aspiring poet and later a leading Victorian/Edwardian man of letters, asked his father to finance a volume of poetry. His father refused if it was to be in the style of his son's friend Myers: 'How can you be captivated by this turgid rant ... do you not see that this style of writing is an utter sham?' (Charteris 1931: 14–15). Yet other critics emphasized the metrical subtlety of the verse, which gave them a chance to parade their erudition:

> The metrical scheme appears to be, that is, 5-stress trochaic, with dactylic substitution in the first foot and truncation or catalexis of the last foot in the second and fourth lines; or perhaps iambic, with anapaestic substitution in the second foot and a feminine ending in the first and third lines. But when many of these stanzas are read in succession, the movement is found to be, that is, 4-stress falling rhythm, with intermixed duple, triple, and quadruple time (Baum 1922: 75–76).

George Meredith more succinctly argued (in the *Fortnightly Review*) that the structure, 'was rhymed fours with an alternating eleven and ten syllable line' (Meredith 1868). And Swinburne himself later attempted the same metrical scheme with his *Mater Triumphalis*. Swinburne, in fact, hovers behind *St Paul* — pagan, intoxicating, sensual. Myers' Paul is a driven sensualist and his absorption in Christ expressed in highly sexual and emotional terms. There is little real argument in the poem. Conviction is generated by the repetitive hypnotic frenzy of alliterative phrasing, and bears the same relationship, perhaps, to genuine Christian mystical experience, as masturbation does to a full sexual union.

In some ways, his greatest legacy to literature may well have been in the impact of his psychical research on the work of writers of the period. This can obviously be traced in the use of SPR material as a source of chilling plot and narrative material. But it can also be demonstrated in more subtle ways in terms of its interaction with the conceptual processes and intellectual debates of the time (Thurschwell 2001, Luckhurst 2002). Some members of the SPR, particularly Myers, were great popularisers and systematisers in this field and provided writers with very useful sources for creative work (Keating 1991: 361). One could even suggest, as in the following example, their narratives were both a source of fiction, and themselves were shaped by it (though Myers and his colleagues were on their guard with regard to this):

> One night on retiring to my bedroom ... I heard a peculiar moaning sound ... there on the grass was a very beautiful young girl in a kneeling posture before a soldier, in a general's uniform, sobbing and clasping her hands together, entreating for pardon; but alas! he only waved her away from him ... had had an illegitimate child ... died broken-hearted (Myers 1904 2: 383).

The vision of the 1880s was later found to relate directly to a tragic event of the 1840s and would have had many resonances and echoes in Victorian literature and painting.

However, there were other areas of fiction where Myers and the SPR had less influence. Whimsical fancy and children's literature were not affected by the work of the SPR. They sprang from a different tradition. In addition, one must be careful when trying to align the work of the SPR with that of great writers like Henry James or R.L. Stevenson. Neither writer was prepared to allow the SPR material to overly influence their creative processes and intentions. Myers sent Stevenson rather peremptory and enthusiastic letters about the *Strange Case of Dr Jekyll and Mr Hyde*. Stevenson was flattered by the attention but did not make any of the changes suggested by Myers, which Myers stated would improve the story and give it the greatness that it so nearly attained (see Myers 4/76–77 and Maixner 1981). His suggestions were largely designed to link the behaviour of Hyde more closely with that of the multiple personalities he had researched in France and, in fact, would have had little effect on the literary merit of the work; except possibly to weaken it by making it more didactic.

Stevenson always stressed the importance of dreams to him throughout his life as an access to his unconscious and as an aid to creativity. Dreams played an important part in the genesis of *Kidnapped*, *Catriona* and *Dr Jekyll and Mr Hyde*. He saw the creative process as the work of his subterranean 'Brownies' who laboured through the night hammering out the main features of his stories to which his conscious self had only to put on the last finish and polish. And sometimes this dream activity seemed to plug into contemporary anxieties and concerns, such as — in the case of *Dr Jekyll and Mr Hyde* — the conflict between Victorian respectability and night- time evil (Walkowitz 1992: 206-207). Myers' friend JA Symonds, who knew all about the double life, expressed the terror and darkness at its heart in a letter to Stevenson: 'The fact is that, viewed as an allegory, it touches one too deeply. Most of us at some epoch of our lives have been on the verge of developing a Mr Hyde' (McLynn 1994: 266). Myers fully recognised, and was excited by, the relevance of Stevenson's creative processes to his theory of the subliminal consciousness, and particularly the upsurge of creative power that characterised genius (Myers 1904 1: 91). Roger Luckhurst has demonstrated how richly both this tale of Stevenson and another one (*Olalla*) feed off and in turn contributed to the development of psychodynamic approaches to the mind in the late nineteenth century (Luckhurst 2006: xiv–xx). George Johnson has also stressed the challenge of Myers' ideas to the psychological orthodoxies of the time, and their appeal to writers at the end of the nineteenth century and beyond (Johnson 2006: 64–68).

Henry James was evasive and reluctant to allow too direct an alignment between the scientific discoveries and narratives of the SPR and his creative work. This was a particular danger, in that he had much closer contact with the SPR, than Stevenson, through his social connections with Myers and the Tennant family and through the work of his brother William (he read William James' Presidential Address to the Society for him). He was very careful to absorb only what he needed and to digest, shape and modify it in his own way. He wrote to Myers, modestly, that 'The T of the S is a very mechanical matter, I honestly think — an inferior, a merely pictorial, subject + rather a shameless pot-boiler' (Myers 2/142: 19.12.1898). This is an interpretation strongly supported by the seasoned writer on psychical research, Brian Inglis (Inglis 1989–90). *The Turn of the Screw* was based on a story told Henry James by the Archbishop of Canterbury, EW Benson, who was familiar with the ethos of the Ghost Club and the SPR (Edel 1987: 426–27). But James was determined not to see the story as empirical fodder for psychical research. He wanted to get into it what he called elsewhere 'the dear old sacred terror' of the ancient ghost story' (Keating 1991: 360). He was, therefore, nervous about the rather dry as dust approach of the SPR and was deliberately vague about the onto-logical status of the events. And Myers did not treat it with the same seri-ousness that he had Stevenson's work. As Myers breezily informed Lodge in 1900: 'Henry James has written a fanciful story of country house life … The little girl feels lesbian love for the partially materialised ghost of a harlot governess' (SPR 35/1520). EA Sheppard, however, has argued that the Society and its work had much more impact on *The Turn of the Screw* than James might have wanted either to recognise or to admit (Sheppard 1974: 1).

The other writer closely associated with the SPR was Arthur Conan Doyle. Doyle had described in the pages of *Light* the powerful impact séances had had on his beliefs (Lycett 2007: 130–31). Myers immediately wrote to him urging him to help the Society in their work, since they needed people like him who were trained to assess evidence carefully. He also encouraged him after Gurney's death to take up Gurney's research into hypnotism and mesmerism (Lycett 2007: 138). This did not happen, in scientific terms, but this interest was certainly reflected in his literary work. Doyle joined the SPR in 1893 and actually investigated poltergeist activity in Dorset with Frank Podmore (Wynne 2006: 223–43). It would probably have been useful for Doyle's later reputation if a little of Podmore's famed scepticism had rubbed off onto him. Myers and Doyle both eventually took an optimistic attitude to what they saw as the best phenomena of the séance room, and after Myers' death, Doyle grew increasingly dissatisfied with what he saw as the narrow, carping meth-odology of the SPR, and he eventually resigned (Anon 1930: 45–52).

Myers also achieved a certain contemporary reputation as an essayist. Occasionally, in second hand bookshops, one can still spot faded copies of one or other of Myers' collections of essays (reprinted from periodicals) — *Essays Classical, Essays Modern,* and *Science and a Future Life.* However, were these, together with his *Collected Poems,* all that he left to posterity, there would be little excuse for reading him, except as part of the archae-ology of minor aspects of Victorian intellectual and cultural life. In *Essays Classical* he published extended essays on Greek Oracles, Virgil, and Marcus Aurelius Antoninus. In *Essays Modern* there were pieces on Mazzini, George Sand, Victor Hugo, Ernest Renan, George Eliot, Rossetti, Seeley (*A New Eirenicon*), and on Arthur Penrhyn Stanley and Archbishop Trench's poems, the latter two now forgotten figures. *Science and a Future Life* contained writings on the main title, on Darwin, on French politics, on Tennyson, on Modern Poets, and the gushing obituary of Leopold, Duke of Albany, already mentioned. A number of these essays had an impact at the time, but probably only the Virgil, the Rossetti, and the George Eliot have enriched later literary and cultural criticism in any significant sense.

A consistent theme emerged in many of these essays, as William James pointed out in his review of *Science and a Future Life*:

> The Essays ... have the same essential aim, which is to show, first, how disconsolately irrational is the view of the world which merely materialistic science and merely mundane history offer to the mind's acceptance ; and, second, how probable certain kinds of neglected fact have made it that the world which science acknowledges is but ... a fragment, of a larger universe of which we, as yet know nothing defi-nite, but which, if known, might satisfy our rational need (James 1986: 107–10).

It was quite natural for Myers, in pursuit of this aim, to have a particular penchant for politicians and writers who operated within a cosmic view of things. This is what he responded to most enthusiastically. He admired individuals who grappled with the great questions of ultimate purposes and value — love, honour, duty, immortality — even if their solutions were different from his own. The essay on George Eliot is celebrated and has often been quoted as an example of dogged Victorian ethics in the light of a meaningless universe. The essay on Rossetti has a sophisticated ratio-nale in that Myers was trying to rescue Rossetti's work from public aware-ness of his difficult and sensational private life, and to point out that sexual desire could lead to, or be transmuted into, genuine aesthetic and spiritual values (Danahay 1998: 379–97). It was written in the context of an exhibition of Rossetti's paintings, and Myers was trying to shift the focus from a merely sensual appreciation of physical beauty in his work, to an understanding of its spiritual dimension. Again, in his essay on Tenny-son, he paid little attention to the verbal craftsmanship and metrical skill, but focused largely on those cosmic aspects in the poet's work which so chimed with his own interest, quoting, 'Star to star vibrates light; may soul to soul/ Strike thro' some finer element of her own?', as an example of telepathy (Myers 1893d: 127–65); and, 'As here we find in trances, men/ Forget the dream that happens then,/Until they fall in trance again', as reminiscent of his and Gurney's discovery of different layers of conscious-ness only accessible through hypnotic trance or automatic writing.

But for contemporaries his essay on Virgil attracted most attention. Mackail, the Oxford Virgil scholar, sent a flattering note to Myers (Myers 3/4: 2.5.1897) thanking him for his support with Latin literature and stat-ing that he thought that Myers had come nearest of any modern writer in writing effectively and sensitively about Virgil. Myers had particularly commented on the character of Dido: 'A nature like Dido's will now repel as much as it attracts us. For we have learnt that a woman may be childlike as well as impassioned, and soft as well as strong; that she may flow with all love's fire and yet be delicately obedient to the lightest whisper of honour' (Turner 1993: 306–308). Turner has described Myers' attitude as expressive of 'the fear of women and the misogyny that so extensively touched late century literature and culture'. But I think, in Myers' case, this is too crude. Myers certainly was not a misogynist. He liked and appreciated women, as we have seen, and worked as a young man for women's social and educational rights. His views in this context resonate with his own experience, the platonic relationship with Annie Marshall, and his belief that the highest love is the spiritualised love of Dante and Beatrice and Petrarch and Laura. It is significant that this essay was printed in the *Fortnightly Review* just two and a half years after Annie's death, and that it was one of the pieces of reading that Myers and Eveleen shared before their marriage. Certainly, the word 'childlike' is revealing in the above quote, but it is too simplistic to attribute misogyny to Myers on the basis of this. There was indeed misogyny — a substantial amount — in late Victorian society, but its type and nature varied, and Myers, though he may have had particular views about the public and private behaviour of the sex, was certainly no woman hater or fearer; quite the contrary.

Much of his work appeared in the *Nineteenth Century*, a periodical founded by Sir James Knowles in 1877, which reflected the ethos of the Metaphysical Society, of which Knowles had been the secretary for almost eight years (Brown 1973: 184–95). Knowles did not publish novels or serial fiction; the emphasis was on debate and fair, dispassionate argument, and early symposia included those on *Morality and Religious Belief* and *The Soul and Future Life*. Victorian heavyweights like Arnold, Galton, Tennyson, and Spencer wrote for it. It was an appropriate vehicle for Myers, both for his literary essays and for the early SPR work with Gurney. He also wrote for the *Fortnightly Review* (liberal in politics), first under Morley and then Escott, but he does not appear to have published anything in it after the egregious Frank Harris took over in 1886. He did not have much in the *National Review*, which was revived again in 1881 as a conservative monthly on political and literary matters, though he did publish two articles in it in the 1890s, one on the state of psychical research and the other on evidence for the survival of death. He also had a small amount of material in other publications: *Macmillan's Magazine*, the *Cornhill*, and the *Contemporary Review*. A number of people felt that his literary essays were somewhat overrated and Havelock Ellis, the psychologist, commented to his lover, Olive Schreiner, that Myers tended to see things through 'a beautiful mist' whereas he and Olive saw things as they actually were (Draznin 1992: 274). The literary essays lack the vitality and the perception of the best Victorian essayists like Leslie Stephen. Myers' finest work, his most speculative, imaginative, insightful and often surprisingly humorous writing, was in the *Journal* and *Proceedings of the Society for Psychical Research*: the former accessible only to members and the latter often buried in the decent obscurity of a library of record.

He achieved a wider fame with his *Wordsworth* published in 1880 in the English Men of Letters series. As Morley pointed out, he was the man for the job, in a position — given his Marshall Lake District contacts with the poet — to 'give us plenty of biographical materials and personal traits' (Myers 3/51: 27.2.1879). However, despite his reference to family letters (Myers 1929: 25), Stephen Gill (Gill 1998: 308) has argued that he relied very heavily on published sources, and that actually there was not much original material in the book. However, his interest in the platonic and pantheistic elements in Wordsworth made him a sympathetic and generally perceptive critic. This is particularly evident in his chapter on Wordsworth and natural religion (Myers 1929: 128). He stated that Plato identified four access points to the spiritual world: through revelation, prayer, art, and 'the lover through his love'. Wordsworth had added a fifth source of spiritual power, insight and energy; 'the contemplation of nature'.

As well as being a poet, an essayist and a biographer in his own right, Myers also had friendships and acquaintanceships with many of the leading literary figures of the day: Browning, Meredith, James, Gosse, Bradley, Swinburne etc. He had contact with — and a huge admiration for — Tennyson, who, characteristically, kept him at a little distance. The relationship with George Eliot, however, was for Myers the most fascinating, intense, and at times painful of these connections. She was interested in the Cambridge milieu, in Myers, Sidgwick, and particularly Edmund Gurney, who made an almost overwhelming impression on her. Myers' most famous anthologised piece of writing (Myers 1897: 268–69) revolves round his meeting with her at Trinity and their walk in the Fellows' garden:

> I remember how, at Cambridge, I walked with her once in the Fellows' Garden of Trinity, on an evening of rainy May; and she, stirred somewhat beyond her wont, and taking as her text the three words which have been used so often as the inspiring trumpet-calls of men, — the words *God, Immortality, Duty,* — pronounced with terrible earnestness, how inconceivable was the *first,* how unbelievable the *second,* and yet how peremptory and absolute the *third.* Never, perhaps, have sterner accents affirmed the sovereignty of impersonal and unrecompensing Law. I listened, and night fell; her grave, majestic countenance turned toward me like a Sibyl's in the gloom; it was as

> though she withdrew from my grasp, one by one, the two scrolls of
> promise, and left me the third scroll only, awful with inevitable fates.
> And when we stood at length and parted, amid that columnar circuit
> of the forest-trees, beneath the last twilight of starless skies, I seemed
> to be gazing, like Titus at Jerusalem, on vacant seats and empty
> halls, — on a sanctuary with no Presence to hallow it, and heaven left
> lonely of a God.

The portentous tone, the heavy, almost ceremonial inevitability of the
prose rhythms, and the phrasing 'that columnar circuit of the forest-trees'
create the sense of some mighty, ultimate cosmic drama being played
out—just a few yards from Grange Road!

Combined with this cosmic self-importance, there is what one can only
call a rather distasteful exclusiveness. He really admired the way Eliot tackled the great and serious themes of life but he felt that there were too many
snobs (in the original sense of common) and vulgar people in them. She
should 'write one book in which all the people should be refined, & where
… tragedy should be unmixed with vulgar elements, & depend wholly on
the collision of high natures, and on such sorrows as are felt most keenly in
the purest air' (Williams 1984: 137). The twenty-first century reader might
be forgiven for thinking that such a book would have been unreadable, and
that Myers was advocating a kind of Bloomsbury Group Society without
that group's redeeming gossip, wit and physicality.

At the end there was just duty and for Myers this was not enough. So,
he found himself (Myers 1961: 16) in her largely secular salon in the early
1870s, puzzled by the materialistic and sophisticated views presented
there, which seemed so out of kilter with the strange world of spiritualistic phenomena that he was starting to investigate. George Eliot herself
came to sense and appreciate something of this. In a letter of the late 1870s
she acknowledged their differences stating that in her reluctance to accept
this extra dimension he perceived, she was perhaps aware of her limits,
and that her own moral powers acted to screen her from these many speculative possibilities (Myers 2/54: 16.11.1877). It was as if she was return-
ing a compliment. He praised her for tackling great themes with
sensitivity, discrimination and insight. She, in her turn, implied, delicately, that he had the courage to go where she couldn't or wouldn't. She
also, on another occasion, pointed out, that in one sense, what he was
doing, if it led to truth, would reverse and negate her life's work and
thought (Myers 26/63/75, Beer 1998: 214). But they were close to each
other and he confided in her, as he had to Mrs Cowper-Temple, the nature
of his relationship with Annie Marshall. Hence the reference in her letter
of congratulation on his marriage to a 'thoroughly sanctioned affection'
(Beer 1998: 213–14).

Chapter Three

A Career in the Seen and Unseen World

Spiritualism and Science

In the 1870s, as we have partially seen, a series of three inter-connected events unfolded which shaped Myers for the rest of his life. He lost his Christian faith, though he continued to use the vocabulary and moral lessons of Christianity, as his letters to his wife demonstrated. Consequent on this, and with the encouragement of Henry Sidgwick, he began to make a systematic investigation of paranormal phenomena. Secondly, after a certain amount of havering and advice from friends, he embarked on a career as one of Her Majesty's Inspectors of Schools. This gave him a certain professional status and income, but was not so demanding that it impeded his other interests and activities. And, finally, his strongly emotional and romantic temperament found expression in two powerful and significant relationships; the platonic liaison with Annie Marshall and his later marriage to the young, rich and beautiful Eveleen Tennant.

It is too simple to represent Victorian England as a pious, fundamentalist land shaken by the advances of a materialistic and iconoclastic science. The census of 1851 revealed that well over five million people did not attend church on Sunday 30th March 1851 (Chadwick 1971: 363–69). Many of them, as first or second generation migrants from the countryside to the industrial cities, found the Established Church of little relevance to their immediate social and economic problems, though it may still have influenced them through less formal methods than Sunday attendance (McLeod 1996: 6–7). It was amongst the educated middle classes and upper-middle classes, who were emancipating themselves from their evangelical roots, that scientific and scholarly advances had most impact. On this group, from which Myers, Sidgwick, Gurney (all of whom had clergymen fathers) and some others of the SPR sprang, the loss of simple faith was particularly devastating.

What was it that led to this shattering of their secure world view? It is quite clear that the process had started well before the impact of Darwinism. Robin Gilmour has argued that, while developments in geology in the 1830s and the new historical approaches to the Bible played a part in this, what really turned many against Christianity was the evangelical emphasis on a God who had 'hell and everlasting punishment' for those of his creatures who persistently sinned (Gilmour 1993: 85–94). We have already seen how Myers' mother, not wishing to expose her son to the full implications of this doctrine, substituted the idea that the wicked were annihilated at death (Myers 1961: 7–8). Other intellectual developments did, however, play their part. The fossil record challenged the traditional timeline of the Bible, and Germanic historical and textual criticism revealed the internal inconsistencies of much of the Bible, particularly the Old Testament. With regard to the New Testament, *Das Leben Jesu* by DF Strauss (1835) put forward the thesis that Christ was a remarkable human being, a model of ethical behaviour and aspiration, but not the divine son of God (Gilmour 1993: 53–58). In addition, Feuerbach's *Essence of Christianity* (translated by George Eliot and published in 1854) also had a considerable influence on the educated public, with its emphasis on the divinity in and not outside humankind (Wilson 1999: 141–44).

Traditional beliefs were also attacked from within the citadel of the Church itself. In 1860 *Essays and Reviews* was published by a group of Anglican clergymen (and one layman). This publication disseminated liberal ideas that had long been discussed in more sophisticated and obscure environments; namely that the Bible should be treated as an historical document like other texts of the past and subject to the same critical scrutiny. The implication (though it was not stated as forcefully as in later generations) was that Christianity had to be able to stand up to the general intellectual trends of the time if it was to survive. The effect of Darwinism, therefore, was all the more devastating as it impacted on an edifice apparently already crumbling from the inside. It was little wonder that Myers described the intellectual scene of in the early 1870s in very bleak terms:

> It must be remembered that this was the very flood-tide of materialism, agnosticism, — the mechanical theory of the Universe, the reduction of all spiritual facts to physiological phenomena. It was a time when not the intellect only but the moral ideals of men seemed to have past into the camp of negation. We were all in the first flush of triumphant Darwinism, when terrene evolution had explained so

much that men hardly cared to look beyond. Among my own group, WK Clifford was putting forth his series of triumphant proclamations of the nothingness of God, the divinity of man. Swinburne, too, in *The Pilgrims* had given a passionate voice to the same conception. Frederic Harrison, whom I knew well, was still glorifying Humanity as the only Divine (Myers 1961: 15).

In addition to its developing intellectual ascendancy, science was beginning to have a massive and even majestic influence on daily social and professional life. The application of the steam engine to production and transport, the laying of electric cable and the expansion of the telegraph, gas and electricity, and the great improvements in health and sanitation, all proclaimed the power of science. Men of science were growing in prestige and were often called upon to act as expert witnesses both in criminal and in patent cases. William Crookes, as editor of *Chemical News*, strongly defended the right of scientists to earn their bread in this fashion (Hamlin 1986: 492). A view of 'science', its methodology and status, later characterised as scientific naturalism, became more visible and powerful in argument and debate (Turner 1974: 8–37). This approach to science opposed the traditional claims of religion to decide and pronounce on the nature of physical reality. Such men of science argued that the structure, function and process of the universe could be explained by clear, physically based laws that did not require any supernatural intervention. They asserted that the scientific method alone could reveal truth. It is important to state a caveat. The individuals particularly associated with this view — Tyndall, Clifford, Huxley *et al.* — were not necessarily materialists. They may have been like Huxley agnostic or like Tyndall vaguely pantheist. What they agreed on, without exception, was that what could be known by humankind could only be known using the scientific method. Tyndall, the physicist, in his famous Belfast address of 1874 (Turner 1993: 196) probably gave the most forceful, public assertion of the prior claims of science over religion to decide on the questions of the world. Yet this hostility, broadly, was not directed against the idea of an unknowable ultimate creator, but against superstition and fundamentalist religion.

As we have seen, Myers seems to have been slow to absorb what JP Williams has called the liberal culture of the 1860s (Williams 1984: 41–64). He appeared to be going against the grain of the time. In the face of a world operating, according to men of science, under the three great laws of the uniformity of nature, the conservation of energy, and evolution, he could only fall back on an intense and subjective faith, whose truth lay in its emotional impact and its effect on moral behaviour, not in demonstrable scientific fact. Yet, the evidence for the truth and validity of Christianity, Sidgwick argued (Sidgwick and Sidgwick 1906: 39–40), should be examined with the detachment of a rational being from another planet. This approach was initially far from the heart of Myers and he tried to repel it in the 1860s with all the emotional ardour, imagination and will at his disposal. He was operating strangely and exhaustingly on two levels at once: as an academic living in a world of increasing rationalism, reform and progress, and as a spiritual reactionary, trying to preserve the miracle and the passion of his faith. But the arguments of others and the triumphs of empiricism gradually prevailed. He could not permanently insulate himself from the contemporary world of progressive ideas.

As a Cambridge academic and with strong Cambridge roots and contacts, he was surrounded by what Noel Annan has called the intellectual aristocracy (Annan 1955: 241–87), that widening network of gifted individuals, often from evangelical backgrounds, who through intermarriage, mutual encouragement, and shared values, acquired considerable dominance over late-Victorian intellectual and cultural life. Their main and broadly shared assumption was a belief in the empirical approach of John Stuart Mill, as outlined in his *System of Logic* (Williams 1984: *passim*). Mill asserted that knowledge was built up from controlled and trained observations based on the evidence of the senses. There were no prior organising categories or privileged insights or concepts. The future progress of society rested on the unfettered application of rational procedures to all aspects of life, by bodies of well qualified men and women from all classes of society, studying and employing the newly developing sciences and social sciences. Myers was slower to absorb this position than Sidgwick, but once no longer a Christian, he fully subscribed to these approaches and adopted them for the rest of his life; even so, the longing to believe, occasionally, temporarily, vitiated his judgment.

The Sidgwick Group

But, even if science and scholarship rendered traditional Christian belief invalid for men like Sidgwick and Myers, was it worth exploring, by using the methods of science, observation and experiment, other evidence for a spiritual dimension to life? Myers posed the question to Sidgwick in his usual portentous terms on 13.11.1871, during a star-lit walk:

> I asked him, almost with trembling, whether he thought that when Tradition, Intuition, Metaphysic, had failed to solve the riddle of the Universe, there was still a chance that from any actual observable phenomena, — ghosts, spirits, whatsoever there might be, — some valid knowledge might be drawn as to a World Unseen. Already, it

seemed, he had thought that this was possible; steadily, though in no sanguine fashion, he indicated some last grounds of hope; and from that night onwards I resolved to pursue this quest, if it might be, at his side (Myers 1901c: 454).

They had both already made some initial forays in this field. Myers had shown an interest in mesmerism and abnormal behaviour in the 1860s. Indeed, as early as 26th June 1863 he had visited a lunatic asylum, but does not appear to have been deeply disturbed, for afterwards he played croquet and went for a walk (Myers 14/1). In February 1867 he visited the London Mesmeric Hospital, and in his diary for the same month there is a reference to Henry Sidgwick's being involved in mesmeric experiments. There were also a number of diary references to his mesmerising or being mesmerised, particularly in May, October and November 1867 (Myers 14/1). This must have been during the full intensity of his Butlerian Christian frenzy, and one wonders how he reconciled the two worlds. Sidgwick had been a member of the Ghost Club at Cambridge, which was a more serious society than its title might have suggested, involving a number of gifted academics and ecclesiastics, including a future Archbishop of Canterbury. He had also been particularly impressed with Crookes' investigation of the phenomena associated with Daniel Dunglas Home, first reported by Crookes in the *Quarterly Journal of Science*, 1st July 1871. As he later wrote to his mother:

> There is so much crass imposture and foolish credulity mixed up with it, that I am not at all surprised at men of science declining to have anything to do with it. On the other hand, no one who has not read Crookes' articles in the *Quarterly Journal of Science*, or some similar statement, has any idea of the evidence in favour of the phenomena (Sidgwick and Sidgwick 1906: 290).

What were these strange phenomena (see Gauld 1995: *passim*), shunned by the rational and sensible, that Myers, Sidgwick, and later a wider group, began to investigate? There were two main sorts. The first was mesmerism, which took its name from Franz Mesmer, a Viennese who made his international reputation in Paris in the 1780s (Crabtree 1993: 3–12). In a less ostentatious form, this was adapted to an English environment by John Elliotson at University College London and, in its hypnotic form, by James Braid in Manchester (Crabree 1993: 109–68). Naturally, showmen and charlatans took these medical phenomena into a show business context, and (mostly using their own stooges but occasionally genuine members of the audience) performed in halls and theatres around the country. Those affected would go into a trance, lose the capacity to feel pain, sometimes develop clairvoyant powers, sometimes share the same sensations that their mesmerisers were experiencing, and often give exhibitionist performances of great dramatic and physical skill. These would be well outside their normal physical competence or their normal behaviour patterns. And, most disturbingly, sometimes, they would appear to be affected at a distance by the will of the mesmeriser. The mechanism behind all this, it was argued, was a powerful fluid, flowing through the natural world, which could develop and increase in potency through the mesmeric passes of the agent.

The second set of phenomena (often linked to mesmeric activity) related to spiritualism. This developed rapidly as a religion from the first odd powers demonstrated by the children of the Fox family of Hydesville, New York, and it eventually arrived in England through the American medium, Mrs Hayden, in 1852. Interest became more widespread with the arrival of another transatlantic visitor, the charismatic and handsome Daniel Dunglas Home, in 1859. A bewildering variety of phenomena were associated with these professional mediums and a number of them were replicated in private sittings or home circles. They included automatic writing and drawing by the medium, or writing and drawing by the spirits themselves, music, scents, the materialisation of objects and sometimes the full forms of spirits, and vague uplifting addresses or, less frequently, clairvoyance and evidences of spirit identity. It was to these happenings, many of them nauseatingly fraudulent and viciously exploitative of human grief, that Myers was referring when he, in fear and trembling, asked Sidgwick, his famous question.

Such a question had, moreover, a certain contextual sense and logic at the time. Increased understanding of magnetism and electricity and their practical applications, and the idea of ether through which light and electricity were transmitted, were well in evidence and discussion by the 1870s. It was not credulous to assume that there might be some empirical and theoretical link between the worlds of the physical and the psychic, provided — and it was a big provided — that it could be proved that some, at least, of these strange phenomena did genuinely exist. Spiritualists had anticipated this linkage, at least metaphorically, by calling newspapers, on both sides of the Atlantic, the *Spiritual Telegraph*. Surely, at the very least, it was worth some proper exploration, by the educated, the rational, the balanced, and, particularly, those of independent minds and means? Richard Noakes has lucidly demonstrated how historians of science have become more sensitive to the fluid context within which nineteenth century men of science operated and how for a number of them the psychical research and scientific research cultures partially merged and overlapped (Noakes 2008: 65–85).

There was, too, increasing popular interest in the whole range of phenomena covered in a popular Victorian survey, *The Nightside of Nature:*

Of Ghosts and Ghost Seers by Catherine Crowe (Crowe 1848), which went quickly through two editions and which explored 'all that class of phenomena which appears to throw light on our psychical nature and on the probable state of the soul after death' (Stein 1968: 1). What is particularly interesting is that Crowe's book was well-written and forcefully argued; it treated with serious consideration material that, on the surface, smacked of a pre-enlightenment age and of the grossest superstition – death wraiths, strange lights, stigmata, premonitions etc (Gauld 1968: 66).

Therefore, this interest by Myers and Sidgwick in mediumship and mesmerism was not as bizarre and isolated as it might appear from a later distance in time. For example, in 1869, the Dialectical Society (an intellectual debating society established in 1867) had set up a committee to examine spiritualism (neither Myers nor Sidgwick were members) and it reported in 1871 that the subject merited more serious consideration than it had previously received (Podmore 1902: 147–51). In 1872 *The Times* (26.12.1872) produced a long and serious leader on the phenomena and in 1874, after several years exposure to the public debates, the Oxford Union voted to add spiritualist literature to its library expenditure (*Spiritualist Newspaper*: 18.12.1874). Probably the most significant catalyst during this period, however, was the interest and involvement of the increasingly celebrated man of science, William Crookes. In 1870 he wrote an article outlining the kind of evidence that a man of science would need, if he was to endorse the existence of such phenomena (Noakes 1998: 174). And later he went on to investigate the most notorious nineteenth-century medium, Daniel Dunglas Home, and to report positively on him in 1871.

It is important to appreciate the significance of Crookes' investigation of Dunglas Home and its impact on the wider public in that year (Brock 2008: 135–53). Crookes had considerable intellectual authority. He had been elected FRS at the age of 31. He had the discovery of the element thallium to his credit and he was the successful editor of two scientific publications, *Chemical News* and the *Quarterly Journal of Science*. Therefore, when it leaked out that he was going to investigate spiritualism, there was considerable expectation on the sceptics' side that he would reveal it for the fraud it undoubtedly was, and on the spiritualist side, high hopes that he would establish the genuine nature of at least some of the phenomena encountered at séances. When he tested Home, he apparently established two things: firstly, that an accordion played by itself and secondly, that Home was able to use what Crookes called a 'psychic force', to exert considerable pressure on a board attached to a spring balance, without himself employing any downward effort. Crookes had taken the precaution of having Serjeant Cox, an experienced investigator of such phenomena, and William Huggins, the astronomer, to be at the sessions

as observers, and to guard against the objection that he had been mesmerised and/or duped. In fact, that was exactly what he was accused of, in
certain quarters. His observations were doubted and he became
embroiled in considerable controversy. Nevertheless, as we have seen,
the interest aroused by his work was a major factor in encouraging Myers
and Sidgwick to make systematic investigations themselves.

For Myers and Sidgwick, the enquiry was, at bottom, fundamentally
moral and spiritual. If they could not demonstrate the existence of a spiritual dimension, if they could not find in the grotesque world of spiritualism some evidence of ultimate meaning and transcendence, then they had
better shut up shop and encourage humanity to think as little as possible
about such questions (Myers 1961: 14). Yet, at the same time, the matter
was of such vital importance, that any investigation had to be carried out
methodically, even ruthlessly, according to the rules of science and evidence in the widest sense. And if the ultimate result of such an enquiry
was to confirm the assertions of the materialists, so be it. Better to know,
and to prove there was nothing beyond the material, than to live in a fool's
paradise. The approach had to be the patient, endless accumulation of
detail and the continual sifting and testing for fraud. Myers fully agreed
with this, but for him it was also more primal. Every fibre in him cried out
for continuing existence, experience and growth. The idea of his extinction, that he would not go on, was for him, from childhood, the most intolerable, the most unsupportable concept. He fought hard to keep this bias
in check but did not always succeed and, through his life, was fortunate
that he had the cooler-headed Sidgwick to keep him grounded.

Myers, as we have seen, had got to know Sidgwick better from 1869
onwards. He began to realise that there was much more to Sidgwick
beneath his initially frosty and nervous manner. They examined together
that year in the Moral Science Tripos (Add.Ms.c. 100/202: August 1869)
and Myers became increasingly impressed by Sidgwick's moral stature
and his intellectual steadiness. He admired Sidgwick's resignation from
his fellowship (in protest at the Church of England's control over fellow-
ships), though he had not thought it was necessary for Sidgwick to do so.
Almost from the start of their long correspondence, ending only with
Sidgwick's death in 1900, one can see them candidly and clearly scrutinis-
ing each other's ideas, attitudes and emotional positions. For Sidgwick,
this was the essence of debate and personal growth. He described the
impact the secret Cambridge Society, the Apostles, made on him: 'I can
only describe it as the spirit of the pursuit of truth with absolute devotion
and unreserve by a group of intimate friends' (Sidgwick and Sidgwick
1906: 34). And it was in this spirit that he engaged in deep individual
friendship with Myers and Gurney, with other members of the group

investigating spiritualism in the 1870s, and, as far as possible, given the disparate constituencies, within the SPR itself.

Sidgwick, although he became a pre-eminent and widely published philosopher of ethics, also had a profound influence, by his personal example, on individuals, their ideas, culture, and behaviour. This was, in fact, what had happened to him in his own life. His father and two siblings died when he was very young, and after an unsettled period, the family stabilised under the guidance and leadership of EW Benson (who was Sidgwick's father's cousin) and they came to live with him at Rugby where he was an assistant master, fully supportive of the reforms of Dr Arnold. Yet, though there was much mutual respect, they gradually moved intellectually away from each other as Benson eventually became Bishop of Truro and, at last, Archbishop of Canterbury (Schultz 2004: 31–39). Benson was always worried at the corrosive effect Sidgwick's sharply analytical intellect might have on his (Benson's) immediate family and friends.

This lucidity was often expressed with an even-handed generosity which made Sidgwick appear sometimes kinder to an individual or their work than perhaps they deserved. Myers spotted this in Sidgwick (a quality quite unlike his own youthful vehemence) and, characteristically, urged him not to waste his time reviewing mediocre publications. In a rather revealing analogy, he argued that it was unworthy of him, in just the same way as if he and Sidgwick were out walking and he (Sidgwick) should flirt with, and pay compliments to, a pretty, but common lower class girl (Myers 12/94: 17.10.1869). Yet, equally characteristically, Sidgwick was careful in his relations with Myers, as with others, not to appear the guru. With regard to Arthur Hugh Clough (one of the leading poets of religious doubt in the previous generation) he wrote, 'I am not a prophet—I have not solved in anything the Gordian Knot he fingered' (Sidgwick and Sidgwick 1906: 227). Though hugely different in temperament then, they nevertheless both had a real gift for intellectual friendship and responded warmly to those friends who had passions and enthusiasms that they could share. Sidgwick particularly enjoyed the brio and energy of Myers' letters, 'My dear Fred, Send me more letters: they are charming'. And after one visit he stated, 'Each day I have wished to write to you how delightful and salutary your visit has been to me' (Add.Ms.c.100/221: 20.11.1871). He also recognised, as had Myers' mother long before, the way that Myers' emotions sometimes ran ahead of his intellect in his impatient search for answers:

> And I feel that your peculiar phase of the 'Maladie' is due to the fact
> that you demand certainty with special peremptoriness—certainty
> established either emotionally or intellectually—I sometimes feel

> with somewhat of a profound hope and enthusiasm that the function
> of the English mind with its uncompromising matter-of-factness will
> be to put the final question to the Universe with a solid passionate
> determination to be answered which <u>must</u> come to something. How-
> ever, in the mean-time we have to live on less than certainty, which for
> you is peculiarly difficult (Add.Ms.c.100/227: April 1872).

Myers, in fact, relished Sidgwick's acuity and admired 'the astonishing
precision with which you insert your pen's point between the convolu-
tions of my cerebral hemispheres' (Myers 12/100: 11.3.1871).

Encouraged by the deepening friendship and support of Sidgwick,
Myers began to make his own personal psychical investigations in 1872
and suggested to Sidgwick that they might research together. Sidgwick
replied describing his own experiences with John King and his ambivalent attitude: 'John King is an old friend, but as he always came in the dark
and talked at random, our friendship refrigerated' (Sidgwick and
Sidgwick 1906: 285). John King was supposed to be the spirit of Henry
Morgan the buccaneer, who, in order to make up for his sins on the earth,
dedicated his time in the spirit world to proving life after death. He was a
most ubiquitous and conscientious contributor to séances and appeared
through most of the well known mediums of the period (Fodor 1969:
190–91). Myers had a sitting with the medium Charles Williams on the
20th November 1873 and in his diary laconically wrote, 'John King shakes
hands' (Myers 14/1). In his autobiography he stated that this was the first
occasion on which he had encountered forces unknown to science (Myers
1961: 15). Eveleen Myers, in an interview given to the spiritualist journal
Light in 1934, provided greater detail, on the basis of what her husband
had told her, of that experience. She stated that a great hairy hand materialised, which Myers bravely grabbed hold of, with both his hands. But in
spite of that, the hand became smaller and smaller like a new-born baby's
and then dematerialised in his very grasp (*Light* 1.6.1934: 332).

More significant than this event, no matter how extraordinary it
appeared to have been, was Myers' visit to Broadlands in May 1874. This
had been arranged by Edmund Gurney who was a distant relative of Mrs
Cowper-Temple. There he was introduced to the Cowper-Temples and
their eclectic spiritual environment; and he also met Stainton Moses, an
Oxford graduate, a clergyman, a man of probity, and above all — as a
medium — a cut above some of the rather squalid figures he had encountered in his investigations so far. Georgina and William Cowper-Temple
had a long and very happy marriage based on their mutual religious and
philosophical interests, which to-day would seem typically New Age.
They were interested in vegetarianism and spiritualism, and from 1869
onwards, when William inherited Broadlands from Lady Palmerston,

they made it a centre of religious and spiritual exploration. A wide variety of assorted believers and their gurus would meet there through the year, and at the annual religious conference they instituted (Burd 1982: 5–8). It is easy to mock the Cowper-Temples (or Mount-Temples as they later became) but Georgina was genuinely kind, sympathetic and tolerant and William often translated his ethical and spiritual predilections into practical action. He established the General Medical Council in 1858. He was also prominent in campaigns to preserve open spaces for the public and to prevent continued enclosures. Possibly, however, his most famous political intervention was the Cowper-Temple amendment of 1870, which prevented denominational religious teaching in schools that were built and funded by the rate-payers (Hoppen 1998: 599).

What Myers and Gurney heard from Stainton Moses beggared belief. Sitting within a small circle of intimate friends he had, he stated, produced some amazing physical phenomena. Myers, naturally, 'asked Moses to sit with us sometimes' (Myers 12/115: 26.5.1874), but there is no record of such a sitting ever having taken place. After Moses' death, however, Myers was to have access to his notebooks and he wrote them up in the *Proceedings* of the SPR (Myers 1894–95 9: 245–352, 11: 24–113). Moses had investigated spiritualism in some detail and also been a medium himself, having developed both automatic writing and physical mediumship. He provided Myers and Gurney on the 9th May with a very vivid account of the way a distant relative of his, Fanny Westoby, had communicated with him after her death through his automatic writing. She gave him her maiden name, her address, and told him (he did not know this at the time but his father later verified it) that she got stuck — to the amusement of all — when trying to get on to his father's roof one day (Myers 1904 2: 597–598).

That such a man was having such experiences galvanised Myers into even more vigorous action, and he put forward the idea of a more sustained enquiry into the area which would include a number of their mutual friends. Gurney, a young fellow of Trinity and Myers' most intimate friend, was, at first, very reluctant to get involved. He was a hugely gifted figure who has left a substantial body of writing on both psychical research and music, but at that time he was uncertain as to the value of the enterprise, and more interested in music, both philosophically, and in performance (Add.Ms.c.100/252: 18.5.1874). He probably needed the more pushy and buoyant Myers to galvanise him into action. Myers eventually persuaded him to collaborate in spite of his distaste for some of the murky environments he might find himself in. This core group of investigators, which one can call the Sidgwick group, since already Sidgwick's guiding and cautious hand can be seen in much of the correspondence that passed between them, was eventually composed of: Myers, Sidgwick, his later wife Eleanor Balfour, Evelyn Balfour (in 1871 the wife of John Strutt, later Lord Rayleigh), Edmund Gurney, Walter Leaf (a Trinity classicist and wealthy business man), Arthur and Gerald Balfour (Trinity men and future politicians), and John Hollond, another Trinity man and an MP (Sidgwick and Sidgwick 1906: 288–91).

This group was determined to be objective and logical, but was aware that too overtly a brisk and scientific approach would alienate the very mediums they were trying to investigate. Myers was acutely aware of this dilemma. The matter was so profoundly important to him that the only way forward was to adhere to truth, logic and science, and not, by even the mildest manipulation of facts or magnification of probabilities, lure himself into a false sense of security (Myers 1961: 37). Yet, he had to keep the mediums sweet. We can clearly see this tension in a letter from Myers to Sidgwick in May 1875 concerning one of their early joint investigations. He enclosed the text he was going to send to a new medium, probably Mary Rosina Showers, who found his request for tight controls insulting:

> I am sorry that I did not make the purpose of my last note sufficiently clear. It was intended to show you how far I was from the position of absolute scepticism to which your previous note had seemed to assign me. Some little evidence as it seemed to me was still lacking to establish these phenomena on a basis of scientific certainty nor was it my intention to slight the testimony of others or to set my own above theirs, but rather to suggest to you that it will not be any encumbrance. Only with a large number of independent testimonies will the world be convinced [of] the reality of the phenomena. I accept with regret your decision against séance on Wednesday next. Should you at any future time be inclined to admit Mr Sidgwick or myself to such a meeting there will be nothing on our minds which can be thought likely to interfere with the success of the manifestations (Myers 12/114: 7.5.1875).

Sidgwick, for his part, had less tolerance than Myers for the time wasting caused by the temperamental inanities, foibles and suspicions of a number of the mediums. He was particularly irritated by Mrs Fay (see next section) and also by Mrs Jencken (one of the Fox sisters, whose experiences had helped to trigger the spiritualist movement years before) and he dropped them both. He wrote to Myers concerning the latter that, 'Mrs Jencken is shilly-shallying and may get me into difficulties about my visits'. He felt the same about Mary Rosina Showers; however she was not a working-class medium on the make, but the daughter of General Charles Lionel Showers, a very high ranking Indian Army officer, who actually wrote to Queen Victoria supporting his daughter's mediumship.

It is not known whether Sidgwick actually sat with her, but certainly Mrs Sidgwick did (Sidgwick 1886: 46) and also Myers. In fact, Sidgwick was aware that his impatience and scepticism often had a negative effect on mediums and he tended to withdraw from an investigation if his involvement seemed to be a problem. He wrote to Myers of Miss Showers, 'I have come to the conclusion — as I daresay you have — that my interference in viz Showers would do more harm than good. Only, when you write to her, please mention (in whatever way may be most rhetorically effective) that I now entertain no doubt (personally) as to the genuineness of her ghosts' (Add.Ms.c.100/249: 8.5.1875). This was mere expedient politeness. Too publicly sceptical an attitude in the early stages of their investigations would debar them from access to many a possible source of evidence.

The Amazing Mrs Fay

Myers was highly taken by the beautiful and sensational Anna (or Annie) Eva Fay, when she arrived in Britain, from America, in the summer of 1874. It was rumoured she had been a pupil of Madame Blavatasky's (Dingwall 1966: 40), though Wiley (Wiley 2005: 250) is not sure that they ever met. She seems to have tailored the explanations for her performances to her audiences — conjuring/mind reading to the cynical, mediumistic to the spiritualists. She was involved in a scandal in Boston in 1874 shortly before she wisely left for a tour of Europe. A Mrs Carpenter identified the tricks she was using and demonstrated them to spiritualist friends. A Mr Boardman — owing to a badly fixed blindfold — also spotted her standing in for the spirits. However, in the *Medium and Daybreak* of 12th June 1874 she claimed that she had been a medium since childhood. She was a very attractive and charismatic individual who could captivate both in a small group and a theatre setting. She gave some private sittings before the opening of her show at the Hanover Square Rooms on the 13th July 1874. Jerome A Paddock was her manager, and her husband Colonel HC Fay of Ohio was also to hand. No spiritualist claims were made at these performances. *The Times* made this clear in its article on 17th July 1874. Colonel Fay (dubious both in rank and reputation) was at the door receiving members of the audience. Her performances lasted till the 29th August (Dingwall 1966: 40-42).

With hindsight it seems amazing that the Sidgwick group should have bothered to investigate her at all. She seemed so blatantly pure 'show biz'. However, Myers moved quickly and enthusiastically and was one of the first to have private sittings with her, on the 18th and 19th June at £50 a time (Myers14/1; Wiley 2005: 130). He had already written to Sidgwick on the 13th June (Myers 12/116) hoping for an extensive series of séances in July, being quite prepared to defer any school visits if they interfered with this. He and Sidgwick planned to investigate her in a systematic and co-operative fashion, using prominent scientists. For them the scientific approach meant not just the application of the scientific method, but also involving practising scientists in the enquiry. The Sidgwick group already had in the family the future Lord Rayleigh—an outstanding physicist, who was married to Eleanor Sidgwick's sister Evelyn—and Myers and Sidgwick attempted to bring Crookes on board as well. They were prepared to make £300 to £400 available (Wiley 2005: 139) for enough sittings to examine the medium's phenomena in depth. Mrs Fay, however, had her own ideas. Over the next eight months, as a professional operator and an excellent reader of character, she manipulated those whom she could and eliminated those impervious to her charms. Sidgwick complained vigorously to Myers that she refused to come to Carlton Gardens (the Balfour family home where Sidgwick paid court to his future wife), and that her manager now called her an 'Entertainer' not a medium (Add.Ms.c.100/136: n.d.). She also made difficulties for Rayleigh, who wrote to Myers, 'I scarcely see my way to asking Mrs Fay here again without a better explanation of her extraordinary conduct' (Myers 2/42: 15.1.1875). She flattered Myers, who was susceptible to female beauty. She indicated, by various stratagems, that Sidgwick and Gurney were not *persona grata* at sittings; and she showed a distinct preference for William Crookes as her scientific investigator (Wiley 2005: 137–45).

There can be little doubt that there was an element of competition, perhaps unconsciously sexual, between Myers and Crookes in this matter. Certainly, Fay was extremely attractive both physically and as a personality. Myers wrote to Sidgwick that, 'The moral evidences of her candour constantly increase. Each accession of intimacy with her leads me to an increased respect for her uprightness, courage, & kindness' (Myers 12/117: 26.11.1874). This smacks more of infatuation than the attitude of a detached investigator. However, there were other factors at work. The Cambridge group had raised the funds to pay for the sessions with Anna Eva Fay and Crookes may well have resented their attempts to deploy what Sidgwick called 'the Common's use of the power of the purse'. Crookes may, too, have been irritated by the involvement of Sidgwick and Myers, neither of whom were professional scientists

It was quite clear that by December 1874 Mrs Fay was inclining towards Crookes as her preferred investigator. Crookes had the international public clout that Myers and Sidgwick lacked, and public endorsement from him would give her great publicity, particularly as the conjurer Maskelyne, was replicating her 'tricks' at the Egyptian Hall (Wiley 2005: 134). Sidgwick wrote to Myers warning him that Crookes might snaffle Mrs Fay from under their noses. Myers replied with the enigmatic statement, 'The lion will not let himself be robbed of his cub — nor the cub of his lion' (Myers 12/118: 3.12.1874). This statement could, of course, be interpreted in two ways! Either the smitten Myers was prepared to fight for his medium, or he recognised that Crookes was determined to proceed with her, regardless of any finance from the Cambridge end. In addition, rumours were beginning to circulate about the past and the probity of her husband. Myers grew increasingly uneasy, writing that, 'There is a crisis in the affairs of Eva. I know not what will happen, but will write again' (Myers 12/122: 9.12.1874).

He then went on to suggest that Sidgwick need not inform Rayleigh what they had found out about Colonel Fay's misdemeanours, since he would not be involved in the séances (Wiley 2005: 143). This was unethical, particularly as Rayleigh was involved in contributing finance to the project. Myers did have a general tendency to push on towards his goal regardless, and occasionally, for a man who prided himself on his high-mindedness, this could involve a certain economy with the truth. Sidgwick, for his part, was worried about the whole affair (Add.Ms.c. 100/256: n.d.) and wrote to Myers expressing a certain unease about Mrs Fay's good faith. It was a difficult and tense period, and at one stage Myers seems to have felt, rather petulantly, that Sidgwick was sidelining him by pushing Lord Rayleigh forward as the sole investigator. Sidgwick replied soothingly that he valued nobody's opinion on these matters more than Myers', but that Rayleigh, as a distinguished scientist, would be very useful in convincing the wider world of the reality of such phenomena (Add.Ms.c.100/198: n.d.). Eventually Myers seems to have lost interest in Mrs Fay and to have ceded control to Crookes. Crookes then went on in February 1875 to investigate Mrs Fay without the support of the Cambridge group, though Lord Rayleigh did attend one session. Crookes, using an electrical test devised by Cromwell Varley, pronounced her phenomena genuine (Wiley 2005: 164–80). There has been some debate as to how she managed to evade Crookes' test and whether or not she had any genuine gifts. But in later years Myers, as he wrote to Lodge, was quite certain that she was a cheat (Wiley 2005: 144).

There have been many theories as to Crookes' behaviour. The most sensational — that he was conducting affairs with mediums under the guise of scientific investigation — seems unlikely; and cultural historians have possibly overplayed the erotic undertones involved in the largely male investigation of mainly young, attractive female mediums (Owen

1989, Tromp 2006). Wiley has probably got it about right. He convincingly demonstrates the fraudulent nature of Anna Eva Fay's activities, but points out that the suggestion that she and Florence Cook had affairs with Crookes (Hall 1962: 99–108) borders on the preposterous (Wiley 2005: 161). Medhurst and Goldney (Medhurst and Goldney 1964: 138) are probably also close to the truth, stating that there was vanity and a touch of megalomania in Crookes' approach. He had discovered, he thought, the psychic force operating in the case of Home and would have believed himself almost uniquely qualified to investigate mediumship.

Certainly, the Cambridge group were not offered an opportunity to sit in on Crookes' sessions with Florence Cook, which in the history of psychical research were the sources of Crookes' fame or infamy, depending on one's perspective. These were the exclusive province of Crookes and his small circle, and throughout his later life he was guarded in revealing information about these early investigations (Brock 2008: 206). However, towards the end of 1878, after Florence Cook had become Mrs Edward Corner, Myers did have thirteen sittings with her and a number with her sister, Kate Cook (Gauld 1968: 130). He possibly came to the same conclusion about them as he eventually did with Anna Eva Fay, though we do not know this for certain. Nor do we know exactly what were Myers' considered views on the whole Crookes/Cook episode. Certainly, there were rumours at the time that Crookes was something of a Don Juan in his behaviour and attitude towards young female mediums. Whatever the truth or not of this, Crookes' investigations into Cook were never published or assessed by Myers and the SPR, probably because of Crookes' status (in 1898 he was President both of the Royal Society and of the SPR), because of the embarrassing and controversial nature of the material, and because Crookes himself grew heartily sick of the whole farrago of claim, counter-claim, jealousy and gossip.

Miss Wood, Miss Fairlamb, the Pettys and 'Dr Slade'

There were, however, plenty of opportunities for the Sidgwick group to access other mediums, by means of advertisements in the spiritualist press and through personal contacts like Hensleigh Wedgwood (the philologist, committed spiritualist, and cousin of Charles Darwin). They certainly had ample funds to pay for them. Sidgwick was particularly generous in this regard. His income had increased considerably on his marriage, his wife bringing with her a legacy of £19,000, an annuity of £500, and half of her mother's estate (Lubenow 1998: 133). They were, therefore, well able both to pay for investigations and, more generally, to make substantial donations over the years in the field of psychical research and other areas; as, too, did Myers, his mother, and his brother Arthur.

The group first began systematically to investigate Miss Wood, Miss Fairlamb, and the Petty Family (all Newcastle mediums of whom they had heard good reports) in the early months of 1875. It was a tedious and unrewarding experience, as Mrs Sidgwick later pointed out (Sidgwick 1886: 45–46). Myers also has a long list of diary entries against the Newcastle mediums — failed, failed, failed (Myers 14/1). But it was during this period that he and his colleagues began to hone the skills that would serve them well in the 1880s. The investigation of Wood and Fairlamb was extensive and thorough. These mediums had emerged through the Newcastle Society for the Investigation of Spiritualism led by Armstrong, Barkas and Mould. It was Hensleigh Wedgwood who introduced the Sidgwicks and Myers to them. Miss Wood had been in service and came to spiritualism through her father; she was eventually employed by the Newcastle Society. Annie Fairlamb was initially Miss Wood's chaperone and then developed as a medium herself. At these séances the spirits of adults and children materialised in a variety of guises and a range of names: 'Pocka', 'Cissy', 'Meggie', 'George' (Owen 1989: 57–58).

Both mediums began to earn a reasonable living from these séances, a better living in terms of income and status than life as domestic servants. It may be that they became too greedy, for Sidgwick, in particular, grew suspicious of them, with their excuses and their constant demands for money. It was no better with the Petty family, the other Newcastle-based mediums. Sidgwick had long and complicated negotiations with them, both for their Newcastle sittings and later when he brought them to Cambridge in the summer of 1875. The Pettys always seemed to be asking for more and Sidgwick thought them grasping (Add.Ms.c.100/141: 1.5. n.y.). Yet, in another letter, while still moaning about the Pettys, he enquired about Eglinton and Sanby — the former one of the most notorious and disputed mediums of the late nineteenth century — as to what they could do and did their ghosts walk about the room? (Add. Ms.c. 100/147: n.d.). There was often a guarded weariness in Sidgwick's tone, but also a certain dogged sense of duty which was admirable. This contrasted at times with Myers' rather over-optimistic and gung-ho attitude.

Though their attitudes and temperaments might differ, there was a common determination to do the job thoroughly, which carried over into the group's work in the SPR in the 1880s. There was also a breathless sense of pace and effort in their letters as they travelled round England in their search for phenomena. Very few people — private or professional researchers—had or have the time, leisure, status and finance to work with mediums in the very intensive way that the Sidgwick group did in the 1870s. Myers, himself, as his diary reveals, had a very large number of sittings, which continued throughout his life and had, even before the founding of the SPR, reached several hundred (Myers 1895f: 61).

However, the mediums did not always repay the time, money and effort devoted to them and did not always behave impeccably. Myers, who at this time was living in London, in lodgings, got Wood and Fairlamb to come to Brompton for séances in April 1875 at the rate of £3.12.0 a week for rooms and board (Myers 12/124: 21.4.1875). Some further sessions were held at 4 Carlton Gardens, the Balfour family home, and again there in July (Sidgwick 1886: 49–53). At one of the investigations at the Balfours' house Miss Wood behaved weirdly after the séance and had to be taken back to her lodgings at 6.15 in the morning, and in another Miss Fairlamb refused to be searched, despite having promised beforehand to allow this. On both occasions it was suspected that the behaviours were designed to conceal or divert attention from possible fraud.

There was a special frisson when the Pettys came to Cambridge in the summer of 1875—on Sidgwick's home territory. In fact Hensleigh Wedgwood was worried for Sidgwick's job and reputation—introducing superstition into academic Cambridge. As Sidgwick put it to Myers: 'Wedgwood is sincerely concerned about our proposed séances at Cambridge. He thinks the Master would be sustained by public opinion if he dismissed me! So there is yet a chance of one's posing as Galileo. What delight!' (Sidgwick and Sidgwick 1906: 296–97). Caroline Jebb was predictably scathing about the whole business, particularly as it involved Myers. She described, in a letter back to her sister in America, how Myers got her husband Richard along to a séance and how he thought that the spirit was just a boy on his knees. She asserted that Myers and Sidgwick saw themselves as breaking new scientific ground, but that they were really just very credulous. That her comment was unfair to Sidgwick and (marginally less so) to Myers, would have worried Mrs Jebb not a jot. She strongly disliked Myers. Yet even dear and close friends were dubious at Myers and his circle throwing themselves quite so wholeheartedly into such enquiry. His old friend Collins wrote: 'All I know about Spiritualism is that the other day I saw Maskelyne and Cook do at Egyptian Hall by sleight of hand all that Spiritualists of old averred they did by aid from above' (Myers, 1/138: n.d.).

Myers held further sessions with Fairlamb and Wood later in the year, at Newcastle, with the John Hollonds and Aksakof, the aristocratic Russian investigator, attending. At one séance Myers saw the figures of the materialised spirit and of Miss Wood, both walking and talking as separate figures: 'I touched both: both were solid – If the Newcastle folk are trustworthy the thing is done' (Myers 12/127: 14.10.1875). But characteristically he immediately suspected, given that there were twenty seven people forming the circle, that a confederate might have been smuggled into the cabinet.

Much of 1876 was overshadowed for Myers by the sad affairs and tragic end of Annie Marshall, but his interest in the Newcastle mediums did not abate and he wrote enthusiastically, from The Turk's Head Hotel Newcastle, in December 1876, of 'very good fresh evidence for all the mediums' and that he had engaged rooms for the Sidgwicks to come and see for themselves. These included an attic for séances, which was 'so grisly an apartment that I do not think they would consider it desecrated if Beelzebub himself appeared there' (Myers 12/136: 8.12.1876). Final sessions were held there with the mediums in January 1877 (separately because they had quarrelled) and Mrs Sidgwick stated laconically, in spite of Myers' earlier and favourable comments, that, 'the indications of deception were palpable and sufficient' (Sidgwick 1886: 53).

The lodgings might be squalid, and the mediums grasping and unpredictable, but at least Myers, Sidgwick, Gurney, Leaf, and their colleagues were helped in their investigations by the expanding railway network. It would not have been possible otherwise for them to travel so widely and to gain so extensive a knowledge of potential mediums. In addition, other developments in technology aided their work. The far flung and scattered British Empire, which was being brought closer together by underground cable and telegraph, provided them with an almost uniquely designed test bed for the examination of telepathic phenomena. Telepathic communications across the world under the influence of powerful emotion and family or friendly rapport could be assessed, verified or disproved by modern, physical methods of communication. The Empire provided a vast network of familial and commercial relationships and – at times – life threatening conditions to do with war, disease, and arduous travel, which might generate such telepathic cries of joy or distress. It could be seen, with pardonable hyperbole, as one vast laboratory for psychical research. This huge reservoir of source material would be explored and exploited in greater depth after the Society for Psychical Research was set up in 1882 (Noyes 1999: 252).

The Sidgwick group began to run a little out of steam after the failure of the Newcastle, Cambridge and London sittings and the impact of the Slade trial in 1876. Dr Slade, a self-styled doctor no doubt, had come to England from America in 1876 and immediately become known for his slate writing mediumship. (Slate writing was a form of mediumship whereby spirits communicated by writing on slates which were either sealed together or apparently not touched by the medium at all.) There was an acrimonious debate about him at a committee meeting of the British Association at Glasgow in August. As chairman, AR Wallace (the co-discoverer with Darwin of the theory of evolution and a supporter of spiritualism) had allowed wide ranging discussion after William Barrett had read a paper on thought-transference. This had led to an animated discussion of Slade's séances and related phenomena. It also resulted in a number of those present calling for a special committee to be set up to investigate spiritualism. Edwin Ray Lankester (a young and highly sceptical biologist) was particularly enraged that his fellow men of science could be taken in by Slade. He determined to expose him. He had a sitting with him, during which he claimed he had spotted that the writing Slade said would be produced by the spirits, had been written on the slate beforehand. He then summarised these experiences in a letter to *The Times* on 16th September 1876.

As a consequence, Slade was put on trial under the Vagrancy Acts with the charge that he had used various subtle methods, 'to deceive and impose upon Her Majesty's subjects'. As was usual in such cases there were many conflicting viewpoints and much uncertainty. Serjeant Cox (the same Cox who had sat with Crookes and Home) had investigated him and reported that strange phenomena occurred. Lord Rayleigh had also had a sitting with him, taking along a magician who could not explain what had happened. Myers (true to form) had four sittings with Slade and experienced significant physical manifestations including table movements and the levitation of a hand bell (Myers 12/134: 21.9.1876, Myers 12/135: 22.9.1876). Sidgwick was much less positive, even a little glacial, and stated with regard to Lankester's letter in *The Times*, 'his account of what he saw is so much in keeping with our previous suspicions ... that I do not think it worth our while to go on with Slade for the present' (Add.Ms.c.100/101: n.d.). He added, however, that those who had had good experiences should go back to sitting with Slade, 'in the fullest consciousness of the point at issue'.

As with all matters of this type the Slade case became mired in claims and counterclaims. The judge ruled much evidence irrelevant, stating that Slade must have used subtle craft to try to deceive Lankester since spirit writing was not possible under the laws of nature. Maskelyne (who never lost an opportunity to make publicity out of spiritualism) popped up again, saying that he could do in the full view of the court what Slade did. The judge also ruled this as irrelevant, though Maskelyne, of course, got the attention he craved. Slade, for his part, received three months hard labour. The verdict was overturned, after appeal, on a technicality, and

Slade left for the continent, probably convinced that he would never receive a fair hearing in England. He did offer to return if given certain personal guarantees by Lankester; but Lankester never replied to his letter (Inglis 1977: 281).

In some ways the Slade affair symbolised all the tensions, irritations and confusions involved in the Sidgwick group's first systematic foray into what later became called psychical research. The publication by two renowned scientists of their researches into spiritualism, William Crookes (Crookes 1874) and Alfred Russel Wallace (Wallace 1874), and the furore caused by William Barrett's paper at the British Association in 1876, aroused very strong feelings. Scientific naturalism went on the offensive. Barrett's paper was simply airbrushed out of history. It did not appear in the 1876 *Proceedings* of the British Association, either in the abstracts or in the index (Stein 1968: 29), and WB Carpenter, the leading psycho-physiologist, fired up by the affair, attempted to squash such credulity once and for all in his 1876 Royal Institution lectures, published in the following year as *Mesmerism and Spiritualism*.

An examination of the detail of Barrett's paper (Noakes 1998: 251) reveals what a stark challenge it was to existing orthodoxy and why it stimulated so much hostility. Barrett had mesmerised an Irish peasant girl. She appears to have read his mind and also to have identified the suit of a card safely hidden in a book. When reading his mind, she could not have been already possessed by a dominant idea (as Carpenter suggested in such cases), since she had no idea what he was to think about. Nor could she have got clues from the unconscious muscular action of his face, since she had been blindfolded. He, therefore, took on directly — as Gurney and Myers were to do later — the establishment explanations authoritatively purveyed by Carpenter for these phenomena. In response, Carpenter in his turn directly confronted Barrett, alleging that he had no expertise in this field, that he and his ilk did not understand 'the nature of their instruments of research', whereas he, Carpenter, had had forty-eight years experience of assessing self-deception (Noakes 1998: 254).

Men of science lined up on both sides of the barricade. It was not necessarily, as one might have expected, the small but growing number of paid and professional scientists who opposed the 'superstition' of belief in spiritualism and related phenomena. Crookes was a self-made professional, as was Cromwell Varley. Wallace, Barrett, and (later) Lodge came from relatively modest backgrounds, and were certainly not Oxbridge. The tradition of the wealthy amateur researcher beholden to no-one, who could seek the truth unswervingly without pressure from public, patron or profession, was also still strong. To some extent, the founders of the SPR carried on this tradition into the 1880s and 1890s, which, as we shall see later, was a source both of strength and of weakness to them. They had money and intellectual independence, but there were those who saw them as out of the same stable as the gentlemen amateurs and genteel ladies of yesteryear, who, with stout shoes, went out gathering and drawing and recording specimens, rather than being qualified exponents of a rigorous science based on mathematical theories and sound laboratory-based experimentation.

So within the scientific community there were several competing claims for intellectual authority and credibility in the investigation of the paranormal. And, to complicate matters further, two additional groups claimed expertise (Lamont 2004: 897–920). One group consisted of conjurers and magicians who argued that they alone had the appropriate skills: scientists were all very well in their laboratories, but only a practising magician would know the tricks of the trade (for mediums were just frauds or part of show business) and would be aware of what to look for. The final group was the mediums and the spiritualists themselves. They asserted, from their vast practical experience, that only they knew the conditions under which genuine phenomena could be created. For scientific researchers, of course, this presented some difficulty at times. They were used to interrogating a natural world which did not talk back, sulk, or withdraw involvement!

Mrs Sidgwick's, as we have seen, is much the coolest and most measured account of the investigations of those years by the Sidgwick circle — and her sense of the wearisome futility and triviality and vulgarity of much that they investigated came to be partially shared by Myers himself. Her conclusions were damning and poured cold water on Myers' initial enthusiasm. Her experience was 'entirely inconclusive' except with regard to the fraudulent and spurious and she had sat with virtually all the mediums (Sidgwick 1886: 45–74). By the late 1870s little positive had emerged from their investigations. They were visibly flagging. But they had at least learnt the need for careful observation and cautious investigation in their engagements with professional mediums. Myers himself believed that he had witnessed a number of paranormal events, but was not in a position to go much further than this in the face of his colleagues' scepticism.

Indeed some of the cases he recorded (though he had not always been able to investigate them personally) totally beggar belief. For example, he wrote to Sidgwick on 17th January 1877 from Liverpool that, 'I have wonderful phenomena to report to you'(Myers 12/141). He had just interviewed Dr Hitchman of the Liverpool Psychological Society, a very experienced spiritualist, 'a big old man with long white hair with a general look of being a character out of Dickens' (Gauld 1968: 129). Hitchman had told him of a very impressive séance with a Miss Clark. She sat in a cabinet with no top and Hitchman was allowed to look down inside it: 'at the top of the cabinet appeared the gigantic head of <u>Wat Tyler</u>. Hitchman stood on a chair & kissed this being & talked to him: looking downwards into the cabinet he saw that Wat Tyler ended in a fringe in mid air while the medium still sat on her chair. Wat Tyler spoke & was warm & had a pulse in his wrist, but ultimately faded away.' Myers stressed that Miss Clark and the other mediums he was given information about, did not take payment for their sittings. One wonders, even with the credit gained for the non-professional nature of the activity, at the Sidgwicks' reaction on receiving this letter. One also speculates on the motives of the leader of the Peasant's Revolt in 1381, in 're-appearing' — almost six centuries later — at a séance in the North of England!

There is additional evidence, in the memoirs of AR Wallace, to support the thesis that the more extreme and sensational of Myers' experiences were not publicised. Wallace visited Myers in his rooms at 3, Bolton Row, Mayfair. He was shaky on the precise dates but he provided a fairly full account of what he said were Myers' personal conclusions derived from the experiments of these years (Wallace 1905: 334–37). He particularly stressed the detailed records that Myers had kept in a number of manu-script books, and the physical controls that Myers asserted had been in place to prevent fraud. He stated that Myers pointed out to him that the Sidgwicks had not attended as many sittings, either in range or in serial depth with individuals, as he had, and had therefore missed those ses-sions at which the most astounding phenomena had taken place. Wallace urged the publication of the full set of records. They were never found and only glimpses of such experiences can be gathered from Myers' letters. They may well have been destroyed by Mrs Myers as part of her general weeding out of the archive after Myers' death. Wallace pointed out the importance of these note books, since otherwise the only signifi-cant account of the researches of these years is the cool and sceptical report of Mrs Sidgwick's already quoted. However, Wallace's picture of Myers as an enthusiastic supporter of 'ectoplasmic manifestations', needs to be read against Myers' statement in his autobiography, that 'my own career has been a long struggle to seize and hold the actual truth amid illusion and fraud. I have been mocked with many a mirage, caught in many a Sargasso Sea' (Myers 1961: 40).

One cannot fault the drive and effort of Myers and his friends in the mid- and late-1870s. They were entering the investigations with the highest of motives, as well as their obvious desire for the demonstration of personal survival, which was particularly strong in Myers' case. They hoped, though they could not logically assume this, that the discovery of a spiritual universe would guarantee and sustain the values that they held dear, as Williams has called them: 'duty, music, poetry and love' (Williams 1984: 119). Myers, particularly, held all his life a powerful intuition that the ultimate spiritual value was platonic, and that love and beauty, stripped of their carnal elements, fused. There was a strong sense here that spirit was higher than matter. Yet, much of what they got in their séances was very physical, even grubby, sweaty, sordid, and distasteful.

The Sidgwick group's efforts faltered and William Barrett, rather than Myers, became for a time the prime mover in the investigation of anomalous phenomena. He was undaunted by the Slade fiasco and the attacks of Tyndall, Carpenter and Lankester. He asked *The Times* readers (22.9.1876) to send him cases of thought-transference, which he then followed up — examples of what later came to be called the higher powers of mesmerism (thought-transference, clairvoyance, willed action of others). As part of this process he discovered the apparently paranormal skills of the Creery family. These experiences, and their dissemination, provided the impetus that eventually led to the founding of the Society for Psychical Research.

Myers himself, always capable of bouncing back, did contribute to Barrett's investigations. It was probably in August 1877 that he and Barrett first met and discussed these matters, when, on his return from a visit to Paris, Myers went to Ireland to investigate a haunted house (Williams 1984: 165). The reading of minds was of particular concern to Myers at this time, because of experiences he had had with two mediums while abroad (Gauld 1968: 130–32). At a sitting with Madame Rohart on July 30th,[1] Annie Marshall apparently communicated, giving her name, her father's name, her relationship to Myers, and a long message in French. Characteristically, Myers with his linguistic skills commented: 'Notice the French, which is anglicised & much resembles the fluent but non-idiomatic way in wh. she talked' (Myers 12/144: 2.8.1877).

Barrett, as well as his Irish experiences, had also (Barrett *et al.* 1882: 47–56) received interesting cases from a number of people in England. Myers followed up on two of these, with the Misses B on the South Coast and with Miss C and her mother in London (October to December 1877). In the London case, mother and daughter were able roughly to transmit a simple sketch and, with greater accuracy, words and phrases (two in foreign languages). In the latter case, on the South Coast, Myers recorded sixteen experiments with the Misses B, some of which were largely successful, others partly so, and some complete failures. In both cases, however, some physical contact was allowed, and the South Coast experiments, in particular, seemed indistinguishable from what later became called

1   See above, p. 46.

'Cumberlandism' or – from a popular party entertainment – the 'Willing Game'. Experiment 15 with the Misses B, for example, strayed dangerously close to Victorian parlour games. Barrett, however, provided an example of an 1876 experiment with the same young ladies in which thought-reading apparently took place, with physical contact only in one of the five experiments cited.

It was extremely important for the investigators to distinguish the 'genuine' cases of thought-reading or thought-transference from mere public and private entertainments. The 'Willing Game' was yet another fad that had crossed over from the United States. While one person was out of the room, the others would decide on an object for them to find, or an action to perform, when they returned. On their return, the group would will them to behave in the required manner. Marie Mallet, one of Queen Victoria's ladies-in-waiting, described one such occasion (Mallet 1968: 24). The Queen wished Marie to try her hand. She was sent out of the room and when she was let back in, after a moment's meditation, she made straight for Lord Knutsford and took off his Jubilee Medal. It was what she had been willed to do. Sometimes, but not always, this willing was accompanied by light physical contact. 'Cumberlandism' was named after Stuart Cumberland, a professional entertainer, who with a combination of touch and shrewd assessment of body language, discovered objects often hidden in the most unlikely and inaccessible places. He had an imitator, one Washington Irving Bishop, who alleged he had a genuine gift, unlike Cumberland who openly proclaimed his own performances as based purely on his practical skills (Barrett *et al.* 1882: 13–15, Inglis 1977: 319–20, 322–23).

Barrett had written up his experiences and published them in *Nature* in the summer of 1881. This, coinciding with the popularity of the willing game and the antics of Cumberland and Bishop, stimulated much public interest and speculation. Myers and Sidgwick, who had shown consistent interest in Barrett's work during the late 1870s, were intrigued (Myers 12/147: 1.9.1877). However, they were cautious about re-engaging in collective activity in this area, mistrusting the investigative abilities of most others, and not sure as to the quality of Barrett's leadership. There were ideological, social and temperamental differences between him and the Cambridge group. Sidgwick had powerful connections to the highest echelons of the Church and the Liberal and Conservative Parties. Myers was a London and Cambridge-based high intellectual and poet, and Gurney was a rather fastidious philosopher of music (Noakes 1998: 255–73). Barrett retained his Christian faith whilst the Sidgwick group had lost theirs. They had no belief in the capacity of the Irish to govern themselves and were, broadly, Liberal Imperialists, whereas Barrett threw his hand in with Mr Gladstone and home rule and contributed much to social and educational reform in Ireland. Socially, the Sidgwick group were elitist and rarefied, and though pro-education, were suspicious of attempts at wider social reform and organised labour movements. Barrett clearly did not share their background. He was educated at grammar school and through private tuition. He did not become a fellow of an Oxford or Cambridge college, but went to work as a lowly technical assistant to John Tyndall, the physicist, at the Royal Institution. After a slightly chequered career he became Professor of Physics at the Royal College of Science in Dublin. So, though he shared their interests, he was divided by geography, education and social background, from intimate and frequent contact with them. These structural differences, mainly latent at this stage, were to have an impact on the Society for Psychical Research as it evolved in the 1880s.

Myers and Her Majesty's Inspectors of Schools

Throughout the 1870s, parallel with his psychic investigations and his literary work, Myers pursued a career as one of Her Majesty's Inspectors of Schools. It had not been his first choice. In the 1860s he had briefly thought of entering the church, but that idea faded with his faith. He had earnest discussions with Sidgwick about his future and his failed attempts to write a novel (at one stage Myers had thought of a completely literary/man of letters future), 'If it is true that you cannot write a novel, I should think it was for the reason (it gives women such a superiority over men in this line) that you do not care enough about little things, and therefore do not observe them enough' (Add.Ms.c.100/203: 11.9.1869). This diagnosis may well have been accurate, but such a deficit should be seen as a little alarming in a future psychical researcher — a field where the devil is in the detail, in the precise, sustained observing and recording of spontaneous phenomena. To be fair to Myers, he recognised this and tried to train himself as an observer and recorder. Myers also considered medicine as a career, but Sidgwick warned him against it, given the sheer time and the nervous and physical energy involved, which would not give him the leisure for his literary activities or for a sustained investigation into the paranormal (Add.Ms.c. 100/214: 29.8.1871). One might have thought Myers would have pursued an academic career, but he intensely disliked lecturing undergraduates (though he enjoyed speaking to wider public audiences) and there seems little doubt that the appeal of London life and London society was strong. As he wrote to Sidgwick, 'I am going to stop lecturing & live in London lodgings in December, reading & writing (but doing as little arithmetic as possible.) I am drawn to the magnetism of 3 million souls' (Myers 12/98: 12.9.1870).

Becoming an HMI seemed a satisfactory compromise. It was socially of high status, it was well paid, and it was worthwhile. Myers clearly had a developed public conscience. He was in negotiations with Octavia Hill in the early 1870s to support her scheme of housing for the poor. He in fact contributed £50 towards it (Myers 2/106: 23.3.1874) and he was involved, as we have seen, in higher education for women and other initiatives of Josephine Butler. It should be stressed that this was not just a peripheral fleeting interest under her enchanted, spiritual influence. It should also be emphasized that though Mrs Butler's methods of winning young men to her cause (a strange melange of sublimated sexuality and religiousity) might be seen as suspect, nevertheless, no one can deny her courage, drive, compassion and final achievement. And Myers contributed not a little, with genuine conviction and considerable energy, to the early stages of her endeavours. It is evident from various sources that Myers' involvement in the woman's movement was more substantial than has generally been appreciated (Tullberg 1998: 38–41). Myers' application for the Chair of English Language and Literature in Oxford in 1885 gives a specific account of this activity: '... those Local Lectures in English towns by University men, in starting which Professor Stuart & I at first were almost alone ... I continued thus lecturing on English Literature & History till 1871, giving courses at Manchester, Rochdale, Southport, Cheltenham, Leamington, Winchester, etc –' (Myers 13/8-9). Sidgwick had also roped Myers into his system for educating young women by correspondence – soliciting his views and then appointing Myers the English specialist. This movement grew rapidly (Sidgwick and Sidgwick 1906: 248–49).

Myers had very supportive testimonials for his application to be an HMI but had to undergo the tedium of acting as an Inspector of Returns in 1871 (essentially checking that the basic statistics schools provided were accurate) before he could get an appointment as a full Inspector in 1872. He was conscious of his own worth and of where he wanted to be, holding out for a posting to the Cambridge district even though greater financial rewards could eventually come to someone who was prepared to go to a less popular area. He achieved his Cambridge district appointment in 1875. The testimonials from Sidgwick, Thompson, Jebb, and FD Maurice (the theologian) were very impressive and clearly demonstrated his potential and capacity for applied action as well as his genuine interest in education. WH Thompson, the Master of Trinity, wrote unequivocally to Myers: 'I am not surprised to hear you wish to become an Inspector of Schools, for since I first knew you you have always taken a lively interest in the cause of education' and 'I have no hesitation in saying that you will become one of the best inspectors ever appointed' (Myers 4/112: 21.10.1871). Myers may have been seen as odd and eccentric at times, and considered a poseur by the less intellectually and imaginatively gifted amongst undergraduates, but he clearly impressed his peers. Jebb stated, 'I have never known anyone who professed in so high a degree at once the powers of the imagination and the powers of the practical intellect' (Myers 5/3). Sidgwick described his great force of character, and declared, 'He is sure to perform any work in which he is strongly interested with a perfectly infectious spirit of energy.' He was also confident he knew 'no one less likely to sink into a merely mechanical execution of routine duties' (Myers 5/5). That interest had, as we have seen, been clearly focused on providing middle-class women with access to higher levels of learning. This was a much more attractive proposition than the inspection of a public system of primary education focusing on low level skills attainment and the technical achievement of certain primitive criteria. On the other hand, his new post required little wide reading and research and enabled him to free his mind for other things.

Myers was lucky that he had such an outstanding university record and such quality testimonials. EM Sneyd-Kynnersley's ebullient memoirs give some insight into the methods of appointment which might, in other circumstances, have worked against Myers. He applied in 1871, the same year as Myers:

> About Easter there came a letter to my father from our old friend …
> H Sandford, who was a cousin of Sir Francis Sandford, Secretary to
> the Education Department, and had become a Senior Inspector. He
> premised that certain officers were to be appointed to make enquiries
> under the New Education Act — and that the nomination of these was
> in the hands of the District Inspectors. He went on to enquire whether
> my father had a son with the necessary qualifications (Sneyd-
> Kynnersley 1908: 3).

Myers' appointment seems to have been purely on merit. He was fortunate, given that the jobs were so heavily lobbied for (Sutherland 1973: 58).

We get from the memoirs of Sir Almeric Fitzroy some general idea of the pressures of the HMI role in the 1870s and the kind of people who became HMIs. He would probably have known Myers since he knew his uncle, Mr Marshall of Patterdale Hall, who lent him a boat to sail on Ullswater. He was appointed to an HMIship just a year after Myers in 1873:

> My duties lay in Wiltshire, with headquarters in Salisbury, where I
> was only fifty miles from my father's place in Hampshire, whither I
> was able to go for the end of each week and have a day's hunting with

Mr. Garth's hounds; later, when I had two horses, I managed, what with odd days and intervals devoted to paper work, to enjoy on average three days a fortnight (Fitzroy 1925: ix–x).

So, in Myers' case there would have been ample time for literary and psychical research work, though not perhaps as much as we might imagine, particularly given the increasing workload from the 1880s onwards, consequent on expanding schools and greater regulation. Also, one must not caricature the situation. Fitzroy was an able man with a first in history who sat the examination for an All Souls fellowship and, as Sir George Kekewich pointed out, it was generally expected that HMIs and Examiners (senior civil servants in the Education Department) would have first class degrees (Kekewich 1920: 6). Gillian Sutherland, however, has argued that while this broadly applied to Examiners, the HMIs (with the distinguished exception of Arnold, Myers, Renouf and one or two others) were not academically outstanding (Sutherland 1972: 62).

Yet, able or mediocre, all the Inspectors operated within a culture set by the Examiners, which according to Sir George Kekewich, who became Secretary to the Education Department in 1890, was narrow, elitist, and unsympathetic to innovation:

> The Department was always on the watch to find something which deserved a lecture or chastisement, but never ready to help, guide or sympathise. The staff of distinguished and aristocratic scholars from the Universities treated elementary education and elementary teachers with contempt. Their cherished creed was that no education mattered or was of any real value except classics and mathematics, for they were University men ... They had no use for village Hampdens, nor any idea that a child from the 'lower' classes might, after all, possess a modicum of brains (Kekewich 1920: 11).

HMIs came from the same class and their positions were seen as carrying the same status. FH Spencer (an impressive figure, who went from being a board school pupil to a pupil teacher to Chief Inspector for London County Council and eventually became HM Divisional Inspector of Schools) described the visit of one HMI, with his black well-made boots, 'symptomatic of the great gulf fixed between the educated upper middle class and the "working class" ... who hardly knew what it was to have anything good in the material world'. And he commented tartly, 'Few of that generation of HMI's had even a theoretical knowledge of the art of teaching, still less of its practice'(Spencer 1928: 87–100).

A similarly bleak picture is painted by EM Sneyd-Kennersley, an HMI in the NW Division, who asserted that the job appeared to have little to do with education: 'In 1871 school inspection was, as a science, still in its infancy. The chief function of HM Inspector was to assess the amount which the Treasury should pay; and this was done by rapid examination of every child above seven years of age who attended 250 times in the school year.' He also stated that 'the great aim of inspector, teacher and children was to finish by 12.30 at the latest'. The main emphasis was on the completion of form IX on which grant calculations were based. The school filled it in but it had to be checked by the HMI' (Sneyd-Kynnersley 1908: 57, 158–59).

This was a piece of nightmarish bureaucracy and may well have caused Myers some irritation and difficulty, leading to certain rumours about his competence and his ethics in the late 1890s which we will examine below. There were, however, Inspectors' assistants who did the bulk of the drudgery and shielded the lofty HMI from too much proletarian detail.

There is no evidence in Myers' letters that he showed any interest in his work beyond performing it competently – though his wife on occasions mentioned how hard he was working trying to juggle both psychical research and inspection. It is unfair, however, to assume that he saw the job as a mere sinecure while he got in with the main business of his life. He was a conscientious inspector and discharged his duties efficiently. However, he strongly guarded his own personal position and affairs, and was only prepared to inspect in certain parts of the country. Cambridge and London were his key intellectual poles. He also tried to free himself from extra work consequent on the introduction of the Revised Code of Inspection in 1883 (Myers 12/87: 25.1.1883), as he also had when the Department had tried to reduce his days available for correspondence in 1877 (Myers 11/215: December 1877). In fact, when school inspection does appear in his letters, it is only as an obstacle or irritant – something that prevents him meeting someone because he was involved in an inspection or invigilating a training college examination. Nor is there any sense that the impressive body of knowledge that he was building up about the human psyche could be used to improve the quality of learning and teaching in schools. He did, however, occasionally remark (see later chapters) on the positive effects hypnosis might have on the individual, recalcitrant child. He also compressed school visits into short blocks of time, once four in one day and five in two. There were several entries in his diary which indicated, apparently with pride, that he had inspected between one thousand and fifteen hundred children in a few days!

No doubt, like his fellow HMIs he exploited his considerable freedom: not keeping a proper diary, not being easy to contact, and not being predictable. There exists a letter from Matthew Arnold asking him for a bit of help, but in a rather sighing and resigned fashion, accepting that he might not turn up (Myers 1/143: 3.6.1885). His friend Collins, trying to track him down on one occasion, went to the Education Department, 'Went to the

Ed office—the only address on your card—but there Joseph[2] was not known save by his voluminous correspondence' (Myers 1/139: n.d.). Certainly, he tended to use the office as a general clearing house for much of his correspondence including psychical research. It was obvious that both Collins, a great personal friend, and Eveleen Myers, thought inspection not worthy of his considerable intellectual powers. Collins wrote, 'So you are a permanent inspector now—I am very glad, as you desired it; but I should like you to undertake something loftier ... as a supplement to your official work' (Myers 1/132: 6.10.1872). Yet the loftier work was to be something, as he remarked frequently through his life, that the intellectual and social elite of the time, or many of them, dismissed as superstition and silly rubbish. He never produced the great history or literature or the contribution to public life that his abilities warranted and a number of his contemporaries hoped for.

There are a couple of incidents that lend some support to the thesis of Myers' occasionally casual approach to his job. Firstly, shortly before his engagement to Eveleen Tennant, he appears to have made a rather cavalier arrangement to swap for a period of time his Cambridge district for Sir Peter Renouf's London one. Reading between the lines, it is obvious that Myers would have had more opportunity to meet the kind of young women who would be a good match for him in London rather than the limited circle in Cambridge. However, a consequence of Myers' rapid engagement and marriage (the whole process took barely five months) was that he wished to work again in Cambridge, living in his new house with his young bride. Renouf was, quite naturally, reluctant to swap back again so quickly. He complained that Myers had put him out of pocket because he, Renouf, had had to hire a house in Cambridge for the whole year and he was also concerned about the disruption to his children's education. The spat continued till the end of March 1880 when Renouf reluctantly agreed to revert to their original inspection districts—Myers having offered to contribute to some of the housing costs involved (Myers 3/168,169,170: various dates). There appears to have been little or no consultation with or involvement by their superiors in this matter!

The second incident concerned a certain Algernon Joy. If this was the same Algernon Joy who was a staunch spiritualist, his gossip may have been stimulated by Myers' criticisms of the excessive credulity of some of the adherents of that movement. It appears that he had been spreading rumours that the reason why Myers had not made Chief Inspector was

---

2   Referring to Myers as 'Joseph' in this context is an allusion to the Biblical patriarch, described in a once-familiar verse as unknown to the Egyptian pharaoh: 'Now there arose a new king over Egypt, which knew not Joseph' (*Exodus* 1.8).

that it was widely known that he had fiddled his returns — in other words was too casual and could not be bothered to get the figures right. Myers, on discovering this, obtained a statement from Kekewich, Secretary of the Board (previously the Department) of Education in his support. This plus the threat of legal action was enough to make the man back down and apologise. 'I am informed by Mr. Frederic WH Myers,' thundered Kekewich, 'that some person has charged him with having at some period "swindled" the Education Office by sending in false returns, or by other means; and that it is suggested that this mal-practice has prevented Mr. Myers' promotion to be a Chief Inspector. There is no truth whatever in any allegation of the kind' (Myers 2/26: 4.7.1900). Myers' solicitor was Montague Crackanthorpe, a well-known Spiritualist and also a supporter of eugenics, and Myers sent him a copy of the grovelling retraction of Algernon Joy after he had received the testimonial and Myers' threat of libel (Myers 2/20: 30.6.1900). Eveleen Myers noted on the documentation that it was an example of great charity that he did not pursue the matter. It may well have been; but it was also wise.

His HMI reports still exist but, as Sutherland states (Sutherland 1973: 66), apart from being better written than the majority of his colleagues', there is little individualisation, and — unlike Matthew Arnold, a finer poet and a better educationalist — Myers exhibited little evidence of real engagement with the educational issues of the time. Yet, when one considers the scale and effort of his writing, travelling, and researching in the cause of psychical research, he would have had to have been superhuman to have been able to make a similar in-depth intellectual commitment to English education. In personal terms, he seems to have had the affection of his assistants and lobbied for them in support of their future careers whenever possible. For example, he pushed hard, without success, to get his faithful assistant Bartlett made a sub-inspector. There is also a moving letter from a teacher, EJ Walker (Myers 4/131), describing the great help and support Myers gave when that teacher was in difficulties. Myers was a man of social conscience, and though given to bursts of irritability, was basically kindly. He was also, of course, keen to protect his own interests, and he realised that, provided the work load could be controlled, the post had considerable advantages. For Sneyd-Kynnersley, the attractions of inspection as a profession were obvious: 'If I were asked to state its principal charm, I should say it is irresponsibility. The income is moderate, but sufficient and certain. In the dim and distant future looms a pension, assuring bread and butter ... But the chief comfort is that there is no personal worry' (Sneyd-Kynnersley 1908: 204–205).

1. Miss Eveleen Tennant
by Sir John Everett Millais, Bt 1829–1896 © Tate Gallery

2. Myers around the time of his tour of
Greece and the Aegean in 1864

3. Myers the Poet

Registered. *Sarony & Co.* Copyright.

1873

4. Myers in 1873

5. Myers with Leo

6. HM Stanley and FWH Myers

7. Henry Sidgwick

ELLIOTT & FRY   Copyright.   55, BAKER STREET. W.
AND AT 7, GLOUCESTER TERRACE. S.W.

8. Eleanor Sidgwick

9. Edmund Gurney

Chapter Four

Myers and the SPR in the 1880s

Foundation of the Society for Psychical Research

William Barrett was clearly the prime mover in setting up the Society for Psychical Research, despite the later Cambridge dominance over it (see Williams 1984: 162–63; Noakes 1998: 259–61). He wished to bring before the scientific community, the anomalous and apparently supernormal phenomena that he had experienced, so that they could no longer ignore them, or react negatively without having properly examined them. He wanted able and educated men to authenticate supernormal phenomena if they existed or, as a service for the general public, expose them if fraudulent. He also believed it was important for investigators to have opportunities to work closely with spiritualists, who were the people most knowledgeable about the range of phenomena that actually or allegedly occurred. The original idea (it is tedious to debate who first thought of it) emerged in discussion when he was staying with Dawson Rogers, a leading spiritualist, at the end of 1881. It was decided to hold a conference to explore the matter in greater depth. This took place at the headquarters of the British National Association of Spiritualists in Great Russell Street, on the 5th and 6th January 1882. The conference adopted a resolution by Stainton Moses, to organise a society for those interested in 'Psychological Research'. A working committee was set up to deal with the details and after several meetings terms like 'occult' and 'psychological' were weeded out, and at the next meeting of the conference on the 20th February the SPR was set up with Sidgwick as the first President.

Barrett may have had the original idea and the spark, but the spiritualists were the practical driving force in the very early days. They provided the rooms and they did the marketing and a substantial proportion of the early individual membership and members of the council were spiritualists of longstanding and experience (Dawson Rogers 1911: 46–47). They particularly welcomed, as Barrett did, the link with the Cambridge group, and the prestige and status that Sidgwick's name as President lent the fledgling organisation. It was in fact touch and go whether Sidgwick, Myers and Gurney, would become involved at all. Myers, though favourable to the setting up of a society was only willing to become heavily committed if Sidgwick led it. In the Barrett papers (SPR 3) in the SPR archive, the names of Myers, Gurney and Sidgwick do not appear to be among the first twenty seven replies to Barrett's proposal, possibly because of the phrasing of the original proposal, which was 'to enquire into the phenomena associated with Spiritualism'.

Yet Myers was often more pro-spiritualist than some of his published work would suggest. He certainly was concerned, like Gurney and Sidgwick, about the quality of the work of such a society, given that there were very few people capable of objective, systematic investigation. But, he, 'secretly ... desired anything which would bind them and myself to systematic work. There was also the hope that the Spiritualists might introduce us to phenomena of "home circles", which we had been vaguely told of' (Myers 26/63/44). This initially seemed possible since Stainton Moses, the most respected figure in spiritualism and a major contributor to *Light*, gave his full support to the SPR. He had originally thought that the intellectual and social differences between the spiritualists and the Cambridge scholars were too great to surmount (Oppenheim 1985: 137–38). But he quickly saw the value of the alliance with Cambridge. On 22nd July 1882 *Light* printed the SPR prospectus and details of its organisation; on the 3rd February 1883 it stated that the SPR was meeting the scientific sceptic by scientific methods; and in a retrospect at the end of 1883, Moses assured his readers that the SPR, 'is rendering a service to Spiritualism which spiritualists will appreciate in the future more than they are able to do now that the processes are so largely hidden'. And later (on 5th January 1884) he specifically acknowledged the impact that the writings of Messrs Myers and Gurney was having in bringing hitherto tabooed facts to public attention, particularly 'among those who influence and lead opinion'.

However, despite initial good will, the early years of the SPR were characterised not just by painful clashes of personality and class but also by conflicts over both methods and areas of investigation. Williams (Williams 1984: 2, 5) has contrasted the liberal epistemology of the Cambridge group (based on rational, elitist, detached enquiry) with the plebeian methodology of the Spiritualists (based on the democratic, anecdotal commonsense of the masses). This, however, is an over simple distinction. A number of the spiritualists were well educated middle class and upper-middle class. It was the precise application and tone of the Cambridge group's methods which irritated them. Rather than concentrate on the immediate activities and experiences of spiritualistic circles, it rapidly became clear to the spiritualists that the SPR was investigating old cases of apparitions and the elusive concept of telepathy, instead of the core issue of individual survival of bodily death, for which, they argued, there was much contemporary evidence. A cogent letter in the SPR *Journal* from GD Haughton set out these concerns. Myers replied to it agreeably, but in a slightly lofty tone, in August 1885 (Myers 1885f: 29–32), defending the logical and evidence-based approach he and his colleagues adopted. Haughton had stated that the Society, 'pursue the inquiry ... like a firm of solicitors preparing a case for a trial'. Well, Myers was delighted by that, since a certain Devon solicitor had criticised the Society for not behaving as stringently as his firm would have done! He and Gurney actually agreed with some of the points Haughton made, but he quite understood Haughton not spotting this since, 'It is only natural that on seeing the too frequently recurring names of Messrs Gurney and Myers at the bottom of an article, he should claim *Toujours perdrix!* and pass on to the next.' Myers, therefore, managed both to imply that Haughton was a little superficial and casual in his approach, and to identify himself and Gurney, by implication, as the real workers.

A certain intellectual arrogance lay behind this approach to psychical research. WC Lubenow's (Lubenow 1998) research on the Cambridge Apostles (though Myers was not himself an Apostle) provides a good insight into the intellectual milieu which formed Myers, Gurney and Sidgwick. It is significant, as Lubenow points out, that 'For much of the century the Apostles operated out of the grandeur and intellectual power of Trinity', the college contributing 92% of the membership in the 1860s (Lubenow 1998: 109–10). Also, as Lubenow indicates, the Society for Psychical Research could be seen in some lights as a natural 'extension of apostolic interests'. Sidgwick, the model apostle, was President and a substantial number of other apostles were members or associates: Roden Noel, Arthur Myers, Arthur Hamilton Smith, Henry Babington Smith, Donald MacAlister, Oscar Browning, Arthur Sidgwick, Roger Fry, and Edward Marsh, for example (Lubenow 1998: 229–30).

In broad terms (with a range of shadings and refinements) they adhered to a political party-free liberalism involving respect for property rights and civil order, while at the same time they defended the right to apply rational thought to all areas of life. They valued (with some reservations) the training that the classical and mathematical tripos gave in developing powers of critical analysis, evaluation of evidence and incisive communication; and that these were transferable to all areas of human investigation and activity (Lubenow 1998: 352–55). They believed, too, in expertise (provided it was not marred by over-specialisation) and the importance of the new applied subjects that were emerging. They had, in addition, a strong conviction of the value of moral excellence and the importance of doing one's duty, which was often translated into work for the public good or in the emerging public sector. They also had a certain suspicion and fear of the masses; and they found the context and ethos of spiritualistic investigations often distasteful and vulgar.

The dominance of Cambridge values, approaches and priorities in the SPR was reflected in the nature of the committee structure established. It was evident that the main focus would be on an examination of the various paranormal properties of mind and not exclusively on the survival question and the physical phenomena associated with spiritualism (Cerullo 1982: 44–45). The committees set up were on: thought-reading, mesmerism, the Reichenbach phenomena (this was the odic force which Baron Reichenbach stated penetrated all things and which certain sensitive individuals could see and feel), apparitions and haunted houses, and physical phenomena associated with spiritualism. There was also a literary committee whose aim was to collect relevant written material for any of the other committees. Therefore, only one of the committees was tasked with investigating spiritualism. Those on thought-transference and mesmerism rapidly emerged as the key ones, together with the literary committee. Myers and Gurney threw themselves with great drive and enthusiasm into the work of these committees, supporting Barrett, who was at this stage the leading figure, and initially on all the committees (Noakes 1998: 261). But they soon supplanted him in power and influence. As Nicol pointed out (Nicol 1972: 345–46), their relative youth meant that they had much drive and energy. All the important contributors to SPR work in the 1880s (with the exception of Sidgwick who was 43) were in their twenties or thirties in 1882. Several of them, in addition, had private incomes, and considerable control over their professional and private time, which enabled them to travel freely and to undertake research.

The committee structure established in 1882 did not last the lifetimes of Myers and Gurney. It relied on the other members of the committees having their own drive and energy and capacity for mastering large bodies of detail. They did not. The haunted houses committee and the physical phenomena committee faded away within two years. The latter was revived in 1886, but again had little staying power. The Reichenbach committee also guttered out. Only the literary committee and later the library sub-committee—because of their emphasis on general information-gathering—had a more sustained existence, and, of course, relied heavily on the input of Myers, Gurney, and Arthur Myers. The general view gradually developed that rather than have large numbers of standing committees, working parties would be appointed to deal with very specific issues (like Madame Blavatsky, the *Census on Hallucinations*, and Dowsing). After their reports were delivered the thought-reading and mesmerism committees were wound up. In the former case because there was some confidence that telepathy had been established, and in the latter case, Gurney, as an individual, continued to lead investigations, in greater depth, on hypnotism and mesmerism. One exception to this general trend was the establishment of a Hypnosis committee in the 1890s, led by medical doctors rather than Myers, because of the increasing interest in this area, an interest partly due to the pioneer work of Myers and Gurney in the 1880s.

There was, no doubt, a lofty sense of social and intellectual certainty about the Cambridge group's judgements which went against the grain for many spiritualists. In spite of the former's generally meticulous efforts to detect fraud and to obtain good corroborative evidence for phenomena, many then and now must have felt that there was a class-grounded interpretation of evidence at work. These quotations, taken at random from early reports — 'The witness was a clergyman of good standing and unimpeachable character personally known to me', 'The boy was loutish', 'The woman large, flabby, sallow' — would make many a reader uneasy today. Myers, in fact, wrote a letter to Lord Acton in which he clearly outlined the class and racially based criteria the society used in initially weighing evidence, which will be considered in greater detail later (Gauld 1968: 364-67). In a strange way these judgements almost foreshadow, or are parodied by, the sweeping confidence of Sherlock Holmes' assertions and deductions. One wonders, a little fancifully, whether Doyle derived elements of the imperious, precise and self-confident tone of his great detective from his reading of the SPR *Journal* and *Proceedings*.

The sense of class difference manifested itself in other ways apart from personal judgements. One of the objects of the Society was that the Council would conduct their investigations as far as possible through private channels (thus avoiding lower class paid mediums) and subscription levels were set at well above what the working class could afford: associate membership at a guinea a year and full membership at two guineas. In addition, Sidgwick, as President, displayed very effective public relations skills, modelled the society on existing scientific society lines and set the appropriate ethos. He cleverly, after a short period, managed to create a situation where the Society expressed no collective views and where publications were clearly seen as being attributed to and the responsibility of the individuals concerned (Williams 1984: 96–97). This tactic allowed the Society, to some extent, to shield itself from individual crises, scandals, bizarre theories and viewpoints, and to retain a broad church coalition. Indeed, under his presidency, the Society expanded rapidly within the intellectual and social elite of the time. Within twenty years the society had over nine hundred members, many of whom had considerable intellectual, social, scientific or literary distinction. Gladstone, Tennyson and Ruskin were honorary members; two Cavendish Professors of Experimental Physics at Cambridge also joined — Rayleigh and his successor J J Thomson (Rose 1986: 5). A number of glittering aristocratic names also appeared on the regularly published membership lists — the Ranee of Sarawak, Lord Bute, the Earl of Caernarvon, and the Earl of Crawford and Balcarres, for example. The list of members also reveals the very high percentage with fashionable London addresses, or comfortable rural or country house locations. In his otherwise valuable book on this period, *The Invention of Telepathy*, Roger Luckhurst (Luckhurst 2002: 1) does not do justice to the status that the society had, even though, of course, it did receive its fair share of ridicule and abuse.

It has often been suggested that the Society for Psychical Research was a desperate, last ditch attempt by nineteenth-century intellectuals to restore some spiritual meaning to the Universe in the face of geological and biological evidence to the contrary, and that they accepted lower standards of evidence than otherwise in their desperation to retain a Cosmos that had meaning. This is to do them a considerable injustice. They had, indeed, individual motives based on emotional needs — Sidgwick had a nagging concern that there should be some set of justifiable ethical principles to underpin human behaviour, Myers had an overwhelming horror at the thought of extinction and Gurney was driven by compassion and empathy for humanity — yet they were quite prepared to face up to the fact that their enquiries could peter out and they would then have to accept an existentially meaningless universe. They had considerable intellectual toughness and persistence and were quite ruthless in discarding evidence that they thought was contaminated or discredited in any way, whatever their inner hopes and fears. As Williams has cogently pointed out (Williams 1984: 98), psychical research as practised by Sidgwick, Myers and their colleagues, far from being 'part of a late Victorian "flight from reason"', was an embracing of reason, an attempt to look rationally — and in a scientific and scholarly fashion — at these strange and dubious phenomena, in the same way as the Bible and the 'miracles' of Christianity had been subjected to thorough examination.

However, once they were convinced that there was something worth investigating, they were determined to communicate this. Sidgwick oversaw a considered approach to the dissemination of the findings throughout the country, with the support of Myers and Gurney, who did most of the actual writing. The *Journal* (from 1884) was private to members but the *Proceedings* were circulated widely to libraries and to mechanics institutes, and eventually to some institutions abroad. Myers and Gurney also adopted a policy of summarising a number of their theories and findings in quality periodicals like the *Fortnightly Review* and the *Nineteenth Century* and Myers, from very early on, utilised his skills as a lecturer, to spread the message to appropriate audiences. There are many tributes to the way his skills in public speaking and social conversation facilitated and publicised the work of the SPR (Masterman n.d.: 67, Salter 1958b: 264).

One mark of this, as Stein has pointed out, is the fact that psychical research had a centrality then which it has never regained, 'Almost anyone who had anything to say in the period had something to say about psychical research, whether he believed there was any truth in the psychic experience or not' (Stein 1968: 8–9). Physicists, psychologists, anthropologists, depending on their temperament and personal experiences, all lined up on various sides of the great debate. Articles appeared in many of the leading and the popular periodicals, from Stead's *Pall Mall Gazette* and *Review of Reviews* to the *Contemporary Review*, the *Fortnightly*, the *Nineteenth Century*, the *National Review*, and even *Mind*. The Archbishop of Canterbury (Benson), and the Bishops of Ripon and Carlisle (Carpenter and Goodwin) all took a keen if cautious (particularly in Benson's case) interest in the field.

They were also prepared to see their work fully informed by the young science of psychology and even to challenge existing paradigms (see below). One particularly important development in this regard, was the burgeoning friendship in 1882 between William James and Edmund Gurney. James was actually in England in 1882, the year of the founding of the SPR, taking a break before starting his great book *The Principles of Psychology*. When their father died, William stayed in England, and Henry went back to make the funeral and probate arrangements. Gurney, who knew Henry, presumed on this to invite James to the December meeting of the Scratch Eight (an informal philosophical society) and from then on a close friendship developed (Epperson 1997: 49–50). It is not known if James met Myers through Gurney at this very early stage, but he would certainly have heard about him and met him if he had not gone back to America in the spring of 1883. Gurney sent occasional letters to James outlining their investigations and the huge amount of work following up the leads — some private, some the result of the newspaper adverts in *The Times* — and it was from this initial contact that the mutually beneficial, intellectual cross-fertilisation between Gurney, James, and later Myers, grew (Skrupskelis *et al.* 1997: 491–92).

Thought-transference, Telepathy and Mesmerism

It is quite clear that when the SPR was first set up the main thrust of Myers' early interest was in thought-transference and related phenomena. Just a few months after the Society's foundation, Barrett, Gurney and Myers were in print in the *Nineteenth Century* with their work with the Creery children (Barrett, Gurney and Myers 1882: 890–900). The Reverend Mr Creery was described as 'a clergyman of unblemished character' and, no doubt, his children were also seen as such. The children had been extensively investigated both at their home and at Cambridge and – in some of the experiments – in situations that would have prevented sensory leakage or the transmission of clues. Under a variety of controlled conditions, they appeared to demonstrate powers of thought-transference, by identifying the concealed faces of playing cards and other objects. They did this on a scale massively above what one would expect by chance. The authors of the article thus vigorously distinguished these phenomena from what they had encountered from Cumberlandism and the willing game, and they tried to eliminate all sensory sources of communication. They were later criticized on this score (Hall 1980a: 58–59) and on the grounds that they took the good faith of the participants too obviously for granted. However, they addressed these points in their second report on thought-reading (Gurney, Myers and Barrett 1882: 70–97).

They stressed that, in their key experiments, questioning the good faith of the Creerys was irrelevant since, 'We based our conviction of the reality of the phenomena on experiments made *when none of the Creery family were cognizant of the object selected*' (Gurney, Myers and Barrett 1882: 71). Myers and Gurney had visited the family in Buxton in April and the second report described, amongst other things, the experiments conducted when Myers invited the family to his new home, Leckhampton House, in Cambridge, the following July. The young Eveleen Myers took part in some of the tests, probably her introduction into the strange new world that would impinge on much of her future domestic life. The enquiry lasted for ten days and, quite often, the children were tested alone, with a thick, closed door separating the guesser from the investigator. Two of the sisters were also assessed by Barrett later in the year at Dublin. The results overall were above chance but not as spectacular as some of the Buxton findings. There were, the report commented, indications that boredom and tiredness could affect the results, a possible indication, one might think, of the trouble later to come.

The second part of the report described the much more spectacular results that Myers and Gurney had with two new subjects, Douglas Blackburn and George Albert Smith, who lived in Brighton. Blackburn had written to *Light* claiming that he and Smith had a remarkable rapport which allowed Smith to read his thoughts and to share the same taste sensations when he ate or drank. Myers and Gurney visited them in December 1882 and the committee reported that, 'The results of these trials give us the most important and valuable insight into the manner of the mental transfer of a picture which we have yet obtained' (Gurney, Myers and Barrett 1882: 78–79). The quality of the results might have given them pause for thought and one wonders what enquiries were made into the backgrounds of Smith and Blackburn. Smith was a stage mesmerist and Blackburn a rather scurrilous journalist with a dodgy private life. In spite of this, Gurney and Myers were particularly impressed by their demonstrations and Gurney, even more so, by Smith's abilities as a mesmerist or hypnotist. Gurney took on the chairmanship of the mesmeric committee in addition to his general duties as honorary secretary of the SPR in order to investigate hypnosis/mesmerism in greater detail. It was an exciting time and they may have got a little carried away. As Constance Buxton, an interested observer, enthused, 'The accounts of the Brighton experiments with Mr Blackburn and Mr Smith are quite wonderful ... I will certainly go on with our experiments on Thought Transference whenever I can get my husband into a sufficiently un-matter of fact state of mind' (Myers 1/107: 11.5.1883).

However, both the experiments with the Creerys and those with Smith and Blackburn were severely questioned in later years. Firstly, Gurney discovered the girls using a simple code (Gurney 1888–89b: 269–70), which ironically was not long after the time that Myers wrote to his wife that the children seemed to have recovered their old form and that he had found that one of them was an excellent hypnotic subject (Myers 8/11: 27.2.1887). From then on, Sidgwick rigorously excluded all their results as possible evidence for telepathy. Barrett strongly protested at this, pointing out that the code only covered situations when the sisters were in sight of each other and that there was plenty of other evidence that telepathy occurred when these conditions did not obtain. He defended his position strongly in later years and gave examples of successful thought-reading where it was not possible to pick up sensory or muscular clues: 'Stringent precautions were taken to avoid any information being conveyed to the subject through the ordinary channels of sense ... one of the percipients, Maud, then a child of twelve years old, was taken to an empty adjoining room and both doors closed. I then wrote down some object likely to be in the house, which we (the family together with myself) silently thought of. No one was allowed to leave their place or to speak a word. The percipient had previously been told to fetch the object as soon as she "guessed" what it was, and then return with it to the drawing room where we were seated' (Barrett 2006: 53–54). The girls performed well on these and other tests but Barrett felt that it was obvious what had happened. The girls had become bored and were also worried that their abilities fluctuated, so they invented the code in order not to disappoint their important visitors. Myers partially agreed with him and wrote to him as late as 22nd November 1900 pointing out that the issue was always, 'how to deal with the later cheating in connection with what I believe, with you, to have been the early genuineness' (SPR3/A4/97).

In later years, the experiments with Smith and Blackburn came in for considerable criticism, in the light of the claims by Blackburn, in the 1900s (in 1908–1909 in *John Bull* and in 1911 in the *Daily News*), that the whole series of experiments had been faked. He had assumed that all the other key participants were dead. Unfortunately for him, Smith was still very much alive and wrote to the paper to insist that there had been no hoaxing. He did not deviate from this position for the rest of his long life. Blackburn's confessions were thought by some to be prompted by a chronic need for cash and the SPR, in a rather lofty way, referred his accusations to the attention of their members, 'We think that those of our members who do not regularly see the *Daily News* may be interested in reading the following letters and articles …' (*Journal* 1911: 115–32).

After all this time it is not possible to state whether Smith was fraudulent or not. There just is not enough evidence. Certainly, he did start out as a hypnotist and mind reader on the Brighton stage and Blackburn was an out and out rogue. Though it should be stated that, later, he showed himself a gifted novelist on South African themes (Hall 1980a: xii). Certainly, Smith had strong show business interests and eventually exploited the world of psychics and spooks as subjects for his film factory at St Ann's Well Garden in Hove (he was one of the earliest silent film makers in England). Yet, to the end he denied fraud, was thought very competent by Gurney, Myers and the Sidgwicks, and remained an associate member of the SPR throughout his life (he did not 'sever his connection with the SPR after Gurney's death in 1888', as Luckhurst [2002: 74] stated). It is also noteworthy that the Sidgwicks engaged in thought-transference experiments with Smith in 1889, that there was a further series in 1890 and 1891, and that Smith was — apparently very satisfactorily — used in a number of roles by the Society, generally without incident or contention. There were, however, on the other side of the equation, two moments of concern. Mrs Verrall, a close Cambridge friend of Myers, mentioned to Alice Johnson (the SPR's research officer) in 1908 that there was some suspicion that

Smith had cheated in the Sidgwicks' 1889 investigations in Brighton. Furthermore, Sir Oliver Lodge told JG Piddington in 1909 that he thought he remembered Gurney catching Smith out on one occasion (Hall1980a: 142). Myers referred to the Brighton reservations in one of his letters to his wife but, given Smith's continued involvement with the Society, the worries seem to have been allayed (Myers 8/275: 6.4.1891).

Alan Gauld (Gauld 1965) in a well balanced survey of the case rightly pointed out that the third report of the committee into thought-transference was rather inadequate, and that the show business element in Smith's background did predispose one to looking much more carefully at him as a character. But he could not find any direct evidence, beyond Blackburn's confession of their joint hoaxing, that Smith was fraudulent. However, a certain sense of residual unease remains in this case. It does give one pause for thought when one reads in *Light* 25th October 1884 an advert on *Thought-Reading or, Modern Mysteries Explained by Douglas Blackburn, Price One Shilling*. Furthermore, the letter Blackburn sent to *Light* in 1882, outlining the extraordinary powers of thought-transference that he and Smith could demonstrate, has all the hallmarks of bait. If it was bait, Myers and Gurney took it. They contacted Blackburn, as we have seen, and carefully examined the paper records and reports he sent to them. They visited Blackburn and Smith in Brighton on the 15th November and on the 2nd, 3rd and 4th December 1882, where they conducted their first experiments with them. Hall was to criticise the sloppiness of these initial experiments. Physical contact, for example, was allowed at times between the two demonstrators. But that, it could be argued, was not naivety but rather the varying of conditions in order to get a better insight into the phenomena (Hall 1980a: 101–103).

But all this was well in the future. At the time the evidence for the new human faculty that they thought they had discovered seemed strong, and they searched for an appropriate terminology — 'thought induction', 'ideoscopy', thought-reading', and 'thought-transference'. Only the last developed any general currency, and even it was superseded by Myers' coinage of the term ' telepathy' which caught on very quickly and soon spread into the language generally (Williams 1984: 172). The birth of this charismatic and puzzling child is described in a letter of Myers to Sidgwick, 'What do you think of the words telaesthesia, telaesthetic, telepathy, telepathetic which I have just invented' (Myers 12/170: 2.11.1882). So Myers and his colleagues now had, to some extent, an empirical fact and a concept, but not even the beginnings of a hypothesis as to how it worked. Did telepathy have a physical or a psychic vehicle as carrier? how, if at all, did it relate to 'the luminiferous ether'? and to the physiology of the brain? Yet, they appeared to have demonstrated that mind was not totally dependent on brain and that there were things beyond the five bodily senses. A crack had opened in the apparently self-sealed and doomed materialist universe.

The third major source of evidence for some form of thought-transfer was the set of experiments carried out in Liverpool by Malcolm Guthrie, early in 1883. Guthrie, the owner of a drapery firm, had discovered that, stimulated by a visit to Liverpool of the stage performer Washington Irving Bishop, two of his female employees could transfer words, letters, numbers, to each other, crucially in some circumstances, without contact. Barrett went to see them in May 1883. Myers and Gurney followed later and eventually, Oliver Lodge, Professor of Physics at University College, Liverpool, became involved. As with the Creery children, the quality of the performance declined over time. But when Myers and Gurney investigated late in the year, they found that the girls, without being hypnotized, could detect with reasonable success, a substance tasted by the experimenter, and also, particularly in one case, six drawings were transferred with a considerable degree of accuracy. Lodge, in his tests, brought all the objects involved in experiments with him, and he alone knew what was to be used. He, too, came to the conclusion that the results were well above chance (Inglis 1977: 324–27).

Therefore, with evidence from the Creerys, from Smith and Blackburn, and from the experiments with Guthrie in Liverpool, Myers and his colleagues felt that they had established, if tentatively, the experimental existence of telepathy. But experiment was based on a lot of hard travelling and a lot of searching for factual information. It meant time and drudgery and there are many letters interchanged between Myers and Sidgwick with hotel rather than home addresses at the top. But they were buoyed up at times by what Myers called the Darien moment, the sense that 'we were the first that ever burst into that silent sea'.[1] This was a period of momentous excitement and exhilaration that even Sidgwick felt at times, and whose atmosphere was well captured by Jane Harrison, a young Cambridge classicist and acquaintance of the Cambridge psychical researchers: 'This was the Psychical Research circle; their quest, scientific proof of immortality. To put it thus seems almost grotesque now; then it was inspiring' (Harrison 1925: 55).

In the *Fortnightly Review* in March and April 1883, Myers and Gurney for the first time brought to the fore the question of telepathy in relation to 'crisis apparitions', seeing in such phenomena another form of operation of the same faculty (Gurney and Myers 1883a: 437–52, Gurney and Myers 1883b: 562–77). That is, they applied the concept of thought-transference

---

1   The allusion is to the final line of Keats' sonnet: 'On first looking into Chapman's Homer'.

or telepathy to the experiences that a number of people appeared to have concerning dreams, impressions, or visions of loved ones and friends in moments of danger or death. It should, incidentally, be noted that they ran these two lines of enquiry together and argued that they reinforced each other: the early reports on thought-transference had sections on spontaneous cases at the end. (During these years Gurney wrote regularly on this topic to *The Times* [17.12.1883] and other papers, both to publicise the SPR and to collect information.) In their articles Myers and Gurney stressed the need to sift, examine and corroborate and the importance of a personal interview with the experient (the individual experiencing the phenomena, as opposed to the agent, the person causing it). However, they stated that sometimes this was relaxed, 'where the testimony of illiterate persons, difficult to reach, has been accepted as genuine, on the authority of the clergyman of the parish.' Myers and Gurney were well aware of the weaknesses in their position and that they couldn't just produce a collection of sensational ghost stories that had no evidence to back them up. They had to pitch it right: 'Our tales will resemble neither the *Mysteries of Udolpho* nor the dignified reports of a learned society.'

Also, in these articles, Myers and Gurney tackled head on the assumptions of some Victorian men of science. They argued that it was legitimate to study these strange, marginal things in the interests of pure knowledge — not everything need immediately lead to utilitarian progress. Their subject matter was not what was conventionally labelled normal or natural. But neither was it miraculous. It was supernormal and would eventually be brought under the operation of the laws of the natural world. In short, their enquiries were perfectly legitimate, just at an early stage of development. But Myers and Gurney were very careful, as usual, not to venture on a physical explanation for telepathy. (They remembered James Knowles' attempt in the *Spectator* in 1869 to put forward a physical explanation for brain waves. His argument was that chemical changes in the brain of the transmitter led to undulations which were then transferred through the universal ether, a substance of incredible fineness and not currently detectable by scientific instruments, to be picked up by the recipient [Stein 1968: 41].) There were just too many imponderables and it was important not to discredit their observations by premature and possibly ridiculous speculation.

Whatever the ultimate verdict on all this and whatever later hidden regrets he may have had, Sidgwick was prepared to go public, concerning these first experiments in telepathy, as early as 28th January 1884 in his lecture at the London Institution. He stressed the weight of evidence that lay behind his account, particularly concentrating on thought-transference, 'numerous other illustrations of this class of evidence followed, the excitement rising as the lecturer proceeded'. *The Times* published the report as a summary narrative without the frivolous and sceptical asides that sometimes accompanied such descriptions. No doubt this was a tribute to the status of Sidgwick, who as *The Times* reported, 'fills the chair of Moral Philosophy at the University of Cambridge'.

As well as establishing the independent status of telepathy, Myers and Gurney were also eager to explore the relationship between it and mesmerism, and the nature of mesmerism itself. This was discussed in some detail in the first report of the committee on mesmerism (Barrett *et al.* 1883: 217–20). They had two central aims. The first was to get the medical profession to admit the existence of mesmerism in its hypnotic aspects. (In fact, one of the later triumphs of the SPR was gradually to increase the medical profession's awareness of hypnosis.) The second was to consider the residue of mesmeric cases, 'where the evidence of a specific influence is hard to controvert'. This was particularly difficult for the wider educated community to stomach. These cases ranged from the ability to make someone turn round by staring at them, to preventing their walking or drinking, right up to the outlandish — but apparently verified — claim by a medical student that he could mesmerise a manservant, as he went to feed the pigs, from almost twenty miles away (Gurney and Myers 1885b: 401–23).

Meanwhile the SPR was able to investigate mesmerism in better controlled experimental conditions through the co-operation of George Albert Smith. After the initial Smith-Blackburn experiments, Blackburn mysteriously disappeared (which suggests the Society may quite early on have found out something about this dubious character), but Smith remained and became of great value to the Society in their exploration of mesmerism. Although very young, only nineteen, he had already demonstrated mesmerism on the stage and had a number of very susceptible subjects, mainly working class lads (the star was one Fred Wells, a baker) whom he got to 'perform' for the SPR investigators. Smith put them through all the usual stage routines but his subjects also exhibited some more puzzling abilities, like the reception of physical tastes and sensations from the mesmerist, which the committee found difficult to explain in terms of hypnotism. These, and the silent control from another room over aspects of the subject's behaviour and the anaesthetisation of individual fingers (which the subject could not see because of an intervening screen), suggested the existence of some kind of influence over and beyond the suggestion/autosuggestion that Myers and Gurney were coming to see as the explanation for hypnotic phenomena.

This was a much more difficult set of phenomena to come to terms with than the general bizarre behaviour of Smith's Brighton subjects, which were and still are the standard fodder of stage hypnotists. For example, 'Wells was given a candle, which he was assured was a sponge-cake. He broke it in pieces, remarking that it was very stale, and actually ate about an inch and a-half of it. Shortly afterwards he began to feel the effects of his unusual meal; and, when pressed, flatly declined to have any more of "Mr Gurney's sponge-cakes"' (Barrett *et al.* 1883: 222–23). And, again with Wells as subject, 'His power of imitation under the influence of a suggested idea was most remarkable. Thus he admirably mimicked at different times a parrot, a worm, a clock, a statue, a bear, and a frog. His leaps under the influence of the last-named impression were so energetic and so reckless that it became necessary to discontinue the experiment, lest he should do himself some injury.' Finally, Wells excelled himself with his virtuoso performance as a nightingale, perching on a high bookshelf, his head pressed against the ceiling and 'ineffectually' flapping his arms/wings. It is not impossible that there was some element of make believe, but Smith was a talented hypnotist and, on many occasions with the Society, showed himself perfectly capable of hypnotising susceptible subjects whom he had never met before.

Of particular interest to the committee (because of its close links to the phenomena that the committee on thought-transference were investigating) was what came to be called 'community of sensation'. In two series of tests (one on 4.1.1883 and the other on 10.4.1883) the sensations of being pricked, pinched, slapped and the tastes of salt, wormwood and ginger, were, in broad terms, successfully transferred from Smith to Wells. The committee stated that they had strongly guarded against the possibility of codes and that the 'mesmeric sympathy' identified had previously been experienced and written about by Professor Barrett in his 1876 paper to the British Association (Barret *et al.* 1883: 227).

The remarkable nature and power of mesmerism was given wider circulation by Myers and Gurney, later in the year, in an article they wrote for the *Nineteenth Century*. They began with their by now standard lament, 'We are really at a loss to account for the small measure of attention which has been accorded to phenomena so eminently impressive' (Gurney and Myers 1883c: 696). They were, therefore, eager to draw the educated public's attention to them. At the same time they had to impress that public with their own detachment and capacity for critical judgement. The language they used, therefore, had a certain ironic distance to it, and the range of references was such as to reassure their readers that they were dealing with gentlemen and scholars. So, for example, in an account of stage mesmerism (obviously witnessed at Cambridge), 'The scene may be a public hall in a university town, the operator a woman of vigorous frame and commanding gaze' and an undergraduate rushes

onto the stage 'flinging himself at the feet of the stern mistress of his desti-
nies' having the previous evening been hypnotised and bidden to attend
the next night. Or, when, 'a ruffianly tanner' is hypnotised in order to see
imaginary angels, he 'clasps his hands, and shows a dark visage concentrated into the dully glowing intensity of a Ribera or a Zurbaran' (Gurney
and Myers 1883c: 696).

But although they emphasized at this early stage in the enquiry that
their aim was the collection and colligation of facts, they found it impossible to avoid some intellectual debate. They could not accept that the phenomena they had discovered were adequately explained by the dominant
psychological thinking of the time, as represented in the work of WB Carpenter. He was a very significant and combative figure, as we have
already seen[2] He was a Fellow of the Royal Society and had been President of the British Association in 1872. His *Principles of Mental Physiology,*
published in 1874, summarised his views concerning the explanation for
abnormal mental phenomena like mesmeric trances and other unusual
behaviours. He argued that the concept of mental reflexes adequately
covered such areas. He asserted that the trance state induced by the mesmerist led to the suspension of the will and that the individual then
responded in an imitative and zombie-like way to the suggestions of the
mesmerist. He was not prepared to accept that the unconscious state actually initiated and controlled human behaviour (Hearnshaw 1964: 24).
Michael Clark, moreover, has argued that this went well beyond Carpenter and was part of the general diagnostic repertoire of doctors in the late
nineteenth century (Clark 1981: 271–312). Abnormal mental phenomena,
hallucinations, a range of automatisms, were pathological in origin, the
consequence of some physical disease or lesion. This caused the will to
lose its grip on the body and the body's perception of the external world.
For Myers and Gurney, this was a travesty of an explanation. They found
phrases like 'automatic mental action' and 'unconscious cerebration'
grossly inadequate for the lively, vital and creative activity displayed by a
good hypnotic subject like Wells, let alone for higher mental processes
like the complexity, creativity and imagination displayed in the work of
the poet and the mathematician (Gurney and Myers 1883c: 699–700).
Moreover, they were gradually coming to the view that the source of this
creativity lay not in normal everyday consciousness, but in an unconscious that was far richer and more dynamic than Carpenter ever dreamt
of.

They had already, and were to gather many more, compelling examples
that indicated there was a powerful intelligence, albeit thwarted or

2   See above, p. 99.

impeded, that was operating in these bizarre cases. For example, as Perry Williams has pointed out (Williams 1984: 190), the impotent fury with which Smith's mesmerised subject struggled to pick up a sovereign offered to him, while forbidden by the mesmerist's command, was certainly not the response of a mindless automaton, only capable of mirror-like imitation. It was also clear that the creation of stigmata, either through religious ecstasy, or deliberate suggestion, were other examples of this creative power. Myers, running his examination of automatic writing in parallel with the mesmeric investigations of Gurney, had in fact as early as 1885 come to the conclusion: 'Coincidently with our normal or primary self there is within us a potential secondary self, or second focus of cerebration and mentation, which is not a mere metaphysical abstraction, but manifests itself occasionally by certain supernormal physiological or psychical activities' (Myers, 1886a: 30).

However, the lofty and assured intellectual tone of these early articles by Myers and Gurney was not always warranted. Sometimes, without realising it, they were skating on very thin ice and their first major fall came in 1884. Those who mocked the Spookical Society were delighted by the Edmund Hornby fiasco, the first of several embarrassing episodes that damaged — but did not destroy — the Society's reputation for investigative competence. Sir Edmund Hornby was a very grand figure indeed. As Fraser Nicol states, 'the case was printed very largely as an act of faith in Sir Edmund's testimony (though ostensibly confirmed by his wife)' (Nicol 1972: 352). And what a case! Sir Edmund had the grand title of Chief Judge of the Supreme Consular Court of China and was based in Shanghai. His customary practice was, the night before he gave written judgements in court, to brief favoured journalists on his verdict, so they could catch the morning press. On one occasion he was awoken, he stated, just after one in the morning by a journalist asking for his judgement. Sir Edmund, though enraged, gave him the report verbally. The journalist said this would be the last time they met. Lady Hornby, aroused by the noise, was told by the Judge what had happened. She later confirmed this. The following day it was found that the reporter had been working on this very story at the time of his death, which was about the time Hornby had seen him in his bedroom. This story was one of the more vivid tales in the May and July editions of the *Nineteenth Century* which eventually reached Shanghai. Upon their arrival a local newspaper editor wrote to the periodical pointing out that Hornby was not married at the time and that the reporter's death had actually occurred between eight and nine in the morning (Hall 1980a: 65–68). Gurney had to withdraw the case and make a grovelling apology for not seeking corroborating evidence, which he should have done by searching 'the files of Chinese newspapers at the

British Museum' (Gurney 1885a: 2–4). Hornby, however, refused to retract his testimony. One explanation, of course, is that it was a particularly vivid dream. Another, more piquant one, is that Hornby was in bed with his future wife before they were legally married and that the incident occurred broadly as he reported it (Lambert 1969: 43–55). But, bluntly, whatever the case, Gurney should not have accepted his word — just because he was a senior judge — without searching for corroborative evidence, as he had done in other cases. The matter was also embarrassing for Myers, in that he received a letter from Harvey Goodwin, Bishop of Carlisle, and a member of the SPR, expressing interest in the article and pointing out that one of the judges mentioned in it was his brother (Myers 1/108: 15.7.1884).

There was, despite such occasional setbacks and failures, a real sense of excitement about the early years of the SPR. They believed they had, as Crookes thought he had with Home, demonstrated empirically — and sometimes under laboratory conditions — the existence of a new force or faculty. What its relationship was to the physical world, however, was much more complex. Balfour Stewart, the physicist, reflected on this when he became President of the SPR in 1887. Did the mind of A act directly on the mind and then the body of B? Or did the mind of A act on the body of B and then the mind? Or did the body of A act through a medium on the body of B and then the mind? Was telepathy transmitted in some way like light through the ether as vibrations which set up corresponding vibration of the molecules of the brain in B? The problem with a physical or quasi-physical basis, however, was that the effect should decline with distance inversely; and why should it, if carried by the ether, be experienced only by one individual? (Williams 1984: 173).

Myers himself speculated at times that a spiritual ether (the metetherial as he called it) was the vehicle of transmission, but he was always careful not to rule out a continued link or bridge between mind and matter (Myers 1886c: 290). Nevertheless, he believed that there had been a breakthrough, in that there was some evidence for the mind's operating beyond the traditional constraints of matter, as the definition in his glossary of psychical research terms indicates (Myers 1904 1: xxii). Telepathy was seen as, 'the communication of impressions of any kind from one mind to another independently of the recognised channels of sense'. The adjective 'recognised' was very sensible. It acknowledged the possibility that there might be other modes of sense-based perception as yet undiscovered. For example, Rupert Sheldrake (using expertise from animal research) has recently postulated the existence of a sixth sense of different physical types based on electrical and magnetic fields, heat-sensing, or miniscule vibrations (Sheldrake 2003: 4). Despite the reservation implicit in 'recognised', Myers was certainly capable of pointing up the spiritual implications of their discovery, expressing towards the end of his life – in forthright terms – that, 'to believe that prayer is heard is to believe in telepathy – in the direct influence of mind on mind' (Williams 1984: 172–79).

Myers, the SPR and Madame Blavatsky

It was, no doubt, with a mixture of excitement and scepticism that Myers heard of the initial reports of Madame Blavatsky and the work of the Theosophical Society. Here appeared to be an organisation which not only had gathered and examined phenomena similar to the SPR's, but which also had adepts who claimed to be able to produce and replicate them under certain conditions. The Theosophical Society had been set up in 1875 in New York by Madame Blavatsky and Colonel Olcott. The former was a Russian aristocrat of considerable intelligence and resource and the latter was a well-meaning but rather credulous seeker after occult and spiritual truths. It was through his friend and fellow SPR Council member, Charles Massey, that Myers became fully involved in the Theosophical Society. This aspect of his life, which has been rather under played, was brought to wider attention by one historian of Theosophy, Leslie Price (Price 1985, 1986), building on the earlier research of Waterman (Waterman 1963, 1969–1970).

Myers had dinner with Alfred Percy Sinnett, the leading English publicist of Blavatsky's ideas, on 16th May 1883, and on 3rd June became a Fellow of the Theosophical Society (Price 1986: 2). So, even before the arrival of Madame Blavatsky in England there had been increasingly close links between some members of the SPR and the Theosophists. Myers, for example, immediately after the dinner with Sinnett, wrote to Massey: 'Sinnett said that he would like to join the SPR. If you will propose him I should like to second him' (Myers 19/6: 17.5.1883). Indeed, Sinnett went so far as to assert in his memoirs that the salon of Gertrude Tennant (Myer's mother in law), was a centre from which interest in Theosophy 'radiated' out into 'London society at large' (Sinnett 1922: Chapter IV). This must have been Myers' influence rather than Gertrude Tennant's. She confided to her journal on 7th May 1884 that Theosophy was 'great rubbish' (D/DT: 2535/5).

Charles Carleton Massey was a strong supporter of Myers' investigation into Theosophy and, like him, tried to put the phenomena he encountered into the context of wider, even cosmic speculation. There were not many people within the SPR with whom Myers could relax intellectually in this way. Massey had trained as a barrister but, because he had a private income, he was able to give up the practice of law, and dedicate his time to research into spiritualism and related phenomena. He joined the Theosophical Society in 1875 and became the first president of the British Theosophical Society in 1878. He had links with a range of occult organizations, dividing his time between the rather feverish and conspiratorial atmosphere of London-based sects and contemplative life in the countryside. Two incidents particularly turned him against Madame Blavatsky. He was dismayed by her apparent plagiarizing of an address by H Kiddle of New York, and incorporating it in a letter miraculously sent to Sinnett by her master, Koot Hoomi. He was further outraged by a letter he was shown in May 1882 (Hodgson *et al.* 1885: 397) which proved that another letter, supposedly sent supernaturally to him by an occult Master, had in fact been put by a creature of mere flesh and blood in a place where he would discover it.

The friendship with Myers was deep and long lasting, despite their growing differences over the way the SPR assessed spiritualist phenomena. Massey was invited to become Leo's godfather after the death of Prince Leopold, his original godfather. Massey was also instrumental in providing Myers with a background in Theosophical and Eastern thought; and he also translated du Prel (Massey 1889) and Zöllner (Massey 1882) into English, furnishing Myers, and sections of the English upper middle classes with some insight into the German mystical and idealist traditions (Williams 1984: 215–17).

Myers' first meeting with Madame Blavatsky, was, as befitted the great lady, in somewhat dramatic circumstances. On 7th April 1884 he attended the London meeting of the Theosophical Society to elect a new President. She burst in at the end of the formal business, arriving sweaty and out of breath. She had been ordered, she said, by the Master to leave Paris and attend. She had walked from Charing Cross station, following her 'occult nose', to the meeting at Lincoln Inn's Field. The minutes of the meeting indicate that Myers used the opportunity of her presence to ask whether any documentary evidence could be obtained from India to substantiate the astral apparitions of the Mahatmas (Sinnett 1922: 54-56, Caldwell 2000: 244-45). She then returned to Paris, but shortly after came back to London and stayed till mid-August with Francesca Arundale at 77, Elgin Crescent, Notting Hill. There — downstairs, in the drawing room, in a big armchair — she received visitors, rolled and smoked her cigarettes, was the centre of certain phenomena, and had another encounter with Myers (Caldwell 2000: 253-58). On 9th August she attended a meeting of the Cambridge branch of the SPR in the rooms of a fellow of King's, Oscar

Browning. Myers and Sidgwick subjected her to sustained questioning for a couple of hours. The following day they had lunch with her. The Sidgwicks formed a reasonably favourable impression (Sidgwick and Sidgwick 1906: 384-85), in spite of the copious decorations of cigarette ash about her person.

Sidgwick, however, had been aware right from the beginning, perhaps more sharply than either Myers or Gurney, that the Theosophists posed a particular problem for the SPR. He raised the question in a letter to Myers (Add.Ms.c. 100/65: 21.6.1883) as to how far the SPR should mix with Theosophists or share rooms with them. He was re-assured by the number of Theosophists who came from the same class background as many members of the SPR, but he was also well aware of the potentially danger-ous overlap in aims between the organisations. For example, one of the objects of the Theosophical Society was eventually stated as, 'to investi-gate the unexplained laws of nature and the powers latent in man'. This could, in some senses, be said to be what the SPR was doing (Dixon 2001: 4). But could Theosophists be trusted to investigate in the same sceptical and balanced fashion as the SPR?

The paranormal phenomena linked to Madame Blavatsky appeared to go well beyond the sporadic and elusive cases of ghostly apparitions the SPR was collecting for what later became *Phantasms of the Living*. The Theosophists claimed that through intense training these phenomena could, under certain conditions, be produced and replicated at will by those who had been apprenticed, as Chelas or pupils, to advanced Mas-ters in the Himalayas. Sidgwick could see that this was an area worthy of investigation—indeed central to the Society's mission—but he was con-cerned that the SPR might lose credibility, as the almost inevitable tall tales and accusations of fraud circulated amongst the wider public. This linkage is clearly demonstrated in two of the appendices of the first report of the SPR committee set up to investigate Theosophical phenomena. They contain an account of the considered and pre-meditated 'astral' projection, on two occasions at night, of a Mr B (verified by the percipient) to a lady friend: all details of which were sent to and held by Gurney (Committee of the SPR 1884: appendices XL, XLI).

The Committee of the Society for Psychical Research Appointed to Investigate the Evidence for Marvellous Phenomena offered by certain Members of the Theo-sophical Society, was established by the Council of the SPR on the 2nd May 1884. It was chaired by Myers. Gurney, Frank Podmore (a senior Post Office employee with an increasingly sceptical view of much of the phe-nomena investigated) and JH Stack (a *Daily Telegraph* journalist) were members, as was Sidgwick, ex officio, as president. Witnesses were inter-viewed in some depth and the committee collected documentary evi-

dence. The committee assumed that all its readers would be familiar with
Sinnett's *The Occult World* (Sinnett 1881), which gives some indication of
the penetration of that book in cultural circles in the early 1880s. However, a short note by Myers, on key theosophical tenets, was added as a
supplementary aid. It should be stressed that, as with all other SPR activity, the views and conclusions of this committee were only those of the
participants and not the collective opinion of the SPR, which did not and
does not have collective institutional opinions. It was not a witch hunt.
The SPR did not set out to 'expose' Theosophy and/or Madame Blavatsky.
Madame Blavatsky was not herself examined directly by the committee
but on two occasions, Myers and Gurney (26.7.1884), and once with William Barrett (5.7.1884) heard the 'astral bell' in her presence. It is worth
quoting part of Gurney's description, because of his trained musical ear:
'In the middle of the conversation the attention of Mr Myers and myself
was caught by a very distinct sweet musical sound, resembling somewhat
the sound which can be made with the nail of a finger against a fin-
ger-glass, but differing in that there was less sharpness of "attack". It was
noticeably a <u>free</u> sound, such as could not be produced by any object
whose vibrations were in anyway damped or checked' (Price 1985: 25–35).
In addition, Myers, after pleading with her, had a separate demonstration
of his own. She asked for a finger bowl and some water and with her
hands folded in her lap and well away from the bowl, several silvery
notes soon resonated through the room. Myers went away saying that he
would never doubt again but was back within a fortnight with possible
alternative explanations, as was his usual response to startling phenomena; enthusiasm and then doubt (Caldwell 2000: 256–57). Not to be out-
done, Eveleen Myers reported experiencing a similar sound at home
while Myers was away, which was 'quite unlike any tinkling sound I have
heard before', and she bravely went downstairs to investigate (Myers
25/137: 2.8.1884).

Myers was at this time on his annual holiday with his brother Arthur.
They went to Belgium and Holland, combining frequent swimming and
bathing with visits to art galleries. They then took the opportunity to visit
Elberfeld in Germany where Blavatsky was staying with the leading
German Theosophists, the Gebhardts. Myers had, on the 16th August,
received from Padshah, a Theosophist, a letter stating that Madame
Blavatsky had seen the astral projection of one of her supporters,
Damodar, who was in India, standing in the corner of her London residence and asking her what she wanted him to do about her trunk (Myers
3/129). Padshah asserted that this was a good opportunity to establish
some independent corroboration of the claim. Myers managed to see an
entry in Blavatsky's private diary for 15th August, apparently written at

the time, which described the incident. He was, however, back in Cambridge before the registered letter, that Damodar had sent from India confirming his astral projection, arrived at Elberfeld on the 10th September. Mrs Sidgwick (Hodgson *et al.* 1885: 388–92) discussed the matter in some detail and showed, theoretically, how with careful forward planning, Madame Blavatsky and Damodar could have pulled off the trick, if trick it was.

Nevertheless, at the time, Myers' visit to Elberfeld had a considerable impact on him. He wrote glowingly to Massey: 'I give list of Elberfeld party as I met them. All save (6) [a boy: there were thirteen adults there in addition to Myers and his brother and he listed and numbered them all] had had experiences. Nothing happened actually in my sight. Mrs Holloway is about the most important witness of the lot: Solovieff the next. They establish to my mind existence and powers of Mahatma KH and Maunjah' (Myers 19/8: 9.9.1884). And more fulsomely: 'I've spent 5½ days mainly in Mme B's bedroom, cross-examining her as to past life etc. … My confidence in her has increased about fourfold'. The ending of the letter was pure Myers. He stated he had signed up four of the Elberfeld party as members of the SPR and he urged Massey to do some recruiting too. Myers was obviously greatly impressed and even Gurney seemed to be swayed in the rather intense and exotic environment that surrounded the Theosophists and their entourage. As a reflection of this, the committee reported in December 1884 that there was a prima facie case for more detailed enquiry. In anticipation of this conclusion, Hodgson had already been sent to India, in November, to investigate on the spot (Hodgson *et al.* 1885: 203).

Yet trouble was brewing for Madame Blavastky. Blavatsky and Olcott had left the Theosophical headquarters, in Adyar, India, earlier in the year to visit their centres of support in Europe. They went to Paris, London and then on to Elberfeld, as we have seen. But back in Adyar, her servants, the Coulombs, were spreading stories (possibly, it was alleged, paid to do so by local missionaries) that Blavatsky had forged letters from her occult Masters and produced phenomena by trickery. In other words, that she was a blatant fraud.

She was unfortunate, too, in the nature of her SPR investigator. Richard Hodgson was a complex, stubborn and highly independent character. He had come from Australia to St John's Cambridge and had taken a high second class degree in Moral Sciences rather than the first he was expected to achieve. With characteristic perversity, he had not followed the syllabus in detail, preferring his own approach. Sidgwick, on the other hand, with equally characteristic generosity, had paid for Hodgson to have a study visit to Germany so that he could improve his German in order to read their philosophy in the original; and he also helped to secure him an extra-mural lecturing position (Hackett 1920: 207–209). Sidgwick valued the directness and practical clarity of his thought and also believed his amateur interest in conjuring and legerdemain might be of use to the Society. But sturdy independence of thought could easily turn into prejudice and Hodgson was notoriously difficult to shift once he had made up his mind. RH Thouless made the same point, in his review of Waterman's later criticisms of Hodgson (Waterman 1963): 'It was I think characteristic of Hodgson that he decided early on in an investigation what was the truth of the matter and then tended to present the evidence in a way which supported the truth, tending to over-emphasize the part of the evidence favourable to his conclusion and to under-emphasize the part of the evidence which made difficulties for it' (Thouless 1968: 344).

Hodgson spent several months in India, building his case against Blavatsky. He sent regular letters back to England outlining his findings. Sidgwick described the process in his journal and his reactions to it: 'We talked over Theosophy, of which Hodgson keeps us amply informed by weekly accounts [from India] of his investigation. His opinion of the evidence seems to be growing steadily more unfavourable; but there are still some things difficult to explain on the theory of fraud. I have no doubt, however, that Blavatsky has done most of it. She is a great woman' (Sidgwick and Sidgwick 1906: 405). In a later entry he noted Hodgson's return (April 30th) and that Hodgson stated that, 'all Theosophic marvels are and were a fraud from beginning to end' (Sidgwick and Sidgwick 1906: 410) . There was, significantly, no reference to Blavatsky's greatness of character this time.

Hodgson based his case against Blavatsky on four key grounds (Thouless 1968: 344). Firstly, that her disgruntled employees, the Coulombs, had documentary evidence showing that she had giving them orders to carry out certain fraudulent phenomena. Secondly, that she had a shrine built at Adyar in which, from her bedroom, she, or an accomplice, could put documents or other objects that would appear as precipitated or materialised apports in another room. Thirdly, that she, rather than supernormal Mahatmas or Brothers, had written the letters that magically appeared offering esoteric or practical advice. Fourthly, that these Mahatmas were really her employees or servants in disguise. Hodgson added a bit of spice (seen most clearly in his preliminary overview of his conclusions in *The Age* 12.9.1885). He argued that Blavatsky's main motives were political not occult. She was a Russian spy and Theosophy was a cover for her part in the Great Game between the British and Russian Empires in Asia. At the end of June 1885 Hodgson read part of his account at a meeting of the SPR and the account was published in full in December 1885.

Both narrative and conclusions were rapidly and widely accepted at the time and for some considerable period to come.

Hodgson was strongly supported by Eleanor Sidgwick (Hodgson *et al.* 1885: 378–96) who went over his handwriting analysis and agreed with his conclusion that Madame Blavatsky had faked the letters. She also demonstrated how Madame Blavatsky could have opened a letter sealed with red and yellow floss silk and put in a note from a Mahatma, without leaving any evidence of interference. In addition, drawing on the Society's extensive experience in assessing evidence for the soon to be published *Phantasms of the Living*, she analysed four cases of astral projection or the sighting of apparitions. She dismissed them all because of the inaccurate observation of the witnesses, the scope for trickery, the psychological state of one witness, 'whose organisation is highly nervous', and lack of corroborating evidence generally.

The result of Hodgson's account was a vigorous and robustly worded conclusion by the committee, namely that Madam Blavatsky 'had achieved a title to permanent remembrance as one of the most accomplished, ingenious, and interesting impostors in history' (Hodgson *et al.* 1885: 207). It is probably the most celebrated quotation from SPR literature and has been well seeded in the wider academic consciousness because of the exotic nature of Blavatsky and her significance for *fin de siècle* cultural and social history. For example, a distinguished writer on nineteenth-century spiritualism and the occult, Alex Owen, could, as late as 2004, describe Hodgson's account as 'devastating' (Owen 2004: 34) without any qualification as to its accuracy or the later, revisionist scholarship that has weakened its authority. At the time, and for a long time to come, it certainly gave the Society a reputation for hard edged, no nonsense investigation, that did it no harm; and it boosted Hodgson's status as a researcher into and assessor of the anomalous and allegedly miraculous that would have significant consequences for the future direction of the Society and for Myers himself. Gurney enthusiastically assured William James of Hodgson's qualities, after James had expressed some reservations: 'But I think, when you see something of him, you will be struck by his really remarkable thoroughness & acuteness in the sort of work he is now doing. His qualities are *absolutely invaluable*; & psychical research ought to insure his life for about a million pounds' (Skrupskelis *et al.* 1998: 192). It was, politically, a very expedient report. The SPR was at a crucial stage in its history, the Society having surmounted a fair amount of initial criticism and gibing. Sidgwick's cautious approach based on the gathering and sifting of very large bodies of evidence was having some positive effect on upper-middle class opinion makers. The Society was well on the way to the publication of *Phantasms of the Living* and it did not want another disaster like the Hornby case (the exposure of the Creery children and concerns about the veracity of Smith and Blackburn still lay in the future) on an even grander scale. Such an occurrence would have severely damaged their credibility and ruined the impact of their first major publication.

Over the last century, however, a number of researchers have cast doubt on several crucial features of Hodgson's research. Beatrice Hastings (Hastings 1937) severely dented the credibility of the Coulombs as witnesses, and Adlai Waterman (Waterman 1963) savaged, in considerable technical detail, Hodgson's assertions concerning the fraudulent shrine. More recently Michael Gomes (Gomes 2005: ii) has re-emphasized this and also the physical impossibility of Hodgson's suppositions in this connection. And Vernon Harrison (Harrison 1997), an expert on forgery and handwriting, pointed out the many weaknesses in the evidence put forward to prove that Madame Blavatsky had counterfeited the Mahatma letters. He also took to task the leading figures in the SPR at the time, who had gone from a rather bemused belief that there might be something in it all, to a complete and uncritical acceptance of the Hodgson Report.

The verdict also played to a certain view of the East by the West, which was not just Hodgson's alone. JH Stack consistently argued that, 'there is no country in the world where confederates and witnesses could be purchased so cheaply as in India and where false testimony is so common' (SPR4/1/8: 17.10.1884). He was alarmed by the way that as late as October 1884 Myers, and surprisingly Gurney, appeared to be susceptible: 'I tried to convert Myers and Gurney yesterday; I am afraid my arguments had not much effect: they are still under the spell of the Blavatsky.' It was almost as if they had been duped by Oriental magic and that Hodgson had released them from their enchantment. Myers, in later reviewing his ideas on the nature of evidence and the trustworthiness of testimony, placed low reliance on orientals as witnesses, largely on the basis of his experiences in the Blavatsky affair (Gauld 1968: 364–67). Blavatsky, in her turn, ridiculed the SPR investigations writing about their, 'ungentlemanly, disgusting, *Scotland yard* secret proceedings' (Dixon 2001: 36) and commented on Hodgson's youth and naivety. But it was a blow, fair or unfair, from which she did not recover. She also complained bitterly to Sinnett about Myers' underhand behaviour. He had promised not to reveal Blavatsky's aunt's name in print but had allowed Hodgson to publish it in connection with his accusations that Blavatsky was probably a Russian agent: 'You ought to expose him before every honourable man, and this action he will not be able to deny, and will stand as a blackguard before many. If you do not do this, then you shall have lost the best opportunity of showing the Cambridge *clique* in its true light' (Barker 1923: letter 61).

The collapse of Myers' hopes and enthusiasm with regard to Theosophy, induced a sobering scepticism, after the heady days of the early 1880s, particularly concerning the possibility of life after death. As Myers put it: 'Gurney up to the time of his death was quite uncertain on this capital point. He still held that all proved phenomena were possibly explicable by new modes of action between living men alone', and, 'the collapse of Madame Blavatsky's so-called Theosophy — a mere fabric of fraud, — had rendered all of us severer in our judgement of the human evidence on which our own conclusions depended. Sidgwick urged that all that we had actually proved was consistent with eternal death' (Myers 1961: 40–41). It would take the news of a new medium from America — William James' 'white crow', Mrs Piper — to re-invigorate the quest.

Sinnett, looking back on the affair years later, blamed poor Colonel Olcott for the start of the rot, and for stimulating the desire of the leading figures in the SPR to disentangle themselves from Theosophy (Sinnett 1922: chapter 4). He asserted that 'the superficial aspects of his personality were of a kind quite certain to set the teeth on edge with Englishmen of the type of those who were leading the Psychic Research movement.' But this was both unfair and inaccurate. As we have seen, the Sidgwicks responded positively to Blavatsky in August 1884, and Myers and Gurney were still alarming Stack as late as October that year by the seriousness with which they were taking Theosophical claims. It was the superficial vigour and coherence of Hodgson's account and concern in case they jeopardised the reception of their mammoth domestic project, *Phantasms of the Living*, that were the most important factors in their disengagement.

Yet, there was one aspect of Blavatsky's influence that Myers took with him, even if he rejected the phenomena associated with her. He had been stimulated to read more widely in Eastern philosophy, and this chimed with and enriched his other metaphysical reading (Williams 1984: 218–22). This was a heady brew: Hartmann on the Unconscious, du Prel on Mysticism, Zöllner on Transcendental Physics, and now Sinnett on Theosophy. He had already a strong strain of Platonic mysticism in his intellectual repertoire (both directly and as filtered through Plotinus [Lambert 1928: 393–413]) and had been encouraged to apply the concept of Darwinian evolution to the spiritual sphere through contact with Alfred Russel Wallace. The encounter with the ideas of Theosophy helped to confirm, enrich and deepen the channels in which his thought already ran; particularly the idea that access to paranormal powers could be part of the destiny of humankind. They also informed his intuition, increasingly expressed in highly wrought digressions in his later writings, of man's continuous evolution through a range of experiences and levels, post-mortem as well as pre-mortem, as part of an unending progression towards the Godhead itself in eternal growth.

Phantasms of the Living

Both rattled and relieved by the apparent exposure of Madame Blavatsky, Myers and Gurney turned with renewed vigour to the collection and sifting of evidence for their own investigation of *Phantasms of the Living*. They had first introduced the public to the concept of phantasms or crisis apparitions and hallucinations linked to death and trauma, in the *Fortnightly Review* in 1883. They stressed the 'laborious quantitative work' involved and their 'systematic collection of facts' and that readers should not treat the publication of such investigations as a manifesto of faith in supernatural agencies. They tried to make an initial catalogue of the types of crisis phenomena: feelings of doom/disaster/apprehension, specific visions, hearing voices, and getting ideas/impressions from objects. They also did some cautious and provisional speculation. They dismissed the idea of physical explanations based on brain-waves, but thought that the apparition might be caused by telepathic stimulation of the cortex which then sent messages to the optic nerve and the visualising centre and that the percipient in some way often modified the primary telepathic impulse (Gurney and Myers 1883b: 562–77).

It was also decided to print cases regularly in the *Journal* so that members would have an opportunity to comment on them. This approach was consistent with the Millian approach to evidence collection and examination that — so Williams (Williams 1984) has argued — particularly characterised the work of Myers, Gurney and Sidgwick. This is a point well worth reinforcing and Podmore has a valuable comment on this in his review of the Sidgwick memoir: ' The aim of the Society, it will be recalled, the conception which marked out its investigation from all previous investigations of the subject, was that it should be *collective* – that the task of appraising the evidence should depend upon no single judgement.' Sidgwick, from his usual largesse, provided the money to facilitate this process: '[He] came forward and defrayed the cost of having the entire collection — which mounted up week by week to almost incredible totals — printed on separate slips, with wide margins for comments and the insertion of additional evidence. In this way it was possible for each member of the Literary Committee to form his or her independent judgment on a case before discussing it in full conclave' (Podmore 1907: 438–39). The 'discussion in full conclave' and the letters from readers of the *Journal* were seen as crucial parts of the assessment of evidence. It ensured the cases eventually printed in *Phantasms of the Living* were not there solely on the authority of the individual investigator, whether Myers, Gurney, Podmore, or the Sidgwicks.

By 1884, 500 cases of impressions and apparitions at moments of death and danger had been collected. It was on these materials that Myers began to display his considerable gifts of organisation, pattern identifying and classification. This analysis of cases and their ordering started in the *Journal* of May 1884 and continued through nine instalments to January 1885. Myers was quite explicit about the way in which the material had been ordered, 'and the direction in which additional evidence is specifically to be desired' (Myers 1884–85: 54). He stated that, 'the cases have been so classed as to illustrate the theory which regards phantasms of the living as a development of Thought-transference. The mode of impact on the percipient's mind has, therefore, been the point primarily regarded'. The first category was that of a feeling of unease or calamity felt by only one person and he urged people to record these feelings and get them corroborated by someone else before it was known whether anything happened or not. One case, from 'a trusted informant', was the Hon Mrs Fox Powys, another was from Miss Agnes M.A.S. of Whepstead Rectory, Bury St Edmunds: reassuring names and addresses. He also made the customary appeal for additional cases of the same or a cognate kind. It was becoming clear to them that these phantasms, or crisis apparitions, came in a variety of forms, even though the dominant category was visual. Myers was later to argue that the type of manifestation might relate directly to the sensory modality (kinaesthetic, olefactory, verbal, visual) which most easily accessed the subliminal consciousnesses of percipient and agent. In fact, throughout his writings he demonstrated an embryonic but developing sense of the widely differing ways in which human beings experienced, processed and transmitted information: a perception foreshadowing the detailed work on human creativity produced by Howard Gardner in the following century (Gardner 1985).

In the *Journal* for December (Myers 1884–85: 213–20), Myers spelt out this classification in considerable detail. There were three divisions: individual cases; neutral cases (the percipient was, for practical purposes, alone, but it was impossible to say-if someone woke or passed by-whether or not they would have seen/experienced the phantasm); and collective cases. These divisions were divided into eighteen classes and then into fifty-seven groups. It was a considerable feat of phenomenological analysis and categorisation and laid part of the basis for Myers' later substantial and sustained reflections on the nature of telepathic impressions and their emergence from the subliminal consciousness.

A number of themes and issues resulted from this first classification which were to exercise Myers and Gurney for the rest of their lives. Firstly, who was the most significant partner in the telepathic process? In experimental cases of thought-transference it appeared that the more gifted the percipient, the better the results. But in the case of death or trauma it might be that only a few individuals suffering that process had the ability to project, in whatever form, a phantasm of themselves (Myers 1884–85: 80–81). Secondly, some reported cases seemed to be examples of clairvoyance rather than telepathy; as when the percipient seemed to be transferred to another scene, in half-trance, drowsy, or in a dream, and viewed that scene from their own perspective. This could more rightly be interpreted as 'an extension of the powers of some one individual mind rather than the result of any communication from another mind' (Myers 1884–85: 143). Thirdly, some of these experiences had no clear friendship or relative link. Cyrus Read Edmonds, the headmaster of the Leicestershire Proprietary Grammar School, told his wife that, in a dream, 'he had seen the Thames Tunnel break through. That the workmen rushed to the staircases or ladders, the means of exit, but one poor fellow … was overtaken by the rush of water and perished.' He had the accuracy of his dream confirmed at a dinner party the following evening. Myers argued, 'The kind of communication which we are now picturing to ourselves no longer resembles a whisper along a tube, but a shout diffused in space and caught by a casual listener' (Myers 1884–85: 122–24). Picking up information about a major event like this would seem to be a radically different process and perhaps implied a cosmic ether, in which all events were retained and registered and were only accessible to the random few individuals with the appropriate sensitivity. Fourthly, though the phenomena were hallucinatory it was important to distinguish them from morbid hallucinations, by the quality of testimony for them and their proved link with specific events. The testimony of the masses, however, was suspect since, 'The class of persons who send their children to public elementary schools is officially defined as including six-sevenths of the whole population' (Myers 1884–85: 188). Fifthly, the nature of the phantasm was very varied and complex (Myers 1884–85: 115). It was very rarely a full physical materialisation occupying space, reflecting light, and seen by different percipients from the appropriate perspective. It could range from a vague physical approximation to full visual hallucination. It could be symbolic or almost completely representational. Myers was to explore all these issues in greater detail over the next seventeen years and attempt to develop a broad, over-arching conceptual framework to explain and make sense of them and their profuse variety. Gurney was also to tackle these issues in his own way in *Phantasms of the Living*.

As the cases mounted, the question arose as to who should be responsible for the big book that was obviously emerging from these detailed records. In terms of first and obsessive interest in the field, it seemed right and appropriate that Gurney should write it, for he seems to have been collecting material from the 1870s, if Lodge's account in his autobiography is to be trusted. Lodge described first getting to know Gurney when Gurney attended his lectures on mechanics in the mid-1870s and how he was invited to lunch with the Gurneys; but he saw little of Mrs Gurney (a recurring theme in their marital history), spending most of his time in Gurney's study, discussing the collection (spread out in packets over the floor) of what Lodge thought were 'a meaningless collection of ghost stories' (Lodge 1931: 270–71). These were first-hand accounts of apparitions that Gurney had already started to harvest and winnow.

Yet Myers, too, had claims in terms of the energy and enthusiasm with which he had committed himself to the Society. There was some suggestion that they should, therefore, write it jointly. But Sidgwick was worried by this. He preferred one author (a secret preference for Gurney one suspects) so that only one reputation would be threatened. As he recorded in his diary, 'I urged this view, but did not prevail: it was a delicate matter as I was palpably aiming at ousting FM and leaving EG as sole author: estimating the superior trustworthiness of the latter in scientific reasoning as more important than his literary inferiority. I could see M was annoyed; but he bore it admirably. Ultimately we compromised thus: M to write a long introduction and G the body of the book'(Gauld 1968: 161). There was little doubt that Sidgwick' assessment was accurate. Gurney had a small but distinguished reputation with his book on the philosophy of music, *The Power of Sound*. He had a wider scientific training than Myers (he had completed the academic work necessary to become a doctor but had been put off by the practice). He was a member of the Scratch Eight, the debating group of distinguished and coming academics, and he had, as we have seen, a growing friendship with the most influential and sympathetic American psychologist, William James. Myers had started to write some impressive papers for the SPR and the periodicals, but for many people he was still seen as a poet and literary figure and—perhaps for some—the memory of his intellectual bumptiousness at university, and negative gossip about the Camden Medal Affair,[3] still lingered.

Myers faced a very difficult task with his introduction (Myers 1886b: xxxv–lxxi). He was introducing a book which went against the current

3   See above, p. 27.

medical and cultural orthodoxy with regard to hallucinations and visions of all sorts. The impact of eighteenth-century rationalism and nineteenth-century positivism meant that the ghost tended to be explained in comfortable psychological and physiological terms. Dickens, in his ghost stories of an earlier generation, usually found a physiological and materialistic explanation for them (Henson 2004). As Scrooge said to Marley's ghost: 'You may be an undigested bit of beef, a blot of mustard, a crumb of cheese, a fragment of an underdone potato. There's more of gravy than of grave about you, whatever you are' (McCorristine 2007: 67–81, quoting *A Christmas Carol*). Ghosts and apparitions were seen by the mentally ill and those who had been temporarily destabilised by illness and injury. To admit the literal reality of the ghost was to move back to the dark ages. In this sense, by using telepathy as the explanation, the SPR were trying to avoid that accusation and give their apparitions a different status and origin from morbid ones. As the first report of the committee on mesmerism stated, 'In virtue of having their real cause *outside* the percipient, and so in a way conveying true information, we may describe death-wraiths and the like as *veridical* hallucinations' (Barrett *et al.* 1883: 217–29).

Myers adopted several strategies to deal with this problem. Firstly, he stressed the aims and objectives of the Society for Psychical Research and the dispassionate and scientific way in which its members examined what for many were strange and distasteful phenomena (Myers 1886b: xxxvii). He argued that science did not stand still and that psychical research was a new science, like anthropology, developing new methods for dealing with anomalous phenomena whose existence had often been ignored or denied throughout history. He carefully but forcefully both separated the Society from Theosophy, 'a *réchauffé* of ancient philosophies' and also refrained from endorsing spiritualism, too closely associated with 'the specific suspicion to which the presence of a "paid medium" inevitably gives rise' (Myers 1886b: xliv–lix).

Secondly, he stressed the importance of the term *Phantasms of the Living*. It clearly signalled that the temper of the book was agnostic. He and his colleagues were neither against religion nor trying to prove life after death. The selection of 'Phantasm' as the key term was important in that it did not signal any premature belief that the apparition/ghost/whatever was the surviving soul of an individual. It was meant to be neutral and imply no specific view as to the ontological status of the phenomenon. The central thesis emerging through the book was that crisis apparitions were produced telepathically by dying persons. This was based on well attested and examined evidence from sane and healthy individuals. These individuals had experienced an hallucination associated with the death or trauma of a distant person; and this had happened more frequently than one would expect from chance. The accounts in the book were the carefully sifted residue from over two thousand depositions investigated. These spontaneous, individual cases of telepathic contact were strongly supported by experimental evidence for telepathy which was also included in the book (Myers 1886b: lx–lxxi).

Statistics were not Myers' forte. The statistical case was argued by Gurney. On the basis of a census he made of people 'in good health, free from anxiety, and completely awake' who had experienced visual hallucinations, he calculated that 1 in every 248 of them had found their hallucination coincided with the death of the person identified in the hallucination. By comparing this to the daily death rate of the country's population he worked out that the odds against the link between the deaths and the crisis visions being purely chance, were in the trillions to one (see Gauld 1968: 167–68). It was therefore vital, Gurney stressed – in the light of such remarkable figures – to make absolutely sure that the original accounts were accurate and valid. The investigators had to check that there was no way the percipient could have had prior knowledge of the impending death/trauma of the apparitional figure, that there had been no deliberate fraud or playful hoaxing, and that there was other oral and written evidence to corroborate the original testimony. Gurney showed particular alertness to all these issues and deliberately headed his first chapter *Preliminary Remarks: Grounds of Caution* (Gurney *et al.* 1886: 1–9).

In one sense, then, the claims made at the end of this vast book were modest: there was some evidence for the existence of telepathy between living people both within the laboratory and, in certain circumstances, spontaneously in the wider world. Sidgwick, however, was very concerned at the possible reception of the book. 'We have reached the real crisis in the history of the Society, for Phantasms of the Living is printed, and advance copies have been sent to the newspapers' (Sidgwick and Sidgwick 1906: 460). Yet he was to be pleasantly surprised. Eveleen Myers wrote to her mother expressing their astonished pleasure at the positive review in *The Times*: 'Mr Sidgwick rushed in last Sunday morning in such a state of excitement & delight at the <u>Times article.</u> I Hope You saw it, it was so <u>very</u> unexpected that they would accept it in <u>that way.</u> – Mr. Gurney too is quite amazed! to have a <u>leading article</u> on it before the Book was out (as one may say) & in such a very friendly spirit & in the one newspaper of importance, was very gratifying, do you not think so dear Mother?' (D/DT2585/1: n.d.). She also stated that they had expected the *Saturday Review*'s mocking notice. William James had noticed that too and commented on it in a letter to Henry: 'What an infamous thing is the Saturday Reviews article (Nov 20th I think) about Gurney's masterly book on Phantasms. (Skrupskelis *et al.* 1993: 54). In fact, selective quotation from reviews has sometimes created a false impression of the book's reception. As Stein pointed out (Stein 1968: 11), Shaw in the *Pall Mall Gazette* and Wilde in the *Nineteenth Century*, made, as they would, witty fun of the whole enterprise, but reviews in *The Times*, as we have seen, and the *Spectator*, were positive, as were others in the provincial press. Gurney was also particularly gratified by a serious review in *Nature* (*Nature* 35, 345: 10.2.1887) and immediately wrote asking its readers to send him more cases.

Trevor Hall has made much of the fact that Gurney handled the attacks on *Phantasms of the Living* without any support from his colleagues. In fact, Gurney was far and away the best person to deal with these attacks as he had written so much of the book, and was so close to it. He faced two main opponents, CS Peirce and AT Innes. Innes (Epperson 1997: 85–97, Hall 1980a: 76–78) argued that there was virtually no evidence of letters written at the time and before the death of the person whose apparition had been seen, which confirmed the linkage. Gurney replied that he could only find three, but it was in the nature of such experiences that people would tell others about it but would not necessarily write it down and formally send it to others as proof and corroboration. Moreover, even without the letters, the incidents had been confirmed, as far as possible, by other documentary evidence, and by individual in depth interviews.

A related charge of Hall's was that Gurney was severely overworked and that he delegated much of the checking in detail to Podmore and George Albert Smith — neither of whom Hall believed discharged the task with much efficiency (Hall 1980a: 74–75). These points have been strongly rebutted by others. Nicol has argued that Smith merely provided secretarial assistance and that Podmore was more thorough than Hall gave him credit for. Nicol in his examination of the book found 185 cases in which the investigator could be identified — Gurney 105, Podmore 30, Sidgwick 14, Myers 5, Mrs Sidgwick, Hodgson and others 3 each, and 16 others one each (Nicol 1972: 353–54). Factored up this was clearly and hugely Gurney's book and he travelled the United Kingdom extensively to interview witnesses, writing to William James about his 'hundreds of personal interviews' (Skrupskelis *et al.* 1998: 194–95).

The debate between Gurney and Peirce was conducted with a certain good humour, though with a little testiness at times on both sides (Gurney 1887 c: 157–79, Gurney 1887d: 287–300 and Peirce 1887a: 150–57, Peirce 1887b: 180–215). Gurney generously declared that, 'The foregoing review has been to me a source of genuine pleasure and profit.' Like Myers, he preferred detailed argument with an engaged sceptic, rather than the indifference so many showed. They both had the capacity to separate their intellectual differences from their personal friendships. Peirce made a number of useful points, particularly in the field of probability theory. His work in astronomy was one of the few areas of science where work had developed in this field. He welcomed Gurney's attempts to apply it to psychical research but felt his approach was flawed. He particularly criticised the huge odds Gurney quoted against the apparition/ death link being by chance. Gurney was prepared to admit the force of some of Peirce's technical points, particularly the need for a much larger survey, but believed that these did not outweigh the sheer volume of the evidence he and his colleagues had presented. Morever, he was able — quite easily, and with a certain amount of low key, gently malicious humour — to show that Peirce had not read the individual cases particularly carefully and that there were many inaccuracies in his remarks. Peirce replied, and Gurney was in the process of completing his response at the time of his death. This was published with a postscript by Myers.

Myers, in his postscript, paid tribute to Gurney's scrupulousness, 'I am absolutely sure that he would never knowingly have allowed a single sentence to stand which overstated his own case in the smallest particular' (Myers 1887e: 300). He addressed Peirce's concern that Gurney had included a number of cases where anxiety might have contributed to the creation of a phantasm. He pointed out that Gurney had been the judge of this and he had excluded such cases. However, he agreed with Peirce that as the percipients had been the judges of whether they were in ill-health or not, there should be tighter controls on this in any future survey.

Spiritualists in particular found these debates arcane and even irrelevant and they could not understand the terminology. Why 'phantasms'? Surely the apparition was the astral body of the departed. Why 'of the living'? Surely the apparition was the spirit of a departed loved one or friend. The authors of *Phantasms of the Living* argued that the apparition was said to be of the living if it occurred within twelve hours before or after death since the precise moment of death or of the telepathic transmission of that event could not be accurately identified. It was also important to set a time limit in order to distinguish the inquiry from one that was out to study communications from the dead, both because the book was not an enquiry into spiritualism, and because only with phantasms of the living was it possible to establish a base-line against which statistical probabilities could be established. Members of the general public were also confused. They did not appreciate the attempt at underlying theory and they found the distinction between phantasms of the living and the dead rather artificial. For them, as the popular journalist WT Stead so clearly appreciated a little later on, these were just real ghost stories.

Apart from the statistical issues with Peirce and the issues of corroboration with Innes, Gurney had also to deal with internal theoretical conflicts within the SPR itself. There was general agreement that individual phantasms of whatever sensory modality were caused by telepathy – difficult though that concept was. There was no such agreement with regard to phantasms experienced collectively. Myers argued strongly, in his note in the second volume of *Phantasms of the Living*, that some kind of physical impact was made when an apparition was seen and that this explained the cases where more than one person witnessed it (Myers 1886c: 277–316). Gurney, in a letter to James, was scathing about Myers' attempted explanation: 'Myers's note seems to me a hopeless attempt to present a frankly material view of ghosts with elimination of the material element' (Skrupskelis *et al.* 1998: 191). But with characteristic honesty he was not at all happy with his own view of some kind of collective telepathy to explain phantasms perceived collectively. In fact, there were many holes in this thesis, particularly the idea of the telepathic infection of other people. In addition, collective apparitions seem to have been seen according to the viewpoints of the individual concerned: for example, side on or head on. Regardless of these difficulties, however, William James had no doubt as to the value of the work, particularly in comparison with what had gone before. In a letter to Carl Stumpf he stated: 'Have you seen Gurney's two bulky tomes "Phantasms of the Living," an amazingly patient and thorough piece of work? I should not at all wonder if it were the beginning of a new department of natural history' (Skrupskelis *et al.* 1998: 205). He also opened his review of it with an uncompromising flourish: 'This is a most extraordinary work, – fourteen hundred large and closely printed pages by men of the rarest intellectual qualifications ...' (James 1986: 24).

However, there have been many criticisms of it in later years (often with the benefit of hindsight and ignoring the poor quality of what had gone on before) pointing out that it was a collection of well-evidenced eye witness accounts but that it was irredeemably anecdotal. RH Thouless may be taken as representative of this school of thought. He pointed out that very few spontaneous cases fulfilled tight conditions. He argued that, 'the observational evidence we have is generally vitiated by the fact that the records were not made until after the verification of the supposed paranormal experience, with all the possibilities of distortion which result from thinking and talking about the event afterwards' (Thouless 1972: 14). He called *Phantasms of the Living* a magnificent collection of stories but felt that this approach underestimated the 'importance of experiment as a method of advancing theoretical understanding'. But this was to misunderstand the initial approach of Myers, Gurney and the Sidgwicks. They were not against experiment and the *Journal* and the *Proceedings* record a wide range over the years at home and abroad. What they were immediately concerned to demonstrate was that something actually existed, something was actually taking place in ordinary, everyday life, that was worth investigating. It was a question of getting people, particularly those in the scientific and educated community, to sit up and take notice. As Gurney wrote to James: 'On the whole, I should say that the great difficulty the whole business has to contend against is not so much contempt as indifference. One's material being human beings, with wills of their own, one is continually baffled by the fact that they have no vision of the subject as a whole, or as a subject at all, & therefore cannot be brought in to tender their item of help' (Skrupskelis *et al.* 1998: 190). One cannot but have huge admiration, particularly for Gurney, in this remorseless, untiring, piling up of the evidence. Myers, the Sidgwicks, Podmore, all had their professional demands; so much fell on Gurney's shoulders, the unpaid honorary secretary of the SPR. In addition, as he wrote to James, just before publication almost the whole edition of *Phantasms* was destroyed in a fire. He had to proof read 1,400 pages again and see a new edition through the press. And this was done in two months, ready for publication at the beginning of November (Skrupskelis *et al.* 1998: 193 n.6).

It should be stressed that a certain amount of work has been done since the publication of *Phantasms of the Living*, pointing out in greater theoretical detail than Gurney and Myers were able to, the complexity of both the phenomena and the explanatory concepts they had developed. Stephen Braude in particular (Braude 1978: 267–301) has explored the difficulties involved in both grasping a possible carrier mechanism for telepathy and matching it against the sheer range of literal, contextual and symbolic meanings that telepathic messages might carry. CD Broad (Broad 1962: 224–49) has exposed in some detail the problems with Gurney's theory of telepathic infection, and Hornell Hart has produced a comprehensive phenomenological analysis of apparitions/phantasms (Hart 1956: 153–239). He examined the six leading theories as to the nature and status of apparitions and argued that, on balance, the evidence suggested that there was an 'objective' element involved supporting Myers' view that in some unknown and complicated way, ordinary space was actually modified or impacted on by the phantasm.

Myers' contribution to *Phantasms of the Living* was limited. He only did a relatively small amount of interviewing. He contributed two comparatively short chapters. He had no expertise to bring to the statistical section or to those aspects of post-publication controversy. What he could give to Gurney, in the long hours of isolation from other people and the possible distancing from his wife, was companionship. They still frequently met each other and they collaborated, to some extent, on mesmeric/hypnotic experiments and on visits to France to meet the French savants. Myers, as the more consistently buoyant character, must have helped his intimate friend through the difficulties he faced. The impression Hall gives (Hall 1980a: 72–78) of his abandoning Gurney to the savage criticism of the outside world is a travesty.

Automatic Writing, Hypnosis and the Multiplex Personality

Parallel with the collection and examination of phantasms, went the collection and examination of other unusual and abnormal phenomena, both naturally occurring and experimentally induced. Myers and Gurney, particularly, saw automatic writing and hypnosis (and later various forms of crystal gazing) as new experimental methods peculiarly appropriate for examining the hidden depths of human personality. Myers also had, virtually on his own doorstop, an interesting individual example in his brother Arthur, who had a strong and informed interest in hypnotism, was a medical doctor and suffered from both *haut mal* and *petit mal*. When suffering an attack, he could apparently continue to function normally to outward appearances, including diagnosing and treating a patient (Williams 1984: 197), but be unable to recall the episode later. Their first significant insights came from Myers' detailed examination of the phenomena of automatic writing and from Gurney's work on mesmerism and hypnotism. However, Myers' conviction that not all these phenomena could be explained by automatic ideo-motor reflexes and unconscious cerebration was greatly strengthened by the visits that he took, sometimes alone and sometimes in conjunction with either or both Gurney and Arthur Myers, to French psychologists in the mid 1880s. In addition Arthur Myers was useful to his brother because of his medical knowledge and his access to medical records (Myers 3/95).

In his first signed articles in the *Proceedings* in 1884 and 1885, Myers, as an individual, began to consider in some detail the implications of these phenomena for knowledge of an increasingly enriched view of the nature of man and as evidence for life after death. This can very clearly be seen in the article 'On a telepathic explanation for some so-called spiritualistic phenomena' (Myers 1884b: 217–37). The telepathic mechanism he mainly focused on was automatic writing and in later articles on the subject he used that term rather than the clumsy original. He argued that, 'in no way can psychical research be better aided than by constant and varied experiments on Thought-transference in every form. We have got, as we hold, a definite fact to start from, a fact of immense and unknown significance' (Myers 1884b: 217). He selected automatic writing for study in this connection since he believed that the partial dissociation caused by automatic writing (in a milder way parallel to thought-transference in the hypnotic trance or somnambulistic state) was a useful tool for studying telepathy and the creative workings of the unconscious mind.

In his examination of automatic writing Myers enthusiastically encouraged his readers to experiment, even pointing out that the SPR had planchettes (devices used for automatic writing) for sale! There was a kind of breeziness about his approach which seemed to imply that no sane, well-balanced member of the English upper-middle classes need have any fears, though he did on occasions offer one or two brief words of caution and advice. He identified five possible theories to explain automatic writing and he stated that he was most reluctant to accept the fifth — the spirit hypothesis — until all the others had been completely ruled out. These were: writing by deliberate conscious will; writing automatically by unconscious cerebration; automatic writing inspired by a higher faculty of one's own; automatic writing inspired by telepathic impact from other minds; automatic writing inspired by spirits or extra-human intelligences. He described four days' experiment in automatic writing by a friend (Mr A) — 'on whose accuracy we believe we can thoroughly rely' — who briefly thought, as well as experiencing other puzzling communications, that he might be in contact with a beautiful spirit, Clelia, who was to be born on the earth in six years' time. What impressed Myers about the above was the complexity of the unconscious processing; for example, Mr A's subconscious memory of Spinoza was worked on, altered, and disguised in a teasing way in an anagram to express Spinoza's statement about life as a revelation of the Deity (Myers 1884b: 227–28).

Myers already suspected, by 1885, that the vast majority of material that spiritualists claimed originated from discarnate beings through automatic writing really came from a hidden intelligence within the conscious personality. In his conclusion, however, he stated quite moderately that, 'some of the effects which Spiritualists ascribe to spirits are referable to the unconscious action of the writer's own mind' (Myers 1884b: 237). This hidden intelligence could produce, without the conscious knowledge of the rational mind, both sense and nonsense, but even when there was evidence of insightful and creative activity, no external source need be posited in the vast majority of cases. It was not really until the arrival on the scene of Mrs Piper, the Boston medium, that he thought there was any substantial evidence for an external source of information. But even in this case, telepathy between sitter and medium needed to be rigorously ruled out first.

In his second paper (Myers 1886a: 1–63) he tested in greater detail the claims that some automatic writing contained information that the writer did not know. He pointed out the absurdity of people paying attention to the predictions that the unconscious mind made through automatic writing: 'One smiles at finding Philip sober thus appealing to Philip drunk, — the waking man guiding his judgement by the capricious utterance of his own unconscious brain.' He argued that the mind had often retained impressions and details that it was not consciously aware that it had and which, in certain circumstances, might be wrongly ascribed to an external source. But in a small number of cases he believed that he had — from automatic writing, as well as from earlier SPR thought-transference experiments — evidence of mind-to-mind contact. He based a substantial part of this argument, in his second paper, on his examination of the private diary of the Reverend PH Newnham. This diary recorded the experiments for eight months in 1871 when Newnham attempted to 'transmit thought voluntarily to his wife'. They established a set of ground rules. They sat about eight feet apart. The husband wrote questions in his notebook, with his back to his wife, and she, not knowing the questions, used the planchette to reply. There were moments of real humour. Newnham stated, on one occasion, that, 'I had to engage a clergyman who was not a favourable specimen of his profession, as I could procure no one else in time to get the Sunday's work done. He was much amused with Planchette, and desired to ask: — How should a bachelor live in this neighbourhood.' The answer came, 'Eating and drinking and sleeping and smoking.' Newnham received over three hundred responses from his wife via automatic writing, often with considerable relevance to the original unseen question, and frequently displaying a mixture of humour, cunning and prevarication when searching or persistent questions were asked.

Myers had his own reflections to make, but he also recorded Newnham's suggestion that there might be a dual state in every brain and that the second state might emerge from the right hemisphere, the untrained side, the side that behaved like a mendacious and cheating child. Myers himself raised the question of terminology, what was this unconscious mind? He distinguished it from the 'complex unconscious cerebration' of his first paper. Unlike unconscious cerebration, which occurred when conscious attention was elsewhere, it presented itself 'as co-ordinate with the conscious action, and as able to force itself upon the attention of the waking mind'. In addition he stated that: 'A secondary self — if I may coin the phrase — is thus gradually postulated, — a latent capacity, at any rate, in an appreciable fraction of mankind, of developing or manifesting a second focus of cerebral energy which is apparently neither fugitive nor incidental merely — a delirium or a dream-but may possess for a time at least, a kind of continuous individuality, a purposive activity of its own'. In a note at the foot of the page he acknowledged a paper by Hellenbach, which reflected much of this view, and its links with his earlier paper in the *Contemporary Review* expressing much the same idea (Myers 1885b). He also referred to Baron du Prel's *Philosophie der Mystik* (Myers 1886a: 23, 27, 30) and pointed out that this line of argument 'has, of course, been advanced, with more or less distinctiveness, by many previous writers'. He was not always so punctilious about indicating past influence, as Carlos Alvarado has pointed out (Alvarado 2003: 13); partly because, as Williams suggests (Williams 1984: 215–22), many ideas were in the general zeitgeist, and also because of a desire to distinguish his work from spiritualistic platitudes. However, Andreas Sommer (Sommer 2008, 2009), has strongly argued the particular impact on Myers of du Prel's work both in its original German and after it was translated into English by Massey in 1889 (Prel 2008).

In addition, Myers linked the telepathic phenomena of the Newnhams with the SPR's growing collection of *Phantasms of the Living* and proposed three hypotheses which he never withdrew for the rest of his life: the existence of a secondary self; telepathy as one of its supernormal activities; and the manifestation of such phenomena through channels usually associated with 'abnormal or morbid vital phenomena' like automatic writing or somnambulism. As a rider to this last hypothesis, he stated that these phenomena could be evolutive or dissolutive. For him telepathy was part of the evolutionary process. He was prepared with Newnham to assume that the secondary self, with its apparently telepathic powers, manifested through the right hemisphere. But he was not prepared to accept that this was the home of the 'untrained moral sense'. He knew of no 'well-recognised doctrine of cerebral localisation' that would authorise that conclusion. Finally, he laid down a challenge to the spiritualists. His argument was that these phenomena showed no 'spiritual influence other than that of the spirits of living and breathing men'. He needed evidence—'cases which they can give on first-hand testimony, and with full details'—that an intelligence other than that of some living man was at work. But in spite of an appeal 'in the leading Spiritualistic news-paper' he had received very little, nor was he to.

Nevertheless, in a later article on automatic writing he softened his earlier position, 'It is by far the most interesting hypothesis, and there are a few cases which tell strongly in its favour' (Myers 1889a: 522–47). Yet it was a mark of the paucity of the contemporary evidence he was receiving from spiritualists that a substantial part of that article focused on the Daemon of Socrates and the voices of Joan of Arc. It was in that context that Myers first developed in detail his concept of automatisms. Firstly, a very wide range of sensory and motor activities came under the heading

of automatisms — not just automatic writing. Secondly, they were independent phenomena and not symptomatic of an organic disease. Thirdly,
they were message-bearing, usually internally from one stratum of the
personality to another. Fourthly, they were active if they found a motor
channel of expression and passive if they found a sensory channel. The
messages from the secondary consciousness would manifest themelves
through the individual's dominant sensory-motor mode, whether auditory, visual or motor.

Myers' growing belief in a secondary self was enriched and consoli-
dated by his visits to France in the mid and later 1880s. He made four significant and substantial visits: to Paris and Nancy with his brother and
Gurney in August and September 1885; to Paris and Le Havre with his
brother in April 1886; to Paris and Lyon with his brother and Gurney in
October 1886; and to Paris and Blois in April 1887 alone.

In *Human Personality in the Light of Hypnotic Suggestion* (1885c) he fed
back — to an England largely ignorant and complacent about European
developments in this field — what he, Gurney and Arthur Myers had discovered. As he stated: 'I have, through the kindness of Drs Charcot, Féré,
Bernheim, and Liébeault, myself witnessed typical experiments at the
Salpêtrière in Paris, in the Hôpital Civil at Nancy, and in Dr Liébeault's
private practice; have been allowed myself to perform experiments (with
the aid of Mr Gurney and Dr AT Myers) on the principal subjects whose
cases are recorded' (Myers 1885c: 6). In a letter back to his wife he
expressed his delight at the reception they received from the French
savants: 'The way in which we were received by savants in Paris was most
gratifying. We are far better known than we expected' (Myers 7/207:
30.8.1885). In the article he tried to strike an appropriate balance between
doing justice to the material and its implications and not alarming his
readers. Stage hypnotism, as in the performances of Donato across
Europe since 1875 (Pick 1996: 149), threatened to discredit the scientific
and medical uses of hypnosis. Myers gave the terrifying example of Mlle
AE 'a very amiable young person', who 'was made by Professor Liégeois
to fire on her own mother with a pistol which she had no means of knowing to be unloaded'. But he immediately stressed that such influence was
highly unusual and that proper precautions should always be taken to
prevent exploitation of the very small number of highly sensitive subjects.
This exposure to the work of Liégeois, Liébeault and the Nancy school,
reinforced his belief that hypnosis was a powerful tool in experimental
psychology and of great potential value in the study of supernormal phenomena: 'Hypnotism is in its infancy; but any psychology which neglects
it is superannuated already.' The examination of the extraordinary states
made possible by hypnotism provided new insight into the mind and, 'we

may return to those normal states which lie open to our habitual intro-spection, having gained a new power of disentangling each particular thread in the complex of mentation, as when the microscopist stains his object with a dye that affects one tissue only among several which are indiscernibly mixed' (Myers 1885c: 2).

The second visit to France with his brother Arthur gave him a deeper insight into the possible links between hypnosis, telepathy, and even clairvoyance. It was one thing to admit the power of hypnosis as a scien-tific method for exploring the mind. It was quite another to accept the reality of *sommeil à distance* (the putting someone to sleep and getting them to perform certain actions) and its implications. Since his own expe-riences as a young man and the later contacts with Barrett and then GA Smith, he had become increasingly aware of the paranormal evidence supposedly associated with the practice of hypnotism and mesmerism. However, this second visit to France gave him his first opportunity for sustained contact with a gifted subject who had already been assessed and tested by reputable scientists. This was Léonie, a middle aged woman, of peasant background from Normandy. When hypnotised by both Dr Gibert and Pierre Janet she appeared to demonstrate *sommeil à distance* and the Myers brothers witnessed and were involved themselves in these experiments from 20th to 24th April 1886 at Le Havre (Dingwall 1968 1: 266–70). There, apparently, Léonie was both sent to sleep from a distance and ordered, from a distance, to perform particular actions, which she did. Hacking (Hacking 1995: 157–58) has implied an alternative explanation for all this, based on her long experience in being mesmer-ised. Namely, that it was a form of learned behaviour. Janet, too, played down the apparently supernormal elements. Myers reported on these experiences in considerable detail in *On Telepathic Hypnotism, and Its Rela-tion to Other Forms of Hypnotic Suggestion* (Myers 1886d: 127–88).

The third visit to France in October 1886, with Gurney and Arthur Myers, was at first less successful. They went down to Lyon to see a Dr Perronet, who appears to have exaggerated both his and his patients' powers. Myers laconically noted in his diary (14/2) for 19.10.1886 'Cold bad: experiments fail. Perronet a bore.' However, on the return to Paris Myers managed to recruit the distingushed Dr Ribot for the SPR and to observe Babinski and Charcot at work in the Salpêtrière, to listen to a paper read by Babinski at the Société de Psychologie Physiologique. He was critical of Babinski's 'account of some experiments in the transference of hysterical symptoms, without suggestion of any kind, but by the aid of a magnet, from one patient to another' (Myers 1886i: 443). He outlined, as on other occasions, the precautions to take in order to eliminate the impact of other factors. He was, however, considerably impressed by

Voisin's work and his account of how, through hypnosis, he cured a criminal lunatic who became a nurse in a Paris hospital, and whose subsequent behaviour was irreproachable (Myers 1887b: 505).

Myers' visits to France plunged him into the middle of the intellectual warfare, concerning the nature of hypnosis, between Charcot's school at the Salpêtrière (the biggest asylum in France and sited on the left bank of the Seine in Paris) and the Nancy school of Bernheim and his colleagues (Gauld 1995: 327–52). The latter believed that Charcot's three specific and almost mechanical stages of hypnosis (lethargy, catalepsy, somnambulism) did not really exist and were the product of suggestion reinforced by the highly orchestrated, authoritarian and theatrical nature of Charcot's observation, diagnosis and teaching (Zeldin 1977 2: 857–66). Myers increasingly came to side with the less pathological and more patient-centred Nancy approach.

Bernheim, a professor of medicine at the modern hospital at Nancy, utilised and then publicised the gentle approach to hypnosis developed by a country doctor, Liébeault. He argued, contrary to Charcot, that there could be many and varied hypnotic stages, that gentle suggestion building on the patient's own resources of attention and auto-suggestion was very effective, and finally, people who were not mentally ill (men as well as women) could be hypnotised to their positive benefit. It was on the basis of this work that Myers began to build his theory that the human personality had inner resources which, if tapped, would have great evolutionary potential.

The final visit in April 1887 was notable for his observation of a particularly sensitive subject. The Commandant of Engineers at Blois, de Rochas, had a considerable interest in hypnotism and his subject, Benoît, through his unusual suggestibility, demonstrated a range of interesting behaviours under hypnosis. He was told that 'three and two make four', and 'Benoît, going next day to the Préfecture, where he is a junior clerk, continued to add three and two as making four, and when his sums were sent back to him, could not discover his mistake' (Myers 1887d: 98–99). He had to be re-hypnotised out of this state. In front of Myers it was suggested that de Rochas' son had come into the room. Benoît addressed the phantasm respectfully. Myers then gave the illusory young de Rochas a box round the ears and 'Benoît stared in amazement at my insolence'. A later reader might wish to comment on several aspects of all this: the fact that it was an amateur who was doing the hypnotising; that a slightly airy view was taken of the impact on Benoît's work (he was only a junior clerk after all); and that Myers himself made no observations on these features.

Myers' views were not only based on direct observation. He read very widely and was particularly impressed by Pierre Janet's account of further work with Léonie, published in the *Revue Philosophique* for March 1888. It was Léonie's later development, when, under Janet's control she exhibited three distinct personalities – Léonie, Léontine, and Léonore – which gave him much additional support for his ideas. He was, therefore, able to challenge the existing intellectual grain in psychology with greater confidence (Gauld 1995: 372-73). As we have seen, the general belief – though this was gradually being modified – was that reflex actions applied from the lowest to the highest activity. And, as Carpenter argued, the automatic action of the cerebrum could account for all abnormal as well as all normal and creative activities. Huxley, while remaining agnostic about ultimate, metaphysical questions, supported this position. He argued that there was no evidence that the mind produced 'molecular' changes, rather the reverse (Cook [Kelly] 1992: 110-18). So, on these two key counts one can see Myers challenging the existing orthodoxy, even before he had fully formulated his concept of the subliminal self. He could not accept the conventional view that unconscious actions that appeared conscious were really just physical reflexes. They certainly were involuntary in the sense that the individual did not consciously will them, but they were not automatic and reflex in the traditional sense (Kelly *et al.* 2007: 303-305). Myers, in fact, believed that there were other centres of conscious activity and purpose in human beings which, at their own level, consciously initiated the so-called reflex behaviour, and that terms like secondary intelligence, or multiplex personality, better explained the phenomena. Already by late 1885 Myers had enough evidence to publish on the hidden secondary self explicitly using the adjective 'multiplex' to describe personality (Myers 1885d: 637-55) and slightly later to coin the phrase 'multiplex personality'(Myers 1886h: 443-53).

He expanded this concept in his paper on *Multiplex Personality* in the *Proceedings* (Myers 1887b: 496-514). The visits to France had encouraged and strengthened his belief in the mutability of human personality and the range of personalities that could exist in one body. He argued strongly that this mutability, this capacity for modification, had hardly been recognised by the scientific establishment, and that what they might call 'morbid disintegration' in abnormal personalities gave us clues as to the nature of the working of the 'normal' personality and that the behaviour changes were 'not all of them pathological or retrogressive'. He described the strange case of Louis V[ivé], who was frightened by a viper at fourteen and completely changed his stable, quiet and obedient personality. This had led to 'a series of psychical oscillations on which he has been tossed ever since' so that 'his character had become violent, greedy and quarrelsome, and his tastes were radically changed'. According to his doctors, he could be made to go through a number of personality changes by the

application of metals which Myers, interestingly, associated with the inhi-
bition of the right or the left hemisphere of the brain. He argued that 'the
alternate predominance of right or left hemisphere affects memory and
character as well as motor and sensory innervation.' Inhibit the left side of
the brain, where the higher qualities resided, and Louis reverted to more
savage and primitive behaviour. Inhibit the right side of the brain and
'there is self-control; there is modesty; there is the sense of duty'. Myers
drew two conclusions from these phenomena — both of which were disputed — but which have been taken up again in recent years.

The first (and Myers had announced his changed view on this in the
Journal of the SPR [Myers 1886g: 226–27] largely on the basis of the Vivé
evidence) was that the right hemisphere of the brain retained traces of its
savage ancestry and that the unconscious self could use that side of the
brain and get its messages through into consciousness. This explained
why cunning, clumsy, sometimes silly and obscene material was often
part of the phenomena observed. The messages, psychological or spiritual, could not get through the logical, academic left brain into full consciousness. Myers further argued, in support of this, that automatic
writing was often full of mistakes, reminiscent of those of aphasic
patients, who had damage to the right cerebral hemisphere. Janet, however, was not convinced that the immorality and oaths and awkwardness
associated with some automatic writing was necessarily linked to the
right hemisphere.

Myers' second conclusion was that these psychological automatisms,
which Janet and others believed were pathological — signs of disease, of
insanity, hysteria, epilepsy — were a clue to humanity's health and
growth, as well as an indication of disease and dissolution. Rightly understood, they could point the way to the releasing of considerable human
potential. However, he took a more pessimistic view than Janet with
regard to the timescale necessary to effect a cure. Janet believed it was
possible to create an integrated personality in one earthly lifetime. Myers
— probably because his concept of the subliminal self, as he later came to
call his interpretation of the unconscious mind, was larger, more complex
and grandiose than Janet's — believed that such unification was unlikely if
not impossible in this world.

It is important to understand that Myers was trying to rescue these phenomena from the dustbin of psychology and physiology. His central and
powerful point was that the study of these phenomena could shed greater
light on the processes of creativity and of psychological health. For example, that appropriately applied, hypnotism could have a moral effect on
character and could be used to discourage bad habits. There is, for example, the amusing story of the idle boy and Dr Liébeault :

On another occasion an idle boy was taken to this potent moraliser, and it was suggested to him that he would henceforth be a model of diligence. The boy did actually work hard for some months, by an impulsion which he could neither understand nor resist, and rose rapidly to the top of his class. But the suggestion wore off, and he obstinately refused to be hypnotised again, having by no means relished his involuntary role. His mother was weak enough to let him alone (Myers 1885c: 18).

For Myers there was huge and optimistic potential in this area, 'We hold the wand of Hermes, which we have not yet learnt to sway' (Myers 1885c: 19).

Myers, in the last part of that paper, sketched out an apparently utopian scenario where hypnotism could be widely used to get more 'work' out of us, improve our creativity, get rid of pain, and reform our characters. Who can deny that a range of new age therapies and strategies, largely based on hypnotic suggestion, has in some ways moved us in the direction anticipated by Myers, over one hundred years ago? Myers believed in man's capacity to renew and remake himself, in his fundamental creative plasticity, which promised a glorious destiny and was in stark contrast to those degenerate views of humankind that others were putting forward (Pick 1996: 1–11). There is of course a danger here. This plasticity that we recognise in ourselves may suggest an element of role playing, a desire to please, in those being treated by hypnosis. Hacking, for example (Hacking 1995: 171–82), has pointed out how Vivé may well have fabricated his states in order to get the rewards he was not able to obtain in any other way. Myers himself was not unaware of this possibility, pointing out how the hysterics in Charcot's Salpêtrière, were all able when hypnotised, to exhibit with uncanny accuracy, as we have seen, the three stages of what Charcot called the grand hysteria.

Myers, in this work in the 1880s and based on his mixed experiences in the 1870s, was always alive to the possibility of fraud, but always balanced this against the need to find as many interesting phenomena as possible. On occasions, he and his colleagues were even prepared to investigate stage performers if they appeared to be trustworthy. They decided to assess the mesmeric skills of H D'Auquier, who seemed to be a gentleman, and on one occasion they brought him and his entourage to Cambridge, paying him well. They exposed his tricks and D'Auquier complained bitterly at his treatment and at, 'the shameful misrepresentations put forward in the SPR *Journal*' (*Light* 19.12.1887 320: 85). They said that he used a code to trick them but, in fact his female assistant was in a deep, mesmeric trance which they verified 'with needles, a galvanic battery, and *ammonia* placed under her nose'. He was not a cheat and was happy to demonstrate and perform 'before any properly qualified committee of gentlemen who may be willing to bear testimony to the truth, whatever they find it to be'. There was the distinct implication in his final remarks that the Cambridge leaders of the SPR neither wanted to countenance the existence of the phenomena, nor — unlike the experienced readers of the pages of *Light* and despite their intellectual pretensions — were they actually qualified to investigate and assess them. But this was an accusation Myers and his colleagues were quite prepared to live with.

By the mid-1880s Myers appeared to be attacking the spiritualists on all fronts. Gurney's work on hypnotism and mesmerism and the visits to France clearly demonstrated the suggestibility of many people and the ease with which distraction and suggestion could create the illusion of the paranormal. Research into automatic writing indicated that the messages, no matter how lofty or sonorous, could often be traced to latent faculties in the writer's mind, or incarnate mind-to-mind interaction. Voices were not spirit voices but messages from the hidden, secondary self. Silly and obscene automatic writing was not the product of evil spirits but of the untrained child lurking in the right hemisphere. Dreams, too, were the dramatic inventions of the internal actor in us all and not an arena in which the spirit world interacted with us. As he developed these ideas, Myers crossed swords with one of the more elevated spiritualists, his fellow poet and Trinity graduate the Hon Roden Noel. They clashed in two lively exchanges in the *Journal* for December 1885 and April 1886 (Myers 1885–86: 122–31, 234–43). Noel resolutely believed that automatic writing and dreams were the vehicle for communication from deceased spirits. Myers criticised him (tangentially) for a lack of general background in medicine and psychology, unlike Gurney, and he lamented the fact that there was no good general textbook of abnormal conditions of mind available to instruct him. With regard to Noel's views he stated that, 'one begins to see the dangers of a too resolute avoidance of any contaminating knowledge of the labours of the materialistic school'. He also pointed out that Noel's definition of consciousness was far too simplistic — either A or not A. There could be more than one centre of consciousness which could express itself both in dreams and in automatic writing. It would be easy, but foolish, to take these as the result of spirit communication. For Myers argued that, most of the time, 'The personages who appear in our dreams … are mere products of our own dramatic faculty.'

Yet at times Myers did express views that could almost make the spiritualists believe that, if not actually one of them, he was a fellow traveller. For example, the accusation was made that his researches and theorising on the nature of human personality led to the negative conclusion that man was just a bundle of fragmentary and competing personalities, with no core or unity. In defending himself, Myers replied: ' My own conviction is that we possess — and can very nearly prove it — some kind of soul, or spirit, transcendental self, which even in this life occasionally manifests powers beyond the powers of our physical organism, and which very probably survives the grave' (Myers 1885c: 2). The spiritualists could be forgiven for feeling intense irritation on reading this. At one moment Myers seemed as hard-nosed as any materialist, and at another, cosmic yearnings seemed to suffuse him. They were perfectly entitled to ask him — 'If our evidence isn't good enough for you, where is yours?'

The Break with the Spiritualists

While Myers was undermining the spiritualist position by attributing most of their phenomena to a psychological source, Mrs Sidgwick and Richard Hodgson were robustly attacking their claims by demonstrating the role of deception and distraction in the production of allegedly supernatural physical phenomena. The investigations of the 1870s had, as we have seen, left Mrs Sidgwick quite jaundiced in this regard (Sidgwick 1886: 45–74). She was particularly rough on William Eglinton, the slate-writing medium, who was viewed very favourably in spiritualist circles. She wrote a substantial critical article on him in the *Journal*, pointing out that items for impersonating spirits had on one occasion been found in his effects, that he had dubious links to Madame Blavatsky, and that on the basis of the reports she had read, she had 'no hesitation in attributing the performances to clever conjuring' (Williams 1984: 235). The spiritualists attempted to get her to retract her statements and when she refused to do so, several of them resigned from the SPR.

She had been reinforced in her belief by Hodgson who pointed out Eglinton's use of distraction as a way of implementing his tricks. She and he were further supported by a young man, SJ Davey, who tried to see if he could deceive his friends in the way Hodgson suggested. He was very successful in this as he explained in a number of places, particularly in a long joint article with Hodgson in the *Proceedings* (Hodgson and Davey 1886: 381–495). It was quite clear to them all that the overwhelming bulk of such phenomena was the product of fraud. It was in vain that spiritualists like Hensleigh Wedgwood protested that their theories and Davey's demonstrations did not, by any means, explain all the phenomena that Eglington produced — the levitations, the writing on two slates that had been sealed together etc. Davey particularly aroused their fury, as he was seen in the spiritualists' eyes as an apostate, a turncoat. He had originally been a believer in Eglinton (Fodor 1969: 121). But after his discovery that some of the simpler phenomena of slate-writing could be replicated by conjuring tricks, he had gone over to the sceptical camp of Richard Hodgson and Mrs Sidgwick and, according to his critics, had only demonstrated his simple conjuring tricks on naïve subjects. What he did, the spiritualists argued, bore no comparison to the full range of phenomena exhibited by Eglinton. And what was more, stated Stainton Moses, who rated him very low, 'he resolutely refused a challenge again and again repeated to meet trained observers' (*Light* 10.8.1889: 377–9). *Light*, in fact, went to considerable lengths to put the record straight, as they saw it, with regard to Eglinton. His defence, 'Mrs Sidgwick, The Society for Psychical Research, and Mr W Eglinton' graced the front page of *Light* on the 16th October 1886 and a copy of it was sent to every member and associate of the SPR.

Myers had no direct involvement in the exposure of physical fraud. He bowed and would continue to bow (for most of the time) to the superior patience and powers of observation of Hodgson and Mrs Sidgwick. However, he was a little alarmed at the situation and felt that contact with spiritualists should be maintained, particularly with regard to accessing opportunities for investigation, which were very meagre. He wrote to Henry Sidgwick, enclosing a letter he had received from Massey, which pointed out the dangerous situation that was developing and that Massey and Stainton Moses might have to leave the SPR. He particularly stressed the variance of views developing about the slate-writing phenomena and the Hodgson/Mrs Sidgwick thesis of always attributing it to 'the performance of clever conjuring' (SPR 49/25: 8.7.1886). In the end though, there was no mass exodus from the SPR. Moses left, but Massey, Wedgwood, Rogers, and Wallace remained to fight their corner from within, possibly to the disappointment of Mrs Sidgwick, who wrote to her husband at this time:

> I really think the spiritualists had better go. It seems to me that if there be truth in spiritualism their attitude and state of mind distinctly hinders it being found out ... we are better and stronger without them, so that if they wish to go I should not like to hinder it ... and people who fly into rages are such a bore ... Their spirit is theological not scientific, and it is so difficult to run theology and science in harness together (Sidgwick 1938: 99).

There was in her an instinctive dislike of the showy, the over-emotional, and the passions aroused by spiritualism.

Part of Mrs Sidgwick' attitude can be explained by the extreme credulity of some of the spiritualist members of the SPR. One of them was at the heart of the Society itself, Morrell Theobald. He was one of the original founders, by profession accountant, and currently auditor of the SPR. He had published a record of spiritualistic activities and manifestations in his own home, which had started after the death of several of his children (only four of whom out of eleven had survived childhood). The phenomena increased in power when a new cook, Mary, joined them. In collaboration with the daughter of the house, Nellie, she found that the spirits were helping them light the fires, lay the table, and make the tea. Even spirit writing began to appear on the ceiling (Owen 1989: 75–106). Morrell Theobald invited Sidgwick and his wife to lunch and allowed them to examine his written narrative of these events. Given his status in the Society, he might, perhaps a little foolishly, have expected supportive treatment. Podmore, who was sent in by the Sidgwicks to investigate, produced a short, dismissive report. In the *Journal* for October 1885 Theobald criticised that report and asserted stubbornly that the phenomena continued. Myers' only contribution in all this had been a passing reference to the case in his reply to Haughton on *Methods of Research pursued by the Society* in August 1885 (Myers 1885f: 29–32). He stated that Theobald had offered to let a member of the Society come and observe on a more intimate basis. Theobald replied saying that the offer, which he didn't remember making (though he had not been against it) was now no longer on the table (*Journal* October 1885: 85). It would be too disruptive and would serve no purpose. Nothing would be seen. He had tried continuous observation, shivering in the cold, waiting to catch the lighting of fires, but to no avail. Poor Theobald. More sinister figures than servant girls in the guise of amiable fire-lighting spirits were later to take advantage of his trusting nature. He became auditor to the infamous fraudster Jabez Spencer Balfour (calling himself J Spencer Balfour to vaguely align himself with more respectable Balfours), and signed off the accounts of Balfour's Liberator Building Society, which crashed in 1892, ruining many small investors and creating much misery and hardship (McKie 2005: 191–94, 225). He was duped, but that did not save him from a harrowing trial and a prison sentence; and he died a few years after serving his term.

For Myers, the spiritualists were not just a threat to the Society because they were credulous and dupes. As Janet Oppenheim has stated, it was common practice for spiritualists to describe themselves as scientific in their approach, because they argued that they demonstrated under repeatable conditions the presence of another world (Oppenheim 1985: 59). Yet for Myers and his colleagues, their use of the word scientific was a travesty. They did not test evidence properly, they did not control conditions adequately, and they were open to exploitation by charlatans and conjurers. He was also concerned that, under the guise of an apparently scientific approach, the Society would become too closely identified with their magical view of the world. Sidgwick's note attached to the bottom of the Objects of the Society was fully subscribed to by Myers and his colleagues and regularly re-iterated by them in letters and articles: 'To prevent misconception, it is here expressly stated that Membership of this Society does not imply the acceptance of any particular explanation of the phenomena investigated, nor any belief as to the operation, in the physical world, of forces other than those recognised by Physical Science' (*Proceedings* 1882 1: 5). The spiritualists again and again reiterated that the apparently bizarre behaviours in the séance room would be revealed as subject to laws as predictable and clear as physical ones. However, they argued that the method of investigation and examination of the phenomena required a specific, respectful and sensitive approach to the situation, taking the views of mediums, sitters, and 'discarnate entities' into account. It was not simply the straightforward application of the existing methods of physical and biological science. The Cambridge leaders of the SPR were broadly sympathetic to some aspects of this viewpoint, but not when it allowed slack control and palpable fraud. They also had considerable intellectual, social and cultural capital, and they had to be very careful how it was spent.

Yet the situation was not clear cut. While resenting the methods represented particularly by Podmore, Mrs Sidgwick and Hodgson, the spiritualists were genuinely appreciative of what the SPR had done to raise the status of enquiry and practice in this field. This was of considerable importance, given the general hostility towards spiritualism which existed in many sections of the community. It has not always been appreciated, in accounts of the period, that the practice was a risky one, both legally and socially, for many people. The involvement of the SPR helped confer some kind of legitimacy and, in certain circumstances, a social and intellectual umbrella, that less fortunate members of the community could shelter under. Leigh Hunt, for example, provided a graphic description of some of the social pressures that the Marylebone Spiritualist Association laboured under when referring to the lack of specific names and records kept by the Association: 'From personal knowledge, I can say that such names were often left unrecorded by the special desire of those concerned, for, to be then known as a spiritualist was to risk one's business, as well as social, position. Even notes of proceedings in Committee, etc, of those times were not kept for any period beyond what was absolutely necessary. But from 1890 things were a little better in this respect' (Hunt 1928: 5–6).

So the spiritualists were grateful for the SPR's raising of the social status of their activities, but what they found difficult to stomach was the arrogance of the SPR and its dismissal of the vast amount of practical knowledge that experienced and intelligent spiritualists had. For example, in 1883 the Central Association of Spiritualists issued a circular on the conduct of physical séances which was designed to deal with the issues of fraudulent séances and stressed the importance of continuous observation by all participants, just as much as the SPR did (*Light* 12.5.1883: 225). This anticipated by several years the article in the *Proceedings* that summarised the sceptics' objections to fraudulent phenomena of the kind Eglinton apparently produced (Hodgson and Davey 1886: 381–495). Furthermore, one of the spiritualist publications, WH Harrison's the *Spiritualist Newspaper*, was funded to promote a scientific approach to the phenomena, and exposed fraudulent mediums in its pages (Oppenheim 1985: 45–46).

Often *Light* criticised a hasty SPR investigation borne of arrogance, for example, Podmore's perfunctory examination of the phenomena in the Theobald household, or, in 1891, the young Cambridge graduate's brief and (from their point of view) ill-informed examination of Edina's automatic writing, or the ring on the wrist of the medium Cecil Husk, which Gurney resolutely refused to accept as definitely proved to have been put there by spirit agency. The last two cases mentioned clearly illustrate the different approaches that the believers and the more cautious Cambridge investigators adopted. A man, hidden under the pseudonym 'Edina', had given in the pages of *Light* an account of his daughter's automatic writing. Myers got a young acquaintance, Withers, a Cambridge graduate and a solicitor, to investigate (Myers 1891f: 100–105). He quickly discovered that the girl, though deaf since the age of eight, was an excellent lip reader and that, with Myers concurring in the interpretation, her messages were garbled memories accessed from the sub-conscious self. Myers, from personal knowledge, was able to point out the inaccuracies in the 'spirit' Livingstone's account of the courtship and marriage of Henry Stanley and Dorothy Tennant!

The outcome of the Husk affair was equally irritating to the spiritualists and is a good example of the way each camp used expert witnesses. The spiritualist, George Wyld, quoted Maskelyne, the great showman and conjuror, as stating that Husk's ring was the most puzzling thing he had seen in spiritualism. Gurney (*Light* 18.4.1885: 224) went direct to Maskelyne to get his views in precise detail. He then reported that what Maskelyne had really said was that (a) it was not possible to rule out that the ring had been put on Husk's wrist by natural means and (b) that the ring was sound, whole and in one piece—no evidence of tampering. Such—to their way of thinking—over fussy precision hugely irritated the spiritualists and *Light* thundered, 'We warn them from a standpoint of knowledge that these things are proven facts before they begin to deal with them' (*Light* 25.6.1887: 286). As Helen Brietzcke wrote to the *Journal*: 'I take my own folding slates, hold these in mid air between the medium and myself, have a friend in her normal condition to sit by and watch with me, and under <u>these</u> conditions get writing in the folding slate. I fail to see here the chance to cheat, and cannot but believe' (*Journal* 1886: 406–407).

The spiritualists did not reserve quite the same fury for Myers as they did for Davey, Hodgson and Mrs Sidgwick. In fact, as we have seen, they found it rather difficult to get a handle on him. For some he was a covert spiritualist who hadn't quite the courage to announce his conversion. For others he was a sceptic who was putting forward psychological explanations to discredit phenomena attributed to the agency of discarnate spirits. Tirelessly, Myers wrote to *Light* to correct these and other misapprehensions: the Society held no collective views; the only common thread in all activity was the careful examination of evidence, particularly that which provided information not known to any person at the séance and which could be later demonstrated as accurate: and that he, as an individual, merely because of the scrupulousness of his approach, was not antagonistic towards them; indeed, 'Various converging lines of evidence have led me individually to think it probable that in some at least of the cases here cited there has been a real agency of deceased persons' (*Light* 19.4.1890: 193).

The Death of Gurney

Myers was not a man who easily gave his heart and his affection to others. With most people he presented a mask of genial distance while managing, though not always quite successfully, to mute the extreme snobbishness of his youth. But to those few whom he saw as intellectual equals and who shared his sense of the importance of addressing the great metaphysical and ethical questions directly, rather than going through life in a complacent daze, he opened up his heart and worked in intense comradeship with them. To no one was he closer than to Edmund Gurney. There may initially have been a homo-erotic element in their early relationship, but the bond in essence was much deeper than physical attraction. Eveleen Myers—though she disliked the visits of Mr and Mrs Gurney, wanting her Fred to herself as a young, newly-wed would—clearly and generously recognised what they meant to each other (see below).

Therefore, the news of Gurney's death, in the Royal Albion Hotel in Brighton on the night of Friday 22nd June 1888, hit Myers in a way that nothing had since the death of Annie Marshall in 1876. This was particularly so since there had been no inkling that anything was amiss. Early June had started well for the Sidgwicks and Myers with the opening of Clough Hall (a considerable addition to the facilities of Newnham College) by the Prince of Wales and the Prime Minister, Nora Sidgwick's uncle, Lord Salisbury (Sutherland 2006: 118–19). Gurney, too, seemed to be stable. He had dined with Cyril Flower at the House of Commons the night before his visit to Brighton, apparently on very good form and displaying none of the symptoms of the manic depression that occasionally engulfed him. There may have been difficulties in his marriage because of his intense workload, but that work itself was going well. His research on hypnosis was attracting the interest of a small but select band of scholars and *Phantasms of the Living* had received a more positive press than was initially thought likely; he had vigorously and effectively defended the book against the criticisms of CS Peirce and AD Innes, while frankly and without rancour accepting valid points. In his memorial account of Gurney's work, Myers was in absolutely no doubt about Gurney's importance and that Gurney knew how valued he was, taking 'deep delight' in work 'done in consultation by a small group united both in personal friendship and intellectual interests' (Myers 1888c: 370).

Myers pointed out the great nature of his achievements (Myers 1888c: 366–70). The middle of the nineteenth century was a barren time for research into hypnosis in England: 'Incredible as it may seem, in all the long interval from (say) 1855 till 1883 — the date of publication of Edmund Gurney's first experiments — there was scarcely an experiment performed in England which added anything further to our knowledge,' and, independently of the French revival in hypnotism from 1875 onwards, 'He devised and carried through (1885–88) a complex series of experiments, surpassed by no other hypnotist in exactness, either of observation of record.' In this he anticipated 'the remarkable papers of a cognate kind' of Pierre Janet'. But Gurney's experiments had been carried out, and largely executed, before Myers had informed him of Janet's results. His other great achievement, of course, was *Phantasms of the Living*, which 'is not only the best discussion in our language, but actually the *only* one in our language'.

It is, therefore, difficult to believe that such a man, at the 'top of his game', should have committed suicide. However, the events of the night of 22nd June were open to a number of different interpretations, one of which might support that hypothesis. Gurney had dined at the hotel and gone to bed around 10.00pm. At 2.00pm the following day, since there had been no response to earlier knocking, the door was broken down. Gurney was found dead in his bed with a sponge-bag pressed over his nose and mouth. A small bottle, with a little chloroform in it, was by the bed. Gurney had either been using it to commit suicide, or by inhalation or direct application, as a palliative for neuralgia. This was quite a common practice but it had its attendant dangers as Cromwell Varley's description of his near-fatal inhalation in 1871 demonstrates. Varley described how, possibly in very similar circumstances to Gurney, he had applied a chloroformed soaked sponge to his face, 'After a little time I became conscious ... and I saw myself on my back with the sponge to my mouth, but was utterly powerless to cause my body to move' (Nicol 1972: 348–49). His wife, sensing something wrong, came in and saved him. This is what could well have happened to Gurney, and as there was no evidence to suggest that he intended to commit suicide, the coroner's jury delivered a verdict of accidental death.

Using a wide range and variety of circumstantial evidence, Trevor Hall has challenged this verdict (Hall 1980a). He argued that the poor reception for *Phantasms of the Living*, the revelation that a number of the Society's spontaneous cases and experimental researches were severely flawed (and he conjectured that Gurney had gone to Brighton to receive evidence that Smith was fraudulent), and the lack of support from Myers and his colleagues, had led an over-worked and manic depressive Gurney to take his own life. This thesis has a surface plausibility but it has been powerfully, and in my view, very adequately taken apart by Gauld (Gauld 1965: 53–62) and Nicol (Nicol 1966: 5–59). There are also two unpublished manuscripts in the Trinity archives which make similar criticisms (Broad 1965 D/17: 297–322 and Broad [notes from Nicol] 1970 D/17: 38–51).

As we have seen, *Phantasms of the Living* was not badly received by the daily and weekly press, and Gurney responded, by his own lights, effectively to the criticisms in the periodicals. The Society was ruthless, quite rightly, in discarding flawed evidence, and no one was quicker to acknowledge mistakes, without taking it personally, than Gurney himself. He, Myers and the Sidgwicks, fully accepted that they were 'learning a new trade' and that it was inevitable that errors and inaccuracies would occasionally occur. A characteristic of them all (except possibly the Sidgwicks in the case of physical phenomena) was their willingness to argue, debate, accept criticism, and modify their original positions without rancour. As Myers said of Gurney, 'He delighted in the fray — delighted in acknowledging a fair stroke or rebutting a foul one; delighted in replying with easy courtesy to attacks envenomed with that *odium plus quam theologicum* which the very allusion to a ghost or the human soul seems in some philosophers to inspire' (Myers 1888c: 371). Finally, there is no evidence whatsoever that Alice Smith, Smith's sister, had summoned Gurney to Brighton to tell Gurney about his deception, while Smith was conveniently away on honeymoon, as Hall alleged (Hall 1980a: 187–90).

Indeed there is a simple reason for Gurney's visit and one available to Hall if he had wished to cite it (Gauld 1979: 186-95). The Society had considerable interest in a haunted house in Brighton at the time. Gurney went there on the 13th June to interview the latest tenant and was impressed by her quality as a witness. In his role as Hon Secretary it was part of his responsibility to follow up on these matters. After his death Podmore interviewed another witness (9th July) and arrangements were made for Smith and his wife, back from honeymoon, to occupy the property, which they did between 17th August 1888 and 27th September 1889 (Podmore 1889/90: 310-13). The matter was organised by Arthur Myers who kept Sidgwick informed (Add.Ms.c. 94/163: n.d.). Gurney would have obviously have negotiated the details with Smith himself had he lived, so any 'mysterious letter' summoning him to Brighton, most probably refers to this.

Writing to her sister and mother shortly after the event, Eveleen Myers gave a vivid account of the discovery of the death, the SPR's fears of the damage that it might do to the cause of Psychical Research, and the impact on her husband:

> Dear Mother it is impossible to describe to you the terrible grief that this is to Fred. — His Mother's death or his brothers would not I think have come quite so terribly because she is 77. and much as he adores her ... still it is to be expected — but Mr. Gurney was so dear to him, for 21 years they have loved each other so completely, telling each other every most secret thought and such an <u>understanding,</u> and love of the same things in work, nature, humour, & it might have been expected that <u>years</u> were before them, — Freds mind and his mind were at a complete <u>unity</u> together. — No words of mine can describe dear Freds grief. Arthur came this morning I was at church with Leo & Silvia. — and he broke the news to Fred and his mother. — Fred will go to the funeral on Tuesday. — & is writing all the notices for the papers but he can hardly do it for the paper is so deluged with his tears, — We are all very anxious that people should not talk unkindly about any of the circumstances, or say that the S.P.R. drove him mad, or anything ridiculous of the kind you know how cruel people are so if you and Dolly will just read this carefully and do not let Hamilton or any one make up any story. — He had been dining on Thursday last at the house of commons with Arthur Balfour and Cyril Flower. — on Friday he went to Brighton. He had been suffering dreadfully from sleeplessness and, & neuralgia tho' he spoke very little about his own discomfort he told Arthur Myers how it reduced his strength the want of sleep. — He went to the Albion Hotel on Friday last the day after the dinner party. — he wrote a letter to Dr. Arthur Myers asking him to

join him there for some S.P.R. experiments.-He did not post this letter, but went to bed & in the morning was found dead with a little bottle of chloroform beside him which he constantly had by his bed side. — he had been taking it on cotton wool and it was still over his mouth. — The letter was found in his pocket and poor Arthur was quickly sent for, as no other address was found, — He had to see all the Drs & arrange all & rush back to London & tell Mr Arthur Gurney at the Church. — & poor Mrs Gurney. She has only known it this bright Sunny Sunday Morning what a day for her! — for she loved him dearly. — and now all is over. — Fred had an important appointment with him for next Friday. He was spending last Sunday at Tarling with Lord and Lady Rayleigh in perfect health. — He was very diffi-cult to affect with narcotics & he must have taken at last a dose too large to leave him power to moderate it. Please do not allow any dis-tortion of these facts to be spoken of in your presence by Hamilton or any one. — & I am sure dear Dolly will also not allow any thing to be said about one so dear to Fred. — especially also as the facts are as I tell you, I am so tired, Yours Evey, I have told Fred to write to Hamilton, as he is so full of gossip (D/DT: 2585/2 n.d.)

This account sheds some very interesting light on past theories and speculations concerning Gurney's death. Eveleen Myers' letter and the verdict of the jury were consistent with each other and with the events as they were known. Had there been strong concerns with regard to suicide she would have explicitly mentioned it to her mother, from whom she kept little or nothing. The letter demonstrates that she was aware that gos-sip about the death could damage the work of the SPR and that Hamilton Aïdé, their socialite cousin, could be unreliable in this respect. But there is no indication at all in the letter that suicide had been suspected. Indeed, she stressed that the real problem was sleeplessness and neuralgia. She also made the revealing point that as a very big man he had a certain resis-tance to small doses of narcotics and probably needed to take a substantial amount. One could interpret this all as a very effective cover story, but it reads more like a straightforward and moving account of an accidental death.

Trevor Hall, in support of his thesis of suicide, has cited the testimony of Alice James, the witty, gossipy sister of William and Henry James. She, possibly because it fitted with her psychological needs, was convinced that it was suicide and wrote to William (Yeazell 1997: 152–54) declaring it to be so, and painting the picture of a rather loveless, almost Pygmalion style marriage, in which a beautiful, empty-headed chatterer was fre-quently put down by a neurasthenic workaholic. She partly blamed Myers. She said he urged Gurney to marry her (this in contrast to Hall [Hall 1980a: 33, 39], who using the unreliable memories of Gurney's daughter, alleged Myers really wanted Kate Sibley/Gurney for himself!). Epperson, on the other hand, paints a more generous picture of their relationship, as did Eveleen Myers (Epperson 1997: 145–46). Yet it cannot be denied that Gurney had his unstable, nervy and difficult side. He drove himself very hard, often to prostration, with periods of tremendous activity followed by burn out and lassitude. He could also be sarcastic and impatient at times with those he thought foolish or trivial. His wife sometimes suffered in this respect. There are a number of references in the Myers-Sidgwick letters to his illness and weakness; and a sad letter exists from Myers to his wife — marked quite private — about certain aspects of Gurney's temperament, '… a moonlight walk with the Coon who feels sadly that he does not get people to feel how much he cares for them & sympathises with them; — owing to something in his manner wh they think sarcastic' (Myers 7/132: 5.7.1884). This may have had something, too, to do with his outward appearance. As Myers described him, 'He was over six foot two in height: thin & loosely built, but upright of being and swift of step; with a face whose features seemed moulded for haughty scorn, but whose expression was of absorbed melancholy with gleams sometimes of sarcastic humour, sometimes sympathetic tenderness' (Myers 26/63).

However, none of this suggests that he was suicidal at that time. In fact, Gurney's determination to research and research suggests that it was unlikely he would wish to take his life and leave unfinished business. C Downing wrote to Myers after his death stating that he remembered asking Gurney how long he would go on collecting evidence, 'and he answered "Till I die,"' which Downing thought strange, subtle and sad (Myers, 2/44: 26.6.1888). There were, too, a number of letters to Myers on Gurney's death, testifying to the wide respect in which he was held. Finally, Fraser Nicol, the writer who has most effectively dealt with Hall's thesis that Gurney committed suicide, has stated that, 'it would be an act of unreason to doubt the propriety of the jury's verdict' (Nicol 1972: 341–67).

There is some danger of tedium in raking over again and again the ashes of this debate. Yet, the devil is in the detail. Hall's skilfully selective and persuasive work has been quoted almost uncritically in a number of quarters by scholars whose main expertise has been literary or cultural, rather than the history of psychical research. This has led to false and simplistic views of the characters and achievements of the early leaders of the SPR amongst the wider intellectual community and establishment of the twentieth and twenty-first century — particularly with regard to Myers' character and to Gurney's achievement. He was the leading researcher into hypnosis in the 1880s at a time when England lagged behind in this field. His loss was felt immensely strongly by Myers and William James and was undoubtedly the greatest blow suffered by the Society in its early years. Myers had great energy and drive and capacity for developing explanatory conceptual schema; but he had other employment. Gurney had equal but complementary intellectual skills and was working full-time for the Society. James' reaction was heart felt, 'Poor Edmund Gurney! How I shall miss that man's presence in the world ... He had both *quantity* and quality, and I hoped for some big philosophic achievement from him ere he should get through' (Skrupskelis *et al.* 1998: 429–30).

Interestingly, some irritation with Myers flared up in Mrs Gurney when she wrote to William James in November 1888 (Skrupskelis *et al.* 1998: 455–56). She explained that she had hoped to send James a photograph of Gurney herself but that Myers had already anticipated this. Myers (Skrupskelis *et al.* 1998: 608) in a letter of 17th October 1888 had sent James a photograph stating that he did so at the request of Mrs Gurney. It is as if in the misunderstanding over the photograph they were symbolically contesting the ownership of Gurney and his reputation — did he belong to Myers and the SPR or to his wife? A year later Mrs Gurney married Archibald Grove and severed all contact with the Society — making no donations to its funds — unlike Gurney's blood relatives.

Taking up Gurney's Torch

Myers rose to the challenge of Gurney's death and the removal of the Society's most gifted full-time worker. He began to discuss, in the pages of the *Proceedings*, in a more considered and systematic way, the nature of ghosts/apparitions and the type of evidence required to support belief in life after death. He did this in three papers which completed material Gurney was working on at the time of his death and which responded to the sceptical arguments of his fellow SPR honorary secretary, Frank Podmore; for after Gurney's death, Myers and Podmore split Gurney's role as honorary secretary of the SPR between them.

In the first paper Gurney (with Myers agreeing) stressed the importance of developing clear criteria to establish that the apparition of a dead person was not just a subjective hallucination. Three such criteria were specified: that more than one person saw or was independently affected by the phenomena; that the apparition conveyed information (which the percipient had never known) and which was afterwards found to be true; and that though the percipient did not know the apparition he/she could give a sufficiently accurate description of it for it to be identified. A number of cases were outlined which met at least one of these criteria.

Completing Gurney's paper (Gurney and Myers 1889: 403–85), Myers commented that the idea of a latent and then emerging telepathic impact from agent to percipient did not seem adequate in all cases. In some cases the idea of telepathic clairvoyance, to explain or describe the transfer from agent to percipient of the agent's actual viewpoint and experience, was more appropriate; and to make matters even more complicated, it could occasionally happen when the agent was dying but not dead. Apparitions could be seen before death:

> About two months before the death of my dear father, which occurred on December the 10th 1887, one night about from 12 to 1 a.m., when I was in bed in a perfectly waking condition, he came to my bedside [the father was dying, bed-ridden and helpless, three floors below at the time], and led me right through the cemetery, stopping at the spot; where his grave was afterwards made … I had at that time never been in that cemetery, but when I went there after his interment the scene was perfectly familiar to me (Gurney and Myers 1889: 450).

Of course, though interesting, there was no independent direct corroboration of any part of this story. Myers further pointed out, using a graph, the fact that the records of recognised apparitions became fewer and fewer the more time had elapsed after death, and, therefore, how vitally important it was to collect and compare all such exiguous records (Gurney and Myers 1889: 462).

In the next paper (Myers 1889c: 13–65) Myers actually began to bite the bullet and to raise the question of survival after death, 'The momentous step, of course, is already taken so soon as we consent to refer any *post-mortem* apparition, — dating even from the morrow of the death, — to the continued agency of the decedent. Few readers will question the assumption that in that unknown journey *ce n'est que le premier pas qui coûte.*' He was well aware that even in raising this he was courting controversy, so in a note at the foot of the page, he stressed he was speaking only for himself: 'Various converging lines of evidence have led me individually to think it probable that in some at least of the cases here cited there has been a real agency of deceased persons. But no one else is responsible for that opinion; nor do I even claim that the evidence cited is enough to prove its truth' (Myers 1889c: 13).

And, for the first time, he discussed in detail what we might mean by a ghost. He pointed out that the popular view of a ghost as 'a deceased person permitted by Providence to hold communication with survivors' was based on a number of 'unwarrantable assumptions'. Firstly, we should not assume that ghosts are exceptions to law, but that they will eventually be found to be in accordance with the laws of the universe. Secondly, that though there may be a causal link with the deceased, we have no right to assume that it is the deceased in any obvious incarnate sense. Thirdly, we must not, over simplistically, ascribe any specific motives to the phantasm. All we can assume is that a ghost is 'a manifestation of persistent personal energy' in some way linked to a 'person previously known on earth'. With his characteristic urge to classify, he ranged the cases, listed in the paper, in descending order from those which showed intelligent purpose, down to those which appeared to be only, in Myers' vivid expression, 'a dead man's incoherent dream'.

Myers provided interesting examples for each category. Some of the ones demonstrating purpose seemed particularly impressive and he often cited them in his lectures and on his country house visits. The apparition of a young girl with a red scratch on her cheek appeared to her travelling salesman brother. He mentioned the scratch to the mother who confessed that she had accidentally scratched the corpse's face when preparing it for the funeral and, horrified, had used cosmetics to hide the mark. The mother died shortly afterwards. The granddaughter of the Earl of Egremont, sliding down the banisters one afternoon, saw an old-fashioned lady who then vanished. Telling the story years later, she was informed she had described her great aunt, 'She came to fetch her brother. He died very soon after.' A husband and wife lying in bed both saw the apparition of his father — long dead — he spoke his son's name warningly and reproachfully. The phantom appeared to have some tangibility since, 'As it passed the lamp, a deep shadow fell upon the room as of a material person shutting out the light from us by his intervening body'. The husband had been about to take some financial advice which if followed, it was later found, would have ruined him. Myers argued that a very small number of cases like these, demonstrated a clear sense of purpose, sometimes even over trivial matters; and the humbleness of the motive was, in itself, no reason for dismissing the account (Myers 1889c: 33). He also, and, almost as an aside, suggested that death-bed visions, 'have very rarely been observed with the right kind of care' and that they should be (Myers 1889c: 24, 18-28).

Myers pointed out that those ghosts like the above, which showed purpose, were few and far between. Many cases were, as Mrs Sidgwick had stated (Sidgwick 1885: 143, 147, of the recurring automatic type, local and connected to a specific property. Either they seemed to be condemned to perform the same ritualistic activities over and over again, almost like the working out of a post-hypnotic suggestion, or they were mere impressions of past action, somehow caught in that specific environment. It was often difficult to investigate these cases thoroughly, and make the appropriate discriminations, since, for obvious reasons, 'the owners of house property … conceal well-attested ghosts as carefully as defective cesspools'.

Having stressed that there was only a residue of good cases, Myers then moved on to provisional explanation. Here he begins for the first time in detail to pull together into a conceptual framework all the phenomena he has examined. Although Sidgwick, above all, had urged the piling up of case after case, evidence after evidence, Myers had an instinctive and driven need to go beyond this and to categorise, classify and explain. He argued that the concepts of telepathy and of multiplex personality — which he believed been adequately demonstrated by the collection of cases by the Society, their experiments in their rooms, and the work in France — could be used to provide some initial understanding of the phenomena (Myers 1889c: 47–49). He hypothesised that just as the telepathic message starts from and impinges on the sub-conscious of both agent and percipient in the flesh, a similar process may take place between the living and the dead. The process by which that occurs may be not unlike that of somnambulism, induced or spontaneous, or that of post-hypnotic suggestion. In all these cases the figure seems to be 'working out some fore-ordained suggestion with little reference to any other mind.'

In his third paper, 'A Defence of Phantasms of the Dead', Myers took the opportunity to rebut Podmore's (Podmore 1889–90: 229– 313) comprehensive explanation of phantasms as the product of telepathy between the living, hallucination and occasional deceit. It gave him an opportunity to deal with philosophical matters rather than the detailed case studies of the previous two papers. He hoped that the division of opinion between the two honorary secretaries might stimulate further discussion and, most importantly, evidence. He put his finger on the central problem: 'It remains, that is to say, to be seen whether Science can accord to honest testimony (of a kind which can rarely be confirmed by direct experiment) a confidence sufficient to bear the strain put upon it by the marvellous matters for which that testimony vouches' (Myers 1890a).

Myers argued, firstly, that Podmore pushed the explanatory power of telepathy too far. It was a first hint of discoveries to come. It was dangerous to pronounce on it too definitely as in the hypothesis that it operated through brain waves vibrating in tune, like the other vibrations traversing space (Myers 1890a: 317). Telepathy did open a 'door way out of which materialism can never be shut'. But its mode of operation and relation to 'a mixed multitude of obscure phenomena' was complex. There was now increasing evidence for clairvoyance, 'some energy exercised by the percipient's mind alone'. He further asserted that though it was incontestable that our conscious powers were tied to the physiological activity of the brain, the manifestations of the unconscious self showed 'a greater independence of certain corporeal conditions'. Indeed, he argued that 'telergic action varies inversely, [rather] than it varies directly with the observable activity of the nervous system or of the conscious mind'.

Podmore asserted that the lack of purpose and motive in most phantasms suggested a hallucination on the part of the percipient. Myers agreed, in one sense, but argued that it was how a voluntarily projected phantasm like those recorded in *Phantasms of the Living* (Gurney *et al.* 1886: lxxxi–lxxxiv, 106–107) would behave. He particularly stressed the case of Mr SHB (Myers 1890a: 319, 322). Myers was especially impressed by this case, which originally appeared in *Phantasms of the Living* and was later cited in *Human Personality and Its Survival of Bodily Death* (Myers 1904 1: 292–96). Mr SHB was able to project an image of himself from his home in Kildare Gardens to the home of two sisters, the Misses Verity, in Hogarth Road, Kensington, three miles away. Both sisters saw and testified to the fact that they had seen the phantasm. The dead might be able to project a simulacrum of themselves in the same way that a very small number of living people appeared able to do. The effort to produce such an image might leave the spirit, incarnate or discarnate, with no energy for anything else. Moreover, the projection in some cases might be involuntary or part of an incarnate or discarnate dream. All this was highly speculative, but for Myers it tied in with what he had observed in some cases of somnambulism, dissociation and hypnosis.

He further argued that there was no evidence for Podmore's assertion that the percipients of ghosts were subjected to regular hallucinations, or that they could telepathically infect others. He did agree, however, that some hallucinations could be latent and appear some time after death. He quoted the example of Miss X (Ada Goodrich Freer),[4] whose experiments in crystal vision demonstrated that the subconscious could produce after-images, whether or not the image had been perceived consciously in the field of vision; and some of these after images might have a telepathic origin. He expressly rejected Podmore's infection theory in the case of the Brighton haunted house investigation. This was a version of Gurney's theory outlined in *Phantasms of the Living*. Podmore suggested that Miss Morris, a previous tenant, had through thought-transference sparked off Mrs G's anxieties about the house. Myers countered that this grossly over estimated the power and regularity of telepathy. Telepathy, as it was known to the Society, was 'rare, fleeting and inconspicuous'. We were not equipped — our basic terrestrial sensory structure being designed for daily survival — to pick up the full range of influences on us. The influences were subtle and evanescent: 'We must look for a miscellaneous interfusion among terrene phenomena of phenomena generated by extra-

4   See below, pp. 231–33.

terrene causes' (Myers 1890a: 330). And it was, therefore, essential to study in detail all the accompanying phenomena around the central phantasm — lights, sounds, etc. Myers here proposed a phenomenological approach to the subject which has only partially been developed in later years.

He provided an outline classification into which the different sorts of phenomena of apparitions/hallucinations/ghosts could be grouped. He identified five types of related phenomena: hypnotic suggestion; telepathic experiments; spontaneous telepathy of the living; phantasms at death; phantasms after death. He argued that each of these types or stages had the same three forms of manifestations: hallucinations of the senses; emotional and motor impulses; definite intellectual messages through automatic writing. The very last category, phantasms after death communicating through automatic writing, was the most significant for Myers. But this was also the one where most care had to be taken, since one could easily be duped by grandiloquent language and messages claiming they emanated from the greatest minds of the past. Finally, he touched on the modern conception of super extra sensory perception: 'It is *conceivable* that thought-transference and clairvoyance may be pushed to the point of a sort of terrene omniscience; so that to a man's unconscious self some phantasmal picture should be open of all that men are doing or have done, — things good and evil photographed imperishably in some inexorable imprint of the past' (Myers 1890a: 337). And that after death a kind of psychic précis of the individual lodged in that universal record.

Myers put that forward, for the sake of completeness, as a theoretical alternative to personal survival; but he was much more interested in the latter. He argued that on an immediate practical level, in order to attempt to prove continued personal identity after death, two things were required, 'first the need of definite facts, given in the messages, which were known to the departed and are not known to the automatist; and secondly, the need of detailed and characteristic utterances; a moral means of identification corresponding, say, not to the meagre *signalement* by which a man is described on his passport, but to the individual complex of minute markings left by the impression of a prisoner's thumb' (Myers 1890a: 337–38). It is interesting that Myers did not tighten the first part and state 'not known to any one alive', since one could argue that the information had been obtained telepathically. This, however, was an oversight since he had mentioned it frequently in his earlier articles on automatic writing. That is also why the fulfilment of the second condition, clear evidence of unique personal identity, while not definitive proof of survival, was an additional pointer in that direction.

Finally, he discussed the strange fact that rather than stimulating false hopes of immortality through their researches, their work was mostly ignored. This was a complaint Gurney had also often made. Many people found the subject distasteful and depressing. Educated people had 'a kind of shrinking from the magnitude of fate'. The discoveries of astronomy had revealed a universe which was not *homo sapiens* centric, 'A soul from which the Christian confidence is withdrawn may well feel that it is going forth into the void, — not as a child to his Father's home, but rather as a spark of sentiency involved amid enormous forces, and capable of unimagined pain.' Yet, he argued, this attitude prevented people from addressing the evidence that he and his colleagues were generating, distasteful, perplexing, even grotesque, maybe. But it was evidence: 'As well might Columbus have turned back when the first drift-wood floated out to him from America, on the ground that it was useless to discover a continent consisting only of dead logs' (Myers 1890a: 340).

It is worth at this point expanding on the relationship between Myers and Podmore, since they were increasingly coming to cross swords as Myers tried to develop a speculative, provisional framework to make sense of the evidence the Society received. There does not seem to have been a personal antagonism. The few letters that survive from Podmore are perfectly friendly ones but they do not suggest such a close and warmly enthusiastic relationship as Myers had with Gurney, James and Lodge. In one early letter Podmore described, with a certain aplomb, and in terms that suggest a degree of intimacy beyond the casual acquaintanceship, a near fatal incident when he got lost in the snow on Ben Nevis (Myers 3/135: 8.5.1883). He also wrote warmly and sympathetically to commiserate with Myers on the death of Gurney (Myers 3/136: 26.6.1888). Yet, one detects a certain distance, as if Podmore was not quite part of the inner circle. He was not as wealthy as Myers or Gurney and did not have their range of social connections. He appeared to spend more time in those slightly raffish and subversive groups — like the first stages of the Fabian Society or the Fellowship of the New Life — that challenged conventional social and political thinking (Mackenzie, Norman and Jean 1977). Indeed Edward Pease, the founder of the Fabian Society, was active for a while in the SPR. Finally, Myers may well have heard rumours (founded or unfounded) that Podmore was linked to the homosexual demi-monde (Hall 1980a: 200–206).

Eveleen Myers was certainly no fan and she thought Podmore parasitic on Myers' ideas and researches. Sidgwick, in fact, eventually drew up a memorandum of agreement between the two to try to clarify certain overlaps and issues, Podmore being quicker into book form than Myers (Myers 3/139: 19.12.1895). Myers was concerned that Podmore, who was proposing a book 'on SPR work', would either steal his thunder (after all he had produced a huge amount of material), or their books would come out at the same time. Therefore, it was agreed that some evidence, like *Phantasms of the Living*, would be common property; that other cases would be specifically for Myers to use (Mrs Piper; the Cheltenham Ghost, for example); while Podmore himself, in the memorandum, did not wish to reserve any material exclusively); that their books should come out at different times, and that Sidgwick should arbitrate if there were territorial disputes. It was likely, however, that there would always be some residual underlying tension between the two of them. Podmore's disposition, and the tone of his writing, was more sceptical than Myers' (Myers called it 'carping' on one occasion to Lodge, when it was proposed that Podmore write up the Palladino episodes). It was obviously easier, in terms of writing for publication, to analyse in a critical and possibly negative and destructive sense, material largely gathered by others. There was not the same level of creative challenge as that faced by Myers: the building up of a huge volume of evidence, based on almost encyclopaedic reading, substantial experimental work, and considerable personal investigation at home and abroad, and then the synthesizing of it into a comprehensive publication.

But by the end of the 1880s, the critical and negative perspective of Podmore appeared more in harmony with the events and results of that decade, than the ebullient optimism of Myers. Hodgson's demolition work on Blavatsky, Eglinton and others, the confession of the Creery sisters, the withdrawal of a number of spiritualists from the SPR, and the death of Gurney, together created in the SPR, if not a defeated, then at least a diffident and cautious mood. Sidgwick's attitude and its effect on Myers has been quoted before, but the point bears expansion: 'He thought it not improbable that this last effort to look beyond the grave would fail; that men would have to content themselves with an agnosticism growing yearly more hopeless, — and had best turn to daily duties and forget the blackness of the end. His words touched many a latent doubt in my own bosom. As I have implied, the question was for me too vital to admit of my endeavouring for a moment to cheat myself into a false security' (Myers 1961: 41). Yet, the Hodgson who was partly responsible for that mood, was also the Hodgson who eventually helped to lift it, by his sustained investigation of one of the most gifted mediums the SPR ever encountered, Mrs Leonora Piper. And Myers, from his own involvement in this, was, he believed, to gain the first convincing evidence of the post-mortem survival of Annie Marshall — and of his intimate friend, Edmund Gurney.

Chapter Five

Myers as Psychologist

Myers, the SPR and the International Congresses of Psychology

Exhibitions, expositions, and international congresses became increasing features of nineteenth-century commercial and intellectual life. The international congresses were sometimes very specific: statistics in 1851, medicine in 1867, and criminal anthropology in 1885 (Rozenzweig *et al.* 2000: 11). But often they were tied, for publicity reasons, to broader commercial and cultural purposes. For example, July 1889 was the centenary of the French Revolution, and congresses on psychology, hypnotism and physiology were held in conjunction with the Paris International Exposition, celebrating that fact and French social, economic and cultural life generally. They afforded tremendous opportunities for networking and breaking down the isolation that workers in new fields often felt. They also allowed specialists to reach a wider audience. The exposition in Paris attracted over 32 million visitors. The World's Columbian Exposition of 1893 in Chicago received over 27 million visitors and had an associated Psychical Congress that Myers and Hodgson attended.

Myers was quick to spot the opportunities presented by this developing trend and pushed for the SPR to take an active part in the Paris congress. Myers was very keen that the ideas about the nature of man that he, his brother and Gurney had developed should be put before the wider, international community. The original idea for an international psychological conference had come from Ochorowicz, a Polish psychologist (Rozenzweig *et al.* 2000: 17). It was taken up in France by Charles Richet (the French polymath and later winner of the Nobel prize), who suggested the SPR's involvement to Myers. He enthusiastically passed the idea on to Sidgwick. Sidgwick wrote to him, 'Your proposal about Paris takes my breath away: but we are prepared to discuss it' (Add.Ms.c.100/ 132: April 25/1889). Myers, energetically, tried to rustle up support from the wider English psychological community. He was keen to get Francis Galton to attend (Myers 2/65/1: n.d.). Galton declined, pleading bad French, but he did in fact go after further consideration and pressure. Despite his ambivalence with regard to séances, Galton was always willing to read and receive SPR literature (Myers 2/66: 14.10.1889). He was also helpful with contacts in the medical profession, putting Gurney and Myers in touch with those of his colleagues who might open doors for them (Myers 2/69/1: 6.11.1886).

The 1889 International Congress of Physiological Psychology was a great success and Myers enjoyed it hugely—particularly for the opportunity it gave him to deepen his friendship with William James. He also relished its unintentional comedy. Eveleen wrote to Dorothy:

> Fred describes his International Congress of experimental Psychology in Paris as a very amusing experience. It was a great success, and a great many eminent men were there But There was much conflict of opinions: and Fred found himself one day compelled to take the chair in a mingelled assemblage of Russians, French, Swedes and Germans all having Different ideas, & all wanting to express them at the same moment! ... Charcot—would not come—which was a great mistake but, he was in such a rage at th Nancy school ... (D/DT 2587: n.d.).

Arthur Myers produced a detailed report of the congress as a supplement to the SPR *Proceedings* (Myers A 1889: 171–82). He pointed out that attendance was variable at the sessions since a variety of other congresses were taking place at the same time. He also colluded with the fiction that Charcot, the President, was indisposed, rather than boycotting the congress through pique. There were six members of the British SPR attending—the Sidgwicks, Myers and his brother, and Messrs Barkworth and Kleiber. Myers' report showed that the contributions of the English contingent and the work of the SPR, which was mentioned in some depth in several places, was taken seriously by a section of the attendees, even if—in other quarters—there was some concern about the threat to the status of experimental, physiological psychology.

Richet, as secretary, outlined the main work of the congress, mentioning hypnotism and hallucinations as two areas where there should be unbiaised collective action and made a graceful tribute to Gurney, 'dont la science deplore la mort prematurée' (Myers A 1889: 172). On the 7th of August the congress agreed to continue to develop the Census of Hallucinations along the lines already started in England, France and America, with a recommendation by Delboeuf that the mental habit—visual, audile or motile—of the subjects should be noted. Myers' report then concentrated on the more animated and extensive debates on hypnotism on the 7th, 8th, 9th and 10th August, with which the SPR were intimately concerned. There was broad agreement that the term animal magnetism should be dropped, with its suggestion of some kind of fluence or force. There was also discussion as to whether particular races or classes of people were more or less easily hypnotisable and whether, as Sidgwick asked, all hypnotisers were of equal power. FWH Myers outlined the striking experiments with Gurney and the baker's boy Wells at Brighton, described in an earlier chapter[1] and which, contrary to the above statement concerning animal magnetism, seemed to suggest some influence emanating from the individual hypnotiser. Delboeuf theorised that Myers' results were due to a hyperacuity of feeling which allowed the subject to distinguish different hands. Myers stated that they had tested the subject for this but had found no evidence of it (Myers A 1889: 177).

In the discussion on hypnosis, Janet doggedly continued to assert that to be hypnotisable was a sign of mental and moral weakness and Richet (as Myers had done before him on many occasions) protested against this (Myers A 1889: 180–81). Delboeuf supported Richet, as did Myers in his description, on the 10th, of thought-transference experiments with a hypnotised subject. He pointedly stressed that the subject was healthy. Richet hoped that Myers' experiments, which produced results much greater than chance, would be replicated widely and with great care. Sidgwick added that such results, though they could be obtained with subjects in normal conditions, tended to be greater when the subject was in the hypnotic state. Therefore, at the end of the congress, the Myers brothers and the Sidgwicks could be well pleased with their first efforts to engage the wider psychological community. There were differences and there was some hostility, but an indication that they had not been marginalised was the decision that the second congress be held in England in 1892 and that Sidgwick was to be its President.

Myers was grateful for the support that Richet had given him at the 1889 congress and their friendship and co-operation deepened in the 1890s. He encouraged Richet to produce a French translation of *Phantasms of the Living* and helped him draft the preface (Myers 12/31: 11.9.1890). He was most determined to get Richet to the International Congress of Experimental Psychology in London in 1892 for which he, Myers, had become one of the joint organising secretaries. (Experimental had replaced physiological as the key epithet, since it emphasized the empirical more forcefully.) This was a major coup for the SPR in terms of publicising their work but both Myers and Sidgwick were very careful to avoid antagonis-

1   See above, p. 124.

ing the physiological school. For example, they chose James Sully as joint secretary to the congress with Myers, since he would be a reassuring figure for the continental psychologists. Myers and Sidgwick also rearranged the dates of the 1892 congress so that people could attend both it and also most of the British Association meeting in Edinburgh. Myers very strongly re-emphasized the importance he and his colleagues attached to Richet's attendance: 'We do very much want you! & your position as the virtual founder of the whole thing just makes your absence rather marked' (Myers12/54: 23.7.1892).

Sidgwick and Myers were very keen to get as wide a variety of English intellectuals as possible to receive visitors and offer hospitality. Sidgwick approached Herbert Spencer, the psychologist, for his support, since he would be the best known to continentals. Spencer replied, a little testily, that he would be happy to join the reception committee provided the definition of experimental psychology meant physio-psychology. He was not prepared to countenance a link with telepathy (Add.Ms.c.95/90: n.d.). Spencer's name, however, is not listed in *The Times* (2.8.1892) as one of the illustrious figures who attended the congress. Sidgwick gave a masterly opening address in which he tried to be fair to different schools of thought; he pointed out some of the difficult philosophical issues involved in the mind/body problem, and defined the term experimental in a broader sense than purely laboratory work. But he stressed that he in no way countenanced unscientific and unsystematic enquiry, and he emphasized the specific organisational arrangements he had made to give due weight to German psychologists. These had felt inadequately represented and acknowledged at the previous congress. This was principally done by arranging parallel sessions so that attendees could avoid those contributions and topics they thought of little value. Myers played a lesser, but socially very useful role, in that he organised a major evening reception for the delegates at his mother-in-law's *grand salon* in Richmond Terrace, on 3rd August (D/DT 2636). The reception was not till ten in the evening, so the delegates certainly needed some stamina.

This second congress was also very successful. Much of that was due to Sidgwick's intellectual deftness and the effective practical organisation of Sully and of Myers. Sidgwick had been particularly careful not to make the work of the Society over prominent and a relatively small number of papers covered psychical research matters — particularly the work on the international survey of hallucinations. Hypnosis was again discussed in depth and it was pleasing to the SPR and Myers that the Salpêtrière view of hypnosis no longer held much credibility. For Sidgwick and Myers, as noted in Sidgwick's report of the congress, the key point was not the acceptance of telepathy or thought-transference by psychologists who attended (Sidgwick 1892: 283–93). There was absolutely no attempt to force this issue. The main significance of the congress for the SPR was that, 'representatives of our Society have claimed a place for their special investigations, as a recognised department in the scientific study of psychology, and have had their claims admitted without opposition'. In fact, apart from the work on the census, the only significant contribution from the SPR was the paper Mrs Sidgwick presented on experiments in thought-transference, and the paper Myers read on the experimental induction of hallucinations. It was gratifying to Myers that Janet corroborated the reality of the kind of facts that Myers had put forward in his paper – namely that through crystal vision, or automatic writing, or some other source, it was possible to induce hallucinations that might contribute to the diagnosis and identification of the underlying causes of fears, obsessions, *idées fixes* (Sidgwick 1892: 290).

The issue of the nature and meaning of hallucinations came strongly to the fore on the Wednesday afternoon when Sidgwick read part of his final report on the Census of Hallucinations. He stressed that amongst the 17,000 respondents only in a very small number of the cases 'was there any observed disturbance of health at the time of the hallucination'. This statement led to a clear polarisation of views in the discussion that followed. William Osler of Johns Hopkins stated that 'the mere fact of experiencing a hallucination implied some serious organic disturbance'. Dr Elizabeth Blackwell pointed out that the word hallucination was being used in a new way, since as normally used in medicine it implied morbidity. Myers strongly objected to Osler's view, in the light of the large number of healthy subjects who had been induced to have hallucinations through post-hypnotic suggestion (Sidgwick 1892: 291–92).

The report appeared both in the *Journal* and as a *Supplement* to the *Proceedings*. In the *Supplement*, Myers' initials as well as Sidgwick's stand beneath the text which, unlike the *Journal*, had general public circulation, and one can detect his influence in the greater stress given to the positive aspects and benefits of hypnotism and its wider acceptance by the scientific community. It was also there in the resounding, classical conclusion, urging them onwards and upwards: 'Just as the conquest of Gaul, which for so long seemed a chimerical hope, became inevitable so soon as the Roman Republic had reached a certain pitch of military force and ambition, so like-wise when Experimental Psychology has filled its ranks and perfected its methods, its bolder spirits must needs enter as conquerors the mountain-guarded region which we are now imperfectly surveying as pioneers of the scientific host' (Myers, Sidgwick 1892: 611).

Another challenge and opportunity arose in 1893 to spread the cause of psychical research at the Chicago World Congress of Religions, which was part of the wider exposition celebrating the four hundred years of achievement since Columbus's discovery of America. Myers tried, without success, to get Richet and then Lodge to go, the SPR offering to pay expenses (Myers 12/59: 8.12.1892). Myers was disappointed but decided to attend himself since, 'I think that it will be very important for prospects of SPR in America at that Congress SPR should take the lead, — not the vulgar American spiritualists' (Myers 12/60: 16.12.1892). His HMI work was demanding but routine and it proved possible to re-schedule his inspection visits. He was the right choice, given his sense of occasion, his dramatic presence, and his gifts as a speaker. He sailed on the *Majestic* in August 1893, not put off by a medium's warning conveyed to him by the over-credulous Stead. Myers wrote to James that 'Stead's wife's uncle's ghost says that the Majestic is to sink on this trip ... He has been trying to dissuade me, but I tell him to think of the "copy" if we do go down' (Myers 11/134/1: 2.8.1893).

His description of the impact of the congress on himself and Hodgson and his own performance smacks of the immodest — but it was, after all, in a private letter to his wife. He wrote from Chicago: 'The Congress is a great success — We have more than any other congress — an enormous meeting this morning to hear me speak on the Subliminal Self' (Myers 9/138: 23.8.1893). He was riding on a great high and enjoyed a considerable personal triumph. He described a later event: 'Last night over 1000 people came and sat in absolute stillness while I held forth about immortality etc, & then cheered me, and rushed up to me, & shook hands, & blessed me, & joined the SPR, & said all kinds of things wh I won't repeat'(Myers 9/139: 26.8.1893). He was impressed by the tremendous energy in Chicago and became convinced, with his usual over-optimism, that Chicago would eventually become the main world centre for psychical research. This was clearly a prediction that the University of Chicago has yet to fulfil.

Owing to the death of his mother in 1896, Myers was unable to attend the third International Congress of Psychology (the earlier adjectives 'physiological' and 'experimental' both having been dropped) in Munich. It, too, was successful in terms of networking, and the numbers attending exceeded the previous congresses (Sidgwick 1896: 295-99). However, not surprisingly given the location, the dominance of the German language and German physiological approaches to psychology, meant there was a much restricted discussion of psychical-related material. There were five topic sections running simultaneously and only section IV discussed material aligned with SPR interests. It was also unfortunate that no representative of the Nancy school of hypnosis, with which Myers and the Sidgwicks had much sympathy, was in attendance to reply to criticisms.

Telepathy attracted only marginal interest and Myers was not there to read his paper on trance phenomena. Mrs Sidgwick was, however, able to present her paper on the sensory hallucinations of persons in good health; and her husband, his, on involuntary whispering and thought-transference.

Neither Myers nor Sidgwick was in a position to make much personal impact on the fourth International Congress of Psychology that met in Paris in 1900. Sidgwick was near death and died in late August and Myers had lost his vigour and was to die a few months later. It was unfortunate that the two leaders were so weak, since they might have been able to check the more enthusiastic expressions of occult and psychical sentiments. The official history of the congress (Rozenzweig *et al.* 2000: 35) states that there was irritation from psychologists that spiritualists, theosophists, occultists etc, tried to dominate the congress. However, the Dutch psychotherapist van Eeden's report and Myers' addendum to it (Eeden, Myers 1901: 445–47) put a slightly different perspective on things. Van Eeden stressed that there had been a change of attitude and that privately participants were much more prepared to take the area seriously. This was over optimistic. The 1900 congress was the last at which there was any significant consideration of such issues and this reflected the growing professionalism of psychology and the increasing predominance of physiological and laboratory-based approaches. Myers gave a more vivid and anecdotal account in a letter to William James:

> The Congress <u>received</u> our speeches and papers on <u>Mrs</u> T[2] extremely well:—largest gathering of all the meetings-séance generall—Richet & I spoke & Van Eeden read a good paper. I found at the last moment that they would not understand English, so had to confine myself to extempore Anglo-French. However they cheered, & then crowded round Mrs T at the evening parties & tried to wheedle séances out of her. She gave very good sittings to Richet & van Eeden. There were various silly spiritualistic papers—no great <u>coup</u> of <u>any</u> kind, I think.

Apart from the excesses of the spiritualists, he was also concerned at the activities of a young Russian of great social gifts and energy, Youssevitch, who had roped a variety of big-wigs (including the Czar) into an institute he had set up for studying psychical phenomena. Myers was worried that he was raising expectations far too high and that eventually these important figures would melt away and lapse into indifference (Myers 11/169: 2.9.1900).

Nevertheless, despite the fears of the subject being tainted by 'silly spiritualists', it was very important for the SPR to present their point of view

---

2   The medium Mrs Thompson (see below, p. 221)

given that the dominant trend in science was to naturalise 'strange' phenomena by medicalising them (Alvarado 1989a: 4–7), by localising individual functions in specific parts of the cortex and by stressing the pathological basis of abnormal phenomena. Unconscious muscular movements and unconscious cerebration were still seen as the explanations for so-called spiritualistic phenomena, and mediumship was linked to insanity and particularly to women undergoing the change of life or the onset of puberty. Hysteria was regarded as the underlying condition that produced the extreme behaviours, including physiological effects, that some attributed to supernormal powers. Myers, at the congresses and in his work on the subliminal consciousness, worked hard to dispel this pathological and morbid interpretation of the phenomena, but he was rowing against a stiff and powerful current. However, Richet in his tribute to him after Myers' death (*Journal* April 1901: 56) gave Myers a central role at the international congresses. He stated that Myers played a large part in ensuring their success and, 'he rescued telepathy, premonitions, thought-transference and kindred subjects from the scientific ostracism which had hitherto excluded them from discussion'. He achieved this, 'not by his audacity, but by his rigid adherence to logical principles and scientific methods'.

Richet's assessment of Myers' centrality may perhaps be unrealistic, but John Monroe (Monroe 2008: 200–201) has emphasised the variety of views and positions expressed at the 1900 congress (and of course in previous ones). In this rather mixed environment, before subject boundaries had hardened, Myers with his command of languages, and his conceptual quickness, could well have played a central and impressive role.

Myers and the Subliminal Consciousness

Myers was unable to present his greatest contribution to psychology – his concept of the subliminal consciousness – in any sustained detail to any of the congresses. He had not worked out the framework till the very substantial articles he published in the *Proceedings* between 1892 and 1895 (which was too late for the first two congresses). He was not present at the third, and in no position by the fourth to contribute in significant detail, for given his illness, what energy he had left was spent on his *Human Personality and Its Survival of Bodily Death*. The Eusapia Palladino investigations,[3] the Ballechin House affair,[4] had all taken their toll, and, apart from the intensive work with the medium Mrs Thompson, he considerably scaled down his investigations into mediumship and related phenomena.

It is worth expanding, in a little more detail, some of the adverse currents Myers had to contend with when developing his thesis about the subliminal. As Bourne Taylor (Bourne Taylor 2007: 13–30) has pointed out, there were trends in psychology which were inimical to him. On the pessimistic side, Nordau's *Degeneration* (published in English in 1895) identified a range of features in art and society which suggested a pathological mental and moral degeneration occuring in the human species. It seemed quite possible for evolution to take a negative turn and downward spiral. This ran quite counter to Myers' frequent asides on the evolutionary potential and ultimate destiny of humankind. From a different perspective, and in different ways, Henry Maudsley, building on the work of the redoubtable WB Carpenter, emphasized the importance of will, control and organisation, and rejected the idea of a richly creative and healing subconscious (though he believed imagination was a useful and productive force: Hearnshaw 1964, 29). According to him, the abnormal behaviours Myers identified as possible clues to artistic and spiritual growth and to healing were symptoms of poor training, unfortunate physical inheritance, and pathological injury. And although Myers stressed on many occasions the importance of a strict, exact, empirical, experimental, scientific approach (Myers 1885c: 1), his own writing sometimes soared too far from that disciplined base. In America, France, especially Germany, and to a limited extent in England, Myers' writings were not perceived generally, either in subject matter or sources of testable hypotheses, as contributing to the programs of experimental physio-psychological laboratories that were gradually being set up.

Aside from these formidable obstacles in the intellectual zeitgeist, Myers had considerable problems with terminology. He was trying to find a way to conceptualise thinking (mentation in the language of the time) that did not take place as part of normal, daily consciousness. He did not wish to use the terms unconscious or subconscious, because he believed that both words carried connotations about the nature of the phenomena. They seemed to suggest that the activity was only operative or in existence when caught in the light or the beam of normal conscious activity. Both he and William James rejected this view, arguing that the processes were continuous and vigorous, whether the conscious mind was aware of them or not. Therefore, the term he used, as a classicist, was

3 See below, p. 212.
4 See below, p. 232.

subliminal —from the word Latin word *limen* meaning threshold. This does not, *pace* Gauld, suggest a passage 'from outer darkness into a well-lit domain' (Gauld 1995: 393). It was meant to indicate relatively easy access from one centre of consciousness into others, from one area of activity into others, and not to carry implications of the torchlight theory of consciousness mentioned above. The word means going across the threshold (*limen*) but should not carry connotations of burrowing down-wards. It has variously been suggested that one sees it as a vertical divi-sion, from left to right, from outside to inside, rather than from higher to lower as, unfortunately, the word still might imply. The other misleading connotation of 'sub' was that it might suggest that the activites and pro-cesses were necessarily inferior and primitive. Myers was aware of this and towards the end of his life started to put forward terms like extra marginal or extra liminal to get round this (Kelly *et al.* 2007: 77–78). For the range of the subliminal, in his thesis, was immense, even awe inspiring. Once within, a whole range of activity would be taking place — the control of the automatic physiological processes of the body at the basic level, communi-cation between different layers of consciousness, highly creative and inspi-rational and problem solving activity, and supernormal processes of a telepathic or external spiritual nature. These activities were not rigidly stratified (even though he sometimes used a geological metaphor). They were miscible. They flowed into each other. They were permeable and the nature and type of the permeability both within and across the threshold varied from person to person depending on their make up.

He continually tried to get closer to the essence of the subliminal by employing one metaphorical device after another. In his glossaries of psy-chical research terms in the *Proceedings* in 1896 and in *Human Personality and its Survival of Bodily Death*, he made its wave-like qualities very explicit: '*Subliminal.* – Of thoughts, feelings, &c., lying beneath the ordi-nary *threshold* (*limen*) of consciousness ... The threshold (*Schwelle*) must be regarded as a level above which waves may rise, — like a slab washed by the sea,-rather than an entrance into a chamber' (Myers 1904 1: xxi). For some, the flow would be auditory, for others visual, or emotional, or expressed in physical movement, or a synaesthetic combination. The extent and nature of an individual's control over his or her subliminal would lead to them being characterised as normal, hysterical, creative, clairvoyant or whatever. For Myers it was part of the evolutionary chal-lenge to develop this huge area of psychological force for the benefit of humankind now and in the future. And one way for this to happen was to use the hypnotic stratum in the subliminal (that part of the subliminal that had the power to exercise a control over the physiology of the body that the waking self could not) to eliminate through suggestion and self-suggestion undesirable characteristics and cultivate positive ones; and even eventually develop supernormal powers of clairvoyance and thought-transference. The main methods for achieving this were through hypnosis, automatic writing and crystal vision. As Henri Ellenberger has pointed out, Myers predicted in the 1880s that hypnosis could be used to improve people through positive suggestion, to act as an anesthetic, and and that these original ideas have been taken up through Coué's auto-suggestion, painless childbirth techniques, and Johannes Schultz's autogenetics (Ellenberger 1994: 174).

Myers' second problem with terminology was in his definition of the self. For Myers, the self that emerged from his reading and experimentation was both unified and multiple. He believed that to meet the needs of daily life we constructed a self that had continuity, reason, character, temperament, consistency and stability. Yet under certain conditions, other personalities could form with a brief or a more sustained existence, and that these would have their own memories and thoughts and attributes. However, Myers asserted that there was a fundamental unity behind these shifting identities. He believed that this essential core was strongly indicated by the fact that in cases of multiple personality there was often one personality that seemed to be aware of all the other selves. Myers was encouraged in this thesis by the celebrated case of Léonie, already referred to.[5] The third personality 'inhabiting' Léonie was Léonore, who was the only one of the three who had knowledge of the other two and who seemed the calmest and most sensible of them all (Myers 1904 1: 322–26).

As Emily Kelly lucidly points out, Myers' views can be more easily and fully understood if one tries to standardise his terminology (Kelly *et al.* 2007: 83). This was something he was keen to do, but occasionally he slipped back into looser usage. It is important to keep the word Individuality and Self (upper case) for the fundamental individual unifying principle. The term subliminal self or selves should be used to describe those temporary or more durable *personae* that exist in the subliminal and the term subliminal consciousness should be applied when describing those conscious processes taking place outside ordinary consciousness. The subliminal is the place in which both the temporary personae and the fundamental Individuality have their being. The Individuality, or Subliminal Self, however, has part of its being outside terrene existence where, in a fashion never defined (who could!), it accesses, in certain circumstances, great gifts and talents. The more the full, rich potential of the Individuality streams across the threshold, the more evolved and developed the self in this life. Myers also uses the term personality to describe the self or

5   See above, pp. 153, 155.

selves, again contrasting it with the core individuality. An extra confusion emerges from the fact that he was not always consistent with his capitalisation; and to add even more to the muddle, the book was titled *Human Personality and Its Survival of Bodily Death*. Therefore, is one talking about the survival of the fundamental Individuality, or the terrene personality, or both? Kelly has argued that a change in the title of the book after Myers' death has compounded this confusion (Kelly *et al.* 2007: 96). The original intention appears to have been to publish the book under the title of *Human Personality in the Light of Recent Research*, which might well have attracted a wider, less spiritualistically flavoured readership.

Myers was eager to welcome fellow workers in the field of the unconscious and warmly acknowledged Freud as an ally (Myers 1893a: 14–15) because he believed that Breuer and Freud's work, from a clinical perspective, supported his view of hysteria. He further expanded this view in 1897 (Myers 1897b: 51–58, 69–70) and in *Human Personality and Its Survival of Bodily Death* (Myers 1904 1: 50–55). For Myers, Freud was a late entrant into a field that Myers, Gurney, and Janet, had already explored in some detail. Keeley (Keeley 2001: 767–91) has argued that Freud was concerned at being seen as a junior partner and grew determined to differentiate his position sharply from that of Myers. Freud, who became a corresponding member of the SPR in 1911, used an invitation to write an article for the SPR, to do just that. This was *A Note on the Unconscious in Psycho-Analysis* (*Proceedings* 1912–13: 312–18) In this article, he forcefully denied that Myers' subliminal was the same as his, Freud's, unconscious. It was merely the preconscious or foreconscious where some lightly latent ideas mingled with normal, everyday consciousness. Freud's unconscious was cut off from normal consciousness and specific techniques, requiring substantial training, were needed to access it. There was no easy permeable membrane or miscible strata. Jones, Freud's biographer, has given a laconic summary of this: 'According to psycho-analysis, the unconscious is a region of the mind, the content of which is characterised by the attribute of being repressed, conative, instinctive, infantile, unreasoning, and predominantly sexual' (Tyrrell 1946: 28). This grim definition bears little resemblance to Myers' essentially optimistic, even romantic subliminal realm. Through the key techniques of psycho-analysis (word association, dream analysis, the examination of verbal slips) the unconscious could, with great difficulty, be accessed. By using methods that were not associated (however unfairly) with late-nineteenth-century spiritualism and mesmerism, and by conceptualising his unconscious in a radically different form from Myers, Freud was putting in place the strategy that would eventually lead to the virtual disappearance (for some considerable time) of Myers from the mainstream historiography of the unconscious in the twentieth century.

As well as suffering from the avant garde, Myers was also attacked by the traditional medical establishment. His cheerful encouragement to the upper-middle-class members of the SPR to experiment with automatic writing was anathema to many doctors. In 1893 there was a spate of articles in the *British Medical Journal* criticising the practice (Shamdasani 1993: 105–106). As one contributor put it, 'Automatic writing, that is undirected ideomotor writing, is common enough in acute insanity. To recognize that such manifestations are seen to their fullest development in the insane, the epileptic, the sexually irritated, the neurasthenic generally is positive proof that they are morbid phenomena.' One of the contributors to the attack on automatic writing, Henry Rayner, went further, and identified the use of hypnotism as a parallel danger: 'On this ground [the reduction of mental phenomena to that akin to animal life] I have always opposed the extensive use of hypnotism, and now oppose the self-induced automatic habit ... The risk of mental deterioration by the frequent induction of states of incomplete consciousness, hypnotic or other, should be ... distinctly taught, and the habit for those of the neurotic diathesis labelled, "Dangerous—this way madness lies"' (Williams 1985: 234–41). Again,the dominant nineteenth-century paradigm reared its ugly head: that the collapse of sensory-motor control, the weakening or suspension of the will, signalled that automatic writing and related automatisms were morbid and pathological.

For Myers, the unconscious was not a mere repository of rubbish or the source of psychological disease. It contained gold. The subliminal had elements of the sublime. From the subliminal emerged the insights, the skills, the inspirations, that one associates with genius and the highest creative achievement. Though Myers may not have used all these specific examples, it is clear that Wordsworth, Coleridge, Shelley, Tennyson, Stevenson and others, all attributed aspects of the creative process to sources not necessarily under their conscious control. The original insight or phrase may have required some mundane and systematic re-styling or re-shaping, but the primitive impulse often came suddenly, unbidden, and sometimes with almost overwhelming emotion and force.

Myers also asserted that mystical insights and experiences came from the same subliminal source: the sense of wonder and of joyous insight into the nature of all things. Nor, for Myers, were these creative and mystical experiences unhealthy or pathological. On the contrary, they were the mark of the highest levels of development and of what mankind generally might become with appropriate reflection, insight and proper training. This applied to extraordinary skills demonstration just as much as to poetic insight. Myers studied a number of individuals with extraordinary powers of calculation and noted that for some of them the powers that manifested in childhood only lasted a number of years and then faded away. He speculatively concluded, along with Wordsworth, that they reflected pre-natal powers, and that, through the subliminal, one was getting in touch with that greater self that was both discarnate and incarnate at the same time.

Most of the sustained criticisms of the concept of Subliminal Self came after Myers' death, but a contemporary one by Arthur H Pierce in the *Proceedings* (Pierce & Podmore 1895–97: 317–32) raised all the old objections that Myers had been fighting so hard against since the early 1880s. Pierce bluntly stated that, 'All writers upon the subject of secondary consciousness seem utterly to forget the well known experiments upon frogs and pigeons that have been repeated time and time again in physiological laboratories. These animals when deprived of their hemispheres will swim or fly, as the case may be, will avoid obstacles, regain their normal position … Here we have acts of considerable complexity with nothing but the lower nervous centres to control them.' There need only be the appropriate stimuli since 'no act is spontaneous'. The secondary consciousnesses identified by Myers were nothing more than automatic habits, created by well-worn nervous pathways. This central doctrine should not be abandoned. Evidence from dreams did not indicate the operation of another self. It was only 'the normal consciousness working under peculiar conditions'.

This approach completely failed to recognise the full potential of Myers' concept and (as Podmore pointed out) that psychological complexities could not be properly explored, let alone explained, using just physiological language. It also failed to recognise our almost total ignorance as to the way physiological and psychological processes related to each other in detail. The most positive critic of Myers' theory was William James who clearly recognised its richness. James expressed these views in his memorial address after Myers' death in 1901. He argued that Myers' first achievement was to address the Subliminal at a time when 'official science practically refuses to attend to Subliminal phenomena' (James 1986: 198). His second was to expand the concept so that it contained both rubbish and gold dust. He further believed that some of the information in the Subliminal 'he could reasonably trace to departed human intelligence' (James 1986: 200). James, as a mere empirical psychologist, declined to comment on that or Myers' general evolutionary conception of the Subliminal, only stating that 'the latter is a hypothesis of first-rate philosophic importance'. Again, it is interesting that neither in the narrow sense relative to survival (outside the work of Gerald Balfour 1935 and

Tyrrell 1954) nor in the broader psychological field, can one find much evidence that James' hopes for Myers' ideas have been fulfilled and implemented. They certainly influenced James, however. Eugene Taylor has asserted that, 'Myers's formulations were, in fact, central to the development of James' psychology and philosophy in the 1890s, and they form the epistemological core of James's scientific activities in abnormal psychology and psychical research' (Taylor 1996: 78–81).

However, other critics were less appreciative. Particularly powerful was the argument of the philosopher GF Stout that Myers' hidden agenda was to find justification for his belief in the paranormal and the survival of the soul and that the various stages of his argument, and the evidence put forward, had been carefully crafted to this end (Stout 1903: 44–64). Stout further argued that multiple personality could be explained on the basis that it was difficult to coherently and automatically access our past experience. The fragmentary and inefficient way that we did this led to the impression of multiple personalities inhabiting the same body. Stout also asserted that by his theory Myers was trying to create a guardian angel out of the subliminal. But Myers himself did not make this claim. He was quite clear about the mixed ragbag of powers and purposes that there were in the subliminal and he did not have a fully worked out framework for it. His ideas were initial attempts to deal with intractable problems (aporia) which others could follow up on. As Gauld has pointed out, the detailed alignment and articulation of his broad theories to the mass of detail he marshalled in support of them, has not been carried through (Gauld 1995: 399–400).

The Subliminal and the Survival Question

This emphasis on the subliminal by Myers has puzzled many people, particularly those, past and present, whose main interest in him and in psychical research, has been the survival question. This is often the case, as we shall see later, when people come to read his posthumous book—*Human Personality and Its Survival of Bodily Death*—and find in it much more evidence of a range of psychological abnormalities than for the survival of death. Emily Cook [Kelly] has addressed this directly. She states that when she went to his original material to consider this question, she was surprised to find that Myers 'did not discuss the survival problem or survival research as frequently or as directly as I had thought he would' (Cook [Kelly] 1994: 41). Myers, in fact, decided that he would have to address wider issues, including the mind–body problem and human abnormal psychology, as well as the results of research into mediums, if he was to develop a satisfactory and persuasive theoretical framework to which others might give, at least, provisional assent or interest. Otherwise, his and the Society's work would be treated as just a better written and better evidenced set of Ghost Stories than those of the past.

Yet, as we shall see, this has meant that *Human Personality and Its Survival of Bodily Death*, his masterpiece, has seemed a little lop-sided — literally Hamlet without the ghost. On a number of occasions in print, Myers asserted that, for him, survival had been proved, or very nearly so. Yet (for confidential reasons) he did not provide all the evidence that was available to him; nor did he argue through in great detail, taking into account and answering in logical form, all the intellectual objections that have been put forward against this thesis. His assertions obviously reflected the tremendous impact of his private sessions with Piper and Thompson, where the discarnate Edmund Gurney and Annie Marshall apparently came through with sufficient verisimilitude to meet his standards of evidence. However, he was caught in a Victorian dilemma. One set of desires, the yearning for the immortal, spiritual universe, was opposed by another set, which was the wish for privacy and the hiding of any evidence that breached the unimpeachable façade of familial and moral behaviour. His need to prove and even preach survival was counterbalanced by his reticence over intimate evidence. After his death, his wife's determination to keep that evidence from public interrogation further inhibited a full assessment of the basis on which he believed in survival (see the final chapter on the Legacy of Myers).

Myers also believed that ultimately the survival question — and the full range of psychic activity — would be brought under an expanded and understandable paradigm, no matter how complex or difficult to erect (Myers 1894a: 422), and that one day, though not in his time, the psychological and physical conditions of their operation would be discovered. He believed ultimately in the unity, continuity and friendliness of the universe. It was friendly in that it was understandable and that it was designed for personal growth and evolution, though with great and continuing challenge for all. Tools existed to examine it, though those that he and others had developed needed considerable refinement. He pointed out how scientific instruments have revealed many key aspects of the physical universe that lay outside our normal perception; and just as the microscope and the spectroscope and the telescope had done this, so, too, automatic writing, hypnosis, crystal gazing etc, could do the same for the spiritual world. His assertions in this area were totally metaphor-based. Our conscious mental life was equivalent to the part of the electromagnetic spectrum that we could see. The infrared end referred to our primitive abilities and the ultra violet end to those we might yet attain through evolution. Each individual would be, to some extent, at a different position along that spectrum and this could well change through life. In an ideal world, humanity would move steadily towards the ultra violet end as lower level abilities became more automatic and internalised. Myers was fully aware that these ideas were speculative and hoped that they would provide lines of investigation for future researchers to explore. Probably the individual who has taken these ideas forward, in a broad sense, with most academic and practical vigour, has been Michael Murphy (Murphy 1992). But there has been remarkably little work expanding, refining, and testing Myers' specific framework since his own time, with the recent exception of *Irreducible Mind* (Kelly *et al.* 2007).

The Cosmic Myers

It is difficult enough to accept the above schema. But the cosmological elements that Myers links to his concept of the subliminal self are probably steps far too far for most readers. The Individuality, the Subliminal Self, the unifying and organising power lying beneath the range of personalities, has enormous potential and a cosmic destiny. He postulated its pre-existence in a Platonic sense as a possible explanation for the great talents that some people seemed to demonstrate at an incredibly early age: and following Plotinus (Lambert 1928), Myers asserted, in certain passages, that the soul, after death, progressed through a number of spheres where eventually, in a way which was a mystery to us, the soul united with the ultimate principle while still retaining its individuality. There was much in this which smacked of spiritualism but also much that was mystical. Myers did not dwell on the frankly materialistic heavens, or levels, that the spiritualists reported on, though he did accept the idea of progression and growth beyond the grave. He had little to say on re-incarnation — a concept which still divides the spiritualist communities.

Yet he was prepared to tackle the even more bizarre problems of retro- and pre-cognition, as part of his enquiry into the ultimate nature of man, and here, no doubt, very few professional psychologists or educated lay people then or now would follow him. However, he was courageously prepared to speculate and to throw out ideas and concepts about ultimate things which fleetingly puzzle people in general and permanently fascinate a tiny minority. Moreover, he was capable of synthesizing these speculations in diagrammatic form in the last of his articles on the subliminal consciousness. This laid out a range of cosmic progressions and relationships which many readers might find imaginatively highly challenging and even bewildering (Myers 1895d: 586). And it was this willingness to speculate, to collate and to classify, spanning both the spiritual and pure as well as the temporal and gross, which makes Myers vulnerable to the mockery of those whose sights are set on more modest and manageable targets.

He himself recognised this and was well aware of his isolation; that, as a man of very high gifts who wanted social and intellectual recognition, he was working in an area that many would dismiss and whose achievements very few would deign to recognise. As he stated in the preface to *Human Personality and Its Survival of Bodily Death*, he owed much to the huge support and intellectual comradeship that Sidgwick and Gurney gave him, since:

> The conditions under which this enquiry was undertaken were such as to emphasis the need of some intimate moral support. A recluse, perhaps, or an eccentric, — or a man living mainly with his intellectual inferiors, may find it easy to work steadily and confidently at a task which he knows that the bulk of educated men will ignore or despise. But this is more difficult for a man who feels manifold links with his kind, a man whose desire it is to live among minds equal or superior to his own (Myers 1904 1: viii).

So, he demonstrated huge courage and persistence and, no doubt much later than he would have predicted, much of his work has demonstrated its considerable relevance, despite his florescent and orotound prose, for those who study the current phenomena and literature of channelling (Klimo 1998: 132–33).

One can see this sense of both achievement and frustrated isolation most clearly in Myers' relationship with the Synthetic Society. Increasingly, towards the end of the 1890s, Myers began to feel that both theoretically and practically he had a better sense of the possible nature of the universe than materialistic scientists or narrow-minded clergymen. He had done the actual fieldwork. This could occasionally lead to controversial outbursts. The Synthetic Society, a debating and dining society, set up in 1896, was, to some extent, an imitation of the Metaphysical Society of the 1870s. The Synthetic was more disposed, however, to the transcendental than the previous society and there was a stronger clerical element in its membership. It discussed fundamental metaphysical issues over and after regular dinners. In general, its members behaved very courteously towards each other in discussing the great questions, so much so that one of the waiters at the dinners believed that the society was called the sympathetic society (Ward 1934: 368).

Myers, with a resurgence of his youthful arrogance, tended to assume that he and his co-workers in psychical research knew far more about the nature and reality of the spiritual world, than those who administered and preached the conventional banalities of the Christian church (Ward 1934: 363–67). There were mutterings amongst the membership about his his attitude and there were suggestions that he should tone things down a little. Ward wrote tactfully to him:

> I have had several letters from H. Sidgwick as to the coming Synthetic session. I fancy that if you made the paper you plan nominally on 'the new religious synthesis,' describing the religion you want, and incidentally making it seem that you consider the limitations of Christianity fatal to its being adequate or ultimate, your paper would quite fit in with the temper of the society. I fancy you will agree with this. A paper simply on 'the limitations of Christianity' would incidentally run into an irritating and apparently destructive tone. The Society being constituted as it is, I should fear it. But your sketch of what you consider a wider religion, including a civilly expressed indication of the limitations &c. as well as an indication of those elements in Christianity which you would retain and develop, would, it seems to me, be free from the special difficulty to which I refer. What do you say to this? (Ward VII 217/3/2 [b]: 27.12.1898).

Lodge, in fact, had raised the whole question of psychical research and its implications in a less vehement fashion than Myers, in his papers of May and June 1896 (Stein 1968: 49). And in a third paper in September 1897, he hoped that 'our common friend Myers' would add a paper to the debate (Stein 1968: 51). Myers did and argued that only science, not intuition and tradition, could unite mankind in its search for ultimate truth, and that the SPR had already discovered the way forward through its investigations into telepathy (Myers 1898a: 187–97). His second paper was a brief reply to a member's objection that mediums might have particular gifts but it did not necessarily follow that they had any moral insight or integrity (Myers 1898b: 212–16). It was in his third paper that he followed up Ward's tactful suggestions and produced, in florid prose, a visionary account of the future life and the evolution and destiny of mankind (Myers 1899a: 264–74). This was re-printed as the epilogue of *Human Personality and Its Survival of Bodily Death* in 1903 (Myers 1904 2: 284–92).

All his life this capacity to startle, this sense of something vehement and exotic at work on the margins, clung to him. This may have been the reason why he never attained the secure intellectual status of those, say, who were members of the Athenaeum (Collini 1991: 15-21) by special election. The Athenaeum was a London Club founded in 1824 for intellectuals, scholars and creative figures of particular distinction. In fact, an unre-

solved question mark hangs over this matter. His wife wrote him a gushing and admiring letter congratulating him on his gaining membership of
the Athenaeum by the ordinary method—no black balls (Myers 6/325:
n.d.). Yet there is no record of his membership of that organization
(Rockall A 2007: p.c.). One wonders, quite naturally, what happened? It
may be, bearing in mind Myers' huge efforts with the SPR and extensive
publications in the *Proceedings,* and his sense of his own worth, that he
thought election by the special method (rule 2) was his legitimate right,
and that he refused to accept the more conventional route to membership.
But this is pure speculation.

From a Photograph by A. Marshall, Arlington Street, Boston, Mass. 1900

10. Richard Hodgson

11. Charles Richet

12. Sir William Crookes

13. Sir William Barrett

14. Sir Oliver Lodge

15. William James

16. Leckhampton House

17. Mrs Piper

18. Frank Podmore

19. Ada Goodrich Freer
(Miss 'X')

20. Mrs Thompson

21. Miss Kate Wingfield

Chapter Six

Myers and the Great Mediums of the 1890s

The Advent of Mrs Piper

Myers' interest in both physical and mental mediumship began to revive as the memories of the 1870s receded into the distance. His approach was both direct and indirect. He made detailed, almost exhaustive studies of the documentary evidence available for the mediumship of Daniel Dunglas Home (this in conjunction with William Barrett) and of that for Stainton Moses. He did not have sittings with either of them (as far as can be ascertained) since Home was out of the country for long periods and Stainton Moses confined his sittings to a very tight circle of friends. He sent a copy of the latter study to his brother, Arthur, who wrote to his mother: 'Fred sends me a proof of his paper on Moses which is very interesting and brings me face to face again with the old problems of Spiritualism — it is very hard to believe the Spiritualistic hypothesis is all false, & very hard to believe it is true. I do not wonder it is causing the Henry Sidgwicks some searching of heart' (Myers 29/34: 27.11.n.y.).

The literary executors of Stainton Moses' estate (one of whom was Myers' close friend Massey) passed his unpublished manuscripts to Myers. Myers produced a very detailed analysis of these documents (Myers 1894-95) and interviewed the small number of individuals who had experienced the phenomena associated with Moses. On this basis, supplemented by the wider knowledge he had of Moses' character, reputation and achievements, he convinced himself of the supernatural nature of much of the phenomena. He was, however, cautious — as usual — about the quality of evidence concerning the identity of Moses' spirit communicators. A number of spirits like Charles Louis Napoleon Bonparte, the

American Abraham Florentine, and Thomas Wilson, Bishop of Sodor and Man, gave a certain amount of information appropriate to their personality and historical context. But as Myers pointed out, one had to have ruled out both the medium's unconscious knowledge of relevant character, and incident and the part played by telepathy and clairvoyance of the living, before one could realistically entertain the survival hypothesis (Myers 1894–95 11: 111–12).

He did not believe the physical phenomena associated with Moses were produced fraudulently. Although he had no personal experience of them, he argued that the character of Moses and his small band of intimate friends was such as to rule this out on moral grounds. The people who sat with him most frequently were Dr and Mrs Speer and, less often, Mr Percival, an Examiner in the Education Department (Myers 1894–95 9: 245–53). Myers does not explore in substantial detail, however, the possible role that both individual and group hysteria or self-deception might have played in the recounting and writing up of these experiences. Certainly, the reader of Myers' papers has a set of stark choices: if fraud is ruled out because of the moral stature of the individuals, the phenomena took place as recorded, or (and only Moses himself had shown the classic signs of dissociation) they were all deluded. If they were not deluded, what was the nature and origin of the phenomena?

Apart from spirit communicators trying to prove their survival, the two main classes of phenomena were sustained and detailed automatic writing by a band of 'high' and ancient spirits, and a whole bewildering extravaganza of physical phenomena. One can more comfortably and reassuringly find a psychological explanation for the former. As a spiritualist Moses often came into conflict with teachings that went against orthodox Christianity, and the messages that he received from 'Imperator', 'Rector', and the like were quite fluent criticisms of the narrowness of the traditional evangelical approach. It is perfectly feasible to argue that these communicators could well have been psychological constructs emerging from Moses' subconscious.

However, the presence of physical phenomena, supposedly witnessed by his friends, is — assuming their sanity and probity — much more difficult to comprehend. Tables were levitated, objects were brought to the séance room through solid walls, intense and glowing lights were observed, strong scents and perfumes were smelt (including some from Moses' head), and music was frequently heard (with no instruments in the room). This last, allegedly, was caused by Grocyn, a musician from the time of Erasmus. Myers was not only prepared to accept the genuineness of these phenomena, on account of the quality of Moses and his friends, he also — and must be one of the very few people ever to do so — tried to develop a theoretical framework to encompass them. Eventually, in *Human Personality and Its Survival of Bodily Death*, he sketched out a complete scheme suggesting the way in which the supraliminal, the subliminal and, finally, discarnate spirits impacted on earthly, physical life (Myers 1904 2: 505–54) . He argued that there was a reservoir of vital force in the metetherial world from which ectoplasm (a term coined by Richet, though Ochorowicz had invented a similar term, 'ectoplasy', also used by Myers) was formed; this led to the materialisation of human forms or limb-like protuberances that could move objects. The dematerialisation of objects, and their being 'apported' through space, was, he suggested, caused by changes at the molecular level, much in the way that 'Maxwell's demons' were said to operate: 'It became plain to me that Professor Clerk Maxwell's Sorting Demons had been already trained — if I may say so — to the very performances which I was now ascribing to spirit power' (Myers 1904 2: 531).

Myers also wrote a detailed account of Daniel Dunglas Home. Again, as with Moses, this was on the basis of the printed records he had available to him. He first visited Home's widow in Paris and checked that the letters of testimony on which she based her book *DD Home, His Life and Mission* were genuine. He (I have referenced Barrett, his nominal co-author, but it is quite clear that the bulk of the research and the writing up was by Myers) also addressed the question of fraud and found — as did Peter Lamont in his recent book on Home (Lamont 2005) — that there was a huge amount of unverifiable gossip, prejudice and hearsay used unfairly against Home. The classic, almost the canonical, example was that of Browning, who based his vicious treatment of Home in *Mr Sludge the Medium* on a 'third-hand, without written record, and at a distance of nearly thirty years' assertion that Home used phosphorous to produce spirit-lights' (Myers and Barrett 1889: 102). As Katherine Porter points out (Porter 1958: 47-50), Browning had his only sitting with Home on 25th July 1855 and took against him violently — as he had a tendency to do with certain people and ideas, using, one might add, superb powers of rhythmical invective against them. In addition to *Mr Sludge the Medium*, one immediately thinks of his sonnet on Fitzgerald's criticisms of Elizabeth Barrett Browning's verse: 'Spitting from lips once sanctified by hers.'

So Myers went behind the gossip and prejudice and asked logically: had Home been convicted of fraud? had he satisfied any properly trained observers under controlled conditions? and were the phenomena observed beyond the competence of the conjurer? The answer to the first was negative. To the second, Myers replied that Home had satisfied the trained man of science, Mr Crookes, that his phenomena were genuine. Though, he rightly pointed out, this needed to be confirmed by other 'savants'. On the third point, Myers asserted that there were a large number of cases where Home produced phenomena which were either the result of hallucination or 'supernormal fact' and which conjurers tended to dismiss *en bloc* rather than explain in detail how the illusion was accomplished (Myers and Barrett 1889: 106–107). Finally, (as with Stainton Moses) he addressed the question of proof that 'communications did actually proceed from the spirits professing to utter them'. He provided, from Madame Home's book, a list of thirty five cases. In his examination of them, he lamented the fact that proper records were not kept and that the sitters did not always appreciate the need to be specific and searching in their requests for evidence of identity from the 'spirits'. His conclusion was less positive than in the case of Stainton Moses. He did not witness the phenomena and could not pronounce them genuine. He would encourage continued investigation in such areas but they should be recorded much more systematically and in much greater detail. Finally, he stressed, as he often did, that such phenomena were to be seen not as miraculous, but as a yet unexplained part of the natural order of things (Myers and Barrett 1889: 116–17).

However, in addition to the opportunity to examine the documentary records of two spectacular physical mediums, Myers also had the chance for direct observation and investigation of a mental medium discovered by William James. Moreover, though taking some money for her services, she was not a fully fledged professional. This was Leonora Piper, the quiet, unprepossessing wife of a man who held a respectable position in a department store in Boston. Richard Hodgson, who in 1887 had been sent over to America with funding from Sidgwick and Myers to energise the young American branch of the SPR, was seen as the appropriate person to investigate her thoroughly and conclusively. Hodgson found the atmosphere in Boston more relaxed than in England and entered on his work with great enthusiasm. To his chagrin he found that in sittings with Mrs Piper information was provided about his Australian roots, which would have been extremely difficult for her to find out. Furthermore, the employment of private detectives to watch her and her family did not reveal that she had set up any system for gaining information about her sitters (Hodgson 1892: 6, Roy 1996: 52–54). Not all of Hodgson's sittings with her were very impressive, but some were, particularly when it was remembered that Hodgson had only been in America for a short period of time. His cousin Fred was named specifically, his skill at leapfrog accurately described and his manner of death clearly outlined: he had injured his spine during gymnastic exercises and died after a series of spasmodic convulsions (Inglis 1977: 372). It was therefore decided, both by Hodgson (after his initial reluctance at losing his best subject) and by James, to send her to England. It would be very useful to see how she might perform in an environment where she had no friends as possible sources of information and no knowledge of the mores, structures, and networks that might enable her to set up systems of enquiry. She, in effect, became a paid employee of the SPR, working almost exclusively for them, and thus avoiding the suspicions associated with the run of professional mediums. AT Baird, in his biography of Hodgson, stated that she received about £200 a year from the SPR (Baird 1949: 45), a reasonably substantial amount in the 1880s. However, the editors of James' *Essays on Psychical Research* asserted that Mrs Piper did a substantial number of additional sittings for which she charged fees, and so was perilously close to being a professional, in fact if not in spirit (James 1986: 395–96).

In *Human Personality and Its Survival of Bodily Death* Myers divided the development of Mrs Piper's mediumship into three stages (Myers 1904 2: 237–38). The first stage was that of control by 'Dr Phinuit' and communication mainly by voice from 1884 to 1891. 'Dr Phinuit' was a rather eccentric spirit of allegedly French origins, who was called a 'control' because he acted as a kind of gatekeeper. It was he who looked for the spirits of other people and communicated information from them to the sitter. The role was quite a common one in séances and appears to have been designed to help the unskilled spirit communicate and keep the mischievous and interfering one out. In this early stage Mrs Piper would often hold the hand of the sitter. This led, then and now (Brandon 1983: 211), to accusations of muscle-reading. That is, the medium could tell whether or not she was on the right track with her information by the tremors in the sitter's hand.

The second stage of her development, from 1892 to 1896, was largely under the control of the discarnate entity George Pelham (George Pellew) and the method of communication was mainly by automatic writing, though occasionally Phinuit would join in using the medium's voice. The third stage, from 1896 onward, was supervised by 'Imperator', 'Doctor'and 'Rector', the impressive communicators through Stainton Moses earlier in the century. They apparently transferred to Mrs Piper after Stainton Moses'death. Myers did not live to see the culmination of this stage. Nor did he have much direct involvement in the investigation and evaluation of Mrs Piper — the vast bulk of that work being undertaken initially by Lodge in England, following Hodgson's early investigations in America, then in much greater detail by Hodgson and James Hyslop back in the States. Myers' only sittings with Mrs Piper were in 1889–90 and on his visit to America in 1893. It was a matter of regret for Mrs Piper and her daughter Alta that there was no further opportunity for his sitting with her again before his death in 1901.

In her biography of her mother, Alta Piper described the very sympathetic way that Myers and Lodge looked after her and her family (Mrs
Piper refused to be parted from her children), both men being written
about rather fondly. There are revealing glimpses of the personal attributes of Myers (Piper 1929: 58). She said that one very happy personal
memory was

> that of Mr Myers playing 'bear' with us and his own three little chil-
> dren Sylvia, Leo, and Harold, in the nursery at Leckhampton House,
> when, on hands and knees and 'growling' ferociously amid shouts of
> laughter from us children, he crawled in and out among the nursery
> furniture until one by one he proved too quick for us and caught us
> all. And, again, his storming of our 'fort,' a grassy mound in the gar-
> den which we all struggled excitedly and valiantly but ineffectually to
> hold against him'.

On her arrival Mrs Piper was taken to Cambridge where the first three
sittings were held by Myers. Lodge wrote (he did not date the sittings but
they were clearly in late November):

> These sittings were held in order to gain familiarity with the phenom-
> ena and no full notes were taken. Various correct statements were
> made about members of Mr Myers' family: that he had a father in the
> spirit and a mother in the body; that he had two brothers, Ernest and
> Arthur, but no sisters; that his father was named Frederic and had
> been a clergyman; that his wife had a father, named Charles, in the
> spirit, and a brother, Charles in the body, and two sisters, Ella (real
> name Elsie) and Lollie (real name Dolly); that his mother had a sister
> Mary, or Marianne, and a brother John (Myers *et al.* 1890: 621).

It is noteable that Mrs Piper actually got Mrs Susan Myers' sister's name
almost right — it was actually Mary Anne. Though impressive, in terms of
strictest science none of the statements could have had the highest evidential value. They could have been researched in advance in America. The
information was, however, fairly precise and it would have taken Mrs
Piper, who did not seem to have had any interest in academic enquiry,
considerable digging to have got at these facts.

A second point worth commenting on is Lodge's almost throwaway
remark that no full notes had been taken. Myers had become increasingly
obsessive about detailed records and one wonders whether the lack of
detail in this case was to avoid the possible emergence of evidence relating to Annie Marshall. It is quite clear, as we have seen, that Eveleen knew
the story, but perhaps did not appreciate its continuing intensity and relevance for him. There was another sitting with Myers on 28th November,
at which Mr E (the initial used in the published report for Gurney) was
stated to be present, and there were fifth and sixth sittings with Myers on

the 24th and 25th January 1890. Of these Lodge stated blandly, 'In these sittings some private facts as to deceased friends were given as to which it was practically impossible that Mrs Piper could have acquired any information' (Myers *et al.* 1890: 645). We can only speculate as to what these were. In his diary (Myers 14/2) Myers has listed EG for the 24th January and a further entry on the 25th, EMS re EG. So there was obviously sufficient material worth discussing with Mrs Sidgwick. The same date has 'A good', which obviously referred to Annie Marshall. There is, in addition, a note on the session for the 23rd January that Evie was affected. This seems to have happened at a number of the séances in which she took part. The charitable interpretation is that she was upset and disturbed by the whole phenomenon of mediumship, and the uncharitable — in the light of the way she later behaved with another medium Mrs Thompson — that she was just plain jealous

Reading Myers' autobiographical fragment it is difficult to be precise, given the cautious attitude taken to private material, as to exactly what were the messages from Annie Marshall and Edmund Gurney and precisely at which sittings he received them. But convince him they did, 'that love has surmounted the sundering crisis, and has lived beyond the gulf of death' (Myers 1961: 40). He wrote that he was in despair late in 1887, that his doubts as to survival had reached their highest intensity (Myers 1961: 40–41) but, 'next year my belief in survival was clenched, I trust for ever, by the message which Edmund Gurney, as elsewhere recounted, sent to me from beyond the tomb'. Again, Annie Marshall died in 1876 and Myers stated: 'Twelve years after her departing a message came. It was repeated; I felt it sure.'

There did, indeed, seem to be some indication that a Gurney persona was trying to communicate. Lodge first published some of the evidence for this in 1890. He described a deceased male friend,

> whom I will call Mr ?, of whom I had handed in a letter. The speaker now called me 'Lodge' in his natural manner (a name which Phinuit himself never once used), and we had a long conversation, mainly non-evidential, but with a reference to some private matters which were said to be referred to as proof of identity and which are well adapted to the purpose. They were absolutely unknown to me, but have been verified through a common friend.

That friend was Myers who, as we have seen, referred briefly to this in his autobiography. That sitting was on 21st December. On Christmas Eve the Gurney persona appeared again and urged Lodge to continue with his work and gave an interesting character description of the rather dodgy Phinuit. In another sitting, he appeared briefly again and urged Lodge not to divulge the secrets of the 21st (Myers *et al.* 1890: 493, 516, 524, 552–53).

Twenty years later Lodge felt able to be more open (Lodge 1909a: 140–62). In his general review of trance mediumship he devoted a chapter to the Gurney control. He pointed out that at that stage Mrs Piper spoke the communications, rather than doing automatic writing, and that 'on the whole, it was rather a lifelike impersonation'. He also pointed out that both the matter and the manner could be coloured by the particular medium that the communicator came through. He further mentioned that at one session the Gurney persona referred to his book *The Power of Sound*. It is unlikely that Mrs Piper would have read, or even heard of, an academic treatise like that and she had never met Gurney, who died before she came to England.

It should be noted, however, that Myers' conviction sprang from the complete sittings he had with Mrs Piper and that initially he was, in fact, more cautious than Lodge. He wrote, 'I gather from your letters that you are satisfied that it really is the Departed who speak through this strange voice. I am not yet clear on that point' (SPR 35/1301: 21.12.1889). As a reminder of the range of sensibilities that might be offended, he pointed out in the following year: 'Most important not to say that Mrs P likes to sit on Sundays.' It would offend public opinion if it were to be known that people communed with spirits when they should be at church (SPR 35/1305: 30.6.1890). As well as the excitement of investigating a high quality medium, Myers was also gaining a new friend in Lodge. This was an unusual experience for a man who kept himself in cordial remoteness from the herd. He wrote to Lodge pointing out what pleasure it gave him that 'you are becoming interested in our joint work'; that he was now one of the small group, like Gurney and Sidgwick, who had joined with him on the task, 'which by the very constitution of my being I cannot choose but fulfil' (SPR 35/1301: 21.12.1889).

Myers described the precautions he took for the first sittings in Cambridge. He hired a servant for Mrs Piper who was totally ignorant of his family affairs. He chose his sitters largely by chance. He brought them in under false names and sometimes after the trance state had begun. And Lodge was a little more extreme than that. He engaged a new staff of servants, locked away the family Bible and other sources of family information including photographs, and, with Mrs Piper's permission, read virtually all her correspondence. He also searched her luggage for possible incriminating material and finally he hired a private detective to see if he could, through normal means, acquire the knowledge, in one particular case, that Mrs Piper appeared to have gained access to supernormally. He employed the ubiquitous GA Smith, who confessed that Mrs Piper had him beaten (Piper 1929: 55–56). Her performance led to the conversion of Lodge, who became Myers' great support in the 1890s after the death of Gurney and who almost single-handedly bore the brunt of popularising the survival message in the early twentieth century. He did this very courageously and without lapsing into the more obvious sentimentalities of spiritualism. Lodge had had an initial familiarisation sitting with Mrs Piper in Cambridge where—after initial vaguenesses—his Aunt Annie, who had been his main spur and driver in childhood, came through. He then, as we have seen, invited the medium to Liverpool under conditions generally of close control. Mrs Piper put him in apparent contact with his deceased uncle, Jerry, who provided him with very specific survival evidence—he identified a watch Lodge had brought with him and told a number of specific childhood anecdotes that were later verified as correct by his surviving brother Robert.

It is difficult to over-emphasize what Mrs Piper meant to the SPR. The most important initial factor was that she was prepared, calmly and quietly, to submit to their general control. As Myers stated:

> Mrs Piper while in England was twice at Cambridge, twice in London, and twice in Liverpool, at dates arranged by ourselves; her sitters (almost always introduced under false names) belonged to several quite different social groups, and were frequently unacquainted with each other. Her correspondence was addressed to my care, and I believe that almost every letter which she received was shown to one or other of us. When in London she stayed in lodgings which we selected; when in Liverpool, in Professor Lodge's house; and when at Cambridge, in Professor Sidgwick's or my own. No one of her hosts, or of her hosts' wives, detected any suspicious word or act (Myers *et al.* 1890: 439).

Yet Myers was very concerned that she was treated well. Myers was aware of the kind of physical tests that had been employed in America, and were to be employed in England, to make sure that Mrs Piper genuinely was in a trance condition and wrote to Lodge urging him to let Mrs Piper have a lady with her in order to reassure her if any medical tests were to take place in Liverpool (SPR 35/1299: 12.12.1889). James, in America, had tested her lips and tongue in trance and reported them insensible to pain. Hodgson had put a spoonful of salt in her mouth and also applied strong ammonia to the nostrils. She was pinched severely. A lighted match was placed against her forearm and James even made an incision in her wrist (the scar of which she bore for the rest of her life) while she was in the trance state (Piper 1929: 65–66). Lodge, himself, in Liverpool pushed a needle into her hand to test the depth of trance. Marina Warner is right to point out that differences in social and economic status allowed investigators controls over mediums that we would find highly distasteful today. However, this should not be pushed too far.

The investigation of physical mediumship in any period often requires quite invasive and potentially humiliating surveillance, regardless of the sex and background of the medium, and to call such investigations 'this psycho-sexual story, about unconscious gratifications' (Warner 2006: 304) is over-simplistic.

During these years, Myers often reflected on the difficulties, particularly the lack of public regard and esteem and the sense of isolation, associated with his enquiries. In the draft of his autobiography in 1891 (Myers 26/63/48–77), he commented on the loneliness of his life-time's quest; how few were his collaborators and how few of his friends had real sympathy with it. He put AJ Balfour, Watts, Tennyson, Ruskin, Gladstone as strongly supportive; Huxley, W Thomson, Clifford, George Eliot and GW Lewes, Spencer, Frederic Harrison, Morley amongst those strongly anti; some men of science like James, Richet, Rayleigh, Macalister, Liébeault as allies (and of course Lodge later); Crookes, Wallace, Stainton Moses, CC Massey, Lady Mount-Temple strongly pro because of their personal experiences; and other friends who would listen but were really rather indifferent to it all, like George Otto Trevelyan and JA Symonds. Yet one notices that even though he lamented the indifference or even contempt of some, he had at least contact with and access to them; he had the opportunity to debate; he was part of the general intellectual life of the times. And he went on to dig away at the reasons for the opposition. How for some any psychical enquiry, no matter what 'scientific' credentials it was wrapped in, appeared to challenge the integrity and validity of the Enlightenment. How for others, like George Eliot, a successful conclusion to Myers' quest would, as we have already seen, render 'worthless' everything she had spent her life teaching.

Therefore, Myers tended to be attracted to able men who shared his interests and had specialist knowledge he could use, and who could break his sense of intellectual isolation. The friendship with Lodge was no exception. Myers picked his brains frequently about the relationship, in terms of scientific laws, between the psychical and the physical worlds. He discussed with Lodge his metaphorical comparison[1] of the role the spectroscope played in the analysis of light with the role the psychoscopes of hypnosis/crystal gazing/automatic writing played in the analysis of the human personality (SPR 35/1353: 14.2.1893). He also consulted with him when writing his *Modern Poets and Cosmic Law* (Myers 1893: 166–210) as to what were the fundamental physical laws or — as he characteristically framed it — what were the fundamental cosmical laws? For his part he believed they were: uniformity of sequence (in other words causality

---

1   See above, p. 194.

and not caprice), conservation of energy and evolution. Thus far the scientific community would have agreed with him. However, when he boldly asserted that another fundamental law might well be the interpenetration of the universes — the psychical and the physical, a law now in the process of being proved by experimental psychology — he was leaving the vast majority of the scientific and the psychological community behind. He also spent some time discussing with Lodge what terms drawn from the real world might be helpful analogies in describing the weird, limb-like ectoplasmic manifestations in séances. Ectoplasm was the mysterious substance emanating from the medium's body from which materialised spirit forms were built up. Myers asked Lodge what he thought of the coinages 'pseudopodia' ' interstitial growth' (SPR 35/1408: n.d.). On another occasion he enquired, 'Do you not suppose that matter goes out of medium? I imagine force to go out also.' And he admitted, 'I am hampered by electrical ignorance & so don't feel sure whether all light attributes to electricity' (SPR 35/1418: 4.11.94). This was part of his attempt to understand inexplicable light effects at séances when all physical sources of light had been extinguished in the room.

Yet while things were going promisingly with Mrs Piper, there was always the fear that hoaxing and fraud might be the real cause of other potentially exciting phenomena. This was, of course, made the more difficult to detect if the hoaxer was 'one of us'. For example, Myers, excitedly let Lodge know (SPR 35/1310: 14.11.1890) that he and the Sidgwicks had been staying with a private gentleman, Mr D, who produced physical phenomena that were absolutely convincing and who was just not the sort who would cheat. Mr D and his wife were going to visit the Sidgwicks in Cambridge at their home, Hillside. Would Lodge like to come and see them? In a second letter Myers asked Lodge, if he could come, would he bring a weighing machine to see if the medium's weight increased during the production of the phenomena (SPR 35/1311: 17.11.1890).

However, Mr D was a fraud. Two ladies, who had attended the sessions, independently wrote to Mrs Sidgwick in 1891 that this was so (Gauld 1968: 222). Henry Sidgwick (Sidgwick 1894: 278) commented, at a later SPR meeting, on this experience as an example of the way in which people of good social and intellectual standing could perpetrate hoaxes for no other purpose than pleasure in their own cleverness and the enjoyment of exposing and relishing credulity in others. This incident, only accidentally revealed by the consciences of two ladies involved, demonstrated how right Myers and his colleagues had been to take every precaution against fraud with Mrs Piper, even though she came with the most glowing testimonies of personal honesty from James and Hodgson (Piper 1929: 28–41).

An Assessment of Mrs Piper's Mediumship

An examination of many of the other records in Lodge's account of the first set of English sittings reveals considerable variation in performance. Walter Leaf, in particular, felt that the sittings could be explained by thought-reading and that Phinuit was a creation of Mrs Piper's subconscious (Myers *et al.* 1890: 436–659). No one imputed deliberate cheating on Mrs Piper's part and Podmore, the arch-sceptic, agreed with this, and also that in certain cases, a supernormal faculty was involved (Podmore 1898–99: 50–78). Yet the SPR was divided as to the extent the spiritualistic hypothesis could be sustained in her case: Myers and Lodge (moving at different speeds) eventually went in the direction of that conclusion; but others were ambivalent, like James, or frankly sceptical like Leaf and Lang, the writer. It was left to Hodgson and James Hyslop, an American psychical researcher, late in the 1890s to build up the case for contact with the discarnate. Mrs Sidgwick, in a short paper in 1900 and in a massive, book-length document during the war (Sidgwick 1900–01: 16-38 and Sidgwick 1915: 1–657), was convinced that the situation was much more complex than the simple spiritualist hypothesis, and that the vast majority of the spirits who populated Mrs Piper's séances were fragments of her own personality. She admitted, however, that it was difficult to explain how the medium acquired certain pieces of unusual or intimate family material, and very late in her life, as we shall see, was prepared to accept a paranormal source for some of this information.[2]

What was particularly important for Myers, however, was firstly, that no physical phenomena were associated with Mrs Piper's trance states, and secondly, that she went into a complete trance. As he put it, 'her supraliminal self shows no traces of any supernormal faculty whatsoever' (Myers 1904 2: 237). She was, he increasingly came to believe, a new type of medium, an example of humankind's capacity to evolve spiritually. She was someone of normal personality and good health, who had the gift of communication, and who was not associated with the low-level physical manifestations created by immature personalities on both sides of the grave. He believed that eventually there would be more and more mediums of Mrs Piper's calibre, working in close co-operation with those who had passed on, to develop their gifts. He noted, as evidence supporting this, that the quality of her communications improved when she was con-

2　See below, p. 301.

trolled by George Pellew (who supplanted the shifty Phinuit); and also how her transitions in and out of trance became much smoother when the Imperator group provided general supervision. Myers was also pleased by the transition from the hand-holding and speech-trance of the early years to automatic writing by the medium with no physical contact with the sitter. This provided a written record that could be scrupulously analysed and re-analysed. It was additionally satisfying, in that it removed the charge of muscle reading, or Cumberlandism, which had dogged a number of the early sittings.

He was fully aware, of course, that this investigation of Mrs Piper, and the conclusions he drew from it and other sources, ran counter to the progressive and enlightened intellectual currents of the last two centuries. He was conscious that it appeared like a reversion to the beliefs of the Stone Age and that 'Such language, I know, again suggests the medicine-man's wigwam rather than the study of the white philosopher' (Myers 1904 2: 251). In his defence he argued that late-nineteenth-century concepts of the afterlife, whether Christian or Spiritualist, were hardly sophisticated or founded on substantial evidence, 'Yet can we feel sure that the process in our own minds which has (as we think) refined and spiritualised man's early conceptions of an unseen world has (sic) been based upon any observed facts?' These were difficult ideas which offended both Christians and Spiritualists. The former were challenged in their uneasy vagueness and the latter in their strangely mundane and materialistic vision of the after-life. In addition, the case of Mrs Piper, though exciting and impressive, had been led up to 'by all our previous experiences'. These supported the idea of survival, that there was a telepathic link between the spiritual and material worlds, and that the surviving spirit 'retains, at least in some measure, the memories and the loves of earth' (Myers 1904 2: 256). There was, of course, the problem of poor and absurd communications from the spirit world. But Myers had explanations for these: both controlling spirits (the gatekeepers) and the vast run of communicating spirits, were often inexpert and needed experience and training. In adddition, gifted mediums were rare, and rapport was necessary between sitter, medium, and discarnate entity. It should be noted, in this context, that from one perspective these statements provided a plausible rationale for the jumble of confused, irrelevant and sometimes precise material that the raw Piper records presented. The alternative interpretation, that the information actually came from skilful fishing, shrewd guess work and careful reading of the sitter's body language could also, to some extent, be substantiated from them.

Myers had further sittings with Mrs Piper in September 1893, after his attendance at the Chicago Psychical Congress. In his view, these sittings provided even more powerful evidence that the spirit of Annie Marshall had survived and wished to communicate with him. In one sitting 'Annie Marshall' was written out a number of times (Gauld 1968: 323). He reported his experiences to Lodge shortly before he returned to England: 'The third (trance) was the best I have ever seen — no Phinuit — but a control personal to myself — we have agreed to call "the Harvard Control", from the place where it appeared & because it is imperatively desirable to keep the identity private' (SPR 35/1372: 13.9.1893). He went on to state in the same letter that: 'I do not say that facts unknown to myself were given: — but facts unknown to Mrs Piper were re constituted and combined in a manner & an earnestness which in Hodgson and myself left little doubt — no doubt — that we were in the presence of an authentic utterance from a soul beyond the tomb.' These records have vanished but the sittings obviously impressed Myers and in his diary the period is underlined in red, as was his habit, when he experienced particularly outstanding events or emotions.

It should be noted that the quality of Mrs Piper's mediumship, and the reputation of Hodgson as an investigator, have both been attacked in recent years (Munves 1997: 138–54). James Munves has argued that Piper's trance condition gave her access to the kind of total memory control that hypnotised subjects sometimes demonstrate, and that this, plus Hodgson's occcasionally lax supervision, allowed her to create a plausible impersonation of the dead. And he strongly criticised the quality of evidence in the case of 'George Pelham' (really George Pellew, a writer with a distinguished English ancestry), which many have found (Roy 1996: 63–68) particularly convincing as evidence for post-mortem survival. David Fontana (Fontana 2005: 127–28) has equally vigorously contested Munves' position. However, Myers was, and would have remained, fairly relaxed about this controversy. He had had his personal experiences with Mrs Piper under conditions that satisfied him, and he fully accepted — even relished — debate over different explanations for the same phenomena. Moreover, he was as concerned to fit the evidence for survival into a general psychological framework of human skills, talents and behaviours, as he was to establish good individual cases of survival. Moreover, the Piper case, during Myers' lifetime, was largely an American affair. These were, essentially, the cumulative researches of Richard Hodgson (Hodgson 1898: 284-582) and his new colleague James Hyslop. Myers had huge affection and respect for Hodgson, but he had little time for Hyslop either personally or intellectually. As President of the SPR in 1900, Myers agreed to help finance Hyslop's enormous report on Mrs Piper as a separate volume of the *Proceedings*. But he found Hyslop, as he wrote to Barrett, 'a pig-headed prolix creature' (SPR 3/ A4/ 93: 18.7.1900).

The Physical Mediumship of Eusapia Palladino

Hodgson was helpful to Myers in the establishment of a favourable attitude towards post-mortem survival, based on detailed records of séances,
under controlled conditions, and with a wide variety of sitters. But they
came into conflict as a result of Myers' decision to plunge back into the
murky waters of physical mediumship. He responded positively, in 1894,
to an invitation from Richet to investigate the medium Eusapia Palladino
(see Alvarado 1983-84 regarding the spelling of her name) on Richet's
island off the coast of Hyères in the South of France. Myers had always
been more interested in physical phenomena than the diffident and
cautious Sidgwicks, and he had been greatly impressed by Richet, his
intelligence, clarity, enthusiasms and—by no means least—his aristocratic background.

Myers first knew of Richet through his writings on hypnosis as early as
the 1870s and then through Gurney's publicising his work on telepathy
and card-guessing in the *Proceedings* and *Phantasms of the Living* (Gurney
et al. 1886: 31-33). He met him in France in the mid-1880s as part of his
investigations into hypnosis and multiple personality, and Richet came to
stay with him in Cambridge in 1889, bringing the multiple Léonie with
him. Eveleen Myers took her photograph (Gauld 1996: 150). Richet and
Myers developed a firm friendship and, as we have seen, supported each
other strongly at the 1889 International Congress of Physiological Psychology. Myers had an open invitation to visit Richet at his country estate
in the South of France at Carqueiranne and appears to have been as much
taken with the feudal grandeur of the place as with the intelligence and
charm of his host. As he wrote to his wife, on one visit, 'Richet is a Lord
in this countryside & everyone is nice to us for his sake' (Myers 12/64:
30.1.n.y.).

Palladino had a long track record of being investigated by, and of mys-
tifying, researchers (Dingwall 1951: 178-87; Feilding 1963: 21-28). She
had an exotic background. She was born in the province of Bari in South-
ern Italy in 1854 and was orphaned at the age of twelve. She was sent to
Naples and was briefly adopted by a family who tried to civilise and educate her. She began to show signs of mediumistic abilities when the family
started experimenting with spiritualism. According to one account, a Mr
and Mrs Damiani, spiritualists from Clifton, Bristol, had attended a
séance at which John King (the ubiquitous spirit communicator we have

already encountered)[3] had stated that he intended to manifest through a new, powerful medium in Naples. The Damianis hastened to Naples and there met Eusapia and became her patrons and protectors. Thus supported, Eusapia became a professional medium for many years but did not really achieve European notoriety until she was investigated by a committee of distinguished scientists at Milan in 1892. These included Lombroso the criminologist and Richet himself. There were further detailed investigations with the Polish psychologist Ochorowicz at Warsaw in 1893 and early 1894.

On the basis of the evidence from these sittings Richet felt secure in asking Myers and Lodge to visit him to see the astonishing manifestations for themselves. They were to go to an island (Île Roubaud owned by Richet) just off the coast of Provence, where they could investigate Palladino under particularly tight conditions. Myers responded with energy and enthusiasm even though he was deep in the writing up of his major series of articles on the Subliminal Consciousness, performing his HMI work, and continuing (though less intensively than before) his sittings with domestic mediums. For example, shortly before they left for the South of France, he wrote to Lodge, 'I have a Training Coll exam at Cam July 4/5/6 – can probably not leave Cam till 6.10 pm July 6 Friday reaching Kings Cross 7.55' (SPR 35/1401: 21.6.1894), but he went on to say that would still leave time for a séance, possibly with Mrs Guppy, that evening! His drive, his brio, his delight in actual investigation, was still considerable and he keenly looked forward to the adventure in France. The story has been vividly told in Lodge's own words:

> On this island the life was rude and rough, but very enjoyable. There was only one house on the island, other than the cottage of the light-house keeper at a far corner. We had meals in the open air under a verandah, the dining-room being cleared and established as a séance-room ... Myers and I roamed the island in pyjamas-it was too hot for anything else – After we had had dinner we went into the living – or séance-room of the little house, and prepared for the sitting ... the occurrences were very memorable, and were my first experience of psycho-physical phenomena (Lodge 1931: 291–306).

Careful attention was taken to control both of Eusapia's hands, though Lodge was not absolutely certain that this was always the case. Ochorowicz had designed an electrical device which rang a bell if Eusapia took one or both feet off it. Sometimes one of the sitters would stand behind her and hold her head. Under these conditions the hand of John King occasionally materialised, 'a big, five-fingered, ill-formed thing it

3   See above, p. 88.

looked in the dusk'. There were also massive raps and bangs on the table, the curtains swelled and bulged though there was no wind, the door key was transported from the lock to the table, Eusapia moved an escritoire from a distance, a melon was brought to the table, and a music box (painted with luminous paint) was sent gently gliding round the circle where it landed on Myers' chest. Myers was also poked in the back by a materialised hand. Myers wrote in excitement to his wife: 'All so wonderful! Eusapia herself an intolerable bore — Can't ask her to stay — would bore you too much-shall try to have her in London lodgings in November' (Myers 9/242: 23.7.1894). However, he did later invite her to Cambridge and poor Mrs Myers had a very trying time.

Such was the profusion of the phenomena that the Sidgwicks were appealed to come and investigate also. They were reluctant to do so because of their past experiences and the trying hot journey ahead of them. But they gamely agreed. As Sidgwick told James Bryce, a fellow Cambridge academic, 'It will be rather a bore, and, I fear, tiring to my wife: but we both feel that it has to be done' (Add.Ms.c. 105/37: 8.8.1894). In the same letter he explained why it had to be done. He bluntly feared for the reputation of the SPR if its most central figures came forward as believers in spiritualistic physical phenomena. So they nobly went to Richet's chateau at Carqueiranne on the mainland, to which the island investigators and Eusapia had now transferred themselves. There the Sidgwicks encountered phenomena which they could not completely explain away and which puzzled them.

Myers was eager to get the report on Eusapia at Île Roubaud in the public domain as soon as possible and he urged Lodge to write it up and get it out. Given Lodge's workload, they had thought of asking for Podmore's assistance, but he was rejected as too carping (SPR 35/1421: 15.11.1894). However, both Hodgson and William James (sharing the Sidgwicks' fears) were alarmed at publication at this stage. Hodgson believed the Île Roubaud sitters had simply been deceived by various physical gimmicks. He even went so far as to have a heavy table made to show how with appropriate hidden devices he could levitate it (SPR 44/1/37). And he wired Lodge peremptorily, 'Don't publish Lodge Eusapia' (SPR 35/1425: 23.11.1894). James wrote in greater detail to Lodge, stressing the need for considerable caution and also advising against publication (Skrupskelis et al. 1999: 552–53). He admired the clarity of Lodge's report (which Hodgson had passed to him), but rightly argued that, regardless of its veracity, it would damage his reputation and that of the SPR, of which he, James, was currently president. Hodgson, with breezy certitude, gave Mrs Sidgwick his verdict on it all: 'Lodge's conviction I do not regard as of special value ... *Myers* (bless his dear soul!) *can* be as sceptical as anyone about some individual person or thing, but if he once gets his sympathies enlisted, — his evidence isn't worth 2 straws. This is part and parcel of his big, poetic divine genuine soul, & he can't help it!' (Gauld 1968: 233).

Myers, however, was unrepentant. He believed that he and Lodge could handle any criticism. He also trusted his own judgement, based on years of experience, that mediums could be both genuine and also cheat when the power left them. As he told Lodge on one occasion, 'I fear Mrs Mellon has cheated. No doubt. But I also still believe in her in bygone days' (SPR 35/1434: 25.12.1894). So, in spite of their advice and protests, Hodgson and James were not able to prevent publication of Lodge's report (Lodge 1894: 306-360) in November under the moderately tame title *Experience of Unusual Physical Phenomena Occurring in the Presence of an Entranced Person (Eusapia Paladino)*.

Hodgson confidently waded in with his criticisms in the April 1895 edition of the *Journal* (Hodgson 1895a: 36–55). In essence, he argued that the reports of the séances were not detailed enough to assure him that hand holding tricks and the use of straps, hooks and rods, were not employed to account for all the phenomena described. Myers (replying for himself and Lodge), Richet and Ochorowicz responded to these criticisms in the same edition of the *Journal* (Myers 1895f: 55–64). Myers pointed out that the investigators were long familiar with the hand holding tricks that Hodgson described and took adequate precautions and, furthermore, that a fraudulent explanation for some of the phenomena would have required Eusapia to have moved from her seat which she did not. He also stated that to assume that Myers would confuse Lodge's 'massive, cool, firm, and muscular hands' with 'the small, perspiring, quivering, sharp-nailed hand of the Neapolitan woman' was absurd. Myers also, modestly, outlined his own expertise:

> I knew all about these little hand-tricks twenty years ago, and I have shown them off to my friends until in the poet's words, — 'Until the thing almost became — A bore.'[4] I blush to add that, even before the SPR was founded, I had already 367 seances recorded in my notebook. If after all this practice I cannot yet be sure of holding my neighbour's hand, I had certainly better stop 'sitting,' — or at any rate take a back seat.

Lodge, from his scientific background, replied to Hodgson's point about insufficient detail and asserted that he had applied the same principles, in the case of the Palladino report, as he did when doing direct observational work in his laboratory and then writing it up. The amount of detail depended on the rarity of the event and opportunities for replication, and

4   Quoting from 'Changed' by Charles Stuart Calverly.

the statements he made were accurate summaries of more detailed visual observation.

In order to settle the affair once and for all Palladino was invited to stay at Myers' house in Cambridge in the summer of 1895. Eveleen Myers confessed her fears to a diary she briefly kept in the 1890s, 'I don't know what we will do with her—for weeks' (Myers 14/6). She thought of providing her with a bicycle and that she would get an Italian conversation book, since Eusapia could not read or write and had no English. Given the distinct mistrust Mrs Myers had for her, for female mediums generally, and the social, cultural and temperamental gaps between her and the Cambridge academics, it can be fairly said that Eusapia was to be investigated in extremely inhospitable circumstances. Yet they did try, in their civilised Cambridge way, to make her feel welcome. Mrs Myers instructed the children to be friendly to Eusapia and to let her cheat at games. She was allowed to cook her own Italian food in the kitchen. She was taken shopping at their expense and, as Gauld records, 'Professor Sidgwick even flirted with her (a fact not made available to the impious) and she was photographed wearing his academic robes'. Eric Dingwall, while clearly acknowledging the efforts to make her feel welcome and comfortable, also stressed that the gap was too wide to be bridged:

> Certainly, Eusapia must have been a somewhat trying guest in so distinguished a literary, philosophical and learned milieu as that in which the Sidgwicks and Mr. and Mrs. Myers moved. To speak plainly, Eusapia was vital, vulgar, amorous and a cheat ... (Dingwall 1951: 189–90).

As well as being accused of fraud, Palladino was also charged with great powers of sexual enchantment. Dingwall has rather a purple passage on her charms:

> the unashamed exhibition of her erotic needs: her tales of her invisible lover and her first child at the age of sixteen—all these features of her character were such that men were both impressed and attracted ... Indeed, it was suggested that her erotic spell was such that when controlled by two men during the séances they were rendered incapable of both criticism and judgement. The Queen had transformed her subjects into slaves.

Such rumours, no doubt, lie behind the spiteful remark of Alfred North Whitehead, when refusing to support an Apostle Society suggestion to debate the question of communicating with the dead, 'such matters are best left to Myers, or his paramour, Eusapia Palladino' (Deacon 1985: 47).

One very much doubts whether these alleged charms had any impact on the whiskery and chilly Sidgwick or the fastidious Myers. Myers tried to enlist as many informed people, especially scientists, as he could in the examination of the phenomena. He approached Sir William Ramsay, later Nobel Prize Winner for Chemistry, to come to a séance, but he declined, pointing out he couldn't desert his guests, and also that his uniform experiences with mediums was that whenever he attended a séance, the phenomena gave him the slip (Myers 3/145 and 3/146). He managed, however, to get two very distinguished scientists, JJ Thomson and Lord Rayleigh, to come to some sittings. The famous conjurors, the Maskelynes, father and son, also attended one.

A small number of informal sittings were held to help Eusapia to acclimatise, and these were very promising. Eveleen Myers wrote to Nora Sidgwick on 31st July 1895: 'We have just had a most striking sitting – in daylight sitting near the window' (SPR 44/1/42). And Myers informed Lodge a few days later, 'Phenomena last night on the whole better than island – but it was a quasi-private séance' (SPR 35/1451: 5.8.1895). It appeared that there had been raps and tilts of the large table and that a small table lifted over and over again. A systematic approach was adopted at the formal sessions, both in terms of controlling Eusapia and also in establishing an agreed record of events. The note taker's role was rotated and all the participants were asked to initial their agreement and to record any additional comments that they wished. Eusapia was searched after each session by Eveleen Myers and both her hands and her feet were controlled, often by Eveleen and her sister Dorothy,who crawled under the table to hold her feet. Young Leo Myers was present at at least one sitting (SPR 44/1).

Some interesting phenomena were noted, but once Hodgson arrived (he had been sent forty pounds to bring him across the Atlantic) things went rapidly down hill. He pretended to be a novice at investigation and encouraged a slack form of control which Eusapia took full advantage of, as he had always said that she would. For Hodgson her key trick was the way she would work her hands (and sometimes her feet) together in order to deceive people into thinking both limbs were still held when only one was, and he allowed her to do this time and again. This was enough for the other investigators and the verdict in the *Journal* later that year was that nothing but trickery had been at work (Sidgwick 1895: 148–59).

A rather unseemly and faintly comic row broke out between the SPR and the Maskelynes as to who could actually claim the credit for exposing Palladino. In the SPR records it in fact appears that Dorothy Stanley was the one who first spotted the fraud (Cassirer 1983: 54–55). Maskelyne had written to Lodge on the 8th August 1895 (Myers 3/21), stating that he could attend a séance and wanted to bring his son with him. He assured Lodge that they would approach 'the investigation with minds as far removed as possible from any taint of prejudice or bias'. After their single sitting he rejected an invitation to a further session since Palladino refused to submit to any satisfactory tests. He and his son believed that everything she did, all the effects, 'were produced simply by the medium's left hand, her feet and her mouth.' He was also scathing about her trance state: 'As to the "trance" we were convinced it was an unmitigated sham. Her dodge of turning the eyes up seemed to us, of itself, sufficient to stamp the thing as nonsense. Watch her carefully, and note the movement of the eye-balls when her eyes are closed.' However, they did not explain the precise detail of the trick in the way that Hodgson, building on what Lady Stanley had seen, was able to do. The rather grotesque drawings the Maskelynes left with Myers – showing a hugely elongated foot and leg producing fraudulent effects – only confirmed what the SPR already knew (Myers 3/19-22).

In a letter to Lodge in November 1895, Maskelyne stated that the SPR had ignored his contribution, and he defended the rather inflated account of his role in the exposure of Palladino that he had given to the press. He asserted that Lodge, as a distinguished academic, and the Cambridge group generally, could ignore public opinion. But for him, 'Public opinion is everything to me, and I am bound to keep myself right with the public at any costs.' That was why he had written his article in the paper, putting it in language that the public could understand, and giving himself appropriate credit! His statement was rather galling and patronising and totally ignored the fact that virtually all the investigators had pretty strong reservations about Palladino. As Lodge's biographer put it: 'Maskelyne understandably obtained much excellent publicity and gave the impression that he alone was responsible for the detection of the trickery' (Jolly 1975: 106). For this very reason the Cambridge investigators had ignored his original offer to pay all the expenses for bringing Palladino over to England, which would have put him in the driving seat (SPR 35/1237: 6.11.1895). Lodge did in fact do his best to clarify the situation for the public and wrote to the Liverpool Daily Post:

> The fact that Eusapia Palladino was detected in trickery at Cambridge has been emphasized in your article to-day under the mistaken impression that Mr Maskelyne performed the detection at his one and only sitting; whereas in reality the detection was performed by others at other sittings by observations to which Mr Maskelyne's visit happened to contribute nothing (SPR 44/1/47: 30.10.1895)

The Cambridge group should, of course, have expected such an outcome, given Maskelyne's history as a self-publicist.

Myers, as on other occasions, bowed yet again to the caution and wisdom of the Sidgwicks and the detailed knowledge of fraud that Hodgson had acquired. But he was not prepared to let the matter drop completely. In reply to a letter from Page Hopps in the *Journal* for November 1895 (Myers 1895g: 164), he made it clear that his agreement that the Cambridge sittings were largely fraudulent, applied to the Cambridge séances alone. By implication, he and Lodge had not changed their mind about the earlier sessions in France. Therefore, when in 1898 he was offered another opportunity to investigate Palladino in Paris he felt that he could not refuse, despite his reluctance to engage again with a medium who had been proved fraudulent. His conclusion was: 'The new phenomena were far more striking than even those of the Île Roubaud; I was convinced that they were genuine' (Myers 1899e: 35). He held to that belief for the rest of his life and Everard Feilding, a very experienced psychical researcher who later led a highly competent team to study Eusapia , also came to this conclusion. Interestingly, Feilding (whom Myers liked) wrote to Eveleen Myers near the conclusion of these investigations in 1908, 'I think she must have changed greatly from Cambridge days (from what I have read of them) ... it would be impossible to imagine anyone more amenable to experiment or control' (Myers 27/20: 11.12.1908). However, it should be pointed out that later investigations in the United States again demonstrated her ability to cheat blatantly when in certain moods and under certain conditions; and the Palladino controversy rumbles on discreetly to this day in the SPR *Journal* (Fontana 1998, Polidoro and Rinaldi 1998, Wiseman 1992, for example).

There has been some debate in the parapsychological literature as to the fairness and objectiveness of the examination of Palladino—over and above the obvious class and cultural prejudices that would get in the way. Manfred Cassirer wrote a paper, after examining the Palladino file at the SPR archive in Cambridge, in which he attempted to get to the root of this (Cassirer 1983: 52–58). He felt that Myers was pressured into accepting, against his better judgement, an old and partially discredited theory. He argued the attempt to keep a detailed record was only partially successful. The notes—from Alice Johnson and Myers and others—were variously over-detailed or confused or vague or indecipherable. This made it very difficult to reconstruct what had actually taken place. He also asserted that the atmosphere was inimical to Palladino, that the deliberate relaxation of control was unethical, and he further argued that some genuine paranormal phenomena went unacknowledged. He found Myers' change of mind particularly hard to grasp, in that the first impromptu session with the Myers had been so impressive, and that Myers himself knew all about the hand and feet substitution trick that Hodgson spotted and would have been on the alert for it right from the earliest sittings. Finally, Cassirer also suggested that Hodgson may have caused confusion by not telling the group before the séances he attended that he would pretend to be a novice and that he would not control her hand properly. Therefore, 'the sitters deceived not only the medium but each other'.

Myers' own words on the matter are interesting, though Cassirer does not quote them: 'I then felt, and I think reasonably, that in view of all this fraud, although still unable to disbelieve wholly in those earlier experiences, I could not ask other persons to take my recollections of the Île Roubaud séances as proving genuineness' (Myers 1899e: 35). One cannot help feeling that his own awareness of previous over enthusiasms and disappointments (Anna Eva Fay/Madam Blavatsky) rather dented his confidence in the face of the resolutely sceptical Sidgwicks and the indomitably self-assured Hodgson. Lodge and Richet, less emotionally dependent than Myers on the Cambridge group, gave not an inch. The plain fact was that Hodgson and the Sidgwicks, for slightly different reasons, had a particularly strong distaste for physical phenomena, and exotic manifestations à la Blavatsky; so while initially prepared to examine them, they did not necessarily do so with the neutral and calm methodology that was supposed to be the Society's forte. They probably saw themselves saving the optimistic and over enthusiastic Myers, yet again, from himself.

However, Stephen Braude has strongly argued for 'the reality of large scale PK' (physical paranormal phenomena) in some of Palladino's sittings, namely part of the Île Roubaud material and especially the 1908 Naples investigation by Feilding and his colleagues (Feilding 1963). Myers and Lodge may not have been as gullible as their colleagues thought them. Braude's detailed analysis of the record (Braude 1986: 108–41) contrasts with Warner's slightly cavalier account of the investigation of Palladino at Cambridge. It is, for example, very doubtful if the full range of supernormal phenomena was 'imitated and therefore exposed' (Warner 2006: 294–95). And it is almost as unlikely that Eleanor Sidgwick would have allowed desire to lead her understanding or shape her narratives in this field, as Warner implies.

The Mediumship of Mrs Thompson

It must have been with both relief and joy that Myers himself discovered an unpaid private medium, based in England, who was to mean as much to him as Mrs Piper, if not more. This was Mrs Thompson with whom he sat one hundred and fifty times. Records of these séances have not survived, but there are detailed accounts of Mrs Thompson's mediumship in the *Proceedings* of the SPR and we can glean from correspondence he had about her with Lodge and James a little of the impact she made on him.

As with many gifted sensitives, Mrs Thompson's strange experiences began in childhood and, as a young married woman, she sought advice about these from FW Thurstan, a Cambridge graduate and acquaintance of Myers. Thurstan ran a spiritualist group, the Delphic Circle, at Hertford Lodge, Battersea. In a letter to Myers, Sidgwick pointed out that Thurstan's circle might generate a sensitive who could be of use to the SPR but they needed to work with her/him in isolation and not as part of a group (Add. Ms.c. 100/173: June 1896). Myers kept a watching brief on the situation and eventually intervened, discouraging the production of physical phenomena by Mrs Thompson. In fact he actively encouraged her to work exclusively for the SPR as a mental medium from 1898 onwards. He stressed in his introduction to the SPR case studies on Mrs Thompson that she was not a paid medium, that her husband was a successful businessman and that both Thompsons wished her gift to be studied for the benefit of science. He further stated:

> Mrs Thompson, I would add, is an active, vigorous, practical person: interested in her household and her children, and in the ordinary amusements of young English ladies, as bicycling, the theatre. She is not of morbid, nor even of specially reflective or religious temperament. No one would think of her as the possessor of supernormal gifts (Lodge *et al.* 1901–1902: 69).

Several issues lay behind these apparently bland remarks. Firstly, he wished to completely distance her from the SPR's disappointing experiences with professional mediums where 'the trance may be simulated and the utterances fraudulent; the facts which they contain having been previously learnt or being acquired at the time by a "fishing" process'. Secondly, he wanted to stress her healthiness and normality. This was both to defend her against the criticisms of Ada Goodrich Freer (see next chapter) who, in her increasing isolation from the SPR, had attacked their practice of working with trance mediums. Myers also wished to put Mrs Thompson forward (like Mrs Piper) as an example of an evolutionary development that might later become of great benefit to humanity:

> I claim that this substitution of personality, or spirit control, or possession, or pneumaturgy, is a normal forward step in the evolution of our race. I claim that a spirit exists in man, and that it is healthy and desirable that this spirit should be thus capable of partial and temporary dissociation from the organism;—itself then enjoying an increased freedom and vision, and also thereby allowing some departed spirit to make use of the partially vacated organism for the

sake of communication with other spirits still incarnate on earth. I claim that much knowledge has already thus been acquired, while much more is likely to follow (Lodge *et al.* 1901–1902: 69).

Statements like this, however, made it increasingly difficult for him to distinguish himself from the conventional spiritualist position, but at this stage in his life there seemed little imperative to do so.

Myers became Mrs Thompson's mentor and in his home at Cambridge arranged sessions with a substantial number of sitters. There does not seem to have been much formality or control about the sittings or any elaborate methodology. This had the advantage of emphasizing the normality of the proceedings and the unsensational nature of her gift, but also the considerable disadvantage of leaving Mrs Thompson open to accusations of either deliberate or subliminal acquisition of information. This was an issue Mrs Myers was quick to raise after her husband's death, as did Richard Hodgson after his own sessions with Mrs Thompson. Hodgson, as ever, was supremely confident that his extensive experience with Mrs Piper qualified him to make sure judgements on other trance mediums, even where the type and nature of the trance was different from hers (Lodge *et al.* 1901–1902: 138–43).

Myers described the process as follows:

> The actual sittings are of the simplest type. I bring an anonymous stranger into a room where Mrs Thompson is, and we simply await her trance. I sometimes ask my anonymous friend to remain silent (if, for instance, his accent should give some clue to nationality) or else we talk together on trivial topics until Mrs Thompson's light trance supervenes, — with no external symptom except a closing of the eyes and certain slight differences in manner. It does not matter where the visitor sits, nor is any contact desired. There is no 'fishing' for information. I usually converse myself with the 'control'; and in some of the best sittings I have been as ignorant as Mrs Thompson herself of the family history, etc, of the sitter (Lodge *et al.* 1901–1902: 72).

The modern parapsychologist might 'twitch' a little on reading the phrase,'we talk together on trivial topics', given the potential, even the most apparently innocuous conversation has, for the skilled fraudulent medium.

The sittings with Mrs Thompson coincided with a significant down turn in Myers' health. He had always been susceptible to flu and colds. He had bad attacks in March 1898 and February 1899. This brought on Bright's disease which eventually damaged his heart and his arteries (Gauld 1968: 332). Towards the ends of both 1899 and 1900 he went south to the softer air of Provence in the hope of improving his health. On the former occasion he met up with the James family at Carqueiranne where

Richet offered hospitality for both families. The loyal and supportive Thompsons followed him there. At first all seemed well and William James commented that Myers appeared to advantage with his family, and that he read sections of *Human Personality and Its Survival of Bodily Death* to James each evening. However, the arrival of Mr and Mrs Thompson in February, and the resumption of sittings, eventually led to considerable tensions in the Myers family and with Mrs Thompson. Both Alice and William James described the affair in amused and slightly horrified detail, only wishing that Henry James had been there to turn it into fiction: 'Mrs Thompson *qua* medium is precious to Myers — as a guest and fellow mortal he cares nothing about her, while Mrs Myers treats her with absolute brutality alternating with the most false professions of friendship.' Myers, it appears tried to keep the peace: 'At last poor Myers panting and trembling ordered his wife to kiss Mrs T as she repented, and while the perfidious Mrs M fell on her neck and kissed her, Mr M kept murmuring "be nice to her, be nice to her!"' William James added: 'The medium is the only natural and wholesome party and there is more human nature in her than in most people I know' (Skrupskelis *et al.* 1994: 102–104).

It is difficult to imagine Mrs Myers' behaviour being prompted by sexual rivalry. Rosalie Thompson was young and personable, as James has testified, but Myers had no interest in her that sense, nor she in him, except in her admiration for his work. Once more, as with Mrs Piper, the séance contact with Annie Marshall suggests itself as the most likely source of her jealousy, made all the more frustratingly intense since she had no weapons to fight it with. Eveleen Myers was a wealthy, poised, attractive woman in early middle age, with considerable charm when she chose to exercise it, and great vitality. However, she had no psychic gifts, nor could she compete with the memory of a dead and still desired lover.

One wonders at the devotion, and at the motive, of Mrs Thompson, travelling across Europe to Provence, only to be treated, when she arrived, with contempt and disdain by Mrs Myers. In a letter to James in October 1899, Myers had an explanation for her willingness to give sittings to him and his friends:

> My first few sittings with Mrs Thompson were in no way remarkable
> ... But one day the little Nelly announced the approach of a spirit 'almost as bright as God', — brighter & higher, at any rate, than any spirit whom she had thus far seen. That spirit with great difficulty descended into possession of the sensitive's organism, — & spoke words which left no doubt of her identity (Skrupskelis *et al.* 2001: 66–67).

Myers went on to explain that the process was one of great spiritual joy for Mrs Thompson and she associated this joy with the communication between Myers and Annie Marshall, hence her willingness to sit for Myers' friends. This, interestingly, is almost the only insight we have into Mrs Thompson's motives. As the wife of a successful businessman there were no financial problems or pressures, and she seemed ready to drop everything to provide Myers with support in his time of declining health and to give a substantial number of sittings. This must have often inconvenienced her and her husband. Braid has suggested another motive — exhibitionism, the desire to be the centre of attention — which, of course, should always be considered in such situations (Braid 1949: 154).

Myers' confidence in Mrs Thompson's abilities did not rest solely on his personal experiences with her. The records of van Eeden's and Mrs Verrall's sittings with her in the *Proceedings* (Lodge *et al.* 1901–1902: 75–87, 164–83) demonstrate the level of performance that excited Myers' interest. Dr van Eeden had brought with him from Holland clothing belonging to a young man who had committed suicide. Mrs Thompson contacted the young man and provided veridical information about him and also spoke Dutch which apparently she did not know. (Later research has suggested that she may have known a little Dutch [Zorab 1976: 59]). Mrs Verrall had over twenty sittings with her and made a careful analysis of what she said. 238 specific statements were made. Mrs Verrall classified them as: 64 not identifiable; 33 false; 141 true. 51 of these true statements could not possibly have been discovered by the medium through research. Also, the Crackanthorpes — Myers' solicitor and his wife — had sittings with Mrs Thompson, and Mrs Crackanthorpe reported back to him that Mrs Thompson had given her, in trance, the specific names of relatives, which she had no normal means of knowing (Myers 2/14: 5.2.1899).

Richet, too, had an opportunity, when Mrs Thompson was at Carqueiranne, to observe her powers:

> Mrs Thompson gave me an excellent proof of lucidity. Myers had brought her to me for experiment. That evening my son Georges handed his watch to her, asking if she could say anything about it. She replied after some hesitation, 'Three generations mixed.' It would have been hard to say anything more descriptive, for the watch had been given by his grandfather, Felix Aubry, to his son George Aubry. After the death of the latter at the battle of Vendôme in 1870, M Felix Aubry had had the watch back, and on his death he had left it to my son Georges (Richet 1923: 157) .

However, Richet refused to accept what he called the spiritist hypothesis and explained her gifts as examples of cryptesthesia — a form of clairvoyance. One could also comment that this was the kind of gnomic remark that a fraudulent but intelligent medium might make, sensitive to Richet's background and France's recent history.

The main dissenting voice with regard to Mrs Thompson was Richard
Hodgson and he expressed his opinions in typically vigorous fashion
both to Myers and to James. Myers was not in the least upset by this,
admiring, as did James, Hodgson's very considerable strengths. It was
one of the great virtues of the core group running the SPR that they were
able to distance argument from personality and pride, and to encourage a
robust approach to the examination of evidence. Myers thought Hodgson
wrong about her (as indeed did Podmore) but he defended and approved
of Hodgson's boisterous opposition to him. Hodgson had six sittings with
Mrs Thompson in July and August 1900 at the SPR Rooms in 19,
Buckingham Street. Hodgson sat with Mrs Barker, who was anxious to
receive communications from her deceased husband. Mrs Barker had
brought with her a parcel containing private letters. At one stage Mrs
Barker and Hodgson left the room and after a short while Myers, who had
been with Mrs Thompson, left the room to call Mrs Barker in for the sitting. Both during Myers' absence and later when she was handling the letters in trance, Hodgson argued that she could have extracted information
which she then presented as spirit communication.

AT Baird, in his biography of Hodgson stated that Hodgson seemed
very hard and unsympathetic towards Mrs Thompson (Baird 1949: 155–61).
However, it is obvious that Myers had placed Mrs Thompson in a very
invidious position. He should not have left her alone with the letters and
more thought should have been given to the formal conduct of the session. Hodgson's attitude was probably also partly conditioned by the
nature of Mrs Thompson's trance. Whereas Mrs Piper's was deep and she
often appeared to be in a state of insensibility, Mrs Thompson's was very
light and she seemed to drift in and out of the two states so easily that,
were it not for the quality of much of the information provided, the
observer might suspect that she was putting on a show. And there was
one very important additional factor that Myers emphasized in his introduction to Mrs Thompson's trance phenomena:

> Most of the best messages, in fact, have been given to absolute strang-
> ers, while persons of whom much could easily have been learnt – as
> Sir W Crookes, Professor and Mrs Sidgwick, Dr Hodgson, etc – have
> obtained practically nothing. I can, however, perceive to some extent
> on what circumstances success depends. Success depends partly on
> the sensitivity of the sitter himself – when such sensitivity happens to
> meet Mrs Thompson's – in some way which we cannot explain. But
> success depends much more on the question whether there is any
> departed friend who is eager to communicate with the survivor, and
> who has also learnt the way in which to do so (Lodge *et al.* 1901–1902:
> 71).

Yet, in spite of the largely enthusiastic verdicts on Mrs Thompson, no mention of her mediumship occurred in *Human Personality and Its Survival of Bodily Death* when it was published in 1903. An anonoymous note in the *Journal* for 1903 (Piddington 1903–1904a: 74–76) stated that Myers had intended to include reference to her in the book but deferred this till he had dealt with Hodgson's objections to her in the *Proceedings*. He died before he could do so and had not in any way changed his favourable view of her mediumship. Piddington also added that Mrs Thompson ceased to give sittings after Myers' death, apart from a few sittings to Mrs Verrall and himself. She did so for reasons of an entirely private and personal nature and not because of unsympathetic treatment by representatives of the Society. To that statement Lodge, as President, added his personal tribute, stressing her remarkable power, her self-sacrifice, and that she worked without recompense or recognition. In fact, poor Mrs Thompson had become caught up in a rather bitter power struggle between Eveleen Myers and some members of the SPR, over the status, ownership and veracity of apparent post-mortem communications coming from 'Myers' through a number of mediums, and she very sensibly decided to bow out. This will be explored in some detail in the last chapter.

Chapter Seven

Myers, Haunted Houses and Miss Goodrich Freer

Myers, the SPR and Haunted Houses

For many people the SPR's activities seemed a little bizarre and esoteric. Crystal gazing, automatic writing, the Reichenbach force, the investigation of multiplex personality, seemed just too abstract to grasp. For much of the public Myers and the SPR were associated with spooks and the Society was often known as the Spookical Society. And it was spooks the public wanted them to investigate and tales of spooks the public wanted to be chilled and thrilled by. Indeed, sometimes Myers played up to this role in social gatherings and in the many lectures he gave over the years (Grant Duff 1930: 126). He frequently recounted, at the dinner table, his more exotic experiences; Lady Dorothy Nevill (a famous society hostess) gave an account of one such incident in her memoirs. He also often dined out on the famous Cheltenham Ghost, though this case was described in the literature as 'The Morton Ghost' (Myers 1904 2: 389–96). As the real location was in Cheltenham, Myers was conveniently able to examine it at first-hand and in detail.

Myers had first met Lady Dorothy Nevill at Lady Battersea's and she found him 'picturesque and striking' (Nevill 1906: 310–13). He told her the tale of the Handschuchsheim ghost (she had stayed there as a child, at the chateau, near Heidelberg). Hard by the chateau was an ancient building which the spirit of a gigantic mediaeval warrior was supposed to haunt. The intrepid Myers visited Handschuchsheim, and sat in candlelight the whole night through, waiting in vain for the appearance of the formidable apparition (Gauld 1968: 197). He had hoped Lodge would accompany him, arguing that he was the only man big enough to deal with the spectre. He had been encouraged to anticipate some manifestation since the father of the current owner had discovered an armoured skeleton on the site, a few years before. Dorothy Nevill herself claimed to have heard footsteps there, when she awoke in the night, and to have seen the building 'blazing with illumination in the dark', even though it was unoccupied.

The Cheltenham Ghost was less thrilling but, for the researcher, was probably better evidenced. The main investigator (who was also the main experient living in the house and who wrote under the pseudonym of 'Miss Morton') was a very self-possessed young woman, Rose Despard, who was training to be a doctor, and who recorded her experiences in a journal which she kept for a number of years, sending it regularly to a friend who lived in the North of England. She saw the ghost – 'a tall lady, dressed in black of a soft woollen material' – on a number of occasions, and even tried to impede its movement by stretching strings across the stairs at different heights. One of the unusual features of the case was the number of individuals who saw the phantom – into double figures – and Myers was unable to find any significant discrepancy between the testimonies he had gathered.

This case was particularly significant for three reasons. Firstly, because it occurred in Cheltenham on Myers' home turf. He knew the layout of the area intimately and he was able to interview the local witnesses in some detail. Secondly, his active involvement started in May 1886 (Collins 1948: 30–31) and he remained in touch with the family for a number of years. The depth of his engagement and the quality of the evidence had a profound effect on his views concerning the reality, nature and interpretation of such phenomena. Thirdly, because a long running controversy between rival 'ghost hunters' over this case, has highlighted some of the social and psychological factors (perhaps minimised by the early investigators) which might create an atmosphere in which phantasms could be psychologically manufactured (Underwood 1988: 170–71, Mackenzie 1988: 25–32).

In the public eye, such investigations were seen to be an important part of the SPR's function – such 'ghost stories' were lapped up – and the Society appealed at regular intervals for interesting cases. However, the investigation of such matters was fraught with difficulties. There could be wide differences of opinion between sceptics and believers and there could also be real problems in terms of gaining access to properties to investigate. Many house owners – both large and small – were reluctant to acknowledge the possibility of such phenomena let alone countenance a full-blown mission by the SPR. The effect on the property's value could be considerable and make it difficult either to sell or to let. Also, there was the ever present danger of the Society's being set up or hoaxed and sustaining a level of ridicule that would permanently damage its reputation and usefulness. Such was the case in the summer of 1897 when a haunted house investigation blew up into a full-scale scandal, which was chewed over in great and loving detail in *The Times*. The house in question was Ballechin House, suitably and gothicly remote in Perthshire, whither, early in 1897, journeyed a motley crew of investigators—led by Ada Goodrich Freer and well funded by Lord Bute—in the pursuit of ghostly phenomena.

The Arrival of Ada Goodrich Freer

The leader of the expedition, Miss Goodrich Freer, was at least as interesting as any of the phenomena she investigated. It is quite clear from Trevor Hall and JL Campbell's research that Ada Goodrich Freer disguised her origins[1] and presented herself to the SPR as a woman of cultured and upper-middle class background (Campbell and Hall 1968: 95–125). The first record of her link with any member of the SPR is a diary entry of Myers for the 5th January 1888 (Myers 14/2). There is no evidence that he knew her before 1888 or that he had been subsidising her as his mistress, as Hall implied (Hall 1980b: 35). It is more than likely that she brought herself to the Society's attention, possibly by direct letter or even by discrete advert in the pages of *Light*, as she did later in the pages of *Borderland*. He first became interested in her particularly because of her abilities with regard to crystal-gazing (Miss X 1889: 486–521), and her detailed knowledge of its history, based on her researches at the British Museum. She was no fool. She was intelligent, had a capacity for hard work, may well have had some psychic gifts, had a charm which worked effectively on many men (less so on women as will appear later), and she was a clear and effective communicator.

Myers was quite open in bringing her home to Leckhampton House, introducing her to the Sidgwicks, and even taking her to stay with his mother. In fact she wrote to Stead's biographer that her paper on crystal gazing, 'was written not at home but when upon a visit to Mrs. Frederic Myers'(Harper 1914: 63). She appeared regularly in his one line diary entries from 1888 onward and seemed to be a refreshing change from the rather squalid professional mediums he had encountered before. She was almost prissy in her attention to the proprieties (she wrote under the pseudonym of 'Miss X') and, as we have seen, she created a pseudo-upper-middle class upbringing sufficiently precise to assure the SPR that she

---

1   Which may partly account for the variations on her name, reflected in this book.

was of their ilk and yet vague enough not to be tracked down and exposed as a social imposter. However, right from the start Myers spotted the fieriness and the desire to be always right in her character. Eveleen Myers wrote vividly to Dorothy about her visit:

> Did Fred tell you about Miss Freer she is without exception the most remarkable and <u>astounding</u> girl I ever met. — she is about 25 [she was in fact over thirty] pretty rather small-She plays <u>divinely</u>, She lectures on any given subject in public. — on Medicine, on Architecture, on (Sanatory) house arrangements on Music. — She knows everything <u>and</u> <u>about</u> everything. It becomes rather <u>fatiguing</u> at last one can tell her <u>nothing!</u> She is wonderful, Fred passed the Tennis Court at last and thought here is something about which she can't instruct us but alas, she said My farther built a Tenis Court Many are the games I have <u>Marked</u> for this is one of the most difficult things to do (D/DT 2585/2: Jan/Feb 1888).

Hall (Hall 1980b: 18) suggested that Myers might have been financially supporting her (to some extent) during these years till she went to work for WT Stead in 1891. That was certainly a possibility. He contributed generously to psychical research investigations. However, as the above quotation shows, he was far from being infatuated by her.

She was much in favour in the early years and impressed Myers with her gifts, since several of his diary entries are underlined in red after their encounters. The most personal one was described in his draft autobiography, 'It was twilight. She looked up towards me, & over my head she saw the gaze of deep blue eyes' (Myers 26/63). Annie Marshall's eyes were blue. She later saw the same eyes in a crystal ball, but as Myers had, by then, revealed the story to her, this could not be seen as evidential. Sidgwick also recorded in his journal that she told Myers — and had shown him the relevant diary entry — of her sense, the weekend of Gurney's death, that Myers was suffering some kind of personal blow. This was several days before she actually heard of the death (Broad 1965: D1/17/322). She was vigorous and intelligent and seemed to have the capacity to initiate and organise investigations — qualities that were much required given Hodgson's absence in America, the loss of Gurney, and the other pressures on Myers and the Sidgwicks. She also had, for a psychic, an unusually detached capacity to describe, analyse and evaluate her experiences.

In these years their relationship was — allowing for her occasional temperamental outbursts — reasonably good. One such eruption occurred when staying with Mrs Susan Myers, and it is quite clear that Myers, her blue grey eyes not withstanding, was not infatuated with her:

AGF had said nothing to my mother. I told her — & she thoroughly & entirely took our view — of course. She pities AGF for having that huffy temper! She will not mention it to anyone — AGF was, I am certain, half ashamed of herself — I altogether <u>dominated the situation</u> when I talked to her! It was Miss <u>Moore</u> who egged her on — she is like a lioness with her cub! Devoted to AGF (Myers 9/62: 12.9.1892).

At this distance from the event, both Myers' self-importance and AGF's 'huffiness' seem rather comic.

Myers was always keen to expand the number of intelligent and committed workers in the field of psychical research and he promoted her career strongly. Myers proposed her to Lord Bute as a valuable support for a SPR enquiry into Second Sight in the Highlands, which Bute was subsidising, and which was faltering. (Myers, in fact, had assiduously courted Bute's financial assistance and had written him a number of flattering, almost fawning, letters. These continued through the 1890s until they fell out over the Ballechin affair [Hall 1980b: 58–59].) She was to work with the Reverend Peter Dewar who had already started the research. She, however, managed rapidly to sideline him and took over the whole enterprise. Bute, in total, financed three tours of the Highlands for Miss Goodrich Freer and her companion, Miss Moore (1894/1896/ 1898), but with little tangible result. She had the energy and drive to conduct a vigorous investigation in the Highlands, but a number of things were against her. In spite of what she later asserted, the local community clammed up (Hunter Blair 1921). She did not speak the language and had little real rapport with the people of the area, in spite of her claim to a distinguished Scottish ancestry. Much that she sent back was cribbed from the work of an honest and straightforward priest, Father Allan McDonald. There were brief interim reports in the *Journal* by her, but nothing of substance. Nothing remotely reaching the quality of *Phantasms of the Living* or the *Census on Hallucinations*, was ever produced (Campbell and Hall 1968: 35–92).

Few alarm bells seem to have sounded in SPR circles concerning either her behaviour or her lack of results. They found her work on crystal gazing, both practical and theoretical, impressive, and Myers frequently cited her 'experiments' as evidence of the subliminal consciousness and as examples of ways in which one could effectively explore the hidden depths of human personality. However, her behaviour, with regard to Lady Burton, could well have given them pause for thought. It appeared that Miss Goodrich Freer had, through automatic writing when 'staying at their country house with Mr and Mrs D', received messages from the late and infamous African explorer, Sir Richard Burton, who asked her to tell his widow that he had communicated from the beyond. She met Lady

Burton in August 1895 where, again, the late Sir Richard, came through, and advised his wife to employ a capable secretary. This would appear to have been a job tailor-made for Miss Goodrich Freer! Unfortunately for her, Lady Burton died early in 1896, but Miss Goodrich Freer was able to turn the experience into good journalistic copy and published it in *Borderland* (Hall 1980b: 52–57). The Burton affair, to an outsider, must have appeared particularly distasteful. It looked as if she was using her gifts to exploit a very ill and confused widow for possible personal gain; and certainly as copy for her paper. Intervention by the family, who threatened legal action, prevented further publication of the details.

The Investigation of Ballechin House

On her death bed in January 1931, in New York, Ada Goodrich Freer (now Mrs Spoer) made arrangements concerning her copy of *The Alleged Haunting of B − House*. It eventually went to the British Museum and, as annotated by her, was a useful key to the names hidden behind the initials in the book (Hall 1980b: 72–73). She was keen to get her view of what happened at Ballechin House straight before she died. These events led to a breach with Myers and a cooling of relationships with the SPR, which had responded to much of her early work with particular admiration. In fact, no-one emerged from the affair with their reputation enhanced, and Ada Goodrich Freer, in spite of certain mistakes springing from temperament and conceit, had some claims to feeling betrayed by Myers and the SPR, as they scuttled for cover in the public storm that broke out over the investigation.

Ballechin House in Perthshire had a reputation for being haunted. It was built in 1806 but no longer exists having been demolished in 1963. According to Miss Goodrich Freer, the major manifestations took place after the deaths of the owner, Major Robert Steuart, and three years later of his young housekeeper Sarah Nicholson, with whom it was rumoured he was having a liaison. Major Steuart loved dogs and he stated (allegedly) that he would haunt Ballechin after death in the guise of one of his dogs. A priest, Fr Hayden, visiting Lord Bute in 1892, told him of his weird experiences at Ballechin and also those of a governess who had worked there some years before. Bute, who it will be remembered had funded the Second Sight Inquiry of 1894, was extremely interested — particularly as in 1896 the family which had rented Ballechin House left the let two months early because of their experiences (real or imaginary). Some members of the family heard loud knockings, and the sound of quarrelling and footsteps. The father wrote later to *The Times* (14.6.1897) denying for his part the existence of ghosts, but stoutly defending the honesty of his family and denying equally that there had been any silly horse play or hoaxing. Bute let Myers know that he was prepared to foot the bill for an investigation and, with Myers' support and Bute's finance, Colonel Taylor, a spiritualist and member of the SPR, together with Miss Freer and her companion Miss Moore, were ensconced in the house. There was to be no shortage of visitors over the next three months, since Bute's generosity had ensured that the house had a full establishment of servants and that all running expenses were covered. There is some hint in the literature that the motives for visiting were mixed — ranging from desire for a ghost hunting lark in a congenial environment, to credulous and excited anticipation of supernatural goings-on, and, for a distinct minority, to sober interest in psychical research (Hall 1980b: 72–73).

The increasing celebrity of Miss X and her connection with Stead's rather sensationalist occult magazine *Borderland* — plus the exotic quest and the sheer numbers of those invited — meant that, realistically, it was totally impossible that the investigation and the experiences of the investigators could be kept secret. A substantial part of the house was Victorian, light and airy, with solid walls encased in wood and with modern plumbing, but it was based on an older property on the site. The investigators were lodged very comfortably, so in one sense the investigation became a giant country house party in which the regular meetings at breakfasts and the sharing of tall tales and outlandish experiences became part of the social entertainment. It was as if the ghost hunting had become just another late-Victorian leisure pursuit like hunting, shooting, fishing, eating, drinking, charades, and cards. People went mountain-climbing and at least one guest turned up drunk. Ada Goodrich Freer clearly enjoyed playing the hostess and shifting her guests from haunted room to haunted room (Bute and Goodrich Freer 1900: 97, 105, and *passim*). She was in control and she relished it. Therefore, there was much discussion of the noises and endless chasings around the house to determine their source. There was the sense of an atmosphere of evil. There was the phantasm of a nun. There were the names Marget and Ishbel traced by the ouija board in the evening. Above all there was the collective hysteria generated by a section of the visitors (Hall 1980b: 72–90).

In such an atmosphere it was surprising that so little effort was taken to eliminate possible sources of the noise. Bute was particularly keen to get scientists to investigate, writing to Lodge that 'the phenomena have been practically continuous' since the beginning of February (SPR 35/279: 17.3.1897). Lodge, after he had stayed a while, thought the noises momentary and infrequent and therefore difficult to observe continuously and get to the bottom of. It should have been possible to record the noises using a phonograph, but there appears to have been a ban on this by the owner of the property; and when it was decided to explore the use of a seismograph, that too was blocked (Bute and Goodrich Freer 1900: 215). One of the guests — later to write a critical article in *The Times* — thought the noises were easily explained by servant movements and the clanking and cooling of pipes. In addition, because of the way it was built, the house was a complete sounding board magnifying the smallest noise (Hall 1980b: 93).

Myers himself visited for a few days in April and some account of his reactions survive in letters to his wife and to Lord Bute. To the former he described, with boyish enthusiasm, his searching for phenomena, and his chargings around the house (Myers 10/72: 21.4.1897). To the latter he provided a detailed account of the things that others said had occurred, that there were phenomena definitely worth examining, and that he, himself, had at last heard the noises (see below) — a point and position he was later partially to retract (Myers 11/91: 21.4.1897). Apart from the noises, most other phenomena seem to have been seen or heard by Miss Freer alone (though there was the testimony of previous occupants) and a number of the visitors obviously had over-heated imaginations. However, all this could have been argued through, without presupposition or prejudice, in the *Proceedings* of the SPR at a later date, had not the whole matter reached the letters page of *The Times*.

On Tuesday 8th June 1897 the storm broke. 'On the Trail of a Ghost: from a correspondent' was published in *The Times* and was a withering attack on the investigation and particularly on the Society for Psychical Research: 'Seen at all close the methods of the Society for Psychical Research are extremely repulsive. What it calls evidence is unsifted gossip, always reckless and malignant; what it calls discrimination is too often the selection from gossip, all worthless, of those portions which fit best into the theory it happens to be advocating.' Letters followed fast, furious, indignant. Miss Freer wrote, as Miss X, to state that visitors were told to keep their experiences confidential and that the letter was a betrayal of confidence and hospitality (*Times*: 9.6.1897). There can be little doubt that Miss X, somewhat puffed with self-importance, had revealed to a number of people her role in a new major investigation by the Society. Though it was not an official Society initiative, and though it was funded by Bute, nevertheless most people would not have troubled with the theological niceties as to the precise position.

Sir James Crichton-Browne wrote contradicting her assertion — no such stipulation relating to confidentiality had been made, at least not to him (*Times*: 12.6.1897). The then owners of the house, Captain and Mrs Steuart, waded in criticising the deception involved in renting the property and were, no doubt, concerned about the impact on the value of the house and difficulties involved in future lettings (*Times:* 14.6.1897, 18.6.1897). They were supported in this by Lord Onslow (quite a grandee, who shortly after this hosted a major reception for important Imperial visitors at Clandon) who described the effect of an earlier investigation by Miss Freer on his property Clandon, in Surrey (*Times:* 19.6.1897). Myers then replied stating that the Clandon Ghost had been spoken of before any SPR investigation and that the SPR had not thought it worth publishing anything on it (*Times:* 22.6.1897). The result of all this was that the senior figures in the SPR closed ranks. A letter from Sidgwick appeared in *The Times* stating that Myers and the SPR Council had decided that there was nothing about Ballechin worth publishing and in the *Journal* there appeared the following statement in July regarding Ballechin House:

> It has been brought to the notice of the Council that, in spite of a disclaimer by the Honorary Secretary in *The Times*, (June 22nd), there is still an impression in certain quarters that the Society is responsible for the hiring of Ballechin House, with a view to the investigation of phenomena alleged to occur there. The Council therefore desire to make it known to all readers of the *Journal* that this impression is altogether erroneous. The question of hiring Ballechin House was never brought before the Council in any form whatever, and they are entirely without responsibility with regard to it. They desire also to impress upon their members the importance, in investigations of the kind in question, of taking all possible care to prevent the publication of names, where there is any reason to suppose that this would cause annoyance. This rule has been strictly observed in all cases in which reports of experiences of this class have been published in the *Proceedings* (Anon 1897: 116).

This was an extremely disingenuous statement. Myers, in many ways, was the driving force of the SPR, and in frequent and intimate contact particularly with Hodgson (briefly back in England) and Sidgwick. It is impossible to believe that the whole process was not known informally to the SPR leadership and it is surprising that trouble was not anticipated. It also had little effect on the wider public readership of *The Times* who had access to that newspaper rather than the *Journal* of the SPR with its circulation of around one thousand. It was exactly the kind of debacle that Sidgwick had fought so hard to prevent happening in earlier years. Decades of patient observation and cautious recording could be undermined by one sustained outburst of public ridicule. It is a tribute to the fundamental ethos that the Sidgwicks, particularly, had established that more damage was not done. However, the SPR's avoidance of greater harm was achieved at the expense of Miss X, who received no public support from the Society. Indeed, it was left to one of the visitors to Ballechin to point out that Myers had only seen a very small part of the journal of evidence that was kept over three months and 'signed by more than twenty witnesses' and that 'during the visits to which he refers, extending over ten days only, both Mr Myers and Professor Lodge testified in writing to their personal experience of the phenomena under observation' (*Times:* 12.6.1897).

In addition, the issue of confidentiality was much more complex than the SPR note acknowledged. Myers had been able to maintain the confidentiality of the Cheltenham haunted house largely because he had been the initial investigator and there had been no social cachet involved in respect of the owner and house. In the case of large scale investigations, particularly one like Ballechin, secrecy was totally impossible. To some extent, right from the very early 1880s, the line had been blurred between scientific investigation and social stimulation and entertainment. Throughout Myers' and to some extent Sidgwick's and Gurney's letters and visits to verify phenomena, there is the uneasy mixture of the scientific and the social, as was demonstrated earlier. On the scale of Ballechin it was a recipe for disaster. There was a further point. If names were revealed much damage could be done to individuals and their property; if names were concealed the activity could be seen as childish and unscientific. One of the later letters to *The Times* criticised the SPR for this approach: 'What value can be assigned to evidence when the names of the witnesses are kept secret? Such proceedings are the caricature of a legal inquiry and the parody of a scientific investigation. The SPR cannot have the remotest idea of the legal or scientific meaning and value of evidence' (*Times:* 12.6.1897).

The Breach between Miss Freer, Myers and the SPR

Myers defended himself vigorously in *The Times* (10.6.1897, 15.6.1897, 22.6.1897) but he did so to the detriment of Miss X's position: the few noises he and Lodge heard did not require scientific investigation; he was always in favour of public testimony but if this was refused the Society would try to get a private statement lodged with them. He did not deal with the question of letting the house on false pretences, except by denying any Society involvement at all. Yet why then did he, Lodge and Taylor – as prominent SPR members – go there? Surely the public conclusion would be that the project was SPR sanctioned? And if the noises were ignored, what was the point of Lodge – in particular – being there at all? Miss X was left out to dry in the wind.

However, not all of the letters were hostile to the SPR and/or Miss X, or dismissive of the theory that Ballechin was haunted. On the former point *Tenez-le-Droit* 10th June 1897 stated that, 'No reasonable and temperate observer could apply to the evidence collected by the SPR in, for example, *Phantasms of the Living*, the designation of "unsifted, reckless, often malignant gossip",' and that Miss X ' is known to the literary world, and to society in general as possessing in a high degree perception of the psychical order ... and as maintaining with regard to the sources of such impressions a thoroughly agnostic attitude'. On the second point, Harold Sanders, who was butler at Ballechin for three months in 1896, stated in *The Times* (21.6.1897) that the house was definitely haunted and described enormous knockings between 12.00 and 4.00 in the morning, a presence in his room, the bedclothes snatched off him and his bed moved. On one occasion he was up at night with five gentlemen in their night-suits with sticks, pokers and one with a revolver, looking for the source of the disturbances. It was interesting that none of the correspondents took up this piece of evidence. By tacit consent the view of a butler in such matters must be mistaken. And in the original article which started the row, the writer mentions the testimony of a maidservant who heard the noises and who seemed honest, 'but as she has seen the ghost of half a woman sitting on her fellow-servant's bed, one takes her evidence with a grain or two of salt'. There was an obvious lack of acquaintance here with the relevant literature (as Myers might have put it), for there were many examples of the partial manifestations of phantasms in the SPR files.

This led to an increasing distance between Miss Goodrich Freer and the SPR. There is also little evidence of any contact directly between her and Myers after this time. Indications of the widening breach are clear in the SPR literature and in Miss Freer's own reaction to this, as expressed in the pages of *Borderland* in July 1897. She spoke of the decline of the SPR since the great days of the 1880s, mentioning Gurney and the Sidgwicks by name, and contrasting this with the spiritualistic influence which she alleged Myers was introducing into the Society (Hall 1980b: 107-108). At a meeting of the Sesame Club in December 1898 (after Podmore had given an address on the Society's work with Mrs Piper), she said she had an aversion to mediums generally but she had a particular sympathy for poor Mrs Piper, whom she felt the SPR had treated cruelly. She later expanded on this in a book:

> The phenomena presented by Mrs Piper, the American medium, are among those classified as 'induced.' At the 'suggestion' of a fee, she passes through a state apparently of epilepsy into one of trance, in which her utterances are regarded in the light of Intimations of Immortality. One is told that the convulsed countenance, the gnash-

ing teeth, the writhing body, the clenched hands, are 'purely auto-matic' and very beneficial to her health, and as Mr Hodgson has induced this condition eighty times in three months, he should cer-tainly be able to judge. Mrs Piper, whom I saw very frequently when she was in London eight years ago, is a gentle, quiet woman, of very domestic tastes, simple, sincere, and possessing considerable faculty of thought-transference, a woman whom it was especially distressing to observe in her induced secondary personality of 'Dr Phinuit,' coarse, cunning, and of evil-speech (Goodrich-Freer 1899: 21).

Hodgson, in his review of Ada Goodrich Freer's later published statements on Mrs Piper, accused her of suffering from an idée fixe and contrasted them with her earlier positive attitude in 1894 and 1896: 'We have learnt many things from Mrs Piper, and are glad to feel she is in hands so thor-oughly capable of making the most of what she has to teach, as are those of Professor James and Dr Hodgson' (Hodgson 1899: 393–96). He could also, had he wished, have quoted the rather romantic record of Miss Freer, in her guise as Miss X, visiting Mrs Piper on 7th December 1889:

> Miss X was introduced, veiled to the medium in the trance state, immediately after her arrival in Mr Myers' house. She was at once recognised and named. 'You are a medium; you write when you don't want to. You have got Mr E's influence about you [as mentioned before, the spirit of Gurney was named E in the early records] ... This is Miss X that I told you about ... You see flowers sometimes ... deli-cate pink roses ... You have them about you spiritually as well as physically.' Miss X has on a certain day of every month a present of delicate pink roses. She frequently has hallucinatory visions of flow-ers (Holt 1914 1: 454–55).

In addition, her first name, Ada, was given, and a number of other personal and accurate statements made .

The 'dirty tricks', however, were not yet over on either side. The furore over the investigation of Ballechin House in *The Times* meant that the book Bute and Freer published on the affair in 1899 went into a second edition in 1900. On the frontispiece of the book Miss Freer placed a quote from Myers' letter to *The Times* of 10th June 1897: 'I visited B— representing that Society (SPR), ... and decided that there was no such evidence as could justify us in giving the results of the inquiry a place in our Proceed-ings.' She placed below it the laconic statement, 'Compare pages 182 et seq.' (Bute and Goodrich Freer 1900: vii). On those pages she quoted a pri-vate letter from Myers which appeared to show how impressed he was with the evidence so far — based only on his reading of the journal that she had kept for the first five weeks and which he had shown to the Sidgwicks. She also used those pages to take a sideswipe at Myers and 'his preference for the experiences of female mediums whether hired or gratuitous' (Bute and Goodrich Freer 1900: 183). Whether this was based on sexual jealousy, or on pique that Mrs Piper had supplanted Miss Freer in Myer's interest, is impossible to say at this distance in time. Miss Freer, however, was not herself immune from the selective use of evidence. In the second edition she contrasted the above quotation from Myers with a statement from Podmore about Ballechin House, pointing out the contradictory views of two honourable secretaries of the SPR and hinting at a house divided against itself. For in his review of the book Podmore had stated that their book was worth publishing. She neglected, however, to quote Podmore's further statement that Myers was right, 'from the evidential standpoint.' Nor, of course, did she quote Podmore's devastating criticism of her journal and her methods: Podmore, in reviewing the book, crisply pointed out the slender basis on which many of the various manifestations rested: 'It was Miss Freer who first saw a ghostly figure; it was again Miss Freer who first heard ghostly noises, and throughout these records it is Miss Freer who is most frequently and most conspicuously favoured with "phenomena"' (Podmore 1900–1901: 98–100).

An examination of Myers' letters to Lord Bute partially justifies his final public position. It demonstrates that Myers was interested in the phenomena and keen to pursue the investigation, but that what he actually experienced and reported was not really significant enough to make a major contribution to the *Proceedings*. In his letter of 14th April 1897 (Myers 11/86) he summarised the experiences of others and particularly described the background and history of Miss Chaston, the medium whom he brought with him. It is quite clear from the tone of the letter that Myers, despite Hall's hints to the contrary, had absolutely no sexual interest in Miss Chaston, and she had been brought along purely because her mediumistic gifts might be useful. As far as Myers was concerned, he saw and experienced nothing of significance till 21st April, which he described as we have seen to Bute: 'At last I have heard unmistakeable knocks myself—I happened to awake at about 4.30 AM; heard 3 series of muffled knocks, each series of about 15, as tho insistently attracting attention' (Myers 11/91). He got up and at his door met Lodge, who had also heard knocking, and together they searched the house for the source, which they did not find. So, their only personal experience of paranormal phenomena was a series of repeated knockings. The evidence of Miss Chaston had the usual ambiguous status of such séances, with regard to information communicated, and much of the other material could be ascribed to the susceptible nature of some of the people involved, or natural causes due to the construction of the house, or the seismically disturbed nature of the environment. So, although he and the SPR did back off with indecent haste—and in terms of support and courtesy, did let

Miss Goodrich Freer down badly — nevertheless a case can be made that by the SPR's own best canons of evidence, the experiences at Ballechin House did not merit writing up.

In spite of all the claims and counter claims, two things at least clearly emerged from the affair. Firstly, that the investigators had not acted honourably — any of them. As Captain Steuart pointed out: 'I may state that Lord Bute unsuccessfully tried to get my father's permission for one or two members of the Psychical Society to reside at Ballechin-house'. Therefore, by implication, Bute had resorted to using a proxy, Colonel Taylor, to access the property for him and all the other investigators were guilty by association. Secondly, that the investigators had not been particularly competent — any of them — in spite of the much vaunted efforts by the SPR to apply scientific methods to the examination of these sorts of phenomena. Competence required training and expertise — and the use of current and relevant physical knowledge, like that of John Milne the seismologist (Bute and Goodrich Freer 1900: 214). He argued that, 'What you require to make the record ... is a Perry Tromometer' (a tromometer was a device for measuring slight earthquake shocks). The ethics of real world observation and the definition of appropriate expertise are issues as relevant in psychical research today as they were then, though in the heat of the debate and the confused excitement of the visits to Ballechin, no-one appeared capable of standing back and addressing them in a detached fashion. In fact, one of the visitors to Ballechin, the writer Andrew Lang felt so embarrassed about the whole affair that he tried to get all reference to him removed from the pending book by Bute and Miss Freer. As Bute stated to Myers:

> Andrew Lang wrote me a very long letter which I have answered, and forwarded to Miss Freer as she has the text before her which I have not. He seemed to wish us to conceal the fact that he had been to Ballechin, this seems to me impossible. He went there quite willingly and the book is a simple narrative of facts with which it would be inconsistent to make such a suppressio veri (Myers 1/86: n.d.).

Ada Goodrich Freer gradually disappeared from the world of psychical research, though she was still about in 1898. Crookes, who was that year President both of the British Association and of the SPR, wrote to Lodge: 'Miss Frere, "X", is to read a paper before the Anthropological Section on Second Sight in the Highlands. This will open the door to psychic matters and there ought to be a good discussion.' It can be assumed that Crookes, who had a high opinion of Ada Goodrich Freer, had facilitated the opportunity for the paper to be read. After the break with the SPR, she also fell out with her lifelong companion Miss Moore and appears to have been caught out in fraudulent mediumship activity (Hall 1980b: 116-17), though the evidence is tenuous. It certainly seems that women, particularly, always had their suspicions of her. Lord Bute's sister, Lady Margaret, tended to view her with a critical and amused condescension (Hall 1980b: 62). However, always the survivor, she continued with some journalism and writing and eventually married (lopping an appropriate number of years off her age) a man many years her junior, whose expertise in folklore encouraged her into a final career as a folklorist of the Middle East. In many ways, but through different methods, she reminds one, in charm, guile and tenacity, of Anna Eva Fay, and how in a strongly masculine dominated society, able women sometimes had to find heterodox methods in order to survive, let alone flourish. The world of spiritualism, the occult, and psychical research, allowed a number to do so.

Chapter Eight

Myers, Science and the SPR

A Scientific Approach to Psychical Research?

One of the claims of Myers and the SPR was that they adopted a scientific approach to their subject. It is important to examine what this means in detail. The initial problem was to justify their belief in psychical research as a valid field of study; that it had as much right to existence as say, anthropology or sociology. Then as now, this hurdle was extremely difficult to surmount. Opponents argued that there was no subject matter to study. Illusion and fraud could explain all cases of apparently paranormal activity (Foster and Parker 1995: 9). Because of this the SPR approach blended, occasionally uneasily, the desire to accumulate facts in order to bludgeon an indifferent audience into taking notice, with the need to establish a sound, evidential base before they could move towards theorising. However, the manner in which they carried this out, and the assumptions on which that methodology was based have, surprisingly, never been examined in sustained detail—that is, with the partial exception of JP Williams' excellent thesis, to which reference has already been made (Williams 1984: 10–41). Ed Kelly, in *Irreducible Mind* (Kelly *et al.* 2007: 582–84), has a short section headed 'Myers's Methodological Principles', but it is not very substantial. He rightly points out that Myers—starting from a basis in classics and literature, and through very wide reading, direct investigation (particularly in France) and detailed discussion with scientists like Lodge—turned himself into a scientist. But we need to ask what this means in terms of actual practice.

Amongst the early leaders of the SPR, there was none of the Keatsian or early Wordsworthian distaste for science and the 'meddling intellect', or, closer to Myers' own time, the early Yeats retreating into a Celtic twilight. Either they were already scientists by training and qualification—Barrett,

Lodge, Mrs Sidgwick, Podmore — or else as academics (Sidgwick, Myers, Hodgson) they fully appreciated and supported the scientific method. In his obituary of Sidgwick, Myers put forward a view of the scientific approach to psychical research from which few could dissent:

> ... we must remember that our very *raison d'etre* is the extension of the scientific method, of intellectual virtues — of curiosity, candour, care, — into regions where many a current of old tradition, of heated emotion, even of pseudo-scientific prejudice, deflects the bark which should steer only towards the cold, unreachable pole of absolute truth. We must recognise that we have more in common with those who may criticise or attack our work with competent diligence than with those who may acclaim and exaggerate it without adding thereto any careful work of their own. We must experiment unweariedly; we must continue to demolish fiction as well as to accumulate truth; we must make no terms with any hollow mysticism, any half-conscious deceit (Myers 1901c: 459–60).

Myers and his colleagues pursued two approaches to psychical research (Gauld 1993), the investigation of specific cases (the idiographic) and attempts at laboratory-based research, so far as was possible, testing and experimenting under controlled conditions (the nomothetic). Regardless of whether in nomographic or idiographic mode, their behaving scientifi-cally (though there would obviously be deviations from this ideal model depending on context and circumstances), meant demonstrating certain key behaviours, and it is important to see how effectively Myers and his colleagues displayed these. They include: a systematic and considered approach to the collection of evidence; the use of appropriate tools and methods of enquiry; the judgement of evidence against objective criteria; the prioritisation of physical explanations over spiritual ones; the elimi-nation of fraud; the use of experiment to identify and establish the condi-tions under which the phenomena can be manifested and replicated; the construction of testable hypotheses; the avoidance of presuppositions and prejudice, particularly those based on class, gender and race; and the publication of results in a scholarly format so they can be publicly scruti-nised. It is accepted that this is an over-simplified model and that in real-ity actual working practices and the pressure of sociological forces may lead to deviations from this ideal model (Ziman 2002; Collins and Pinch 1998; Becher and Trowler 2001; and especially Sheldrake 2003: 165–77). Nevertheless, claims to behave scientifically require assessment against general criteria such as the above.

The Collection of Material

An essential characteristic of Myers and his colleagues was their infinite capacity for taking pains. Gurney dedicated his life to research, perhaps at the expense of his marriage. Myers travelled ceaselessly at home and abroad to investigate promising cases while still holding down the important position of a senior inspector of schools. The Sidgwicks, particularly Mrs Sidgwick, produced extensive, thoughtful, detailed and cautious analyses of phenomena, the equivalent (as also in Myers' case) of a number of large published tomes. Alan Gauld (Gauld 1968: 313) has calculated that of the 11,000 pages that made up the *Proceedings* and the *Journal* to 1900, Myers and his intimate friends must have produced fifty or more per cent; and of that group, only Gurney and Hodgson could be considered to be full-time.

It was vital for them to demonstrate that these strange, wayward phenomena, sometimes manifesting in sleazy and shabby contexts, actually existed and deserved to be studied seriously. This, in itself, was no easy task given the swirling currents and counter currents of Victorian culture. It was particularly difficult in that the scientific community, as we have seen, was gradually establishing itself in terms of authority and methodology and distinguishing itself from the work of the rich, amateur and clerical. Men of science had no wish to replace one superstition with another and must have viewed with a certain unease the number of clergymen and their wives who provided testimony to the SPR in the early years. As both Nicol and Oppenheim have pointed out, the SPR may have appeared to many a sceptical Victorian, as a refuge for the disillusioned Anglican; the last chance to restore the spiritual, the miraculous, in an increasingly dark and materialistic world (Oppenheim 1984: 119, Nicol 1972: 346).

Therefore, the methods of the law court, the police, the private detective, the journalist and the historian were used in order to establish the fact that something had actually taken place. Sidgwick in his addresses (1882ab, 1883, 1884ab, 1888, 1889), Gurney in his chapter on caution in interpreting evidence at the beginning of *Phantasms of the Living* and in his chapter criticising the evidence for spontaneous telepathy (Gurney *et al.* 1886 1: 1–9, 114–72), and Myers in many places throughout his extensive series of articles in the *Proceedings*, emphasized canons of evidence. Myers himself, apparently the most emotionally involved, was one of the most thorough in thinking through criteria for evidence with regard to the specific phenomena under observation. In generic terms, this involved above all direct interviews, the checking of names, dates, times, places, against other people's evidence and documentation, adjusting for observational error and possible bias, and always searching for some form of independent corroboration of the phenomena beyond that of the original observer or experient. Myers was continually through his career urging people to have the presence of mind to record accurately what was taking place. There was much emphasis, as one might expect with academics comfortable with the written word in several languages, on the examination of documentary evidence. Myers himself furnished particularly thorough examples of these in his examination of Reverend Mr. Newnham's diary, Stainton Moses' extensive records, and the written statements (Barrett assisted him with this) that Mrs Home had gathered to confirm the phenomena associated with her husband, Daniel Dunglas Home. There were frequent, tedious difficulties. Sometimes the witnesses had died, moved away, did not wish to write out an account, or would refuse to testify because of embarrassment or — in the case of hauntings — because it might damage the value of their property. But Myers and his colleagues, with a very few unfortunate exceptions, were relentless and thorough. He, Gurney and the Sidgwicks, travelled extensively in the United Kingdom through the 1880s to interview witnesses. He, his brother, and Gurney made several trips to France; GA Smith was dispatched to Florida and Hodgson to India. Many thousands of miles were covered in the name of psychical research.

Lord Acton was particularly interested in the activities of the SPR in this area because he felt it might help him with his work on Christianity — specifically the handling and treatment of miracles. He asked two questions of psychical researchers: 'How they deal with miracles when they meet them?' and 'what light your experience tends to throw on mine' (Myers 1/7/1: 6.3.1892). In reply, Myers sent him a detailed statement on canons of evidence based on their work to date (Gauld 1968: 364–67). In this reply he clearly distinguished those activities for which there was no known explanation from those which had now been brought under known laws or which were capable of empirical reproduction. The distinction in the second half of the sentence is interesting. One could explain an eclipse. One could not explain the production of stigmata by suggestion; but one could empirically reproduce it. This was rather over optimistic of Myers but it did point to an interesting debate about what one might mean by replication (Williams 1984: 11).

The collecting and checking of other people's experiences made Myers and his colleagues acutely aware of the need for accurate record keeping and that often in very difficult, real world, conditions. They did not always live up to this but they tried. They took recording seriously and when stenographers became available these were employed (especially in relation to Mrs Piper) to capture extra detail. They also developed the idea that observers were there not just to record but also to observe what else was going on in the séance room, including each other. Myers and Sidgwick were also prepared to finance direct investigation, particularly if they trusted the observer, and George Albert Smith was particularly useful in this respect. He was, on one occasion, sent to Florida to examine a particularly important and gifted subject, Mr Skilton, a train driver, whose premonitions several times saved him from death (Myers 1895d: 559). After Smith's honeymoon, as we have seen, the SPR paid for him to live in a haunted house with his new wife and make investigations. One wonders what the new Mrs Smith thought about this as an introduction to married bliss. AT Myers, for example, wrote to Sidgwick that he had 'just talked the Brighton arrangements over with Smith and he is inclined to guarantee that Mrs Smith will not be inconvenienced by (being) there and will not break off a year's residence there' (Add.Ms.c.94/163: n.d.). Smith was also keen to get a London/Brighton season ticket so that he could work with Podmore and on hypnotic subjects in both places. And as already mentioned, Lodge was later to pay him to see if, through normal detective work, he could find out the same personal details about Lodge's family that Mrs Piper had in trance.

Appropriate Tools of Enquiry

A very important part of methodology is establishing appropriate tools of enquiry and knowing what weight could or could not be placed on the evidence gathered because of the methods used. Myers argued that just as new scientific techniques had opened up medicine, astronomy and chemistry, so too, parallel techniques were needed in the field of psychical research. Just as one had developed instruments for investigating the chemical composition of objects or the interior of the human body, so too one had to find appropriate mechanisms for exploring the human psyche. He believed that these techniques existed and he labelled them psychoscopes. He saw them as the psychical equivalents of telescopes, microscopes and spectroscopes. These methods included: the use of hypnosis to initiate altered states, automatic writing, crystal visions, the planchette, table tilting, the study of dreams, and so on. They were ways of accessing the unconscious mind and exploring the various permeable strata of the multiplex personality.

Doctors (as we have seen) gravely warned of the consequences for sanity of indulging in such unhinged practices, particularly automatic writing. But Myers approached automatic writing and the other mechanisms with a much cooler head and indeed encouraged the members of the SPR, their relatives, and the educated wider community to experiment themselves. In this he almost seems to be in the tradition of early medical scientists who used to test ether, chloroform and cocaine on themselves in small doses. There was considerable insouciance in his approach. Another method, also previously discussed, was the use of crystal vision either in or out of hypnosis. He traced the method back to the Elizabethan scryer and magician, John Dee. He accepted that the crystal or speculum pictures, could partly be explained by a partial, self-induced trance and/or by *point de repère*, tiny little marks that could stimulate and suggest pictures to the observer. But this did not cover all cases and the experience seemed more complex than that, and often provided access to the symbolic and occasionally supernormal faculties of the subliminal (Myers 1904 1: 237–39).

The Judgement of Material

Judgement requires criteria against which sound assessment can be made. Myers called this the establishment of canons of evidence and he frequently worked through and published such canons in the *Journal* and *Proceedings*. An early example of this approach occurred in the paper that Myers jointly wrote with Edmund Gurney on higher aspects of mesmerism (Gurney and Myers 1885b: 401–23), particularly with regard to its ability to alleviate pain:

> The canons of evidence which may reasonably be applied to this class of phenomena are such as even laymen may venture to indicate,
>
> 1) That the case should be reported throughout by a medical man ...
>
> 2) The case should be reported, as nearly as may be, at the time and publicly ...
>
> 3) The case must be one in which no other form of medical treatment has been been concurrently employed.
>
> 4) The recovery should be such as cannot reasonably be attributed to the *vis medicatrix naturae*.
>
> 5) The influence of imagination should be, as far as possible, excluded.

He and his brother applied similar criteria (Myers and Myers 1893) when they investigated the alleged miracles at Lourdes. Obviously, they applied the same canons of evidence to apparitions of the Virgin as they would apply in their general investigations into phantasms. However, they needed specific criteria for judging the reports of miraculous cures and the Myers brothers argued that these cases should always be first-hand, detailed, medical experts should be involved, and there should be objective records. Over one hundred years later, Dean Radin (Radin 1997: 149) was still pointing out the failure of alternative medicine providers in this field. In essence, what the Myers' were saying was that there was a need for accurate medical description pre-miracle and post-miracle — otherwise the evidence, no matter how superficially impressive, was worthless. Again, with regard to the use of magnets to treat French patients, both Myers and Gurney were hugely sceptical, believing that much could be explained by suggestion and auto-suggestion, so that Myers (Myers 1886d: 132) carefully outlined the canons of evidence required to judge effectively whether magnets had any impact on patients or not.

The Prioritisation of Physical Explanations over Spiritual Ones

One essential element in the demonstration of the physical reality of the phenomena studied was the application of statistical techniques to them to prove that they happened more frequently than by chance. Unless this was done they would be unable to convince the scientific community that there was anything worth investigating. As Hacking has pointed out (Hacking 1988: 427–51), Myers and the SPR were starting to grapple with problems of sampling and probability before many other parts of the scholarly community, even if by modern standards their initial work appears unsophisticated. For example, Gurney and Myers' acceptance of the randomisation of the Miss Wingfields' telepathic experiments, and Peirce's criticisms of Gurney's statistical conclusions in *Phantasms of the Living*, both reveal errors of different sorts but they were errors from which the SPR tried to learn (Hacking 1988: 443–48).

A further important point was to accept that there was a number of cases of apparent paranormal activity which could be explained by existing scientific knowledge, and that these cases should be eliminated from enquiry or any statistical analysis. For example, as JP Williams has pointed out (Williams 1984: 14), cases of thought-reading where people had physical contact and many of the movements of tables in table-tilting and turning could be explained by unconscious and involuntary muscular movements of the participants. Yet, the fact that some phenomena could be understood in this fashion was not to be used as a device, for explaining away everything. Sidgwick and Myers were particularly aware of the tendency for a number of men of science, particularly the powerful and lucid Carpenter, to operate in this fashion.

The fundamental problem that Myers and his colleagues faced was that for many in the scientific community—particularly the developing community of psychologists—what they were doing was not science. Psychology was the study of the physics and chemistry and biology of the body and the impact of that on mind. Matter and its laws were dominant and it produced the illusion of mental activity and individual volition. Others adopted a middle position of psycho-physiological parallelism, where both physical and mental processes were seen to be correlated with each other but where it was not possible to say anything about their interaction. Myers, however, wished to challenge both these positions, believing that they had some—albeit limited—evidence for the independent operation of mind. Such a challenge required a scrupulous approach to the collection of evidence, and a considerable respect for the existing knowledge paradigm.

Myers, in fact, accepted many of the tenets of scientific naturalism. The SPR was not founded in opposition to this. He believed in scientific knowledge and its public examination and assessment, and in its laws. Where he parted company with a number of scientists was in his attitude towards the anomalous. If an observation conflicted with the known physical laws, this did not mean a return to a magical view of thinking, just recognition that it might be linked to laws and principles as yet unknown. The scientific naturalists saw this as a way of smuggling superstition and magic back into the debate. Myers, however, shared with Gurney the idea of the tertium quid, the need to move beyond dichotomous positions—each of which might have something useful to say for itself—to a third position that transcended them both (Epperson 1997: 98–100). It was this concept that sections of the scientific community were so reluctant to embrace.

As to physical laws, none of the SPR investigators would claim that they had found definite laws in this area—not even Myers. The most they would claim would be that there was some evidence for telepathy and that provisional hypotheses like the subliminal consciousness were useful for guiding future investigation. Indeed as James himself stated, in a letter to the psychologist Münsterberg, in July 1891, there were no theories in psychology itself which yet had definitive value: 'The man who throws out most new ideas and immediately seeks to subject them to experimental control is the most useful psychologist, in the present state of the science' (Skrupskelis *et al.* 1999: 180). That quotation applied equally to the field of psychical research. Gurney and Mrs Sidgwick, in particular, were the great experimenters in the sense of repeated, controlled experiments to establish the existence of certain hypnotic and telepathic phenomena and to subject spontaneous phenomena to accurate observation and examination of testimony. Myers, much to James' relish, was the thrower out of new ideas par excellence. However, it was in the bridging laws (which exist in abundance in the macroscopic Newtonian world) that there was and still is a huge gap.

Myers was not just a theorist. He was always careful to tie in his work with what he knew of other disciplines. For example, he invoked current knowledge of the structure of the cortex and the optic nerve in his explanation of the telepathic origin of hallucinations. He referred to retinal hyperaesthesia in trying to explain bright lights linked to the appearance of a phantasm in a darkened bedroom. He examined in detail existing theories of unconscious cerebration and reflex mental action when developing over time his theory of the subliminal subconsciousness. Though Myers and his colleagues were attacked by the scientific establishment, they did try to eliminate all physical explanations before positing supernormal ones. They were certainly prepared to consider that there might be physiological and pathological explanations for most if not all unusual behaviours: Broca on aphasia, Charcot on hysteria, and Binet and Janet on dissociation. But they reserved the right to accept or reject them in the light of their own reading and research.

This can be seen particularly clearly in Myers' alignment of certain features of automatic writing with contemporary work on double brain hemisphere issues (Harrington 1987: 137–45). Building on his own examination of the automatic writing of the wife of the Reverend Mr. Newnham, and his readings of Pitres, Bernard, Bérillon and Hughlings Jackson, he considered the links between aphasia/agraphia and automatic writing. He suggested there were considerable similarities, both in the ways that words were mangled and in the tendency to swearing and obscenity – this latter possibly indicating the less evolved and primitive nature of the right brain. As we have seen, he was hesitant to assume too positive a relationship without further confirmation, and he felt, to some extent, he had received this in Bourru and Burot's detailed case study of Louis Vivé. The point is that, rightly or wrongly, he was concerned at each stage of the development of his argument, to base it on evidence from the latest medical and physiological research.

With regard to crystal visions, he was as keen to link them to existing physiological laws as to speculate on what they might indicate about the nature of the subliminal consciousness:

> We still want to know more on every point connected with these visions. How far, for instance, do they follow optical laws? Is there any tendency to complementary colouring, so that a green picture would be seen after a red? Are they magnified by the interposition of a magnifying glass? and, if so, is this a mere result of suggestion, or of the presence of something in the field of view which is really magnified? ... I can imagine no fitter problem for research in a psychological laboratory (Myers 1904 1: 239).

Myers and his colleagues were eager to involve professional psychologists and men of science generally in their work, and to learn from them. We have already discussed the visits of the brothers Myers and Gurney to Charcot, Janet, Binet and other leading figures in France, and their extensive practical and theoretical knowledge of hypnosis. The list of scientists who joined the SPR was considerable and in his personal correspondence Myers reached out to as many more as he could. We have also seen the considerable involvement that he and Sidgwick had in the early international psychological congresses, and his enthusiastic support for Freud's early work as a confirmation of his own ideas.

The group of SPR leaders relied heavily on two concepts in the establishment of their case that, after all existing physical explanations had been exhausted, there was still something worth examining. These were the ideas of 'residual cases' and of 'faggots', or collective bundles of evidence. Williams has clearly outlined the first: 'when all cases explicable by known causes have been eliminated, if there still remains a residue of cases, then the existence of an unknown cause is proved'(Williams 1984: 15). Gurney stated the second concept in *Phantasms of the Living*: 'The true metaphor is the sticks and the faggot ... The multiplication of such examples (good but not perfect individual cases or sticks), therefore, makes a faggot of ever-increasing solidity' (Gurney *et al.* 1886 1: 169–70).

The Elimination of Fraud

However, in order to establish a basic core of unusual cases, fraud as well as physical explanations needed to be considered in some depth (Williams 1984: 15). Ruth Brandon in her book *The Spiritualists* (Brandon 1983: 255–86) has a detailed appendix on methods of trickery that fraudsters used to gull the credulous. Yet she is not sufficiently generous with regard to the SPR's role in detecting fraud. Myers, Gurney and Sidgwick went to great pains to avoid being taken in and were honest in admitting it on the rare occasions when it did take place; and they took care to improve their procedures. They certainly made a mistake in the case of Mr D, as we have seen, but for each failure there were a number of successes in exposing fraud, and where they incurred the wrath of the spiritualists, as in the case of Eglinton or Husk, they thought that that was a price worth paying. Also, according to Inglis (Inglis 1983: 209–12), Brandon's book is vitiated by a number of inaccuracies and examples of *suppressio veri*, particularly with regard to Daniel Dunglas Home and Eusapia Palladino, but not only them. For example, Brandon stated that Mrs Piper gained clues to the kind of statements she should make by fishing for evidence, or using the indicators she obtained from holding the hand of the sitter. Berger made it absolutely clear that this was not a feature of many of the best sittings and described the considerable lengths Professor Hyslop and Hodgson went to prevent Hyslop giving her any sensory clues that might provide evidence she could use to fabricate spirit communication:

> Hyslop would arrive in Mrs Piper's home in a closed coach. Before entering he donned a mask which covered his entire face and which he wore as he entered the house and sat with the medium. Hodgson introduced him to Mrs Piper as 'Mr Smith,' the name Hodgson used also to introduce all strange sitters to her. Sitters like Hyslop were were instructed to say nothing so that voice, in addition to face, was concealed. Like Hyslop, sitters merely bowed when introduced to the medium. During the sitting they never spoke in a normal tone. Moreover, during the sittings Mrs Piper was never touched by a sitter so as to avoid any muscular suggestion. Nor were clues given by questions asked in order that facts obtained might not be suggested by questions. Finally, the sitters stood behind the medium so that she could not see them or their movements (Berger 1988: 24).

It is also worth pointing out, in this context, that orthodox science itself was and is not immune from accusations of fraud. William James has an amusing section in his *Confidences of a 'Psychical Researcher'* on the problems scientists face when demonstrations of their experiments go wrong — the demonstrator who drove a nail through a machine to keep it steady, the physiologist who pretended to kill a rabbit, and James, himself stated, for teaching purposes, 'To compare small men with great, I have myself cheated shamelessly' (James 1986: 364). Fraud is a hazard in all aspects of intellectual life — both the relatively harmless low-level fraud of the teacher or lecturer to 'improve' the demonstration of some scientific principle, and the more serious high-level cheating in the interests of mammon and ego. But it is quite unfair to accuse the leading SPR figures of not being alive to the issue. Despite his emotional longing for the certainty of survival, Myers believed the matter was too important to be settled by easy belief. Phenomena had to be probed, examined and discarded, no matter how comforting, if they failed to meet the standards of evidence required.

However, it could be argued that at times, Myers particularly, could be both a little over enthusiastic and careless. His judgement was certainly affected by the physical attractiveness of Anna Eva Fay. There must, too, be some suspicion that in his handling of those séances with Mrs Piper and Mrs Thompson that were under his supervision, the boundary between the social and the scientific was occasionally blurred, thus allowing, at the very least, the potential leakage of information. Yet, though not professional parapsychologists, he and his colleagues were aware of many of the issues outlined in modern guides to psychical research (Milton and Wiseman 1997: 32–51). And, to be fair, they had no extensive, pre-existing resource base, no community of international researchers easily accessible through email or the internet to support them. They did the best that could be expected of them, given the fact that they were at the start of the discipline, that there were still considerable transport and communication problems to face, and that the network of fellow researchers in the USA, France and Germany, was miniscule.

The Place of Experiment in Early Psychical Research

RH Thouless (Thouless 1972: 15) has criticised the early leaders of the SPR for not having a proper concept of the nature of scientific experiment. Yet that statement is perhaps unfair and again made with the benefit of hindsight. It also takes a narrow view of the meaning of the term experiment. An experiment is not just a designed intervention into the natural order. It can also be deliberate and careful observation intended to reveal particular information (Ziman 2002: 93–94). The SPR, as we have seen, was also labouring under particular difficulties and trying to ride a number of horses at the same time — to demonstrate the existence of paranormal phenomena both in the world at large and under controlled conditions. Their experiments were initially designed to demonstrate the existence of something and not to explain it. They had not the control over their phenomena that physical scientists generally had (Gurney *et al.* 1886 1: 6–9). Nor had they a theoretical base comparable with that in physics, chemistry and biology, which would easily elicit specific hypotheses that could be tested under laboratory conditions and accepted or rejected. In fact, ignoring the sensational elements like Home, Moses, and Blavatsky, it could be argued that all the pioneers of psychical research like Myers and Gurney ever fundamentally claimed was this: that their observations, experimentally based and historically collected on an individual basis, allowed them to assert, '*the ability of one mind to impress or be impressed by another mind otherwise than through the recognised channels of sense*' (Gurney *et al.* 1886 1: 6).

As Harvey Irwin has shown (Irwin 2004: 49–50), right from their investigation of the Creery sisters (which slightly pre-dated the setting up of the SPR), Myers and his colleagues were moving towards the concept of 'a controlled test in a laboratory situation'. Their first efforts focused on the careful observation of a situation in which they selected material, inaccessible to the percipient through normal sensory channels, and through themselves, or someone else, hoped to transmit the information. They increasingly became aware of the number of variables that needed to be controlled if they were to feel secure that no normal method of communication had been utilised. They also quickly realised that they should benchmark successes and failures against what could be ascribed to random chance. In the Creery case they often used playing cards (1 to 52, 1 to 13) to establish this. It was Gurney, building on the research of Richet (Gurney *et al.* 1886 1: 31), who first stressed the importance of very large numbers of trials.

Myers was quite aware of the appropriate procedures, and of the way scientists said they worked. He knew that 'We must, in the first place, vary our actual deliberate experiments as widely as possible; in turn introducing and excluding as many separate conditions as seem likely to have a bearing on the result' (Myers 1884b: 217–18). That parallels Broad's remark, ' But all experience in other branches of science suggests that such discoveries are most likely to be made by deliberately varying the conditions under which recurrent phenomena take place and noting concomitant variations in those phenomena' (Broad 1962: 19). Yet, as stated above, the phenomena did not obligingly recur in the way that basic physical phenomena did. The experimenters did not have control over the conditions of recurrence. Gifted subjects were rare, temperamental, and elusive and their powers waxed and waned under laboratory conditions. As for spontaneous phenomena—well, the detective always seemed to arrive after the crime scene had been cleared! In addition, the temperaments of all involved could have an impact on the success or failure of the experiment—including of course the hypothesised discarnate spirits who might or might not be able or prepared to co-operate. Broad also suggested (Broad 1962: 20), eighty years after the founding of the SPR, that the use of hypnotic suggestion as a key variable, which Myers and his colleagues utilised frequently, was still one of the most promising and undeveloped lines of enquiry.

In addition, it could be argued that they had already, to some extent, taken up the concept of a physiological/psychological laboratory that was developing in Germany and America (Mauskopf and McVaugh 1980: 13) and from the 1870s onwards applied it to psychical research. It has been suggested that the rooms in Dean's Yard were, de facto, one of the first psychological research laboratories in the UK (Katz 2005: 129). The SPR gradually improved its protocols and had built up much useful experience after Barrett's early researches. Myers was involved in the early experiments but his interests shifted into more philosophical mode later on. Some early experiments, of course, were the attempts to see if any individuals were sensitive to and could detect the influence of powerful magnets. Leading figures in the SPR took this very seriously and completely blacked out one of the rooms in Dean's Yard in order to test whether or not, in the complete darkness, subjects (over forty were tested) could detect by sight, or some physical effect on them, the influence of the electromagnet (Myers 1904 2: 483). They found three who could, and three individuals who experienced discomfort when brought close to the magnet. Barrett (Barrett 1917: 93–94), who led the investigations, believed in these powers. There has been some later support for this view (Karagulla 1978: 149, Targ 2004: 119–20) but no widespread, mainstream replication, to my knowledge.

A further consideration was the need to take the phenomena out of a show business or sensational context. Barrett, Gurney and Myers all disapproved of the excitable environments created by 'thought-readers' like Bishop and Cumberland and stage mesmerists. Myers also, as Williams has pointed out, viewed the dramatic manifestations at Charcot's Salpêtrière, with a certain distaste and suspicion (Williams 1984: 17–18). The taking of rooms for the SPR with space for both discussion and the calm examination of phenomena was an essential part of the strategy to remove the theatrical and spiritualistic elements that might distract from accurate observation and assessment.

The Construction of Testable Hypotheses

The Sidgwicks, Hodgson and Podmore, in particular, did not see their role as a speculative one. They believed that their main function, essentially, was to examine anomalous phenomena without preconception or bias, in order to test if there was anything in them or not, and the crucial part of 'anything in them' was whether they existed or not. The Sidgwicks till Myers' death had a limited belief in telepathy. Sidgwick fretted that he could not get the least idea, or 'working hypothesis' as to how telepathy operated (Sidgwick and Sidgwick 1906: 473), but he realised that the time was not right for theorising. Hodgson, with the evidence of an enormous amount of Piper material, moved towards the spiritualist hypothesis. Podmore operated as and remained a well-informed sceptic, though he acknowledged the existence of telepathy between the living, and certain puzzling features of the trance phenomena of Mrs Piper and Mrs Thompson. Myers alone took up the challenge, always expressing the inadequacy of his efforts and their provisional nature, to try to create an intellectual framework which would make sense of the phenomena and which could lead, eventually, to more detailed experimental work. This can be seen in his articles on the subliminal consciousness in the 1890s, in *Human Personality and Its Survival of Bodily Death*, and perhaps most clearly in his work on the vocabulary of psychical research which he first published in the *Proceedings* in the 1890s (Myers 1896a: 166–74).

He identified three types of words or concepts that were used in psychical research: words with a standard philosophical/medical meaning which were used in the same way in psychical enquiry, those which were used in a special way in psychical research, and, finally, new coinages which he and others created. A listing of these last shows how much the psychical research community has been indebted to Myers for helping to create a vocabulary to take investigation forward. The words include: dextro-cerebral and sinistro-cerebral, entencephalic, hypnopompic, metetherial, methectic, panaesthesia, paramnesia, preversion, promnesia, psychorrhagic diathesis, retrocognition, supernormal, telepathy, and telaesthesia.

It interesting that Myers did not claim ownership for the term subliminal[1] but that he did claim credit for using and extending it in a particular way:

> Excitations are termed *subliminal* when they are too weak to rise into direct notice; and I have extended the application of the term to feeling, thought, or faculty, which is thus kept submerged, not by its own weakness, but by the constitution of man's personality. The threshold (*Schwelle*) must be regarded as a level above which waves may rise, — like a slab washed by the sea, — rather than as an entrance into a chamber' (Myers 1904 1: xxi).

---

1   Confirmed by *OED*, which attributes the first use to Ward (1886) as well as giving later quotes from Myers (1892) and Podmore (1902).

Unfortunately, the classical associations of *limen* – the threshold of the room – still, as a metaphor, created and continue to create some confusion of interpretation here.

Several of the terms Myers coined are still in general use – dextro-cerebral, sinistro-cerebral, hypnopompic, retrocognition, supernormal, telepathy, and to some extent telaesthesia. Others either never caught on or have fallen out of use. Myers' glossary was meant to be a provisional attempt to make some sense out of a strange, contradictory and muddled field and he hoped that others, more professionally qualified, would generate from it more precise concepts, generalisations and hypotheses that could be explored with experimental rigour.

However, Myers was very concerned lest in an attempt to frame testable hypotheses, psychology (and psychical research as part of psychological enquiry) should narrow down to relatively trivial laboratory-based research projects. He expressed this concern (Kelly *et al.* 2007: 583) in his reviews of *L'année psychologique,* the annual French review of psychological developments. His main focus, however, (indeed all he had time for in one busy life!) was to experiment in the sense of making accurate and reliable observations to demonstrate that something was actually taking place; experiment in the sense of exploring a number of operational hypotheses under a range of very tight laboratory-controlled conditions, in order to explain and predict and replicate, was certainly understood by him and hinted at on occasion, but it was not his main priority or forte. In addition, he was always concerned that the methods of the physical sciences, while there was much to admire and emulate in them, should not be applied without sensitivity to the real world, spontaneous phenomena studied in psychical research.

As we have seen, Thouless has argued that the early SPR researchers were not experimentally minded in the sense of testing a range of hypotheses under controlled conditions to further their understanding. They certainly tried to draw conclusions from a range of gathered spontaneous experiences and from their limited tests for the existence of telepathy, whether under hypnosis or not. Mrs Sidgwick's account *On Hindrances and Complications in Telepathic Communication* is a good example of this (Sidgwick E 1923: 28–69). But there was no consistent and planned programme of laboratory-based research. Gurney had died; Myers was heavily involved in continuing to prove the existence of physical and mental phenomena; the Sidgwicks were fully committed to the development of Newnham College; Podmore (like Myers and the Sidgwicks) had a day job and had cast himself in the role of SPR sceptic rather than active researcher; Lodge was building up a very successful business and academic career; Barrett was in Ireland; and Hodgson was becoming totally absorbed in the Piper phenomena. Had Gurney survived the situation might have been different. However, this is again perhaps too critical. Psychological laboratories were themselves a very new concept, with probably the first one being set up by Wundt in Germany in 1879; there wasn't the equivalent at Oxford till the mid-1930s (Hearnshaw 1964: 181).

In terms of 'hard' knowledge, however, one could argue that neither their careful investigation of individual cases (the idiographic approach) nor their experiments under controlled conditions (the nomothetic approach), contributed significantly to establishing a knowledge base, in the algorithmic way that mainstream science operates. John Ziman has stressed that 'science generates knowledge', and that this knowledge is encoded in scientific theories that are 'widely held to be primarily exercises in *algorithmic compression*' (Ziman 2002: 5). John Barrow (Barrow 2005: 10–11) has described this as a process whereby massive amounts of observational data are summarised in shorthand formulae which, through pattern recognition, create meaning out of the original information. It also allows the prediction of future physical patterns and the conditions under which those patterns will manifest. It has also meant the creation of cumulative bodies of knowledge to which new knowledge has to conform, or by its overwhelming persuasiveness, lead to a modification of the knowledge base. Myers, with characteristic intellectual honesty and generosity, would have acknowledged that psychical research had contributed little to this: knowledge, certainly, in terms of research methods, but not in terms of secure and codified theory leading to the prediction and replication of psychic phenomena. He did, however, assert that their immense labours proved that there was something worth investigating, and that his provisional speculations suggested worthwhile places to look, and instruments to employ when looking. It could be argued (Alvarado 1996: 221–34) that the inevitable and quite natural emphasis on proof in this field has, right from the beginning of systematic work in psychical research and parapsychology, led to a neglect of process issues (understanding, replicating, predicting) and the accumulation of agreed bodies of knowledge. This again is perhaps unfair. But it is a tension that continues to resonate down to the present day.

The Avoidance of Presuppositions and Prejudice

In their public statements, the leaders of the SPR promoted the image of the dispassionate observer. This was a concept that would play a very important part in the battle for the support of educated opinion and was an effective strategy for differentiating themselves from undesirable occult and spiritualistic elements. It was particularly stressed in the Constitution and Rules — 'membership does not imply the acceptance of any particular explanation of the phenomena investigated, nor any belief as to the operation, in the physical world, of forces other than those recognised by Physical Science' (Anon 1882: 5). However, this was a little difficult to square with Sidgwick's statement in his inaugural address that, 'it appeared to us that there was an important body of evidence — tending prima facie to establish the independence of soul or spirit — which modern science had simply left on one side with ignorant contempt' (Sidgwick 1882a: 7–12). This could give critics ammunition to claim both that the SPR did not really approach phenomena without preconceptions and also that they were encouraging a return to the old superstitious days. This was a false argument, as Sidgwick pointed out, and reminiscent of the debate twenty years earlier about the examination of Christianity in the light of modern evidence — when some insisted that the religious attitude could only be preserved by careful abstention from dangerous trains of thought. Nevertheless, it could be argued, even allowing for all Sidgwick's legendary reputation for balance and caution, that the phrase 'tending prima facie to establish the independence of soul or spirit', was somewhat of a hostage to fortune.

However, despite this slight slipping of their guard, the Sidgwicks, Myers and Gurney stressed again and again that they had no presumptions for or against the origin of the phenomena. Their only presumption was that there was something worth investigating. Their method, as we have seen, was to eliminate all cases explicable by known causes and then to build up a powerful residue to present to the educated community. In the final analysis, the aim was to drive the objector to admit the inexplicability of the phenomena or 'accuse the investigators either of lying or cheating or of a blindness or forgetfulness incompatible with any intellectual condition except absolute idiocy'(Sidgwick 1882a: 12). This is what lay behind Myers' incessant — almost frenetic — efforts to establish appropriate conditions and canons of evidence for each of his areas of investigation and discussion, Gurney's paper on the nature of evidence in matters extraordinary (Gurney 1884–85: 472–91), and Mrs Sidgwick's sustained and cool approach to the whole subject (Johnson 1936: 53–93).

Yet they may not have been as objective and without presupposition and prejudice in their practice as they would have liked to have been. One of the most extraordinary members of the SPR in the twentieth century was Eric J Dingwall, who took rather an iconoclastic approach to the SPR establishment. Susan Blackmore provides a vivid account of him in her autobiography, with his vigorous and perceptive interventions, at her first SPR AGM in 1978. Apart from her criticism of Arthur Ellison, the chair of the meeting, which seems a little unfair—by all accounts he was a decent and courteous man—Dingwall's capacity to draw attention to himself and to take a different line from the established 'old guard' of the SPR seems well caught (Blackmore 1996: 209).

One of Dingwall's persistent themes was that Myers and Gurney occasionally forsook their own canons of evidence and accepted stories about spontaneous phenomena without corroborating evidence because of a 'naïve belief that the social or academic standing of witnesses is sufficient to substantiate the stories they tell'. He cited as examples of this the Hornby case, which was encountered in a previous chapter,[2] and the Aberlour Orphanage case, where a clergyman stated that the warden of the orphanage was a reliable witness. The warden had related how he saw a cloud of light over a child's bed in the night and the following morning the child had told him his dead mother had been to visit him. However, the physician to the Orphanage in the mid 1890s stated that the warden was an inveterate liar (Dingwall 1961). Another gifted member of the SPR, J Fraser Nicol, also criticised the early leaders of the SPR on the same general point, but in a rather more understanding fashion:

> The Society's double standard of evidence arose in the following way. The Society's leaders were members of the middle and upper middle strata of society. When faced with the problem of estimating the value of evidence, they divided the world into two classes: (a) Members of their own class (Ladies and Gentlemen in the Victorian sense) whom they tended to treat trustingly; (b) Members of the lower classes, whom for brevity we may call the Peasants: them they treated with suspicion. This division of the British nation into 'goodies' and 'baddies' was never acknowledged in print but it was plainly carried out in practice. I do not think that snobbery had anything to do with it; rather this was the era—or nearly so—of Disraeli's 'Two Nations' in which one nation did not know how the other one lived, thought or behaved. And what the SPR people did not understand they feared (Nicol 1972: 351–53).

In support of this contention, Nicol contrasts the way that the medium Mrs Piper ('wife of a Boston shop assistant'), GA Smith, the hypnotist and agent in telepathy experiments ('son of a boarding house keeper'), and the young female Liverpool telepathists ('shopgirls'), were closely watched and in some cases put under surveillance, with the laxness with which the Countess of Radnor's friends—the Miss Wingfields (mediumship/telepathy experiments), the Reverend PH Newnham (telepathy/automatic writing), and Myers' near neighbour and friend Mrs Margaret Verrall

2   See above, p. 127.

(telepathy/automatic writing) — were treated. The situations were not in all cases entirely comparable but prima facie it is a serious charge to answer.

Their attitude, in essence, was a disposition to trust the educated over the uneducated. An amusing example of this was the clash between the young Butler Yeats and Frank Podmore over the value of testimony from different classes of society. Roy Foster, the biographer of Yeats, stated that Yeats did not become an associate member of the SPR till 1913 (Foster 1997: 462). This may be so in terms of formal membership but Yeats certainly attended a general meeting as early as 29th November 1889 (*Journal* 1889: 172–74) and at that meeting he vigorously opposed the common belief that the evidence of educated people was to be preferred to that of the uneducated. To compound his folly, in that rather dry environment, he stressed that the materialistic theory of apparitions was still held by many Irish. He described his collection of ghost stories from peasants in the West of Ireland and that there was coherence and theory behind them. He hinted at a lack of humility in the approach of scientific men. Yeats was twenty four at this time and one wonders at the reception of this fey exotic by the leading intellectuals of the SPR. But he directly challenged one of their basic premises and Podmore took him head on, as Myers would have done had he been present: 'In answer to Mr Yeats, Mr Podmore said he preferred the evidence of educated to that of uneducated persons: and he would not, as a rule, choose to base a scientific theory of ghosts on folk-lore and the fairy tales current amongst peasantry.'

Nevertheless, the criticisms of Dingwall and Nicol have to be taken into account. For example, Myers, basing his views no doubt on his HMI experience, stated that some testimony would come from the 6/7ths of the population who sent their children to board schools,[3] and he raised the question of what amount of credit could be given to uneducated witnesses in matters of this kind: 'But although a poor ignorant man's evidence is good enough to hang his neighbour, it is hardly good enough (if I may say so) to raise him up again' (Myers 1884–85: 188–89). There was a need for corroboration by a mind more carefully trained. And, for Myers and the SPR, this would often mean a local clergyman or doctor. Though this may sound like snobbishness to a twenty-first-century reader, one has to consider the position with regard to the education of the mass of people in the 1870s and beyond. It was obviously very difficult to get the balance right and one can sympathise with their difficulties.

It is interesting to compare Myers' response to the Devon solicitor (mentioned in an earlier chapter),[4] with his reply to Mr Barkas' letter on

3   See above, p. 140.
4   See above, p. 113.

the medium Madame d'Espérance (Myers 1885e: 407–409; Myers 1885g: 117–18). The former was treated by Myers with considerable respect. The latter must have aroused in Myers and his colleagues memories of the unprofitable séances of the 1870s—some of whose leading mediums Barkas had introduced them to at Newcastle—for neither Mr Barkas nor the medium were given much time or consideration, beyond the minimal public courtesies. There can be little doubt that the files of the SPR are saturated with class based judgements. Some of them are obvious and easily discounted with their comments on appearances and the loutishness of persons of the lower orders and, to be fair, it is not unknown even today for a sensitive middle class democrat to say something similar in private. Other statements suggest an alarming gap and lack of comprehension, as when Myers hoped that people would report on the sighting of Voltaire's ghost at the Chateau de Prangins in Switzerland, as the place was easily accessible (Myers 1889c: 53). Certainly it was, but only to the privileged upper-middle classes (Davies 2007: 9).

As has been said before, Myers was a snob, and this could well have affected his judgement at times. For example, he reacted quite virulently when his wife expressed an interest in palmistry, and her mother Gertrude appeared to be flirting with the idea of inviting Cheiro, the celebrated palmist, to lunch. 'As to Cheiro, all that I can say with certainty is that he is quite fraudulent', pronounced Myers (Myers 10/86: 14.7.1897) and then, in a second letter on the same day, he thundered: 'I hope your mother won't have Cheiro to lunch ... I think he is really too low ... He is, I suppose, originally, on about the footman level' (Myers 10/87: 14.7.1897) In certain situations scientific and social certainties could blend conveniently together.

This prejudice can be over stated, however. The comments about the working class tended to be rather throwaway and descriptive, applying to their person and character and not necessarily to the quality of their evidence, and the upper-middle class context of much of the evidence did not generally mean that that evidence was sifted and evaluated with less thoroughness. The small number of cases in which the Society was mistaken or hoaxed was not necessarily because class blinded them in their judgement but because of other factors. It is also quite easy to point to cases in the twentieth century when scientists have been hoaxed, and where class has not been a factor. It can be argued as inevitable that there should be a strong class-conscious element visible to us and less so to them, but that that did not fundamentally flaw the work that they did. The number of cases where they made mistakes or were 'duped' is very small indeed compared with the total examined and investigated.

Yet, and yet ... At times reading through Myers' correspondence one does get a sense of the investigations as heavily class-biased and psychical research as a kind of hobby pursued with congenial upper-middle class and upper class friends. Myers certainly enjoyed attractive female company in comfortable surroundings. He wrote to his wife from Hurstbourne Park in October 1890: 'Lady Malmesbury has become my special pal here, She has joined SPR & I have not yet invited her to Cambridge but feel that it may be unavoidable' (Myers 8/242). Early in 1893 he was with Lady Radnor at Longford Castle, Salisbury, and later that January he was at Thornes House, Wakefield: 'I have found a true comrade in Lady Mabel Howard (wife of Henry Howard of Greystoke) who gets very good automatic writing, and is very nice' (Myers 9/88, Myers 9/89).

There are also vivid accounts in memoirs of the time of his holding forth on the subject at the dinner table and at soirées — the very model of a modern psychical researcher. He had a strongly histrionic side to his character and obviously through his life enjoyed being the centre of attention. In 1890 ME Grant Duff recorded in his diary:

> Mr F Myers was of the party, and talked much of the Psychical Society. He confirmed what I had previously heard — that they found the evidence for appearances of deceased persons at the moment of death very strong indeed, but could make much less of the stories about haunted houses, the difficulties in the way of enquiring into them being extremely great! (Grant Duff 1930: 126).

Edward Marsh's memoirs mentioned Myers' table-talk more mockingly (though he had considerable respect for Myers' general literary skills):

> In my last year I was included in a very choice dinner party at the Jebbs'. It began with Frederic Myers telling us the social gossip of the next world about which he had exclusive information: George Eliot, he understood, had lately been seeing a great deal of Wordsworth (Marsh 1939: 17).

In defence of Myers, he clearly felt, as he himself stated, that since he went about a fair bit in society he had a role as a kind of ambassador for the cause, as awareness raiser and information provider; but if he was not careful, this could sometimes spill over into the posturing and the comic, particularly in front of unsympathetic or sceptical audiences.

Myers was very keen to involve members of the public, not only by having their awareness raised in this field, but also, as we have seen, by taking part themselves in basic experiments in telepathy and reporting carefully recorded spontaneous cases to the SPR. That is an approach which faded away in the early twentieth century, but in recent years Rupert Sheldrake has imaginatively revived this methodology, based on public engagement through carefully designed but simple experiments, particularly with regard to telephone telepathy (Sheldrake 2003).

The other main criticism was (and is) that they made judgements on the basis of race as well as class. Though never strongly explicit in their written work, one cannot help but feel that elements of an unreflecting racism in the work of the SPR show through at times. The draft of Myers' letter to Acton[5] clearly indicates a hierarchy in terms of trustworthy and untrustworthy sources of evidence. It is, however, anachronistic to describe this as sweeping bigotry, as Bart Schultz does in his biography of Sidgwick (Schulz 2004: 316–17). Myers was really talking in terms of education and scientific attainment, rather than making a wholesale condemnation of other societies. It is true, of course, that he contrasted the ease with which some races could be hypnotised/mesmerised — the French, the Indian — compared to the sturdy Anglo-Saxon. But, in general terms, Myers was not an active racist, and displayed no more than the normal, unreflective language of the educated upper-middle class at that time. An early letter to Sidgwick, for example, describing the visit of an Indian Guru to Cambridge and Oxford is completely without any racial tinge to it: 'I must say this, that a more charming, a serener, a holier man than the Baboo[6] I think I have never seen: if we are to have Theism developed into an organised religion I think he is your man' (Myers 12/97: 22.5.1870).

The Publication of Results in a Scholarly Format

The final characteristic of their work that marks it as 'scientific' was the determination of the leading members of the SPR to publish their findings in a scholarly form and to expose their views to public intellectual debate. Myers fully accepted these standards and his articles are well referenced and backed up by detailed evidence and the sources on which they were based. However, once these conditions were met, he was usually prepared to publish, confident in the quality of his evidence and his arguments. The Sidgwicks (continuing to be rooted in the Cambridge academic world) and William James (at the cutting edge of modern psychology) were more cautious. James was always acutely aware of what we might now call 'the boggle factor', particularly when it came to

---

5   See above, p. 115.
6   One should note that Myers was clearly using the term Baboo/Babu in its primary meaning as a term of respect, rather than in the secondary and more derogatory sense of an Indian clerk who wrote in English.

endorsing physical phenomena; his attitude during the Palladino affair,[7] as we have seen, is particularly revealing. On 4th October 1894 he wrote to Lodge, advising him against the widespread publication of the endorsement of Palladino by himself, Myers and Richet, 'and by no means send it to Nature, Science, or the XIXth Century'. He clearly pointed out that, having got rid of the more extreme spiritualists in the 1880s, the Society could now be in danger of exchanging places with them:

> We are changing places with a set of beings, the 'regular' spiritualists, whom we have hitherto treated with a species of contempt ... and we are since using ... language towards our hard-hearted colleagues almost identical with that which we have so often heard the aforesaid spiritualists use to us (Skrupskelis *et al.* 1999: 553).

Though Myers published a great deal, he was always against unnecessary, sensational and simplified popularisation. For example, Myers needed to keep some contact with the spiritualists and their periodicals in order to gain access to events, incidents and individuals that had an apparently supernormal element to them. Yet the Society's reputation for scepticism and even unfairness led to a number in that community shunning them. There was also a particular issue with WT Stead, the crusading journalist and publisher of *Borderland*, who in 1891 was proposing to take many of the SPR's cases and to publish them as part of his *Review of Reviews*, which had been founded in 1890 by himself and George Newnes, the editor of *Tit-Bits* — a publication hardly calculated to appeal to the austere and academic tastes of the SPR. This had the merit of bringing the SPR to wider attention, but carried the danger of possibly discrediting it by associating it with mere sensationalism. Writing to Richet, Myers hoped that he had got round this problem since 'he [Stead] has allowed me to insert a letter explaining that the SPR is not responsible for what he prints' (Myers 12/47: 9.11.1891.). This had little effect on Stead who published the material as 'Real Ghost Stories' a title with much more punch than Myers' cautious disclaimer.

Finally, discussion — free and fearless — was seen as an essential part of the scientific process, in order to test the strength of evidence in a collective forum. While the SPR held no collective views, it was agreed that nothing would be published unless it first met the standards of the Council. Papers to be published were read at general meetings and the floor was opened to questions afterwards. The great joint publications, *Phantasms of the Living* and the *Census on Hallucinations*, were both subject to what Gurney (in the context of the former) had called a 'great grind'. There were also frequent private discussions at Cambridge outside the

7   See above, p. 215.

formal confines of SPR meetings. Myers relished such discussions and believed in the Millian merits of free, dispassionate debate.

Discussion, however, required something to discuss, and there was an intense and admirably sustained strategy on the part of the SPR leaders to disseminate information, as has been indicated. Libraries were built up — a general one on psychical research, and later the Gurney library on hypnotism — for the use of the membership. The *Proceedings* were circulated nationally to the main scientific bodies and 'as far as is found practicable to Free Libraries, Mechanics' Institutes and Literary Institutions' (Cerullo 1982: 86 and note 20). Substantial donations of books and money were made, particularly by Myers and his family and by the Sidgwicks. The *Journal*, from 1884 onwards, enabled members to examine and make contributions to specific cases and phenomena investigated by members of the Society. Finally, as we have seen, a policy of publishing in quality periodicals (often material almost verbatim to that in the Proceedings) was adopted by Barrett, Gurney, and most completely by Myers. All the major periodicals — *National Review, Fortnightly Review, Nineteenth Century, Contemporary Review, Cornhill* — had articles and/or letters on psychical research in them; as did the more popular *Pall Mall Gazette, Light*, and Stead's short-lived *Borderland*.

John Ziman (Ziman 2002: 97–102) has lucidly pointed out how important the publication of results in an appropriate format is, and has been, for establishing trust into individual and group testimony. Reports should be written up according to standard conventions, so that they provide the person studying the report with all the information necessary to recreate the procedures and processes in order to replicate the original result. It is interesting that deviation from this procedure is still pounced upon. For example a recent letter in *Nature Biotechnology* complains of 'a lack of documented methodology and information that is essential to faithfully reproduce the science claimed ...' (Noseda and McLean 2008: 26–28). There is little doubt that the early leaders of the SPR tried to follow this model, based as it was on the emerging science journals and practices in the late nineteenth century. They provided their readers with guides and supplements to the use of the planchette, crystal balls, thought-reading experiments, and the tabulation of results. They wrote up their experiments in ways which would allow their readers to try to replicate their results and to criticise their procedures. However, they only claimed to have demonstrated the existence of certain phenomena under certain conditions and not to have provided a guaranteed formula for their replication, or a theory for their explanation. Their work could be criticised by modern standards, but they were starting a fresh discipline not inheriting a well-developed and secure one.

Sidgwick, Myers and Gurney sometimes speculated on how much evidence was necessary to gain the attention of the scientific community, let alone win them over. The first stage was to get enough evidence to refute or at least weaken Hume's argument against miracles. Hume stated we have the universal experience of all ages that miracles do not happen and against this a small amount of human testimony that they do. We have no experience that miracles happen and plenty that human testimony is fallacious; consequently it was highly unlikely that supernatural phenomena existed. Sidgwick argued in his addresses as President (Sidgwick 1884a: 153–55, Sidgwick 1889: 1–2) that a large and substantial amount of evidence, that was carefully tested and sifted, could weigh against the inherent improbabilities of miracles. It is difficult to fault this as an approach or to think of any other line that they could have taken, but no amount of testimony gathered by them could prevail against those who thought them deluded, their methods suspect, and that they had not the authority, the right, the training, or the credentials, even to investigate — let alone make judgements in — this field.

The Problem of Interpretation and Explanation in a World of Contested Expertise

There was a considerable and confused debate over who had the right to assess the phenomena in this area. Richard Noakes (Noakes 2004: 23–43) has vividly illustrated this in his account of the clash between WB Carpenter and Sir William Crookes over the investigation of spiritualism in the 1870s. Carpenter argued that Crookes' expertise in one area of science did not prevent him from being deceived and deceiving himself in the swirling murkiness of the séance room. He knew nothing of the physiology and pathology of the human mind and its inveterate tendency to self-deception. Crookes, for his part, stressed his technical expertise with scientific instrumentation and his trained powers of observation. It should be noted that the same issues and conflicts arose in France and Germany as investigators pursued similar aims to Myers and his colleagues (Treitel 2004, Monroe 2008). So, who was to adjudicate between these conflicting claims? And what expertise could Myers and his colleagues appeal to in justification of their conclusions?

With some exceptions, the core Cambridge group at the heart of the SPR had built their intellectual authority on a detailed and expert knowledge of a relatively small number of classical texts, and a shared high Victorian literary, historical and philosophical culture. What they were doing, in the 1870s and 1880s, was moving away from that narrow context and undertaking detailed field research in a difficult, contested and ambiguous region. In moving outside their home territory they bumped up against other types of expertise. These included the tacit, practical and experiential knowledge of both the spiritualist community and the showmen who could expose and duplicate the trickery, as they saw it, of mediums. They also collided with the new world of professional science, which may well have seen the SPR's approach as misguided and anachronistic: they were reviving the old-fashioned approaches and methods of Natural History — where gentlemen, gentlewomen and clergymen tried to demonstrate God's natural order, by deploying the lower-level scientific skills of description, collection, and classification — not this time on flora and fauna, but on ghosts and bogies.

This made them especially vulnerable to the charges of people like Carpenter and Henry Maudsley,[8] and they tried to guard against this, as we have seen, by a rigorous methodology and a retreat from the obviously entertaining, melodramatic and stagey, and by an intensive programme of self-education in the sciences, particularly in the cases of Myers and Gurney. They also utilised appropriate expertise, for example, FY Edgeworth on the calculus of probabilities applied to psychical research (Edgeworth 1885, 1886) and they cultivated leading scientists of a broadly sympathetic disposition, like Lodge, Rayleigh, and J J Thomson.

What made the issues more difficult to grapple with was the woolliness and softness, and sometimes distastefulness, of the subject matter. For many people, the grand successes of Victorian Physics — the steam engine, the railway, the telegraph — carried all before them. The laws, on which these achievements were founded, were demonstrable and validated every day. In contrast the phenomena the SPR studied were evanescent and not easily replicable. To many outside observers, they strongly suggested self-delusion, even temporary insanity, and often fraud. The obvious conclusion then, was that the alienist should deal with the former and the conjuror and police with the latter. Conjurers and reformed fraudsters asserted time and again that, 'The scientist may be versed in certain lines of scientific subjects, but their knowledge in those lines will not be of service to them in their investigation of the "medium"' (Dingwall and Price 1922: 131). It was greatly to the SPR's credit that faced with attitudes like this, they managed to make out a strong case for psychical research as an important area of study in its own right. They argued strongly that only by applying and adapting scientific procedures to this

8   See above, p. 187.

difficult field, could hard won expertise be built up, which entitled an individual to have his or her conclusions taken seriously.

Chapter Nine

The Legacy of Myers

Human Personality and Its Survival of Bodily Death

Sidgwick died in August 1900 and Myers just a few months later. The last letters between them were tender and courageous. Myers was ordered abroad again to the Riviera to ease his symptoms, but Bright's disease[1] was beginning to affect his heart and arteries and his gasping for breath was only relieved by copious draughts of nitro-glycerine (a not uncommon medical practice of the time). Mrs Thompson had predicted that he would pass over in 1902 and one sometimes gets the rather unsettling picture of Myers, with an almost cheery relish, monitoring his final illness against that prophecy. As Sir Lawrence J Jones described it:

> I well remember on this occasion going for a walk with Myers and the turn of the road at which he stopped and said to me: 'I have four hundred and fourteen days to live.' I gazed at him in astonishment. 'Yes,' he said, 'my death has been definitely predicted to me for a day in February 1902. I have made all my arrangements on this basis. I have divided up the work that still remains to do on my book into twelve parts, and I am going to do one part each month. I shall then finish the book and have a few weeks before my time comes' (Jones 1928: 43).

He died earlier than that in Rome on 17th January 1901, where he and his family had gone in order to take the same treatment that William James was having. James had been receiving a fashionable remedy consisting of injections of products from various parts of goat, including the testicles (Blum 2006: 250). Although Myers also underwent this, he continued to decline, but retained his curiosity and intellectual energy to the last. There is a vivid, almost inspirational account (like Evangelical accounts of good

---

1   See above, p. 223.

Christian deaths) of his end in Axel Munthe's *The Story of St Michele* (Munthe 1937: 299–301), and one by William James, a more reliable source altogether. James wrote to Mrs Sidgwick

> Poor FWHM, as you will ere this have learned, died here on the 17th of pneumonia supervening upon all his other troubles. His serenity, in fact his eagerness to go, and his extraordinary intellectual vitality up to the very time that the death agony began, and even in the midst of it, were a superb spectacle and deeply impressed the doctors, as well as ourselves. It was a demonstration *ad oculos* of the practical influence of a living belief in future existence (Skrupskelis *et al.* 2001: 412).

Yet, in some ways, the personality, spirit and ideas of Myers seemed to be just as lively and influential after his death, as before. This legacy and influence can felt in three ways: firstly, through the posthumous publication of *Human Personality and Its Survival of Bodily Death*; secondly, the role of Mrs Myers as the custodian of his memory and reputation; and thirdly, the evidence presented for his alleged survival after death through the cross-correspondence phenomena and messages from a number of other mediums.

According to the editorial note at the front of *Human Personality and Its Survival of Bodily Death* (Myers 1904 1: x), Myers had completed the text to halfway through volume 2 and in 1896 had made arrangements for Hodgson to finish putting together the work if he died. Virtually all the book had been written in one form or another, and the main task was that of arrangement, editing and proof reading. In fact Alice Johnson, who had been designated to complete the appendices and see the book through the press, probably did more than her fair share, given Hodgson's preoccupation with Mrs Piper and his dislike of Mrs Myers. This was to be a bone of contention between Hodgson and Mrs Myers, and also a partial explanation for some omissions in the survival evidence printed at the end of the book. There was considerable ill-feeling about this and in a letter to Mrs Thompson, Alice Johnson explained that she was not able to make use of Mrs Thompson's material in the book because of Hodgson's opposition (*Light* 28.3.1903: 151–52). This was probably the only matter on which Mrs Myers agreed with Hodgson. She constantly complained of his delays in spite of the fact that he had been very well paid. The following extract of a letter from her to William James gives something of the flavour of Mrs Myers in action:

> I told this to Mr Hodgson—he is absolutely *indifferent*,—and sends no work & no reply.—Mr Longman will stand this no longer—Is Mr Hodgson's conduct that of an honourable man? ... Can you help me?—Will you write *now at once* to Mr Hodgson? (Skrupskelis *et al.* 2002: 94–95, August 1902).

Poor James was caught right in the middle, between a frantic and manipulative Mrs Myers determined to get her husband's magnum opus out as quickly as possible and at all costs; and a dogged and obdurate Hodgson who bowed the knee to no person and who was still obsessively researching Mrs Piper.

There now follows a summary of the book, identifying and drawing out the salient points, without going over the detail of the previous chapters in too much depth. Some repetition is, however, inevitable, as much material in *Human Personality and Its Survival of Bodily Death* is incorporated from Myers' earlier work in the *Proceedings*. The preface (previously quoted)[2] is very moving since it accurately describes Myers' natural desire to have the approval of his peers, not in a showy or crowd pleasing fashion, but in the sense of being a man of worth at work on a topic of worth. It was painful for him to feel that he was seen by some of his contemporaries as at the margins of intellectual and cultural life, grubbing around in trivial and strange pursuits. Therefore, in this isolation, the support and encouragement of two highly gifted men like Gurney and Sidgwick meant everything to him (Myers 1904 1: viii).

Myers' approach in the book was to provide a full survey of the range of humankind's faculties before culminating in a section which argued that these faculties in their highest form demonstrated the independence of the mind, the individuality, from the brain, and its ultimate capacity, bodiless, to survive death. At each stage in the book he recapitulated the main argument, and showed how each element of the unusual phenomena he was describing, fitted into his overall thesis. He was particularly concerned to counter the argument of Leaf and others (Oppenheim 1985: 260) that all he had done was to describe the fracturing of personality into sets of discrete behaviours. His aim was not to destroy personality, but to demonstrate that an examination of the ways in which personality disintegrated provided clues as to its potential integration, and access to higher powers currently fitfully and unpredictably displayed by sinner, sage and saint. It is not clear that he managed to do this or to adequately substantiate the thesis in his title—*Human Personality and Its Survival of Bodily Death*. His own death had a part to play in this and had he lived one could have expected a more robust synthesis in the last part of the book and a more thorough and evidenced section from mediums on the continuing existence of the personality after death. Yet, even with these reservations, it is the work of a very powerful and creative intelligence and still has considerable relevance.

2   See above, p. 196.

Myers looked at the disintegration of the personality first from the *idée fixe* onwards, working through a range of behaviours in abnormal psychology, before looking at its higher-level manifestations in the performance of the genius and of highly gifted psychics and mediums. He raised the question of how far we could have mastery of ourselves and our talents, and to what extent these faculties and talents were acquired through earthly effort or accessed through a spiritual source that both pre- and post-dated existence. There was a Platonic element in all this that sat uneasily with the idea of developmental skills and Myers never fully clarified the ambiguity. However, despite these internal tensions, Myers strongly opposed the degeneracy school of Nordau. He focused on humankind's potential, through the control of the subliminal, for the highest personal growth and he looked forward to a century hence when his ideas would become the orthodoxy. He was over optimistic in the sense that psychical research is still a heavily contested area and it is argued (again contested) that there has been no linear and incremental progress in the way that this has occurred in other areas of science. But his second point—about personal development—chimes quite effectively with aspects of the self-help movements that have proliferated in the second part of the twentieth century and on into the twenty first.

In his chapter on sleep, Myers significantly anticipated the work of Jung and Freud in the sense that he saw sleep, not as the psychological by-product of daily activity, a kind of mental excreta, but as a subject profoundly worth while studying in its own right. Dreams contained amongst their undoubted garbage, many creative insights that were highly valuable and which hinted at an unguessed reservoir of imaginative power. He raised the question—discussed by many later commentators—as to what extent we could gain power over our own dreams, and therefore access our own unconscious faculties. While he accepted that much dreaming was a reversion to an earlier stage of development and that its main purpose was reparative, he also believed that a careful study of dreams and dreaming was a way of understanding the language of the subliminal. Through this study one could find the solution to personal problems, stimulate artistic creativity, and access supernormal messages. He gave a number of examples of this, including, as we have already seen, Robert Louis Stevenson[3] and his Brownies (Myers 1904 1: 121–52).

He then moved on to forms of somnambulism and eventually hypnosis, celebrating the victory of the Nancy School over the Salpêtrière. Hypnosis could be defined as suggestion and self-suggestion but he admitted that these were merely names to disguise our ignorance. We did not know

3   See above, pp. 72–73.

why suggestion and self-suggestion worked. He referred to his and his brother's work on the Lourdes phenomena and how they felt that all the so-called miracles could be brought under the heading of suggestion. There was, too, the question of how many levels and layers of personality could be created by hypnotic trance and how stable were these. Myers did not really go into detail over this, though he stated that Mrs Sidgwick found eight or nine (Myers 1904 1: 171). As far as he was concerned, in theory no limit could be assigned to this multiplicity (Myers 1888d: 387). This was an area where a greater theoretical depth and clarity from him would have been useful. It could be argued that sometimes he had too much information, and the digesting of this into a broad, overall framework prevented the undoubtedly speculative but highly valuable attempt to work out connections and relationships in greater detail.

Certainly he was well aware of the potential of hypnosis as a developmental tool. He defined education as a mixture of repression and stimulation: hypnotism could repress the undesirable characteristics and stimulate the positive. His comments on this topic are particularly interesting and seem, in some respects, to anticipate the much later movement of accelerated learning. He argued:

> The work of stimulus or dynamogeny is even more difficult to execute properly than that of inhibition. We know pretty well what we wish to prevent the child from doing. It is harder to discover all that a judicious education might advantageously teach him to do. The very first lesson we have to impress upon him — attention — is really of unknown scope. We are usually satisfied with the inhibitory side of the lesson; with the restraint of wandering thought. The intensity of the attention thus steadied is a different matter; and I shall presently quote certain experiments which point to possibilities in this direction as yet seldom realised. Intellectual education, rendered possible by attention, includes the training of perception, memory, and imagination; and all these faculties' will be found to have been sometimes much heightened by hypnotic suggestion (Myers 1904 1: 174).

He was also in advance of his time in thinking that hypnosis could help with alcoholism, kleptomania, violence, and sexual problems, and even the particular bogy of late Victorian England, the morphine addict. He had an interesting comment on sex, given his personal history, stating that it could be transformed into something higher and, 'that instinct for union with beauty which manifests itself most obviously in sexual passion may be exalted into a symbolical introduction into a sacred and spiritual world' (Myers 1904 1: 177). That may well be true, but it could be argued that such a view, held by the wrong person, could give licence to a certain sort of spiritual seduction.

Myers also considered the transposition of senses that could sometimes (this is contested) be demonstrated through hypnosis and linked this with synaesthesia and Gurney's experiments. He was on dangerous territory here, particularly when he stated that the perceptive power might be independent of the specialised sense organs and that hypnosis could stimulate telaesthesia or clairvoyance. Yet, these ideas anticipated work done in Eastern Europe both before and after the Second World War (Ostrander and Schroeder 1999: 240–41, 255–57). And in *Irreducible Mind* (Kelly *et al*. 207: 108) there are references to work in this field in the 1960s, 1980s and 1990s. At the end of the section, Myers speculated on where this source of great power came from. In doing so, he provided one of his few detailed statements on the relationship between the physical and spiritual worlds. He argued that our ethereal world drew power from the spiritual world — the metetherial — and that this 'ultimate vitalising Power' lies beneath the chemical energy 'by which organic change is carried on' and that we will all eventually learn to access it as part of our cosmic evolution (Myers 1904 1: 215–19).

In his section on sensory automatisms, Myers paid tribute to Gurney (Myers 1904 1: 228) as the first person to raise the study of apparitions above the level of a collection of mere ghost stories. But Myers wished to move beyond the study of spontaneous hallucinations to discover the methods that could be used to induce them — hypnosis, crystal vision, waking dreams — and to consider their relationship to the physical world, for example to existing optical laws. Furthermore, he wished to probe behind the individual or collective examples of telepathy from the living and the dead, and speculate on the underlying mechanism. He was fully aware of the difficulties of suggesting that telepathic messages were carried by brain waves rippling through the ether. Yet, Myers believed that in some cases there did occur a phantasmogenetic impact on reality (as when all the people in a room saw an apparition) caused by some kind of *psychorrhagic diathesis* on the part of the original initiator of the image. This extremely ugly term referred to Myers' view that sometimes a part of the psyche could break free from the body (often involuntarily and unconsciously but occasionally willed and aware). This, in itself was not physical but it gave the appearance or illusion of physical impact, and its source was the 'ultimate vitalising power' mentioned above (Myers 1904 1: 264–65). He gave some examples of willed self-projection by individuals, which seem to anticipate the work on astral bodies by Carrington, Crookall and Monroe, which became increasingly influential in certain circles through the twentieth century and beyond (Myers 1904 1: 294–96).

In volume 2 of *Human Personality and Its Survival of Bodily Death*, Myers moved, in the chapters on 'Phantasms of the Dead', 'Motor Automatism', and 'Trance, Possession and Ecstasy', towards the culmination of his argument. He posed the central question and one that occupied the attention of all really thoughtful members of the SPR: what conditions did a visual or auditory phantom have to fulfil before it could be regarded as prima facie evidence for the influence of a discarnate mind? (Myers 1904 2: 10). In his final chapter he stated that he saw possession as a more developed form of motor automatism. He clearly acknowledged that this, at the beginning of the twentieth century, brought one back to the concepts of the Stone Age, the shaman and the medicine man. But he believed that the difference was that there were now the tools available to start to access higher spiritual states and that we could eventually learn to develop trance as part of the evolutionary process. The chapter ended with some examples from Piper, Swedenborg, Stainton Moses *et al.*, but, as Salter[4] stated, it appeared to lack the final clinching evidence on which Myers based his assertions, and which underpinned the extraordinary resilience and optimism of his death bed.

The immediate commercial reaction to the book was very positive. It was published in the UK, in America, and in Europe. The first edition was in February 1903. It was reprinted in March and June of that year and again in September 1904. There was even a translation into Hindi. But its size daunted and an abridged edition appeared after the First World War with an introduction by Leo Myers (Myers 1919/1992) and another abridged edition in the 1960s (Myers 1961/2001). The reviews were, predictably, very diverse in reaction and tone. William James (James 1986: 203–15) was fair and generous. He recognised Myers' huge skills at classification, categorisation and — on the basis of this — his development of the concept of subliminal consciousness, with its potential powers of explanation and synthesis. Yet he was also aware of the gaps in detail and he was not particularly appreciative of the high flown rhetorical element in Myers. He also made the point that Myers had perhaps relied too heavily on a small number of exceptional cases and that he had not explained clearly how the subliminal could be both rubbish heap and treasure house.

Other reviews were less flattering; for example that of GF Stout (Stout 1903: 44–64) in the prestigious *Hibbert Journal*.[5] It was pretty disparaging and summarised Myers' views rather unfairly. Stout parodied the subliminal self as a kind of guardian angel and revived the old concept of unconscious cerebration to explain material emerging into consciousness from the so-called subliminal. He refused to consider as worthy of examination the supernormal material that Myers had so laboriously put

4   See below, pp. 285–86.
5   See further above, p. 192.

together and he showed in his concluding section that he had, like many other scientists, not really engaged with the material. Nor had WH Mallock done so. Mallock, the witty and reactionary author of *The New Republic*, thought Myers was just describing two — and two only — distinct consciousnessnesses, and accordingly ridiculed him for this (Mallock 1903: 628–44). Myers had been irritated by Mallock in life, and long before had put him on the list of the small number of people whom he intensely disliked (Myers 26/63/77) — a distinction Mallock shared with Oscar Wilde and Sir William Harcourt amongst others.

One has had to wait around a hundred years to get a fuller appreciation of the quality of the book, its anticipatory nature, and its continuing relevance for our own times and beyond. It was unfortunate that the dominance of other schools of thought assigned Myers and his work to the lumber room of psychology, but there has been more recently increasing appreciation of Aldous Huxley's comment in his foreword to a later abridgement:

> His account of the unconscious is superior to Freud's in at least one respect; it is more comprehensive and truer to the data of experience. It is also, it seems to me, superior to Jung's account in being more richly documented with concrete facts and less encumbered with those psycho-anthropological-pseudo-genetic speculations which becloud the writings of the sage of Zurich (Myers 2001: xv).

Much the fairest, most analytical and detailed estimate of his work and ideas occurs in Ed Kelly's *Irreducible Mind* (Kelly *et al.* 2007). Kelly has particularly urged the importance of not being put off by surface aspects of the book which he argues were characteristic of Myers and his time (Kelly *et al.* 2007: 581–82). This is indeed true, but even in Myers' own time his language was found to be over rhetorical and florid on occasions, and this inhibited proper appreciation of the evidence and ideas he put forward. Nevertheless, as Kelly states, the ensuing century or so has produced more detailed evidence of the phenomena Myers studied which fits into his 'basic descriptive framework'. Moreover, the experimental processes that he urged people to develop — hypnosis, automatic writing, crystal gazing — still have potential as methodological tools. One might add here the particular variant of crystal gazing which Raymond Moody has recently developed through his psychomanteum (Moody and Perry 1993). In addition, the expansion of anthropology has indicated the existence of automatisms across the world like those displayed by Myers' subjects. Hypnotic experiments have been replicated; substantial work has been done on dreams as carriers of information, and on the Ganzfeld experiments; exceptional individuals have been identified in all the categories Myers covered (Karagulla 1978, Treffert 1989); and (*pace* Stevenson

1990) there has been no decline in the apparently paranormal, which has always been there for those who have been prepared sensitively to adapt their approaches to individual needs and contexts. However, and quite rightly, its ontological status is still fiercely challenged and contested.

There have been outstanding individual mediums, since his time, who have given evidence of survival at least as good as Mrs Piper's and Mrs Thompson's. New areas (either not explored or only briefly foreshadowed by him) have developed, including evidence from cases of apparent reincarnation and near death experiences. Also, since his time, the study of drop-in communicators and the increasingly sophisticated use of proxy sitters have provided evidence that strains the telepathic link between sitter and medium and the super-psi interpretation almost beyond credibility. Yet there still remains the logical impasse described in *Irreducible Mind* whereby, in theory, apparent evidence of survival can be explained in terms of psi processes only involving the living (Kelly *et al.* 2007: 597). However, the fact that evidence is frequently organised in ways which suggest the conscious and characteristic involvement of a particular personality, does weaken, though not totally invalidate, the super-psi hypothesis.

For many people, however, the ultimate stumbling block is Myers' metaphysical position. It is quite possible to follow his argument for much of the way with regard to his explanation for a range of psychological phenomena and their inter-relationships. It is also possible, for many, to argue that aspects of his research and work provide some evidence that something survives bodily death. However, his view of the evolution of humankind and its ultimate destiny, soaring as it does, speculatively, hopefully, into the cosmic, the mystical, the ultimate, is more difficult to accept and it is grounded clearly in the occult tradition of Plotinus (Myers 1904 2: 289–91). As Gibbons has put it:

> At the heart of Myers' thought is a belief that is also the core of the occult philosophy: 'That which lies at the root of each of us lies at the root of the Cosmos too. Our struggle is the struggle of the Universe; and the very God-head finds fulfillment through our upward striving souls' (Myers 1904 2: 277, Gibbons 2001: 106–107).

Yet, it cannot be denied that for those of a certain temperament, imaginatively and emotionally it has a huge appeal. Myers believed that evolution was an endless process and that new capacities and talents would emerge both on this and on the other side of 'The Great Divide'. He appeared to think that these new capacities were not so much produced by organic change as released from the subliminal or metetherial realm (Myers 1904 1: 118), whether as a set of ideal Platonic Skills and Talents to which humanity and all creation aspires, or as vitalising energies, or a mixture of both, is not clear. He also argued that this growth would only be achieved through considerable effort and with the co-operation of the spirit world. He suggested the vivid image of children looking through a keyhole at the first moves in a game of chess (and wondering as to its nature and rules), as an analogy for our current limited perception of the huge potential for growth that lies outside our blinkered, limited, terrene (as he would call it) perspective:

> The chessboard in this parable is the Cosmos; the pawns are those human faculties which make for the preservation and development on this planet of the individual and the race; the pieces are faculties which may either be the mere by-products of terrene evolution, or on the other hand may form an essential part of the faculty with which the human germ or the human spirit is originally equipped, for the purpose of self-development in a cosmical, as opposed to a merely planetary, environment (Myers 1904 1: 93–94).

This unsubstantiated and, for many scientists, windy and untestable speculation about ultimate purpose and destiny goes a long way to explaining the decline in Myers' reputation in the twentieth century. Yet, the writers of *Irreducible Mind* have done much to resurrect and substantiate the key elements of Myers' beliefs, and at least rescue them from the rather exotic spiritualistic accretions that time has gathered round them. They have striven to support Myers by finding current evidence that backs up his view of the richness of human personality and the complex and non reductionist relationship between mind, body and brain. Specifically, they argue that many of the original observations of Myers and his colleagues, have been amply confirmed in the succeeding century: the impact of the placebo, of faith healing, the production of stigmata, physiological changes induced by hypnosis, distant mental influence on living systems, and other phenomena.

There is also an analysis by Alan Gauld (Kelly *et al.* 2007: 241–300) of the conflict between the brain-based view of memory and the post-mortem survival of memories and some of the issues to be tackled in resolving this conflict: neither an approach based on an over-simplified view of memory as brain-based memory traces, nor a credulous approach to survival, will work. There is support for Myers' view of an underpinning self behind multiple personality states, with evidence both from dissociative identity disorder and the examination of the production of hypnotic personalities. The authors also stress that there has been a considerable amount of largely corroborative work on Near Death Experiences since Myers' time, hugely expanding the relatively small number of case histories he had, and strongly suggesting some independence of consciousness from brain

(Kelly *et al.* 2007: 367–421). This contradicts the conventional view that the basis for conscious experience is high frequency gamma band EEG oscillations (30–70 Hz), and that the absence of such activity (as in cardiac arrest and general anaesthesia) means absence of consciousness. They finally move on to support a view of human personality rather like that of Myers, with its huge potential for growth in talent and spiritual insight. They argue, too, that the psychology of the future will be based on a transmission theory of mind. In other words, the brain acts as a filter for and not a producer of consciousness, which, has its origin elsewhere. On the survival question, they do not, in an academic work, write with the confidence of the later Myers, but argue that the best accumulating evidence has now shifted the balance of probabilities marginally away from the super-psi hypothesis to that of some kind of post mortem survival. How limited or extensive that survival might be, and of what nature, is another matter. (Kelly *et al.* 2007: 595–99).

Mrs Myers and the SPR

We have discussed the legacy of Myers in terms of the rise and fall of his influence across the twentieth century and beyond. But there is another sense in which his legacy can be construed and examined. There was, not unnaturally, great public curiosity (within the appropriate communities) as to whether the leading light of the Society for Psychical Research had himself survived bodily death. Intriguing evidence was not long in coming, but this process and its evaluation were to some considerable extent impeded by the attitude of Mrs Myers.

Eveleen Myers was worried about the revelations concerning Annie Marshall; she resented the appropriation of the name Myers by all sorts of mediums; and she was very sceptical about the quality of much of the material. It should be stressed, however, that she was not hostile to all psychical activity. She did not, for example, resent a message from Alec Yorke — one of Queen Victoria's courtiers, an amateur medium in private, and a personal friend — to the effect that Myers was resting and settling well into life on the other side:

> I was at Valescure for a few days with the Wingfields on my way out [Kate Wingfield had earlier given Myers a number of séances shortly before his final journey to Rome] & we had 3 very comforting sittings. Fred is resting so peacefully but no circles much disturb him yet but friends of his and ours are guarding and helping him. I am so deeply touched by his thought of me. I always loved and admired him and

wished to be nearer to him in his work-but our lives ran in different grooves (Myers 23/23: 27.2.1901).

It should be noted that Kate Wingfield was a gifted private medium of 'good family', who had provided Myers with a range of interesting paranormal evidence over the years, but who, at the request of her family, gradually focused her gifts purely on automatic writing that conveyed spiritual teachings.

Mrs Myers' reaction was quite a complex one and, although she was not a totally sympathetic character, one can have some understanding of her position. She was jealous of the mediums her husband had consulted before his death and also of those he appeared to communicate through after death. She even tried to rival the mediums Thompson and Piper and become a medium herself. She told James that she had been reading a book on trance mediumship and had started to go into trances in which she heard Myers' voice and that the trances frightened her children (Skrupskellis *et al.* 2001: 622–23). She used his diary to record her thoughts after his death and there are entries referring to these attempts at mediumship 'Trance coming — Power gaining. Trance. F near me. Called back by children' (14/2: 18/19.2.1901).

She could not understand why her husband had to communicate through other women and not directly through her. She was distressed at private material, which could be mishandled and misinterpreted, being revealed at séances, and she greatly resented the public appropriation of her husband's name and reputation. She frankly found it vulgar and offensive. She would have particularly disliked WT Stead's later claim that 'both my son and Mr Myers are actively interested in making this bureau a success' (Myers 27/67: 5.5.1909). This referred to Stead's setting up of Julia's Bureau, a kind of central contact point for communicating with the dead, through a co-operative of mediums. Her Fred was a great man and should be recognised as such. She lobbied the National Portrait Gallery to get his portrait (by William Wontner) permanently on display there. They tactfully replied that there was a ten year process of sifting and only original portraits rather than copies could be placed there (Myers 25/32 May 2nd n.y.) Myers did, in fact, eventually make it.

Much of her opposition to the alleged early post-mortem communications was not made public at the time, but is described in the unpublished memoirs of WH Salter, the doughty long-term secretary of the SPR, who wrote them in 1955 while recovering from an operation. It was clear from these memoirs that there was little love lost between Salter, a number of the key SPR personnel, and Mrs Myers, and one must be careful in allowing for bias. However, the fact that at times she appears to have been a very difficult personality comes across from not just this one, but from a number of sources. On the other hand, the desire to obtain the fullest possible evidence for Myers' post-mortem survival may well have led Lodge and Salter, particularly, not to take seriously enough her genuine personal concerns. It is not, for example, difficult to feel sympathy for her when her husband could write ecstatically to Lodge in 1899: 'This year 1899 – after 23 years of such endeavour – has brought me certainty – Far more finally than has Mrs Piper, and I have gained from Mrs Thompson the conviction that a Spirit is near me who makes my religion and will make my heaven' (SPR 35/1528: 3.1.1899). She may never have read that particular letter (though there is evidence that she read much of his correspondence) but something of that emotion may well have leaked out and it would have been hurtful even to a personality less jealous than she. The other issue was Myers' projected legacy to the SPR. His mother and brother had given substantial sums. It was, therefore, a surprise that Myers left nothing in his will to the SPR, despite statements to friends during his lifetime that he would do so. Later, according to Sir Lawrence Jones, Leo Myers flew into a rage when Jones mentioned that he was surprised that his father left nothing to the SPR (Salter 1955a: 12–13). The implications are obvious, namely that a will in which money was donated to the SPR was destroyed and that Leo's rage was the rage of the guilty. But they are only implications. It should be stressed that there is no evidence but this gossip. Leo's rage could equally have been stirred by what he thought was an impertinent and intrusive enquiry.

Salter's unpublished memoirs succinctly described what he took to be Mrs Myers' state of mind when, after her husband's death, she read the private biography that he had deposited with her and some close friends:

> Here, he was, declaring to six friends, and requesting them to make known to the world, the fact that the great event in his life, the turning point in his spiritual development, was not his love for the woman who had been his wife for 20 years, had born him three children, and had contributed largely to his social success, but a married woman whom he had known for three years, and who had been dead for 25 (Salter 1955a: 14).

Salter was not accurate in this respect since Myers had told Eveleen about Annie shortly after his marriage. But she was possibly not aware of the full depth of his feelings until she read the autobiography. And Salter made the further point: 'To make matters worse there was Mrs Thompson giving messages from Phyllis [Myers' name for Annie Marshall] to Myers while he lived, and messages from Myers about Phyllis since his death.' Mrs Myers, who had always been both suspicious and jealous of Mrs Thompson, now felt able to attack her, as Salter put it 'bona fides' without the restraining influence of her husband. She wrote to various people pointing out that the mediums — and she included Mrs Piper in this — had often sat at Leckhampton in her husband's study and could easily have got information this way and that Mrs Thompson was an attention seeker and did what she wanted without regard for her husband. In short, as Salter said, she tried thoroughly to discredit her.

She fought tigerishly both to preserve her view of her marriage and to prevent the Annie Marshall story being made public. There seems little doubt that she destroyed her husband's records of both Piper and Thompson sittings. William James, writing to Flournoy after his sitting with Mrs Thompson in November 1899, stated: 'Myers himself is making a monographic study of an excellent medium (unpaid) whom he saw in London and who on the whole seems as good as, and in some respects is better than, Mrs Piper' (Skrupskelis et al. 2001: 113). And as he wrote in February 1900 to Mrs Morse: 'The unfortunate circumstance is that with Mrs Thompson as with Mrs Piper, the most striking evidence of her powers is too private for publication' (Skrupskelis et al. 2001: 147–48). This unusual combination of quality and intimacy in the evidence must have been very threatening to Mrs Myers.

She was also determined to round up all the existing copies of Myers' autobiographical fragment which contained details of Myers' relationship with Phyllis/Annie Marshall. In the draft of this fragment Myers had made it clear that — though he did not want it published in full while Walter Marshall lived, or during his wife Eveleen's lifetime if she objected to publication — nonetheless: 'I expressly wish the <u>whole</u> to be ultimately published' (Myers 26/63). Lodge, however, was afraid that if she had all the copies back, this would never happen. He held out until the bitter end, determined that a document of considerable relevance to psychical research should not be destroyed or tampered with. Nor did he return Myers' letters to her, in spite of her saying that she needed them for a possible biography. Mrs Sidgwick was put into a panic (in so far as that splendid person was ever panicked) by her request and wrote, 'I am rather disturbed by what you say about a sealed envelope for I have not found one' (Myers 18/8: 17.3.1901). Mrs Myers showed her a copy, so that she would know what to look for, and Mrs Sidgwick replied reassuringly, 'Of course I will not say a word to Arthur Sidgwick or anyone about the "fragment of inner life" that you showed me' (Myers 18/11: 13.7.1901).

However, undeterred by Lodge's attitude, Mrs Myers continued to work tirelessly to get all copies of the autobiography back. In a memorandum to Leo, Silvia and Harold, she summarised the situation (Myers 18/75: 19.10.1907). She had, now in her possession, twenty one of the original twenty five and she was working on the remainder. Lodge was particularly concerned that the softer-hearted James (who had in fact returned his own copy) would be vulnerable to her appeal and support her claims. So on hearing of Hodgson's death at the end of 1905, Lodge warned James that she would try to get Hodgson's copy back: 'I am sorry to write thus, but I write in confidence and in mistrust, or more accurately I write to you in privacy that I mistrust the relict of FWHM' (Skrupskelis *et al.* 2003: 123). In June 1906, his resolve duly stiffened, James wrote firmly to Mrs Myers stating that Myers' letters to Hodgson and Hodgson's copy of the autobiographical fragment would not be returned to her; and that Hodgson had told James he would not return it. 'I think your memory must have played you false, when you say that Hodgson promised to destroy it, or return it to you' (Skrupskelis *et al.* 2003: 238–39). Leo Myers then appealed directly to James, but to no avail (Skrupskelis *et al.* 2003: 254–55). Apart from Lodge's warning, James had earlier been made suspicious by Mrs Myers' publication, in October 1904, of her husband's *Fragments of Prose and Poetry*, which included an expurgated version of the autobiographical fragment. James queried the substantial omissions she had made, but she replied, with a certain guile, that James seemed to have forgotten how brief the autobiography was (Skrupskelis *et al.* 2002: 629–30).

The battle between Lodge and Mrs Myers, over the autobiographical fragment, went on for years, but strangely it didn't prevent her from asking Lodge to be the godfather to Harold's son, born in 1928. Lodge managed to get out of it. In 1930 he returned again to the fray: ' — don't you think that the dramatic moment has come for withdrawing your repudiation of his attempt to give evidence. Thirty years has made a considerable difference; and your attitude has been a difficulty which we have had to overcome, largely without success' (SPR 35/1296: 7.7.1930). Years later, after her death, Salter as secretary of the SPR tried again to get the autobiography published in full, but Silvia and Harold still refused to countenance this. It was not finally published in its entirety till 1961. The enduring family opposition was difficult to understand. Taking the document on its own terms, and accepting the views of Myers' most intimate friends as to his character, unless there is still undiscovered evidence to the contrary, he behaved with nobility and restraint. He was not married at the time. He supported Annie through her difficulties and he emphasized the spiritual and platonic nature of the relationship. He remained in close contact with Walter Marshall and his children till the end. This was hardly the behaviour of a cad and a seducer.

Another of Mrs Myers' objectives was to sit herself with the great Mrs Piper and see what evidence she could obtain. So, accompanied by Leo, she went to America from the autumn of 1901 to the spring of 1902. The records of these sittings have survived and reveal a mixed and complex situation. William James, writing to Lodge, commented on the early ones:

> Mrs Myers is here, returned from California, & about to sail home in the Oceanic, April 2nd. She read me yesterday reports of 2 ½ sittings with Mrs Piper. Myers came very poorly in the first one; but I confess that the dramatic impressions which I received from the latter two were favourable as regards sincerity of effort to communicate. The turn which the Myers Communications here have lately taken improves in my estimation the probability that they may be real (SPR 35/947: March 23 1902).

This was, of course, farther than James was ever prepared to go in public. Mrs Myers herself vacillated considerably, and in private was often prepared to be more positive than in her public statements. One can see why. It seemed, at times, as if every Tom, Dick and Harry, was claiming communication from the late FWH Myers and she quite naturally felt sullied and worried by this process. It was almost a kind of spiritualistic paparazzi that was hounding her.

Her general thesis was that all the mediums — Thompson, Piper, Verrall, as we have seen — had visited him at Leckhampton and been in his study where his diary, books and papers were easily accessible (Myers 18/104/1: n.d.). Nevertheless, some communications gave her pause. The Myers/p persona (the standard format was to add the initial of the medium — in this case Piper — to the name of the alleged communicator) had stated: 'Do you remember the place where we found the boot?' Her comment on this was interesting:

> I consider The Rat Incident good. The circumstances are these. In the night about 17 or 18 years ago, a Rat carried downstairs one of my Husband's boots which was put outside his door to be blacked. In the night we were awakened by a thud thud — and were much perplexed. At 7 AM my husband went out for an early run, and found the boot by the fire in the hall with a bit gnawed out of the boot (Myers 20/41/1: n.d.).

There was, however, a little too much about Annie Marshall in the scripts and on one occasion, in the very early stages, the Myers persona stated: 'Annie is taking my place as I am unable to make myself clear' (Myers 20/22/1: 12.3.1901). This must have been particularly galling for Mrs Myers. And she certainly did not like the modest comment that he found that he was not so much better after all than others in communicating. She put two red crosses, one each side of the section, and scrawled 'not like him' (Myers 20/26/1: 20.3.1901). Her Fred, dubbed, as we have seen, 'Myers the superb' at Cambridge, must surely be able to rise to this supreme challenge.

She certainly vacillated quite a lot in her evaluation of the evidence she received. She wrote to GO Trevelyan in 1903, asking for his help with one or two details that came up in connection with his name and more generally that, 'When I was in America — I sat with Mrs Piper the medium — and some very wonderful things were told me — some only known to myself — some not known to myself but since found to be correct' (Myers 25/109). This was in marked contradiction to the letter she wrote to *The Times* (23.10.1908) which stated that she and Leo had found nothing of value in the various 'spiritualistic messages' that the papers had published, 'purporting to come from my husband, the late FWH Myers'. Her rather variable attitude seemed to stem from the fear of personal details emerging that would embarrass her and her family, and from 1904 onwards her focus was very much on what the automatic scripts of Mrs Verrall would reveal. Myers was close to Mrs Verrall intellectually and Eveleen was probably jealous.

The Verralls and the Myers had been good friends and lived close to each other. Myers and AW Verrall (a classical scholar with wide literary interests and an outstanding lecturer) admired each other. While still alive, Myers had encouraged Mrs Verrall in automatic writing and crystal gazing, so although sceptical, she now decided to make a systematic practice of automatic writing, to provide the deceased 'Myers' with the opportunity to communicate. The tension between Mrs Myers and Mrs Verrall really started to intensify in 1904. Myers had often urged people before their deaths to put a message in a sealed envelope which their discarnate self could then reveal, thus — not conclusively, but with a high degree of probability — proving their continued existence. In 1904 Mrs Verrall received an automatic message saying Myers directed that his sealed envelope be opened and that it would contain the phrase, from Plato's *Symposium*, about love bridging the gap between God and Man. In December 1904 the envelope was opened at a private meeting (Anon 1905–1906: 11–13), and the letter read that if Myers could revisit the earth it would be to Hallsteads he would go. At the time this was accounted a failure. However, Mrs Sidgwick perceived some relevance to the message in Mrs Verrall's automatic script, because she had by this time found and read her husband's copy of the autobiography. She realised that the love of Phyllis for Myers (and his for her) was strongly platonic and Hallsteads, where they met frequently, played a central part in that. Mrs Sidgwick lent Mrs Verrall the autobiography and Mrs Verrall came to believe that that interpretation was a valid one. Yet only public quotation from the unexpurgated autobiography could evidence this and it was impossible that Mrs Myers would sanction it. Indeed the others, fearing problems, had not even invited her to the opening of the sealed envelope.

Mrs Verrall's automatic writing continued to prove a particular source of irritation to Mrs Myers. Mrs Verrall was about to publish a substantial account of her work in the SPR *Proceedings* and as an act of friendship and courtesy she showed Mrs Myers the proofs. The latter immediately demanded the excision of all references to Myers. This led to the end of their friendship. As Salter related, Mrs Margaret Verrall reluctantly consented 'to Mrs Myers' demand that references to communications from Myers should be deleted' (Salter 1955a: 21). When Mrs Myers had consulted the wise and unflappable Mrs Sidgwick about her concerns, the latter replied that she could not understand the problem (Myers 18/17: 6.1.1905). With her usual transparent honesty, she stated that wives had no claim to control messages coming from their discarnate husbands unless they revealed their (that is the wife's) private affairs (Myers 18/18: 10.1.1905). She obviously did not think that the limited references in the scripts merited such censorship. Mrs Myers continued battering away at the issue. Mrs Sidgwick again replied, this time after she had read Mrs Verrall's full paper, 'I have read Mrs Verrall's paper very carefully, but I really do not think there is anything in it which would suggest to any ordinary person any private matters about Mr Myers,' and, more forcefully, she stated that it was 'Not right to suppress it' (Myers 18/24: 23.7.1906). Mrs Myers also tried to stop the publication of a book by Miss HA Dallas in 1910 (Dallas 1910) in which there were references to post-mortem communications from Myers. On this occasion Mrs Sidgwick replied, 'I will enquire at once about Miss Dallas's book. I am afraid the SPR Council would have no right to prevent her quoting from the published Proceedings' (Myers 18/26: 3.1.1910).

The onslaught on Mrs Verrall had indeed been very intense. Eveleen Myers reeled off a string of accusations against her: that Mrs Verrall could have got much of her information subconsciously from the time she helped Mrs Myers sort Myers' papers after his death, and that her writing contained none of the tests of identity agreed on between her and her husband (Myers 18/29–39/1: early 1905). Most powerfully: 'I admitted you almost exclusively into the intimacy of my home, and of my great sorrow and you incur a grave responsibility if you publish it' (Myers 18/63: June 1906). Some of the most extreme expressions of her distress and disgust were in draft letters that she may never have actually sent. In this she was rather touchingly following Myers' advice from years before, for he was often worried by her emotional outbursts: 'Resolve once for all never to write letters of <u>abuse</u> of anybody … There is no power like self-control.' When he himself wrote such letters to relieve his feelings, he then burnt them (Myers 9/10: 27.1.1892).

Eveleen Myers retained a certain status in London society to the end. For example, the increasingly famous Bernard Shaw promised to come to visit Dolly and her and cheer them up 'for a long afternoon' after their husbands' deaths (Myers 24/1: 26.5.1905). Yet, as her grand-daughter pointed out, she grew increasingly remote from the world of the bright young things and lived more and more on her memories and kept the Myers' papers locked away in the smaller house she moved to at 12 Clevedon Row after she left Cambridge and her son Harold married (Myers 29/70). It must, however, have been gratifying to her to be recognised as the Mrs Frederic Myers. Ada St Aubyn wrote in embarrassment to her after one tea party that she didn't catch her name and was covered in confusion when she got home and read the card and realized that she had been speaking to Mrs Frederic Myers: 'I have his *St Paul* always on the shelf in my room' (Myers 23/109: 4.7.1929).

Yet she never dropped her guard in terms of protecting, as she saw it, the purity of her husband's reputation. She belonged to a press agency which provided her with all the latest clippings in the field of psychical research and possible misuses of his name. She read memoirs that mentioned his name, copied out favourable references, and challenged the uncomplimentary or inaccurate. She severely criticised the writer Douglas Sladen (another Old Cheltonian) for his inaccurate description of Myers' deathbed scene:

> At your request I put down for your Book "Twenty Years of My Life" a long paragraph about my dear husband – & I was much distressed – at the strange inaccuracies that were printed about My Husband's last Hours in Rome. And not what I had sent you. – I never left My Husband day or Night – and he died in my arms – I never was in Rome before – but I never went out – or left him for one moment – I saw nothing, – & have never been back to Rome (Myers 27/57: 1917).

She also pointed out to Sladen (who was known for his carelessness) the highly embarrassing fact that he had Henry Sidgwick quoting poetry to Mrs Myers to comfort her as Myers lay dying. Sidgwick had died four months before! The letter is marked 'draft', but one somehow has the feeling that the original was sent!

Her later years were also somewhat marred by a bitter quarrel between her and Dolly (and to some extent Charles Coombe Tennant) over their mother's will. Eveleen had always felt that Dolly had been their mother's favourite and, as often happens, sibling rivalries manifested themselves in a particularly unpleasant form when fuelled with the expecations, or otherwise, of inheritance. Firstly, Charles Coombe Tennant refused to continue to pay Eveleen the £200 a year that Gertrude had consistently paid her since her marriage to FWH. Secondly, Eveleen claimed half of the securities that Gertrude had gifted to Dorothy, arguing that Gertrude always meant to divide them, only leaving them all to Dorothy as a way to avoid tax. One of Eveleen's letters was sent on 11.11.1918 but there was no hint in it that the war had just ended. The war that absorbed all her attention was of a different nature; and Dorothy, in fact, at one stage threatened to correspond with her only through a solicitor (RMCA 5970: 8.5.1918).

The Cross-Correspondences

As already noted, Mrs Verrall, although sceptical about the reality of paranormal phenomena, started in 1901 to systematically practise automatic writing, on the hypothesis that if Myers had survived death, she might be an appropriate vehicle through which he could communicate. The early efforts were gibberish but gradually she produced material from which it seemed possible to deduce some kind of meaning. Several other women had also started automatic writing and receiving messages. Like Mrs Verrall's, these messages individually made little sense; but collectively — after careful independent examination and tracing of sources (historical, classical, literary) — they seemed to have coherence and meaning.[6]

Mrs Thompson was only briefly involved at this stage because of Mrs Myers' opposition. Miss Wingfield (known as Miss Rawson in the literature) was withdrawing from mediumship and began to concentrate on the transmission of spiritual philosophy. Mrs Piper was across the Atlantic and part of a larger research project involving Hodgson and Hyslop. Thus it was highly opportune that Mrs Verrall was prepared to try to open up a possible channel of communication. In fact, from the first coherent script on 5th March 1901 to her death in 1916, she produced over one thousand messages. The first hint that one or more mediums might be used in collaboration occurred when Mrs Verrall, in a script of 31st January 1902, got references to sphere and spear which had occurred in a Piper sitting with Hodgson three days before. Then in 1903 Mrs Verrall was asked by her scripts to send material to Hodgson (August/September) and eventually she saw in a letter from Hodgson on the 20th January 1904 that the indirect references to syringa, in a script from 5th October 1903, meant much to him, as Myers had received this through Mrs Piper in America, in 1893, from 'Phyllis'. In his autobiography Myers had written, with regard to Hallsteads, that, 'There for many a twilight hour I have paced alone, and shaken from the thick syringas their load of scent and

---

6   Only a brief outline of these complex phenomena can be given here.

rain' (Myers 1961: 28). At this time, however, the connection was completely unknown to Mrs Verrall (Salter 1948: 4–7). In 1903 the small group of automatists was added to by Mrs Holland (Alice Fleming, sister of Rudyard Kipling) who, having read *Human Personality and Its Survival of Bodily Death* in India, restarted the practice of automatic writing left off a few years before. From June onwards she was in contact with Alice Johnson of the SPR, and late in the year sent her a script (written on 7.11.1903) which had the phrase 'My Dear Mrs Verrall' and the instruction to send to 'Mrs Verrall 5 Selwyn Gardens Cambridge'. Mrs Holland did not know Cambridge, did not know Mrs Verrall's address, and was unaware of her special interest in Myers. However, she had read *Human Personality and Its Survival of Bodily Death* and there were several references to Mrs Verrall in that (Salter 1948: 7–8, Saltmarsh 1975: 43–4).

It appeared increasingly likely to Johnson and to Lodge that messages/clues/problems might be being divided up and being communicated through more than one medium, though it required a certain deferred gratification, patience and accurate recording to see this unfold, since the process could take several years. For example, in 1904 JG Piddington of the SPR sealed an envelope containing the phrase that if he were a spirit he would try to transmit the number seven in some form or another (Salter 1961a: 175–81). Over the next few years six mediums received scripts playing with the number seven in various ways and on the 27th January 1909, Mrs Verrall wrote: 'Has he (Piddington) found the bits of his sentence scattered among you all?' Mrs Verrall did not get to know of Piddington's sealed letter till 30th March 1909. This, of course, destroyed the purpose of Piddington's original sealed envelope, which was intended to provide some kind of after-death puzzle which the discarnate Piddington could solve, thus 'proving' his survival. However, it did suggest discarnate awareness of the process and some element of co-ordinated design to demonstrate that awareness.

A very powerful automatist joined the group in 1908. This was Mrs Willett, Winifred Coombe Tennant, who was married to Myers' brother-in-law Charles. She had lost a beautiful and intelligent child, Daphne, and tried to communicate with her through automatic writing. Her later scripts provided some of the most powerful and apparently convincing evidence for survival, but added an extra complexity as we shall see. In 1910 Mrs Holland stopped automatic writing but Mrs Lyttelton became involved in 1913, Mrs Wilson in 1915, and Mrs Richmond in 1919. AW Verrall died in 1912 and his wife in 1916. However, their daughter, Helen, continued automatic writing for a number of years. The main weight of interpretation was initially on Miss Johnson and Oliver Lodge, with some support from Mrs Verrall herself. However, from about 1912 onwards most of the work was undertaken by Piddington and GW Balfour. The scripts began to peter out around 1930/31 (Salter 1961b: 183).

What was the nature of these cross-correspondences? Why were they adopted? Was there a consistent and over-all message or plan and to what extent was that plan carried out? Could the whole activity have been the product of the over-fevered imaginations of a cloistered elite? The question of fraud and collusion was also raised, of course, but the automatists were geographically dispersed and there was certainly no financial imperative to spend many years on such a laboured and long-winded project. Elements of delusion, of loss and longing, of fabricating meanings, of nostalgia for a settled late-Victorian past, or yearning for post-war peace and stability, may help us to understand the motivation, but they do not explain away the material.

What does require addressing is the method adopted by the *soi-disant* communicators, and also an assessment of whether the pattern stated by the interpreters to be in the material is substantively there or just the product of over-reading or imagination. All so-called mediumistic communication has to face the objection that the material transmitted could come from the mind of the sitter or somebody else living (telepathy); or that through clairvoyance the medium had access to physical records or events related to such messages and obtained the information that way. The interpreters of the material believed that the communicators devised increasingly complex cross-correspondences to get round these objections. There were simple correspondences when two mediums appeared to be talking about the same subject matter at the same time. There were complex correspondences where the communicators succeeded in getting references and indirect clues introduced through more than one medium, which only made sense with a final or extra clue at a later date. This suggests a high level of collective design and purpose, implying character, intention and personality. Alice Johnson (Johnson 1907–1909: 166–391) was the first to discuss this theory in detail. She stressed that she had not found the idea in the writings of Myers before his death, nor was it suggested by the automatists in their 'normal' state. She argued that it emerged clearly as a student of the scripts read them through and that 'it suggests an independent invention, an active intelligence constantly at work in the present, not a mere echo or remnant of individualities of the past'. It should be noted that there was, in fact, a reference to collaboration between incarnate and discarnate entities to prove survival of death, in the posthumously published *Human Personality and Its Survival of Bodily Death* (Myers 1904 2: 274). Finally, there were super complex cross correspondences where the discarnate entities appeared to be communicating a future plan for the earth and seeding this with a number of predictions that their incarnate colleagues could verify.

It was argued more generally, as part of this whole intricate process, that a range of devices was used to circumvent allegations of telepathy and clairvoyance. Sometimes an important word would be slipped in between mixed up phrases of Latin and Greek; sometimes symbols disguising a real person and a real name were used — the Lily, the Wheel, the Knight, the Palm Maiden, Beatrice, the Laurel, the Peacock, Phyllis, the Fish, Marc Antony etc, etc (Salter 1961b: 186–89). There were frequent quotations and allusions of a literary nature, often drawn from books that the automatists knew but on occasions, and more convincingly, from sources they did not (Balfour 1918). The whole process seemed at times like a giant Victorian word game (anagrams, cryptic puzzles, strange puns and rhymes) of which, in fact, Myers and his colleagues, Gurney, Jebb, Hodgson, were inordinately fond.

There now follow further expanded examples of each of the types of cross-correspondence. The first example is of a simple cross-correspondence. In April 1907 Mrs Verrall, Mrs Piper and Mrs Holland (in India) all received, in ignorance of each other, messages on the theme of death and dying: 'Thanatos, Mors, Pallida Mors etc, etc' (Roy 1990: 251). There were more developed kinds of the simple cross-correspondence, including what has come to be called the Lethe case. George Dorr in Boston had asked Myers through Mrs Piper what the word Lethe meant to him. He received a string of references largely referring to Lethe in the context of Ovid's *Metamorphoses*. Lodge later asked the same question of Mrs Willett. Through her, the Myers persona replied with a detailed set of Lethe references largely based on Virgil's *Aeneid*, which Myers had written about and knew virtually by heart (Saltmarsh 1975: 90–97). The Myers persona pointed out that it was important to give different information; otherwise telepathy between the two mediums would have been the most obvious explanation.

As an example of a complex correspondence (and also of co-operation from investigators on this side) one can cite the Hope, Star, Browning case (Saltmarsh 1975: 66–71, Piddington 1908: 59–77). This fully involved Mrs Piper, who came over from America in 1906–1907 to see if she could assist. A Latin message was read to 'Myers' through Mrs Piper (who knew no Latin). It asked Myers to transmit to A and to B two different messages, and then one to C which would reveal the hidden connection. Piddington also suggested that words/phrases that were significant for a cross-correspondence should have by them a triangle inside a circle. This came through in a script of Mrs Verrall's on 28th January 1907. There was a reference to a star, to a winged desire, and to Abt Vogler. On 3rd February a star was drawn in Helen Verrall's script (daughter of Mrs Verrall) and a reference to rats in Hamelin town. On the 17th February, through Mrs Piper, came 'Look out for Hope Star and Browning'. Browning was the clue, through the third medium, which led to his poem 'Abt Vogler' given by the second. When he read Abt Vogler, Piddington found that one stanza, the only one with star in it, had two lines particularly apt to describe the cross-correspondence and what the investigators had requested in the Latin message: ' That out of three sounds he frame, not a fourth sound but a star ... Give it to me to use! I mix it with two in my thought'. Finally, at the urging of Piddington for some further confirmation, in the session on 24th April with Mrs Sidgwick, 'Myers' drew a star, and gradually got out AB, then ABt, then Volugar, and finally, Vogler, and his final message was 'Now, dear Mrs Sidgwick, in future have no doubt or fear of so called death, as there is none' (Dallas 1910: 111).

It was asserted by the interpreters of the scripts that simple and then complex predictions were seeded through the automatic writing. Lodge commented that he and Myers and Sidgwick had often discussed the importance of consistent, veridical predictions, as providing good prima facie evidence for some form of survival. In fact one of the earliest of these involved Myers' close friend, and the first significant automatist, Mrs Verrall. On 11th December 1901 she wrote of someone reading Marmontel on a cold night by candle light. Below the script was an attempt at Sidgwick's signature. The following March a friend of hers, Mr Marsh, told her he had recently read Marmontel by candle light on a cold night, and two names (mentioned in a later automatic script by Mrs Verrall) Passy and Fleury, also occurred in the passages he was looking at (Lodge 1909b: 155–59).

However, the cross-correspondences eventually turned into one giant, over-arching predictive cross-correspondence, called the Plan. Here one enters an arena where, if not already severely challenged, the reader's tolerance will be stretched to breaking point. The plan, contained in the Salter archive at Trinity (Salter 1948: 18–27, Roy 2008: 553–56) and in a number of other collected sets of the cross-correspondences in England and America, was to bring to birth, through some kind of psychical genetics, supervised by the biologist, Francis Balfour, a new Messiah, who would help bring peace to Earth through a New World Order. This it appears was Henry Coombe Tennant, a soldier, spy and later a monk, and the younger son of Winifred Coombe Tennant (Mrs Willett). This is an over simplified version of what Salter himself puts in his privately printed but unpublished *An Introduction to the Study of Scripts* (Salter 1948) and it can easily be mocked and ridiculed. Salter clearly stated that the discarnate Cambridge group were part of a much wider plan to support the development of international peace after the coming war and to encourage the birth of souls who would work for that. However, even with that modification, the language used and the predictions made, tended to suggest the subliminal yearnings of this world, rather than necessarily the systematic purposes of discarnate entities.

Mrs Willett has, within psychical research circles, a reputation as an outstanding automatist, who contributed greatly to the cross-correspondences and work on the psychology of mediumship generally. However, there is one central issue that must be addressed in her case which does not relate to the other automatists. She, alone, as Salter clearly pointed out, began to write under the pressure of great personal loss and grief — she lost a girl Daphne in 1908 and later a son Christopher in the First World War. She had a strong maternal streak and since much of the detail of the Plan occurred in her scripts it is easy to see them as a detailed, complex and yearning exercise in wish-fulfilment by her subliminal, to assuage her loss. It should also be noted that she was a staunch Liberal and in 1922 became the first woman member of the British delegation to the League of Nations Assembly. It is important, therefore, in an assessment of the scripts, to see to what extent materials related in her scripts are foreshadowed in the scripts of the earliest automatists like Mrs Verrall and Mrs Holland. Salter has argued that there was some evidence of this (Salter 1961b: 187–207).

An additional complication of the cross-correspondences is that interpretations changed radically over the years as further information came to light. The major and, to many people the most impressive, example of this is the Palm Sunday Case, where information transmitted by Mrs Willett appeared to reveal the secret love between Arthur Balfour and Mary Lyttelton and gave examples of the way in which he memorialised her death (Roy 2008: 196–224). He was very secretive about this and some of the details were not known even to his brother Gerald and his sister Eleanor. (However, RJQ Adams has cast some doubt on the intensity of the relationship, particularly on Balfour's side [Adams 2007: 29–33].) This led to the assessors of the scripts trawling back through to the earliest materials from a decade before and considerably revising their interpretations. A minor example of changes in interpretation is the 'Muirhead' case of 1915 (Johnson 1914–15: 50–76), where Miss Johnson first thought that a reference to Alexander's tomb referred to Alexander the Great but later, with additional evidence, she ascribed it to Alessandro de Medici's tomb in the Sagrestia Nuova in the Church of St Lorenzo in Florence. She had also at one stage assigned — in a script of Mrs Holland's — the phrase 'Alexander Moors Head' to Dr Alexander Muirhead, who was involved in the development of wireless telegraphy. She knew that Mrs Holland had some interest in/or connections with this field. Interestingly, Myers was in Florence in December 1869 and visited San Lorenzo (on the 28th). He also visited Florence again the following December 1870 (Myers 14/1). All this could lend some support to the theory that the cross-correspondences functioned like a kind of verbal ink blot and that one read into them what one wanted to find: were it not, however, for the fact that the levels of cross-correspondence were at times powerfully striking and relatively unambiguous and occasionally provided verifiable information not consciously known by the automatist. And were it not also for the fact that a number of the communications displayed, particularly in the scripts of Mrs Willett, something of the general characteristics and intellectual powers reminiscent of the communicators when alive.

Joseph Maxwell (Maxwell 1912–13: 57–144) and, most recently, Christopher Moreman (Moreman 2003: 225–42, 2004: 60–61) have explored the key question as to whether or not the cross-correspondences were generated by chance. In short, it has been argued that intensive hard work and over-imagination on the part of the investigators plus the inevitable links, associations, coincidences arising from a vast body of automatic writing, were enough to explain the apparent pattern, without positing any supernatural agency. Moreman asserted that he was able to get a convincing set of cross-correspondences by providing students with pseudo-scripts to assess based on passages from works of literature. It should be noted that WH Salter, years before (Salter 1928: 525–54), had tried a similar experiment to Moreman's and had come to the opposite conclusion. Moreman has been strongly criticised by Keen and Roy (Keen and Roy 2004: 57–60) who stated that he had not paid sufficient attention to specific veridical material later found to be true, and which had not been known to the transmitting medium. Further, that he had totally ignored the elements of general messages/instructions/communications/discussions/interactions contained in the 'genuine' cross-correspondences (which were evidence of character and personality); and that his article failed to cite the best examples of cross-correspondence that were least vulnerable to the charge of over-reading.

One further and very major stumbling block to an assessment of the existence of a post-mortem Myers, particularly with regard to the cross-correspondences, has been the sheer mass of material produced. A complete set of automatists' scripts runs to nineteen volumes (Roy 2008: 569–70); there are two additional volumes of Mrs Willett's automatic writing; and there are nine volumes of notes, commentary and index. The communicating language is English but the frequent quotations from Latin and Greek (and other languages), the extensive references to literature and history, and the dense and convoluted symbolism, make a thorough assessment of the material very difficult. It also, if subjected to a cost-benefit analysis, makes many potential investigators query value and reward in terms of effort put in. Indeed, although a number of commentators have seen the cross-correspondences as clever attempts by the discarnate to circumvent the objection to spirit-communication that it can all be explained by telepathy, clairvoyance, or Super ESP, others have felt that such effort would have been more wisely spent in trying to communicate absolutely first-rate evidence of personal survival (Braude 2003: 95–100) – and that these should be based on the kind of persuasive criteria that Braude outlined in the last chapter of *Immortal Remains* (Braude 2003: 284–88). He argued that the cross-correspondence approach just multiplied obscurities which then led to more contested and competing interpretations. Yet a defender of the method would counter that that was the price one paid to try to minimise the power of purely telepathic or super-psi alternative explanations.

The Myers persona has not just been encountered in the cross-correspondences. Depending on one's point of view, the idea of Myers has been a conceptual, emotional, symbolic resource for mediums to draw on across continents and over the years, virtually up to the present day; or the actual Myers, after death, has displayed exactly the same energy, determination and tenacity he demonstrated in life, to proof the continuation of human personality. A Myers personality appeared in Oliver Lodge's sittings with Mrs Leonard in the First World War and most widely and evocatively expressed in Lodge's book on his son *Raymond* (Lodge 1915: 90–95). There first seemed to be warnings – references to Horace's *Odes* – that Lodge would suffer something and that Myers would help protect him. Shortly after this, Lodge's son Raymond was killed in the war and later, again through Mrs Leonard, the message came that Myers was acting as the young man's guide and support after death. In addition, and still through Mrs Leonard, a book test was set up with Sir William Barrett (one of the surviving founders of the SPR) on 5th August 1921, at the wishes of the discarnate Myers (Fodor 1969: 34). He gave instructions where the book was to be found. He could not give the title but stated that on the cover he got a sense of progression and that two or three books along the shelf from this book were books that linked to Barrett's studies in his youth. The initial book turned out to be *Middlemarch* whose title had a sense of progression in its second part. (Since it was one of Myers' favourite books/writers, it was strange he could not get this through, but names/titles etc seemed particularly difficult.) Two or three books away was *Heat and Sound* by John Tyndall (whose assistant Barrett had been in his youth).

In the mid 1920s Geraldine Cummins, who was to remain the outstanding automatist in the UK up until the 1950s, started to receive material from an alleged Myers, which was eventually published in two volumes: *The Road to Immortality* and *Beyond Human Personality*. The preface to the 4th edition of the former, written by Geraldine Cummins, stated that shortly after its publication, Sir Lawrence Jones, a close friend of Myers and his wife, came to visit her and made her an extraordinary offer. He said that Eveleen Myers had bought twenty-seven copies of the book to give to her friends, since she was sure the communications were from her husband, and Sir Lawrence offered her, on behalf of Mrs Myers, the chance to live on the top floor of Mrs Myers' house so that she might receive communications from her husband. Miss Cummins refused the offer, very wisely no doubt (Cummins 1967: 7). The writing, ignoring the content for a moment, is fluent and articulate, and Mrs Myers must have caught, what few other scripts achieved, a sense of the intellectual and imaginative nature of her husband. The scripts were also completely free of any personal detail (since they were about cosmic philosophy and life after death in general) so were not threatening to her. The first book seems to accord well with other channelling sources (Klimo 1998) and could be seen as good standard spiritualistic fare, but the second, while having elements in common with the first, moves into descriptions of life on other planets which would probably lose those readers who hadn't already been put off.

The Myers persona has managed to sustain himself beyond this, however. *Swan on a Black Sea* (Cummins 1965), another substantial piece of automatic writing by Geraldine Cummins, contained the apparent post-mortem communications of Myers' wife's sister-in-law Winifred Coombe Tennant (the medium Mrs Willett). There are frequent references to him there. He also makes an appearance in *The Barbanell Report*, alleged communications from Maurice Barbanell (Beard 1987: 56, 122), a major spiritualistic journalist of the mid-twentieth century. He stated that he had met Myers several times and that he retained his seriousness, his drive and his firecracker mind. Perhaps the most dramatic sighting of the Myers persona has been during the extraordinary sustained series of paranormal events occurring at Scole, in Norfolk, in the mid 1990s and collectively summarised both in the book *The Scole Report* (Solomon and Solomon 1999) and in much more detail in the *Proceedings* of the SPR of the same year. Much accurate material was transmitted concerning Myers and his life, and puzzles were set for the sitters to solve which contained characteristics of the cross-correspondences of ninety years before, though much other activity focused on the creation and transmission of physical products. There have been a number of criticisms of this report, though the final adjudication by the arbiter appointed came down in favour of some element of paranormality. No trickery was detected by the investigators. However, with regard to Myers, virtually all the information relating to him, could have been accessed from one book by Oliver Lodge (Lodge 1909b), and for this reason the evidential quality of the material pertaining to Myers was considerably weakened.

One unfortunate effect of the cross-correspondences, because of the above factors and the amount of highly private information apparently disguised and packaged in the scripts, was that the SPR came to be seen as the private, rather arid vehicle for communication with the world beyond by a family group in Fisher's Hill, Surrey (Arthur and Gerald Balfour and their sister Nora Sidgwick plus devoted friend Piddington), with additional support and back up from Alice Johnson. They seemed to have little sympathy with the simpler and more mundane survival and grieving concerns of the mass of the population. This was unfortunate and perhaps a little unfair, but the feeling was there, and may still have lingered post Second World War, and formed a residual, subliminal motive for the onslaught by Hall and Jarman on Myers' reputation.

We have already considered the major objection to the cross-correspondences: that they were the product partly of the subconscious of the automatists and partly of the latent desires and wishes and over-reading and over-analysis of the interpreters. One would hope that the debate continues. But it doesn't. The culture that provided the time and money to produce and study them no longer exists. One book (Roy 2008) has been written on certain aspects of them and is vivid and moving, but it is not a comprehensive evaluation of the cross-correspondences. Nor has there been any replication of such activity, by later mediums, in such a sustained and intricate fashion. The vast collection of cross-correspondence scripts (available only in the printed volumes, the thousands of original handwritten documents having been destroyed) are a monument to a particular period in history. To those who have studied them more than superficially, they are at the least, a vehicle that tells a number of love stories embedded in the aspic of upper-middle class lives nearing the end of Empire, a memorial to a high culture that has long since passed; they could be a collective confabulation on (perhaps) both sides of the grave, or the most convincing demonstration of life after death yet realised. As with the rest of this book, interpretation and meaning must rest with the reader. I have tried, as Myers himself would have wished — in selection, tone, and structure — to avoid the extremes of silly credulity or of knee-jerk and unthinking scoffing. Above all, I have tried to evade that most damaging position, a patronising attitude towards a past, which without our resources and our hindsight, quite often has made a better and more honest fist of things than we ourselves.

The Summing Up

Was Myers' quest successful? In personal terms it was. He became convinced, on the basis of the intimate sittings he had with both Mrs Piper and Mrs Thompson, that he had communicated with human beings (however different their nature and post-mortem existence) who had survived bodily death. This belief was underpinned by his wide ranging reading and research in paranormal and abnormal activity across Europe and in the United States. It led to him bearing the onset of death with a kind of joyous resilience, almost even insouciance: a death (as described by William James) which many a holder of traditional Christian belief might have admired. However, his wider hope, that detailed methodical investigation – over the next hundred years or so – would establish human immortality, or at least some form of life after death, has not been realised. Parapsychology is still challenged by many, even at the level of its right to exist as a genuine discipline, and the same debates, issues and wrangles still plague the subject as they did in the late nineteenth century. In a more general sense, however, his achievement has been considerable. He has, through his massive and impressive co-ordination and synthesis of material in *Human Personality and Its Survival of Bodily Death*, kept alive, in stimulating and challenging form, the key issues of the mind–body relationship. He has been a force for good in terms of opposition to over simple mechanistic and reductionist approaches to the human psyche.

He pointed out in his review of James' *The Principles of Psychology* (Myers 1891a) that celebrated cases like that of Dr Wiltse (an American physician who had been investigated by Richard Hodgson in 1889) challenged the view that mind and consciousness were totally dependent on the effective functioning of the body, and until such phenomena have been 'fully worked' (and they still haven't) all assertions as to the mind/body relationship must remain provisional and tentative. It should be noted that Dr Wiltse had had a particularly vivid 'near death experience' encountering many of what have now become classic characteristics of that phenomenon (Kelly *et al.* 2007: 367–421).

Possibly his most suggestive insight, mentioned in a number of places throughout his writings but most clearly in his 'A Defence of Phantasms of the Dead'[7] (Myers 1890a: 320), was that subliminal activity, particularly in its paranormal aspect, varied inversely in relation to normal conscious-

---

7   See above, pp. 173–74.

ness. If one looks at much current parapsychological literature, dominated by the standard nomothetic model of investigation, one can't help feeling that this valuable perception has not been fully and systematically followed up, except perhaps with regard to the Ganzfeld experiments and Moody's psychomanteum (the former focusing on visual and aural sensory deprivation and the later on a version of crystal gazing: Carter 2007: 53–67, Moody and Perry 1993: 164–183). It is true that Targ (Targ 2004: 37) has denied the kind of link between altered states of consciousness and psi that Myers asserted but there is evidence to the contrary (Kelly *et al.* 2007: 108). Myers also urged the importance of recording the descriptive, particular detail of individual experiences (the phenomenological approach), as a way of shaping investigation (ideally in conjunction with lab-based research), but, this, too, has only been partially implemented in the century or so after his death (Irwin 2004: 8–9).

But there was and is a lot of opposition to such a shift. Myers was aware as early as the 1890s of the dangers of the ways in which psychology might develop (Myers 1893f) and of the influence of the Wundtian approach to experimental psychology which dominated the American scene for many years (Sommer 2009: p.c.). This is a paradigm which is still immensely powerful, and is reflected in the refusal of many psychologists, despite the efforts of Myers and the SPR (and later research surveys), to accept that hallucinations can occur to the sane, well-balanced and healthy, and their determination to define them as irredeemably subjective and linked, very often, with schizophrenia: for example, Kircher and David state: 'Hallucinations must be considered as internally generated perceptions without an objective correlate in the outer world' (Kircher and David 2003: 371).

Though he personally became convinced by the evidence that there was life after death, Myers was intellectually honest enough to realise that this might not fully persuade others. He had two broad tranches of evidence to put forward. Firstly, the huge array of sifted and checked testimony as to the existence, the veridicality, of apparitions/phantasms of the dead. He called these, as we have seen, sensory automatisms. He asserted: 'The *sensory automatisms* with which we have dealt in this and the preceding chapter have proved to us, in my view, the connection of definite apparitions with individual men, both during bodily life and after bodily death. They have, in short, proved by logical reasoning the existence and the persistence of a spirit in man' (Myers 1904 2: 76). His second source of evidence was motor automatisms, the speaking and writing by gifted mediums that gave testable information about the personality that survived death. As mentioned earlier, he had two criteria against which he judged these phenomena:[8] 'first the need of definite facts, given in the messages, which were known to the departed and are not known to the automatist; and secondly, the need of detailed and characteristic utterances; a moral means of identification corresponding, say, not to the meagre *signalement* by which a man is described on his passport, but to the individual complex of minute markings left by the impression of a prisoner's thumb' (Myers 1890a: 337–38) Anyone who has investigated mediumship or spontaneous phenomena in any depth realises the difficulty of unambiguously meeting those standards. Too often the facts prove to have been in the public domain (and potentially at least accessible to the medium) before the paranormal experience and the assessment of the evidence for character and personality can be notoriously subjective. Increasing awareness of these factors over the years has weakened, though not destroyed, the impact of *Phantasms of the Living* and *Human Personality and Its Survival of Bodily Death*. Finally, Myers was unable to publish the detailed Thompson records that so convinced him, and presumably met both of his key canons of evidence. His death and the combined opposition of Eveleen Myers and Richard Hodgson, meant that his great book concluded rather lamely. Another notable omission is the topic of reincarnation, which has attracted research interest since Myers' time. He rather loftily dismissed the subject — 'Yet for reincarnation there is at present no valid evidence (Myers 1904 2: 134) — probably generalising from the investigation by Flournoy of Mlle Hélène Smith (Myers 1904 2: 134, Playfair 2006).

Myers also urged imaginative pre-planning in order help prove life after death. He was particularly impressed by one

> direct experiment, — a test message planned before death, and communicated after death, by a man who held that the hope of an assurance of continued presence was worth at least a resolute effort, whatever its result might be. His tests, indeed were two, and both were successful. One was the revealing of the place where, before death, he hid a piece of brick marked and broken for special recognition, and the other was the communication of the contents of a short letter which he wrote and sealed before death (Myers 1904 2: 182–85).

However, his own attempt to do something similar had rather mixed results (Salter 1955b) and the history of such efforts has not particularly fulfilled his hopes (Oram 1998: 155–61).

On the other hand, he and his colleagues in the Society for Psychical Research, performed a major service in exposing fraud after fraud. He was more inclined initially to give the medium the benefit of the doubt

---

8   See above, p. 175.

and to become emotionally and spiritually involved in the proceedings. Yet his powerful intelligence was always at work on some level and always pulled him back. As Walter Leaf has stated, 'Emotion and intellect worked in alliance instead of civil war. To many men the final victory means the death of one or other; with Myers they both had conquered when peace was proclaimed' (Leaf 1905: 345).

Would he and his friends and family have thought this limited achievement an adequate expression and measure of his gifts and talents? By his mid-twenties he had won all the glittering prizes and was a poet with a national reputation. By his mid-forties that poetic brilliance had guttered out and he was seen, in certain circles, as a brilliant, slightly dubious figure, who had never lived up to his early promise. Through his connections with the Sidgwicks, and his entry into the salon world of Mrs Tennant, he had close and regular contact with the late-Victorian cultural and political elite. There must at times have been a view that, no matter how ultimately important his enquiries were in a metaphysical sense, in terms of worldly achievement, less gifted contemporaries had outstripped him. But, supported by the intellectual comradeship of a few close friends, Gurney, Sidgwick, Lodge, Richet and (after his initial suspicion) William James, he ploughed his narrow furrow to the end. He had the consolations of a stimulating social life. He had the money and position to be at the heart of contemporary cultural activity. He read widely, attended the theatre (including the early work of Ibsen) and private art views, and was well up on the latest French literature (Zola, Maupassent, Daudet, Huysman). Indeed, it cannot be sufficiently stressed that though a classicist, he was fully alive to the literature and ideas of his age, was enormously well-read, and, often at the forefront of taste. For example, he did more than anyone else at the time to publicise and take seriously the work of George Sand (Thomson 1977: 212–13) and he produced one of the first really thoughtful pieces on Swinburne (Hyder 1995: 188).

He was sustained too by the sometimes rather overpowering love of his wife, and his love for his children (though the developing gap between himself and Leo pained him). He had a real relish for life and was no back room experimenter. As he wrote to William James:

> But do not compliment me on tenacity! Any more than you praise the male frog who does not release his embrace when his head is cut off. I am—as you surely know—no more than an insatiable lover of life & love, to whose earthly existence a kind of unity is given by his passionate effort to project his life & love beyond the tomb. This is not ethical, but organic (Gauld 1968: 326–27).

In fact his zest for life, whether in his appreciation of physical beauty or the intellectual challenges of psychical research, was enormous. As he wrote cheerfully to James: 'An endless Life & a merry one! Girls and ghosts & plenty of them' (Myers 11/148: 29.11.1894). This could easily be mis-interpreted and AC Benson, in his diary, thought that behind the high-minded Myers lurked the Satyr in the bushes (Newsome 1980: 236). But there is no direct evidence (or rather no evidence has survived) that he was the kind of philanderer that Hall and Jarman (Jarman 1964, Hall 1980ab) have suggested. Indeed, the language he used to describe his relationship with Annie Marshall (in a document clearly not intended for publication) suggests quite otherwise:

> And what gratitude do I not owe to each creature who has shown me a virtue! To her whose brave blue eyes instructed me that man must bear his destiny with a smile; not with Orestes' mad bewilderment, nor even with Prometheus' cry, but like the 300 warriors who with combed hair in festal fashion, stood up in Thermopylae to die, or like the disciples on their Lord's last day, who 'when they had sung a hymn, went unto the mount of Olives' (Myers 13/22).

In fact, Myers, despite the sheer range of his physical and intellectual gifts, felt that they counted for little unless they were deployed in the service of a great cause. On the personal level, that might be the support of Annie Marshall locked in a difficult relationship with a manic depressive and syphilitic husband. On the cosmic scale, it was the work of the SPR, which gave meaning and coherence to his efforts, and allowed him to fully mobilise his great personal resources. He spelt this out in some detail to his wife as he described his obsessive involvement in psychical research : 'I could not be happy unless I had some great cause to work for. I had all my life been longing for some definite call. Read "Mazzini" [one of his essays] again in the light of this — & see how I longed for a life like his — of labour and exertion for a great impersonal end' (Myers 7/162: 11.10.1884).

This heroic exuberance, this sense of the world as a tremendous drama in which he played a central part, and which he could not conceive of losing to black, permanent unconsciousness, was both, perhaps, his greatest strength, and (in spite of Leaf's comments) his greatest weakness. It gave him the energy to continue. It provided him with huge reserves of drive and stamina as he went from medium to medium, from phenomenon to phenomenon, and wrote his experiences up in the *Proceedings* and *Journal* of the SPR. But it was also, possibly, his Achilles heel. As his mother spotted, in his very early years, he tended to give way to, and trust too much in, 'mere' feeling. The effect on him of beautiful people and beautiful ideas was almost overwhelming. He realised this, and by a considerable act of will, and much self-education and training, he turned himself into a psychologist committed to the application of the scientific method.[9] He managed to hold these opposing forces in balance until the end. Even in the overwhelming séance with Mrs Piper in late 1893, as we have seen, he commented that no facts unknown to him were communicated, only that they were expressed and re-combined in a way very characteristic of the spirit of Annie Marshall. Yet one gets a sense that ultimately his conviction sprang from an emotional, mystical, possibly even narcissistic base, and no matter how much evidence he gathered, how vividly and persuasively knitted together and expressed, this spread of sustaining feelings and intuitions was what lay at his heart, and what would carry him safely across the great, dark waters of death. As he put it in his strangely prophetic poem *The Renewal of Youth* (Myers 1882b: 213-214):

> Ah, welcome then that hour which bids thee lie
> In anguish of thy last infirmity!
> Welcome the toss for ease, the gasp for air,
> The visage drawn, and Hippocratic stare;
> Welcome the darkening dream, the lost control,
> The sleep, the swoon, the arousal of the soul!

9   See above, p. 212.

Bibliography

Note: when two dates are given, the earlier is the first edition and the later is the one cited.

Adams, R.J.Q. 2007. *Balfour. The Last Grandee.* London: John Murray.

Almeder, Robert. 1992. *Death and Personal Survival.*Maryland: Littlefield Adams.

Alvarado, Carlos S. 1983. A century of psychical research: comments on Renée Haynes's *The Society for Psychical Research 1882-1982: A History. Journal of Parapsychology* 47: 145-161.

Alvarado, Carlos S. 1983-1984. Palladino or Paladino? On the spelling of Eusapia's surname. *Journal of the Society for Psychical Research* 52: 315-316.

Alvarado, Carlos S. 1989a. Nineteenth century medical explanations of psychic phenomena. *Parapsychology Review* 20: 4-7.

Alvarado, Carlos S. 1989b. Dissociation and state-specific psychophysiology during the nineteenth century. *Dissocation* 2: 160-168.

Alvarado, Carlos S. 1996. Proof and process approaches to the study of spontaneous parapsychological phenomena. *Journal of the Society for Psychical Research* 61: 221-234.

Alvarado, Carlos S. 2002. Dissociation in Britain during the late nineteenth century: The Society for Psychical Research 1882-1900. *Journal of Trauma and Dissociation* 3: 9-33.

Alvarado, Carlos S. 2003. The concept of survival of bodily death and the development of parapsychology. *Journal of the Society for Psychical Research* 67: 65-95.

Alvarado, Carlos S. 2003. On the centenary of Frederic W.H. Myers' *Human Personality and Its Survival of Bodily Death. Journal of Parapsychology* 68: 3-43.

Alvarado, Carlos S. 2004. Frederic W.H.Myers on the projection of vital energy.*Paranormal Review* 30: 23-28.

Alvarado, Carlos S. 2006. Human radiations: concepts of force in mesmerism, spiritualism and psychical research. *Journal of the Society for Psychical Research* 70: 138-162.

Alvarado, Carlos S. 2008. The term 'supernormal'in writings by nineteenth century spiritualists and psychical researchers. *Paranormal Review* 45: 24-27.

Angoff, Allan. 1962. F.W.H. Myers-poet, essayist, researcher. *International Journal of Parapsychology* 4: 25-40.

Annan, Noel. 1951. *Leslie Stephen. His Thought & Character in Relation to his Time.* London: Macgibbon & Kee.

Annan, Noel. 1955. The intellectual aristocracy: 242-287. In *Studies in Social History. A Tribute to G.M.Trevelyan*.Ed. J.H.Plumb.London: Longmans, Green.

Anon. 1882. Objects of the Society.*Proceedings of the Society for Psychical Research* 1: 3-6.

Anon. 1894. A.T.Myers. *Journal of the Society for Psychical Research* 6: 195-197.

Anon. 1897. [Ballechin House]. *Journal of the Society for Psychical Research* 8: 116.

Anon. 1901-1902. The newspapers on Mrs Piper. *Journal of the Society for Psychical Research* 10: 142-143,150-152.

Anon. 1905-1906. Opening of an envelope containing a posthumous note left by Mr. Myers. *Journal of the Society for Psychical Research* 12: 11-13.

Anon. 1930. Sir Arthur Conan Doyle's resignation. *Journal of the Society for Psychical Research* 26: 45-52.

Anon. 1950. Leonora Piper. *Journal of the Society for Psychical Research* 35: 341-344.

Anon. 1959. Mrs W.H. Salter. *Journal of the Society for Psychical Research* 40: 98-99.

Appignanesi, Lisa. 2008. *Mad,Bad and Sad. A History of Women and the Mind Doctors from 1800 to the Present*. London: Virago.

Arcangel, Dianne. 2005/2008. *Afterlife Encounters. Ordinary People. Extraordinary Experiences*. Virginia: Hampton Roads.

Armstrong, Margaret. 2002. *Linen and Liturgy. The Story of the Marshall Family and the Parish Church of Keswick St. John*. Keswick: Peel Wyke Publications.

Asquith, Margot. 1962. *The Autobiography of Margot Asquith*. Ed. Carter, Mark Bonham. London: Eyre and Spottiswoode.

Assagioli, Robert. 1965/1993. *Psychosynthesis. A Manual of Principles and Techniques*. London: Aquarian Press.

Baird, A.T. 1949. *Richard Hodgson. The Story of a Psychical Researcher and His Times*. London: Psychic Press.

Balfour, G.W. 1918. The Ear of Dionysius: further scripts affording evidence of personal survival. *Proceedings of the Society for Psychical Research* 29: 197-243.

Balfour, G.W. 1935. A study of the psychological aspects of Mrs Willett's mediumship and of the statements of the communicators concerning process. *Proceedings of the Society for Psychical Research* 43: 41-318.

Balfour, Jean. 1958-1960. The 'Palm Sunday' case: new light on an old love story.*Proceedings of the Society for Psychical Research* 52: 79-267.

Bantock, G.H. 1956. *L.H. Myers. A Critical Study*. London: Jonathan Cape.

Barker, A.T. 1923. *The Letters of H.P.Blavatsky to A.P.Sinnett and Other Miscellaneous Letters*. New York: Frederick A.Stokes.

Barrett W.F., Gurney E. and Myers, F.W.H. 1882. Thought reading. *Nineteenth Century* 11: 890-900.

Barrett, W.F. *et al.* 1882. First report on thought-reading. *Proceedings of the Society for Psychical Research* 1: 13-64.

Barrett, W.F. *et al.* 1883. First report of the committee on mesmerism. *Proceedings of the Society for Psychical Research* 1: 217-229.

Barrett, W.F. *et al.* 1882-1883. Preliminary report of the Reichenbach committee.*Proceedings of the Society for Psychical Research* 1: 99-100.

Barrett, W.F. *et al.* 1883. First report of the Reichenbach committee. *Proceedings of the Society for Psychical Research* 1: 230-237.

Barrett, W.F. 1883. On some phenomena associated with abnormal conditions of mind. *Proceedings of the Society for Psychical Research* 1: 238-244.

Barrett, W.F. 1884. Pseudo thought reading. *Journal of the Society for Psychical Research* 1: 10-11.

Barrett, W.F. 1886-1887. On some physical phenomena commonly called spiritualistic, witnessed by the author. *Proceedings of the Society for Psychical Research* 4: 25-41.

Barrett, W.F. 1905. C.C. Massey. *Journal of the Society for Psychical Research* 12: 95-99.

Barrett, W.F. 1911/2006. *Psychical Research*. Montana: Kessinger.

Barrett, W.F. 1918. Note on telepathy and telergy. *Proceedings of the Society for Psychical Research* 30: 251-260.

Barrett, William F. 1917. *On the Threshold of the Unseen. An Examination of The Phenomena of Spiritualism And of The Evidence for Survival After Death*. London: Kegan Paul, Trench and Trubner.

Barrett, William. 1924. Some reminiscences of fifty years' psychical research. *Proceedings of the Society for Psychical Research* 34: 275-297.

Barrington, M.R. 1965-1966. Swan on a black sea: how much could Miss Cummins have known? *Journal of the Society for Psychical Research* 43: 289-300.

Barrow, Logie. 1986. *Independent Spirits. Spiritualism and English Plebeians. 1850-1910*. London: Routledge and Kegan Paul.

Barrow, John D. 2005. *Theories of Everything: The Quest for Ultimate Explanation*. London: Vintage.

Battersea, Constance. 1922. *Reminiscences*. London: Macmillan.

Baum, Paull Franklin. 1922. *The Principles of English Versification*. Cambridge, Mass.: Harvard University Press.

Bayfield, M.A. 1911. [Review of *The Newer Spiritualism* by Frank Podmore.] *Proceedings of the Society for Psychical Research* 25: 70-89.

Beard, Paul. 1987. Ed. *The Barbanell Report Transmitted to Marie Cherrie*. Norwich: Pilgrim Books.

Beard, Paul. 1992. *Inner Eye, Listening Ear. An Exploration into Mediumship*. Norwich: Pilgrim Books.

Becher, H.W. 1984. The social origins and post-graduate careers of a Cambridge intellectual elite 1830-1860. *Victorian Studies* 28: 97-127.

Becher, Tony and Trowler, Paul R. 1989/2001. *Academic Tribes and Territories*. Buckingham: Society for Research into Higher Education and Open University Press.

Beer, John. 1998. *Providence and Love. Studies in Wordsworth, Channing, Myers, George Eliot, and Ruskin*. Oxford: Oxford University Press.

Beer, John. 2003. *Post-Romantic Consciousness. Dickens to Plath*. Basingstoke: Palgrave Macmillan.

Beidler, Peter G. 1989. *Ghosts, Demons and Henry James. The Turn of the Screw at the Turn of the Century*. Columbia: University of Missouri Press.

Beloff, John. 1993. *Parapsychology. A Concise History*. London: Athlone Press.

Benson, Arthur Christopher. 1911. *The Leaves of the Tree. Studies in Biography*. London: Smith, Elder.

Benson, E.F. 1930. *As We Were. A Victorian Peep-Show*. London. Longmans, Green.

Bentley, Michael. 2001. *Lord Salisbury's World. Conservative Environments in Late-Victorian Britain*. Cambridge: Cambridge University Press.

Berger, Arthur S. 1988. *Lives and Letters in American Parapsychology. A Biographical History, 1850-1987.* North Carolina: McFarland.

Blackmore, Susan. 1996. *In Search of the Light. The Adventures of a Parapsychologist.* New York: Prometheus Books.

Blackmore, Susan. 2003. *Consciousness: An Introduction.* London: Hodder and Stoughton.

Blum, Deborah. 2006. *Ghost Hunters. William James and the Search for Scientific Proof of Life After Death.* New York: The Penguin Press.

Blunt, Wilfred Scawen. 1921. 2 Vols. *My Diaries: Being a personal narrative of events.* London: Martin Secker.

Bobbit, Mary Reed. 1960. *With Dearest Love to All. The Life and Letters of Lady Jebb.* London: Faber and Faber.

Brandon, Ruth. 1983. *The Spiritualists. The Passion for the Occult in the Nineteenth and Twentieth Centuries.* London: Weidenfeld and Nicolson.

Brake, Laurel. 1994. *Subjugated Knowledges. Journalism, Gender & Literature in the Nineteenth Century.* New York: New York University Press.

Braude, Stephen. 1978. Telepathy. *Nous* 12: 267-301.

Braude, Stephen E. 1986.*The Limits of Influence. Psychokinesis and the Philosophy of Science.* London: Routledge and Kegan Paul.

Braude, Stephen E. 1995. *First Person Plural. Multiple Personality and the Philosophy of Mind.* Maryland: Rowan and Littlefield.

Braude, Stephen E. 2003. *Immortal Remains. The Evidence for Life after Death.* Maryland: Rowan and Littlefield.

Braude, Stephen E. 2007. *The Gold Leaf Lady and Other Parapsychological Investigations.* Chicago: University of Chicago Press.

Brett, Maurice. 1934. *Journals and Letters of Reginald Viscount Esher. Vol 1 1870-1903.* London: Ivor Nicholson and Watson.

Broad, C.D. Papers.Trinity College Library, Cambridge: Broad D/1 etc.

Broad, C.D. 1938. Henry Sidgwick and psychical research.*Proceedings of the Society for Psychical Research* 45: 131-161.

Broad, C.D. 1953. Phantasms of the living and the dead. *Proceedings of the Society for Psychical Research* 50: 51-66.

Broad, C.D. 1962. *Lectures on Psychical Research.* London: Routledge and Kegan Paul.

Broad, C.D. *et al.* 1970. W.H.Salter. *Journal of the Society for Psychical Research* 45: 203-211.

Brock, William H. 2008. *William Crookes (1832-1919) and the Commercialisation of Science.* Hampshire: Ashgate.

Brocklebank, Lisa. 2006. Psychic Reading. *Victorian Studies* 48: 233-239.

Broughton,Richard S. 1975. Psi and the two halves of the brain. *Journal of the Society for Psychical Research* 48: 133-147.

Brown, Alan Willard. 1948/1973. *The Metaphysical Society. Victorian Minds in Crisis 1869-1880.* New York: Octagon Books.

Brown, Frederick. 2007. *Flaubert. A Life.* London: Pimlico.

Browning, Oscar. 1910. *Memories of Sixty Years at Eton, Cambridge & Elsewhere.* London: Bodley Head.

Burd, Akin van. 1982. *Ruskin, Lady Mount-Temple and the Spiritualists.* London: Brentham Press.

Burns, Michael. 1993. *Dreyfus. A Family Affair 1789-1945*. London: Chatto and Windus.

Burrow, J.W. 2000. *The Crisis of Reason. European Thought 1848-1914*. Newhaven and London: Yale University Press.

Burt, Cyril. 1963. Jung's account of his paranormal experiences.*Journal of the Society for Psychical Research* 42: 163-180.

Bute, J.P. and Ada Goodrich Freer. 1899/1900. *The Alleged Haunting of Ballechin House*. London: C.Arthur Pearson.

Butler, Josephine. Papers. University of Liverpool Library, Liverpool: JB/1/1 etc.

Caine,Barbara. 1993. *Victorian Feminists*. Oxford: Oxford University Press.

Caldwell, Daniel. 2000. *The Esoteric World of Madame Blavatsky. Insights into the Life of a Modern Sphinx*. Wheaton: Quest Books.

Campbell, John L. and Hall, Trevor H. 1968. *Strange Things. The Story of Fr Allan McDonald, Ada Goodrich Freer, and the Society for Psychical Research's Enquiry into Highland Second Sight*. London: Routledge and Kegan Paul.

Cannadine, David. 1998. *Class in Britain*. Newhaven and London: Yale University Press.

Carpenter, W.B. 1877. *Mesmerism, Spiritualism etc. Historically & Scientifically Considered*. London: Longmans, Green.

Carter, Chris. 2007. *Parapsychology and the Skeptics. A Scientific Argument for the Existence of ESP*. Pittsburgh: Sterlinghouse.

Cassirer, Manfred. 1983. Palladino at Cambridge. *Journal of the Society for Psychical Research* 52: 52-58.

Cerullo, John J. 1982. *The Secularisation of the Soul. Psychical Research in Modern Britain*. Philadelphia: Institute for the Study of Human Issues.

Chadwick, Owen. 1966/1971. *The Victorian Church Part I*. London: SCM Press.

Chadwick, Owen. 1970. *The Victorian Church Part II*. London: A. and C. Black.

Chadwick, Owen. 1975. *The Secularization of the European Mind in the Nineteenth Century*. Cambridge University Press: Cambridge.

Charteris, E. 1931. *Life and Letters of Sir Edmund Gosse*. London: Heinemann.

Clark, Michael J. 1981. The rejection of psychological approaches to mental disorder in late nineteenth-century psychiatry: 271-312. In *Madhouses, Mad-Doctors, and Madmen: The Social History of Psychiatry in the Victorian Era*. Ed. Scull, Andrew. London: Athlone Press.

Coleman, M.H. 1992. The death of Edmund Gurney. *Journal of the Society for Psychical Research* 58: 194-200.

Coleman, M.H. 1998. [Letter on Mrs Piper.] *Journal of the Society for Psychical Research* 63: 62-63.

Collini, Stefan. 1991. *Public Moralists. Political Thought and Intellectual Life in Britain 1850-1930*. Oxford: Clarendon Press.

Collins, Abdy. 1948. *The Cheltenham Ghost*. London: Psychic Press.

Collins, Harry and Pinch, Trevor. 1993/2003. *The Golem. What you should know about Science*. Cambridge: Cambridge University Press.

Committee of the Society for Psychical Research Appointed to Investigate the Evidence for Marvellous Phenomena offered by certain Members of the Theosophical Society. [First Report].1884. London: Society for Psychical Research.

Cook, Emily Frazer Williams [Kelly]. 1992. *The Intellectual Background and Potential Significance of F.W.H. Myers' Work in Psychology and Parapsychology.* Ph.D.Edinburgh: University of Edinburgh.

Cook, Emily Frazer Williams [Kelly]. 1994. The subliminal consciousness: F.W.H. Myer's approach to the problem of survival. *The Journal of Parapsychology* 58: 39-51

Cook, Emily Frazer Williams [Kelly]. 2001. The contributions of F.W.H.Myers to psychology. *Journal of the Society for Psychical Research* 65: 65-90.

Cook, Matt. 2003. *London and the Culture of Homosexuality,1885-1914.* Cambridge: Cambridge University Press.

Cooper, Suzanne Fagence. 2001. *The Victorian Woman.* London: Victoria and Albert Publications.

Coulton, G.G. 1944. *Fourscore Years. An Autobiography.* Cambridge: Cambridge University Press.

Crabtree, Adam. 1992. Dissociation and memory: A two-hundred-year perspective. *Dissociation* 5: 150-154.

Crabtree, Adam. 1993. *From Mesmer to Freud. Magnetic Sleep and the Roots of Psychological Healing.* Newhaven and London: Yale University Press.

Crabtree, Adam. 2003. 'Automatism' and the emergence of dynamic psychiatry. *Journal of the History of the Behavioural Sciences* 39: 51-70.

Crookes, William. 1874. *Researches in the Phenomena of Spiritualism.* London: J. Burns.

Crossley, D. 2005. Spiritualism and survival: Bradley on A.R.Wallace. *Collingwood and British Idealism Studies incorporating Bradley Studies* 11: 7-38.

Crowe, Catherine. 1848. 2 Vols. *The Nightside of Nature: Or Ghosts and Ghost Seers.* London: T.C.Newby.

Cummins, Geraldine. 1932/1967. *The Road to Immortality.* London: Psychic Press.

Cummins, Geraldine. 1935/1952. *Beyond Human Personality.* London: Psychic Press.

Cummins, Geraldine. 1965. *Swan on a Black Sea* .Ed. Toksvig, Signe. Foreword Broad, C.D. London: Routledge.

Dallas, H.A. 1910. Introduction Barrett, W.F. *Mors Janua Vitae? A discussion of certain communications purporting to come from Frederic W.H. Myers.* London. William Rider & Son.

Danahay, Martin A. 1998. Dante Gabriel Rossetti's virtual bodies. *Victorian Poetry* 36: 379-397.

Davies, Owen. 2007. *The Haunted. A Social History of Ghosts.* Basingstoke: Palgrave Macmillan

Davis, Philip. 2002. *The Victorians. The Oxford English Literary History. Volume 8.* Oxford: Oxford University Press.

Dawson Rogers,Edmund. 1911. *Life and Experiences of Edmund Dawson Rogers.* London: Office of Light.

Deacon, Richard. 1985. *The Cambridge Apostles. A History of Cambridge University's elite intellectual secret society.* London: Robert Royce.

Desmond, Adrian and Moore, James. 1991. *Darwin.* London: Michael Joseph.

Dingwall, E.J. and Price, H.1922. Eds. *Revelations of a Spirit Medium.*(Facsimile of 1891 original St Paul, Minnesota: Farrington & co.). London: Kegan Paul, Trench and Trubner.

Dingwall, Eric J. 1951. *Very Peculiar People. Portrait Studies in the Queer, the Abnormal and the Uncanny*. London: Rider.

Dingwall, Eric J. 1961. British investigations of spontaneous cases. *International Journal of Parapsychology* 3: 89-97.

Dingwall, Eric J. 1966. *The Critic's Dilemma*. Crowhurst: privately printed.

Dingwall, Eric J. 1967/1968. Ed. Vol I. *Abnormal Hypnotic Phenomena. A Survey of Nineteenth-Century Cases*. New York: Barnes and Noble.

Dingwall, Eric J. 1968. Ed. Vol IV. *Abnormal Hypnotic Phenomena. A Survey of Nineteenth Century Cases.*New York: Barnes and Noble.

Dixon, Joy . 2001. *Divine Feminine. Theosophy and Feminism in England*. Baltimore: John Hopkins University Press.

Draznin, Claire Yaffa. 1992. *My Other Self: the Letters of Havelock Ellis, 1884-1920*. New York: Peter Lang.

Edel, Leon. 1987. *Henry James. A Life*. London: Collins.

Edgeworth, F.Y. 1885. The calculus of probabilities applied to psychical research 1. *Proceedings of the Society for Psychical Research* 3: 190-199.

Edgeworth, F.Y. 1886. The calculus of probabilities applied to psychical research 2. *Proceedings of the Society for Psychical Research* 4: 189-208.

Eeden, F. van, and Myers, F.W.H. 1901. The fourth international congress of psychology. *Proceedings of the Society for Psychical Research* 15: 445-448.

Ellenberger, Henri F. 1970/1994. *The Discovery of the Unconscious*. London: Fontana.

Epperson, Gordon. 1997. *The Mind of Edmund Gurney*. New Jersey: Associated University Press.

Evans, Joan and Whitehouse, John Howard. 1959. Eds. *The Diaries of John Ruskin 1874-1889*. Oxford: Clarendon Press.

Feilding, Everard. 1963. Introduction Dingwall, E.J. *Sittings with Eusapia Palladino and Other Studies*. New York: University Books.

Fitzroy, Almeric. 1925. *Memoirs Volume 1*. London: Hutchinson.

Fodor, Nandor. 1934/1969. *Encyclopedia of Psychic Science*. New York: University Books.

Fontana, David. 1991-1992. The Feilding report and the determined critic. *Journal of the Society for Psychical Research* 58: 341-350.

Fontana, David. 1998. Polidoro and Rinaldi: no match for Palladino and the Feilding report. *Journal of the Society for Psychical Research* 63: 12-33.

Fontana, David. 2005. *Is there an Afterlife? A comprehensive overview of the evidence*. Hampshire: O Books.

Foster, Jeremy J. & Parker, Ian. 1995. *Carrying Out Investigations in Psychology. Methods and Statistics*. Leicester: BPS books.

Foster, Roy. 1997. *W.B. Yeats. A Life. 1. The Apprentice Mage*. Oxford: Oxford University Press.

Freud, Sigmund. 1912. A note on the unconscious in psychoanalysis. *Proceedings of the Society for Psychical Research* 26: 312-318.

Fulford, Roger. 1957. *Votes for Women: The Story of a Struggle*. London: Faber and Faber.

Gamble, Cynthia . 2008. *John Ruskin, Henry James and The Shropshire Lads*. London: New European Publications.

Gardner, Howard. 1984/1985. *Frames of Mind. The Theory of Multiple Intelligences.* London: Paladin.

Gauld, Alan. 1964. Frederic Myers and 'Phyllis'. *Journal of the Society for Psychical Research* 42: 316-323.

Gauld, Alan. 1965. Mr. Hall and the S.P.R. *Journal of the Society for Psychical Research* 43: 53-62.

Gauld, Alan. 1966. Reply to the pamphlet *Dr Gauld and Mr. Myers* by Archie Jarman. *Journal of the Society for Psychical Research* 43: 277-281.

Gauld, Alan. 1968. *The Founders of Psychical Research.* London: Routledge and Kegan Paul.

Gauld, Alan & Cornell, A.D. 1979. *Poltergeists.* London: Routledge and Kegan Paul.

Gauld, Alan. 1983. *Mediumship and Survival. A Century of Investigations.* London: Paladin.

Gauld, Alan. 1992/1995. *A History of Hypnotism.* Cambridge: Cambridge University Press.

Gauld, Alan. 1993. Presidential address. *Proceedings of the Society for Psychical Research* 57: 253-273.

Gauld, Alan. 1996. Notes on the career of the somnambule Léonie. *Journal of the Society for Psychical Research* 61: 141-151.

Gay, Peter. 1984. *The Bourgeois Experience. Victoria to Freud. Education of the Senses.* Oxford: Oxford University Press.

Gay, Peter. 1994. *The Bourgeois Experience. Victoria to Freud. The Cultivation of Hatred.* London: HarperCollins.

Gay, Peter. 2001. *The Making of Middle Class Culture 1815-1914.* London: Allen Lane.

Gaythorpe, Elizabeth. 1950. Ed. *Unpublished F.W.H. Myers' scripts (selected from the Richmond material).* C.P.S. Paper 4. London: College of Psychic Studies.

Gill, Stephen. 1998. *Wordsworth and the Victorians.* Oxford: Clarendon Press.

Gilmour, Robin. 1993. *The Victorian Period. The Intellectual and Cultural Context of English Literature 1830-1890.* Harlow: Longman.

Gladstone, Mary. 1930. Ed. Masterman, Lucy. *Mary Gladstone (Mrs Drew). Her Diaries and Letters.* London: Methuen.

Goldstein, Robert. 1992. Inclined towards the marvelous. Romantic uses of clinical phenomena in the work of Frederic Myers. *Psychoanalytic Review* 79: 577-589.

Gomes, Michael. 2005. *The Coulomb Case.* Theosophical History Occasional Papers X. Fullerton: Theosophical History.

Goodrich Freer, Ada. 1899. *Essays in Psychical Research.* London: George Redway.

Gosse, Edmund. 1923. *More Books On The Table.* London: Heinemann.

Grosskurth, Phyliss. 1964. *John Addington Symonds. A Biography.* London: Longmans.

Grant Duff, M.E. 1930. Ed. Bassett, Tilney A. *A Victorian Vintage.* London: Methuen.

Gunn, Peter. 1964. *Vernon Lee. Violet Paget 1856-1935.* Oxford: Oxford University Press.

Gurney, E. 1884a. The stages of hypnotism. *Proceedings of the Society for Psychical Research* 2: 61-72.

Gurney, E. 1884b. An account of some experiments in mesmerism. *Proceedings of the Society for Psychical Research* 2: 201-206.

Gurney, E. 1884c. The problems of hypnotism. *Proceedings of the Society for Psychical Research* 2: 265-292.

Gurney, E. 1884d. Hallucinations and dreams [circular].*Journal of the Society for Psychical Research* 1: 14.

Gurney, E. 1884-1885. Nature of evidence in matters extraordinary. *National Review-II* 4: 472-491.

Gurney, E. 1885a. Retractions and alterations of view. *Journal of the Society for Psychical Research* 2: 2-4.

Gurney, E. 1885b. Hallucinations. *Proceedings of the Society for Psychical Research* 3: 151-189.

Gurney, E. 1887a. Peculiarities of certain post-hypnotic states. *Proceedings of the Society for Psychical Research* 4: 268-323.

Gurney, E. 1887b. Stages of hypnotic memory. *Proceedings of the Society for Psychical Research* 4: 515-531.

Gurney, E. 1887c.Remarks on Professor Peirce's paper. *Proceedings of the American Society for Psychical Research* 1: 157-179.

Gurney, E. 1887d.Remarks on Mr Peirce's rejoinder. *Proceedings of the American Society for Psychical Research* 1: 287-300.

Gurney, E. 1888-1889a. Recent experiments in hypnotism. *Proceedings of the Society for Psychical Research* 5: 3-17.

Gurney, E. 1888-1889b. Note relating to some of the published experiments in thought-transference. *Proceedings of the Society for Psychical Research* 5: 269-270.

Gurney, E. & Myers, F.W.H. 1883a. Transferred impressions and telepathy. *Fortnightly Review* 39: 437-452.

Gurney, E.& Myers, F.W.H. 1883b. Phantasms of the living. *Fortnightly Review* 39: 562-577.

Gurney, E. & Myers, F.W.H. 1883c. Mesmerism. *Nineteenth Century* 9: 695-719.

Gurney, E. & Myers, F.W.H. 1884a. Apparitions. *Nineteenth Century* 15: 791-815.

Gurney, E. & Myers, F.W.H. 1884b. Visible apparitions. *Nineteenth Century* 16: 68-95.

Gurney, E. & Myers, F.W.H. 1885a. Aspects of mesmerism. *National Review-II* 5: 681-703.

Gurney, E. & Myers, F.W.H. 1885b. Some higher aspects of mesmerism. *Proceedings of the Society for Psychical Research* 3: 401-423.

Gurney, E. & Myers, F.W.H. 1886.Collective hallucinations. *Journal of the Society for Psychical Research* 2: 154-158.

Gurney,E. & Myers, F.W.H. 1887. Statement of the literary committee of the Society for Psychical Research.*Journal of the Society for Psychical Research* 3: 1-8.

Gurney, E. & Myers, F.W.H. 1889. On apparitions occurring soon after death. *Proceedings of the Society for Psychical Research* 5: 403-485.

Gurney, E., Myers, F.W.H. *et al.* 1882. Report of the literary committee.*Proceedings of the Society for Psychical Research* 1: 116-155.

Gurney, E., Myers, F.W.H. & Barrett, W.F. 1882. Second report on thought-transference. *Proceedings of the Society for Psychical Research* 1: 70-97.

Gurney, E. Myers, F.W.H. & Barrett, W.F. 1883a. Third report on thought-transference. *Proceedings of the Society for Psychical Research* 1: 161-215.

Gurney, E., Myers, F.W.H. & Barrett, W.F. 1883b. Fourth report of the committee on thought-transference. *Proceedings of the Society for Psychical Research* 2: 1-11.

Gurney, E., Myers, F.W.H. & Barrett, W.F. 1883c. Second report of the committee on mesmerism. *Proceedings of the Society for Psychical Research* 1: 251-262,284-290.

Gurney, E., Myers, F.W.H. & Barrett,W.F. 1884. Third report of the committee on mesmerism. *Proceedings of the Society for Psychical Research* 2: 12-23.

Gurney, E., Myers, F.W.H. *et al.* 1884a. Second report of the literary committee. *Proceedings of the Society for Psychical Research* 1: 43-55.

Gurney, E., Myers, F.W.H. *et al.* 1884b.Third report of the literary committee-a theory of apparitions part 1. *Proceedings of the Society for Psychical Research* 2: 109-136.

Gurney, E., Myers, F.W.H. *et al.* 1884c.Fourth report of the literary committee-a theory of apparitions part 2.*Proceedings of the Society for Psychical Research* 2: 157-186.

Gurney, E., Myers,F.W.H. & Podmore, F. 1886. 2 Vols. *Phantasms of the Living*. London: Trubner.

Hackett, J.T. 1919/1920. *My Commonplace Book*. London: Fisher Unwin.

Hacking, Ian. 1988. Telepathy: Origins of randomization in experimental design. *Isis*. 73: 427-451.

Hacking, Ian. 1995. *Rewriting the Soul. Multiple Personality and the Sciences of Memory*. Princeton: Princeton University Press.

Haight, Gordon S. 1968. *George Eliot. A Biography*. Oxford: Clarendon Press.

Haight, Gordon S. 1978. Ed. *The George Eliot Letters. Volume ix 1871-1881*. Yale University Press: New Haven and London.

Hall, Trevor H. 1962. *The Spiritualists*. London: Duckworth.

Hall, Trevor H. 1964/1980a. *The Strange Case of Edmund Gurney*. London: Duckworth.

Hall, Trevor H. 1968/1980b. *The Strange Story of Ada Goodrich Freer*. London: Duckworth.

Hall, Trevor H. 1968. *The Strange Case of Edmund Gurney*. Some comments on Mr. Fraser Nicol's review. *International Journal of Parapsychology* 10: 149-164.

Hamlin, Christopher. 1986. Scientific method and expert witnessing: Victorian perspectives on a modern problem. *Social Studies of Science* 16: 485-513.

Hannavy, John. 2008. *Encyclopedia of Nineteenth Century Photography*. London: CRC Press.

Harper, Edith K. 1914. *Stead: The Man. Personal Reminiscences*. London: Rider.

Harrington, Anne. 1987. *Medicine, Mind and the Double Brain. A Study in Nineteenth-Century Thought*. Princeton: Princeton University Press.

Harris, Jose. 1993. *Private Lives, Public Spirit. A Social History of Britain 1870-1914*. Oxford: Oxford University Press.

Harrison, Jane Ellen. 1925. *Reminiscences of a Student's Life*. London: The Hogarth Press.

Harrison, Vernon. 1997. *H.P. Blavatsky and the S.P.R: An Examination of the Hodgson Report of 1885*. Pasadena: Theosophical University Press.

Hart, Hornell. 1956. Six theories about apparitions. *Proceedings of the Society for Psychical Research* 50: 153-239.

Hastings, Beatrice. 1937. *The 'Coulomb Pamphlet'*. Worthing: privately printed.

Haynes, Renée. 1982. *The Society for Psychical Research 1882-1982. A History.* London: Macdonald.

Hearnshaw, L.S. 1964. *A Short History of British Psychology 1840-1940.* London: Methuen.

Heitland, W.E. 1926. *After Many Years.* Cambridge: Cambridge University Press.

Henson, Louise. 2004. Investigations and fictions: Charles Dickens and ghosts: 44-63. In *The Victorian Supernatural.* Eds.Bown,Nicola, Burdett, Carolyn, Thurschwell, Pamela. Cambridge: Cambridge University Press.

Heyck, T.L. 1984. *The Transformation of Intellectual Life in Victorian England.* Beckenham: Croom Helm.

Heywood, Rosalind. 1959. *The Sixth Sense. An Inquiry into Extra-Sensory Perception.* London: Chatto & Windus.

Hilton, Tim. 2002. *John Ruskin.* Newhaven and London: Yale University Press.

Hinshelwood, R.D. 1991. Psychodynamic psychiatry before World War 1. In *150 Years of British Psychiatry.* Eds. Berios,G.and Freeman, H. London: Royal College of Psychiatrists.

Hinshelwood, R.D. 1995. Psychoanalysis in Britain: points of cultural access 1893-1918. *International Journal of Psychoanalysis* 76: 136-151.

Hoare, Philip. 2005. *England's Lost Eden: Adventures in a Victorian Utopia.* London: Fourth Estate.

Hodgson, Richard. 1885. The Theosophical Society. Russian intrigue or religious evolution? *The Age.* Blavatsky Study Centre: www.blavatskyarchives.com.

Hodgson, Richard *et al.* 1885. Report of the committee appointed to investigate phenomena connected with the Theosophical Society. *Proceedings of the Society for Psychical Research* 3: 201-400.

Hodgson R.& Davey, S.J. 1886. The possibilities of mal-observation and lapse of memory from a practical point of view. *Proceedings of the Society for Psychical Research* 4: 381-495.

Hodgson, Richard. 1892. A record of observations of certain phenomena of trance. *Proceedings of the Society for Psychical Research* 8: 1-168.

Hodgson, Richard. 1895a. The value of the evidence for supernormal phenomena in the case of Eusapia Paladino. *Journal of the Society for Psychical Research* 7: 36-55.

Hodgson, Richard. 1895b. Remarks on Eusapia Paladino at general meeting. *Journal of the Society for Psychical Research* 7: 132-135.

Hodgson, Richard. 1898. A further record of certain phenomena of trance. *Proceedings of the Society for Psychical Research* 13: 284-582.

Hodgson, Richard. 1899. [Review of *Essays in Psychical Research* by Ada Goodrich Freer.] *Proceedings of the Society for Psychical Research* 14: 393-396.

Holbrook, Jackson. 1913/1976. *The Eighteen Nineties. A Review of Art and Ideas at the Close of the Nineteenth Century.* Brighton: The Harvester Press.

Holt, Henry. 1914. 2 Vols. *On the Cosmic Relations.* Baltimore and New York. Houghton Mifflin.

Honan, Park. 1981. *Matthew Arnold. A Life.* London: Weidenfield and Nicolson.

Hoppen, K. Theodore. 1998. *The Mid-Victorian Generation 1846-1886.* Oxford: Oxford University Press.

Houghton, Walter E. 1957. *The Victorian Frame of Mind 1830-1870.* New Haven and London: Yale University Press.

Huby, Pamela M. 1970. New evidence about 'Rose Morton'. *Journal of the Society for Psychical Research* 45: 391-392.

Hunt, Leigh. 1928. *The Story of the Marylebone Spiritualist Association (1872-1928)*. London: MS Association.

Hunter Blair, David. 1921. *John Patrick Third Marquess of Bute, K.T. (1847-1900). A Memoir*. London: John Murray.

Hyder, Clyde K. 1995. *Algernon Swinburne: The Critical Heritage*. London: Routledge.

Hynes, Samuel. 1968. *The Edwardian Turn of Mind*. Princeton: Princeton University Press.

Inglis, Brian. 1977. *Natural and Supernatural. A History of the Paranormal from Earliest Times to 1914*. London: Hodder and Stoughton.

Inglis, Brian. 1983-1984. [Review of *The Spiritualists* by Ruth Brandon.] *Journal of the Society for Psychical Research* 52: 209-212.

Inglis, Brian. 1984. *Science and Parascience. A history of the paranormal,1914-1939*. London: Hodder and Stoughton.

Inglis, Brian. 1988. Sir William Barrett. *Journal of the Society for Psychical Research* 55: 16-24.

Inglis, Brian. 1989-1990. [Review of *Ghosts, Demons and Henry James* by Peter G. Beidler.] *Journal of the Society for Psychical Research* 56: 240-242.

Inglis, Brian. 1989. *Trance. A Natural History of Altered States of Mind*. London: Grafton.

Innes, A.T. 'Where are the letters?' 1887. A cross-examination of certain Phantasms. *Nineteenth Century* 22: 174-194.

Irwin, Harvey J. 2004. *An Introduction to Parapsychology*. North Carolina and London: McFarland.

Jalland, Patricia. 1996. *Death in the Victorian Family*. Oxford: Oxford University Press.

James, William. 1896. President's address. *Proceedings of the Society for Psychical Research* 12: 2-10.

James, William. 1901. Frederic Myers's services to psychology. *Proceedings of the Society for Psychical Research* 17: 13-23.

James, William *et al.* (Lodge, Flournoy, Leaf). 1903-1904. [Reviews of *Human Personality and Its Survival of Bodily Death*.] *Proceedings of the Society for Psychical Research* 18: 22-61.

James, William. 1960. *William James on Psychical Research*. Eds.Murphy, Gardner and Ballou, Robert O. New York: Viking Press.

James, William. 1986. *Essays in Psychical Research*. Eds. Burkhard, F.W.,Bowers, F.,and Skrupskelis, I.K. Harvard: Harvard University Press.

Jarman, Archie. 1964 (contains both Jarman's articles). *Dr. Gauld and Mr. Myers*. Hertfordshire: privately printed.

Jeal, Tim. 2007. *Stanley: The Impossible Life of Africa's Greatest Explorer*. London: Faber and Faber.

Jebb, Caroline. 1907. *Life and Letters of Sir Richard Claverhouse Jebb by his wife Caroline Jebb*. Cambridge: Cambridge University Press.

Jenkins, Romilly. 1961. *The Dilessi Murders*. London: Longmans.

Johnson, Alice. 1907-1909. On the automatic writing of Mrs Holland.*Proceedings of the Society for Psychical Research* 21: 166-391.

Johnson, Alice. 1914-1915. A reconstruction of some 'concordant automatisms'. *Proceedings of the Society for Psychical Research* 27: 1-156.

Johnson, Alice. 1936. Mrs Henry Sidgwick's work in psychical research. *Proceedings of the Society for Psychical Research* 44: 53-93.

Johnson, George M. 2006. *Dynamic Psychology in Modernist British Fiction.* Basingstoke: Palgrave Macmillan.

Johnson, Raynor C. 1964. *The Light and the Gate*. London: Hodder and Stoughton.

Jolly, W.P. 1975. *Sir Oliver Lodge. Psychical researcher and scientist*. New Jersey: Associated University Presses.

Jones, Lawrence J. 1928. Presidential address. *Proceedings of the Society for Psychical Research* 38: 17-48.

Jordan, Jane. 2001. *Josephine Butler*. London: John Murray.

Kaplan, Abraham. 1964/1998. *The Conduct of Inquiry. Methodology for Behavioural Science*. New Brunswick and London: Transaction Publishers.

Karagulla, Shafica. 1978. *Breakthrough to Creativity*. California: Devorss.

Katz, David S. 2005. *The Occult Tradition From The Renaissance to the Present Day*. London: Jonathan Cape.

Keating, Peter. 1989/1991. *The Haunted Study. A Social History of the English Novel 1875-1914*. London: Fontana Press.

Keeley, James P. 2001. Subliminal promptings: psychoanalytic theory and the Society for Psychical Research. *American Imago* 58: 767-791.

Kekewich, Sir G.W. 1920. *The Education Department and After*. London: Constable.

Kelly, Edward F., Kelly, Emily Williams, Crabtree, Adam, Gauld, Alan, Grosso, Michael & Greyson, Bruce. 2007. *Irreducible Mind. Towards a Psychology for the 21st Century*. Maryland: Rowan and Littlefield.

Keen, Montague, Ellison, Arthur & Fontana, David. 1999. The Scole Report. *Proceedings of the Society for Psychical Research* 58: 150-392.

Keen, Montague and Roy, Archie E. 2004. Chance coincidence in the cross-correspondences. *Journal of the Society for Psychical Research* 68: 57-59.

King, Greg. 2007. *Twilight of Splendour.The Court of Queen Victoria during Her Diamond Jubilee Year*. New Jersey: Wiley.

Kircher, Tilo and David, Anthony. 2003. *The Self in Neuroscience and Psychology*. Cambridge: Cambridge University Press.

Klimo, John. 1998. *Channeling.Investigations on Receiving Information from Paranormal Sources*. Berkeley: North Atlantic Books.

Knight, David. 2004. *Science and Spirituality. The Volatile Connection*. London: Routledge.

Lachapelle, Sofie. 2008. From the stage to the laboratory: magicians,psychologists and the science of illusion. *Journal of the History of the Behavioural Sciences* 44: 319-334.

Lambert, Angela. 1984. *Unquiet Souls. The Indian Summer of the British Aristocracy*. London: Macmillan.

Lambert, G.W. 1928. The psychology of Plotinus and its interest to the student of psychical research. *Proceedings of the Society for Psychical Research* 36: 393-413.

Lambert, G.W. 1957-1958. The Cheltenham Ghost: a reinterpretation of the evidence. *Journal of the Society for Psychical Research* 39: 267-277.

Lambert, G.W. 1959. Frank Podmore. *Journal of the Society for Psychical Research* 40: 1-4.

Lambert, G.W. 1969. Stranger things: Some reflections on reading 'Strange Things' by John L. Campbell and Trevor H Hall. *Journal of the Society for Psychical Research* 45: 43-55.

Lamont, Peter. 2004. Spiritualism and a mid-Victorian crisis of evidence. *Historical Journal* 47: 897-920.

Lamont, Peter. 2005. *The First Psychic: The peculiar Mystery of a notorious Victorian Wizard.* London: Little Brown.

Lang, Andrew & Sidgwick, Eleanor. 1911. [Review of Tanner, Amy E: Studies in Spiritism.] *Proceedings of the Society for Psychical Research* 25: 90-108.

Lazlo, Ervin. 2004/2007. *Science and the Akashic Field. An Integral Theory of Everything.* Vermont: Inner Traditions.

Leaf, Charlotte M. 1932. *Walter Leaf. Some Chapters of Autobiography With a Memoir.* London: John Murray.

Leaf, Walter. 1905. [Review of *Fragments of Prose and Poetry* by F.W.H. Myers.] *Proceedings of the Society for Psychical Research* 19: 342-345.

Ledger, Sally and Luckhurst, Roger. 2000. Eds. *The Fin de Siecle. A Reader In Cultural History c.1880-1900.* Oxford: Oxford University Press.

Lees-Milne,J. 1986. *The Enigmatic Victorian: The Life of Reginald, 2nd Viscount Esher.* London: Sidgwick & Jackson.

Leese, John. 1950. *Personalities and Power in English Education.* London: Arnold.

Leighton, Mary Elizabeth. 2006. Under the influence: crime and hypnotic fictions of the fin de siecle: 203-222. In *Victorian Literary Mesmerism.*Eds. Willis, Martin and Wynne, Catherine. Amsterdam: Rodopi.

Lightman, Bernard. 1997. Ed. *Victorian Science in Context.* Chicago and London: University of Chicago Press.

Littlewood, R.and Bartocci, G. 2005. Stigmata, magnetic fluids and conversion hysteria: one survival of 'Vital Force' theories in scientific medicine? *Transcultural Psychiatry* 42: 596-609.

Lodge, Oliver. 1894. Experience of unusual physical phenomena occurring in the presence of an entranced person (Eusapia Paladino). *Journal of the Society for Psychical Research* 6. 306-360.

Lodge, Oliver. 1901. In memory of F.W.H.Myers. *Proceedings of the Society for Psychical Research* 17: 1-12.

Lodge, Oliver *et al.* (Myers, Wilson, Hodgson, Johnson, Verrall). 1901-1902. Reports of sittings with Mrs Thompson. *Proceedings of the Society for Psychical Research* 17: 61-244.

Lodge, Oliver (Anon.). 1905. Opening of a envelope containing a posthumous note left by Mr. Myers. *Journal of the Society for Psychical Research*: 11-13.

Lodge, Oliver. 1909a. Report on some trance communications received chiefly through Mrs Piper. *Proceedings of the Society for Psychical Research* 23: 127-285.

Lodge, Oliver. 1909b. *The Survival of Man. A Study in Unrecognised Human Faculty.* London: Methuen.

Lodge, Oliver. 1911. Evidence of classical scholarship and of cross-correspondence in some new automatic writings. *Proceedings of the Society for Psychical Research* 25: 113-175.

Lodge, Oliver. 1916. *Raymond or Life after Death.* London: Methuen.

Lodge, Oliver. 1930. *Conviction of Survival. Two Discourses in Memory of FWH Myers.* London: Methuen.

Lodge, Oliver. 1931. *Past Years. An Autobiography.* London: Hodder & Stoughton.

Lubenow, W.C. 1998. *The Cambridge Apostles. Liberalism, imagination and friendship in British intellectual and professional life.* Cambridge: Cambridge University Press.

Lubenow, W.C. 2005. Intimacy, imagination and the inner dialectics of knowledge communities. The Synthetic Society 1896-1908: 357-371. In *The Organisation of Knowledge in Victorian Britain.* Ed. Daunton, Martin. Oxford: Oxford University Press.

Luckhurst, Roger. 2002. *The Invention of Telepathy 1870-1901.* Oxford: Oxford University Press.

Luckhurst, Roger. 2006. Ed. *Robert Louis Stevenson. Strange Case of Dr Jekyll and Mr Hyde and Other Tales.* Oxford: Oxford University Press.

Luckhurst, Roger. 2008. *The Trauma Question.* London: Routledge.

Lycett, Andrew. 2007. *Conan Doyle. The Man Who Created Sherlock Holmes.* London: Weidenfeld and Nicolson.

Mackenzie, Charlotte. 1992. *Psychology for the Rich. A History of Ticehurst Asylum.* London: Routledge.

Mackenzie, Norman and Jean. 1977. *The First Fabians.* London: Weidenfeld and Nicolson.

Mackenzie, Andrew. 1978. [Review of *Hauntings* by Peter Underwood.] *Journal of the Society for Psychical Research* 49: 837-841.

Mackenzie, Andrew. 1982. *Hauntings and Apparitions.* London: Heinemann.

Mackenzie, Andrew. 1988. Continuation of the record of a haunted house. *Journal of the Society for Psychical Research* 55: 25-32.

Mackinnon, W. Papers. School of African and Oriental Studies: London: Mackinnon Box 94, Emin Pasha File 60/IBEA Co.file.

Maixner, Paul. 1981. Ed. *Robert Louis Stevenson. The Critical Heritage.* London: Routledge.

Mallet, Victor. 1968. Ed. *Life with Queen Victoria by Marie Mallet. Marie Mallet's Letters from Court 1887-1901.* London: John Murray.

Mallock W.H. 1877/1975. *The New Republic.* Leicester: Leicester University Press.

Mallock, W.H. 1903. The gospel of Mr. F.W.H. Myers. *Nineteenth Century* 53: 628-644.

Marsh, Edward. 1939. *A Number of People. A Book of Reminiscences.* New York: Harper.

Masterman, C.F.G. n.d. *In Peril of Change.* New York: Huebsch.

Mauskopf, Seymour H. and McVaugh, Michael R. 1980. Afterword J.B. and L.E.Rhine. *The Elusive Science. Origins of Experimental Psychical Research.* Baltimore and London: John Hopkins.

Maxwell, Joseph.1912-1913. Les correspondances croisées et la méthode expérimentale. *Proceedings of the Society for Psychical Research* 26: 57-144.

McCorristine, Shane.2007. 'Dreaming While Awake': the evolution of the concept of hallucinations. *The University of Edinburgh Postgraduate Journal of Culture and the Arts*: Special Issue 1 evolutions: 67-81.

McLeod, Hugh. 1996. *Religion and Society in England, 1850-1914.* Basingstoke: Macmillan.

McKie, David. 2004/2005. *Jabez. The Rise and Fall of a Victorian Rogue.* London: Atlantic Books.

McLynn, Frank. 1991. *Stanley. Sorcerer's Apprentice.* London: Constable.

McLynn, Frank. 1994. *Robert Louis Stevenson*. London: Hutchinson.

McCue, Peter A. 2002. Theories of haunting: a critical overview. *Journal of the Society for Psychical Research* 66: 1-21.

Medhurst, R.G. and Goldney, K.M. 1964. William Crookes and the physical phenomena of mediumship. *Proceedings of the Society for Psychical Research* 54: 25-156.

Meredith, George. 1868. Critical Note on Saint Paul by Frederic H. Myers. *Fortnightly Review* (January) 3: 115.

Middleton, Judy. 2003. *Encyclopaedia of Hove and Portslade*. 12(S) Part 1: 72-75.

Milton, Julie and Wiseman, Richard. 1997. *Guidelines for extrasensory perception research*. Hertfordshire: University of Hertfordshire Press.

Mitchell, T.W. 1920. [Review of *Papers on Psychoanalysis* by Ernest Jones.] *Proceedings of the Society for Psychical Research* 31: 94-102.

Monroe, John Warne. 2008. *Laboratories of Faith. Mesmerism, Spiritism, and Occultism in Modern France*. Ithaca and London: Cornell University Press.

Moody, Raymond with Perry, Paul. 1993. *Reunions. Visionary Encounters With Departed Loved Ones*. New York: Random House.

Moorehead, Caroline. 2000. *Iris Origo. Marchesa of Val d'Orcia*. London: John Murray.

Moreman, Christopher M. 2003. A re-examination of the possibility of chance coincidence as an alternative explanation for mediumistic communication in the cross-correspondences. *Journal of the Society for Psychical Research* 67: 225-242.

Moreman, Christopher M. 2004. A letter re the cross-correspondences. *Journal of the Society for Psychical Research* 68: 60-61.

Morgan, M.C. 1968. *Cheltenham College. The First Hundred Years*. Buckinghamshire: Richard Sadler.

Morton, R.C. 1892. Record of a haunted house. *Proceedings of the Society for Psychical Research* 8: 311-332.

Moses, William Stainton. 1883/1912. *Spirit Teachings*. London: London Spiritualist Alliance.

Munthe, Axel. 1937. *The Story of St Michele*. London: John Murray.

Munves, James. 1997. Richard Hodgson, Mrs Piper and 'George Pelham': a centennial reassessment. *Journal of the Society for Psychical Research* 62: 138-154.

Murphy, Michael. 1992. *The Future of the Body. Explorations into the Further Evolution of Human Nature*. Los Angeles: Tarcher.

Myers, A.T. 1888. Recent experiments by M. Charles Richet on telepathic hypnotism. *Journal of the Society for Psychical Research* 3: 222-226.

Myers, A.T. 1889. International congress of experimental psychology. *Proceedings of the Society for Psychical Research* 6: 171-182.

Myers, A.T. & Myers, F.W.H. 1893. Mind-cure, faith-cure, and the miracles at Lourdes. *Proceedings of the Society for Psychical Research* 9: 160-209.

Myers, Frederic. 1848/1883. Introduction Myers, F.W.H. *Catholic Thoughts on the Bible and theology*. London: Wm. Isbister.

Myers, F.W.H. Papers. Trinity College Library, Cambridge: Myers 1/1, 2/1 etc.

Myers, F.W.H. 1867. *St. Paul*. London: C.J. Clay.

Myers, F.W.H. 1868. *Books to read: a lecture*. Cambridge: Cambridge University Press.

Myers, F.W.H. 1870. *Poems*. Macmillan: London.

Myers, F.W.H. 1873. Jebb's translations. *Fortnightly Review* 20: 645-655.

Myers, F.W.H. 1877. George Sand. *Nineteenth Century* 1: 221-241.

Myers, F.W.H. 1878. Guiseppe Mazzini. *Fortnightly Review* 29: 513-528, 710-728.

Myers, F.W.H. 1879a. Victor Hugo. *Nineteenth Century* 5: 773-787, 970-995.

Myers, F.W.H. 1879b. Virgil. *Fortnightly Review* 31: 163-196.

Myers, F.W.H. 1880/1929. Wordsworth. London: Macmillan.

Myers, F.W.H. 1881a. Ernest Renan. *Nineteenth Century* 9: 949-968.

Myers, F.W.H. 1881b. Renan and miracles. *Nineteenth Century* 10: 90-106.

Myers, F.W.H. 1882a. *Marcus Aurelius Antoninus* 37: 564-586.

Myers. F.W.H. 1882b. *The Renewal of Youth and Other Poems*. London: Macmillan.

Myers, F.W.H. 1882c. A new eirenicon. *Fortnightly Review* 38: 596-607.

Myers, F.W.H. 1883a. *Essays Classical*. London: Macmillan.

Myers, F.W.H. 1883b.1897. *Essays Modern*. London: Macmillan.

Myers, F.W.H. 1883c. Rossetti. *Cornhill* 47: 213-224.

Myers, F.W.H. 1884a. Personal recollections of the Duke of Albany. *Fortnightly Review* 41: 611-624.

Myers, F.W.H. 1884b. On a telepathic explanation of some so-called spiritualistic phenomena. *Proceedings of the Society for Psychical Research* 2: 217-237.

Myers, F.W.H. 1884-5. Specimens of the cases for 'Phantasms of the Living'. *Journal of the Society for Psychical Research* 1: 54-56, 77-83, 94-103, 114-130, 142-152, 157-165, 182-193, 213-220, 238-245.

Myers, F.W.H. 1885a. Case of monition, succeeded by certain mesmeric phenomena. *Journal of the Society for Psychical Research* 1: 310-312.

Myers, F.W.H. 1885b. Automatic writing or the rationale of the planchette. *Contemporary Review* 47: 233-249.

Myers, F.W.H. 1885c. Human personality in the light of hypnotic suggestion. *Proceedings of the Society for Psychical Research* 4: 1-24.

Myers, F.W.H. 1885d. Human personality. *Fortnightly Review* 38: 637-655.

Myers, F.W.H. 1885e. Reply to Mr. Davies' criticisms. *Journal of the Society for Psychical Research* 1: 407-409.

Myers, F.W.H. 1885f. On the method of research pursued by the Society. *Journal of the Society for Psychical Research* 2: 29-32.

Myers, F.W.H. 1885g. Mr. Barkas' medium. *Journal of the Society for Psychical Research* 2: 117-118.

Myers, F.W.H. 1885-1886. Further notes on the unconscious self. *Journal of the Society for Psychical Research* 2: 122-131, 234-243.

Myers, F.W.H. 1886a. Automatic writing-II. *Proceedings of the Society for Psychical Research*: 1-63.

Myers, F.W.H. 1886b. Introduction: xxxv-lxxi.In *Phantasms of the Living*.Vol.1. Gurney, E., Myers,F.W.H., & Podmore,F. London: Trubner.

Myers, F.W.H. 1886c. Note on a suggested mode of psychical interaction: 277-316. In *Phantasms of the Living*.Vol.2. Gurney, E., Myers, F.W.H. & Podmore, F. London: Trubner.

Myers, F.W.H. 1886d. On telepathic hypnotism, and its relation to other forms of hypnotic suggestion. *Proceedings of the Society for Psychical Research* 4: 127-188.

Myers, F.W.H. 1886e. [Remarks.] *Journal of the Society for Psychical Research* 2:155-157.

Myers, F.W.H. 1886f. Planchette writing. *Journal of the Society for Psychical Research* 2: 192-194.

Myers, F.W.H. 1886g. Automatic writing and moral duality. *Journal of the Society for Psychical Research* 2: 224-229.

Myers, F.W.H. 1886h. Multiplex personality. *Nineteenth Century* 20: 648-666.

Myers, F.W.H. 1886i. Multiplex personality. *Journal of the Society for Psychical Research,*2: 443-453.

Myers, F.W.H. 1887a. Automatic writing-3. *Proceedings of the Society for Psychical Research* 4: 209-261.

Myers, F.W.H. 1887b. Multiplex personality. *Proceedings of the Society for Psychical Research* 4: 496-514.

Myers, F.W.H. 1887c. Note on certain reported cases of hypnotic hyperaesthesia. *Proceedings of the Society for Psychical Research* 4: 532-539.

Myers, F.W.H. 1887d. Remarks on a case of post-hypnotic suggestion. *Journal of the Society for Psychical Research* 3: 98-100.

Myers, F.W.H. 1887e. Postscript to Mr Gurney's reply to Professor Peirce. *Proceedings of the American Society for Psychical Research* 1: 300-301.

Myers, F.W.H. 1888a. Darwin and agnosticism. *Fortnightly Review* 49: 99-108.

Myers, F.W.H. 1888b. Matthew Arnold. *Fortnightly Review* 49: 719-728.

Myers, F.W.H. 1888c. The work of Edmund Gurney in experimental psychology. *Proceedings of the Society for Psychical Research* 5: 359-373.

Myers, F.W.H. 1888d. French experiments on the strata of personality. *Proceedings of the Society for Psychical Research* 5: 374-397.

Myers, F.W.H. 1888e. Remarkable instances of automatic messages. *Journal of the Society for Psychical Research* 3: 214-221.

Myers, F.W.H. 1888f. Further cases of automatic writing. *Journal of the Society for Psychical Research* 3: 230-233.

Myers, F.W.H. 1888g. The disenchantment of France. *Nineteenth Century* 23: 661-681.

Myers, F.W.H. 1888h. Multiplex personality. *Journal of the Society for Psychical Research* 3: 319-320.

Myers, F.W.H. 1889a. Automatic writing- IV. The daemon of Socrates. *Proceedings of the Society for Psychical Research* 5: 522-547.

Myers, F.W.H. 1889b. Tennyson as prophet. *Nineteenth Century* 25: 381-396.

Myers, F.W.H. 1889c. On recognized apparitions occurring more than a year after death. *Proceedings of the Society for Psychical Research* 6: 13-65.

Myers, F.W.H. 1889d. Review of *Automatisme Psychologique* by Pierre Janet *Proceedings of the Society for Psychical Research* 6: 186-199.

Myers, F.W.H. 1889e. Binet on the consciousness of hysterical subjects. *Proceedings of the Society for Psychical Research* 6: 200-206.

Myers, F.W.H. 1889f. Review of *Das Doppel-Ich* by Max Dessoir. *Proceedings of the Society for Psychical Research* 6: 207-215.

Myers, F.W.H. 1889g. Dr Jules Janet on hysteria and double personality. *Proceedings of the Society for Psychical Research* 6: 216-221.

Myers, F.W.H. 1889h. Duplex versus multiplex personality [a letter]. *Journal of the Society for Psychical Research* 4: 60-63.

Myers, F.W.H. 1889i. The probably continuous activity of what is known as our secondary consciousness [a letter]. *Journal of the Society for Psychical Research* 4: 77-78.

Myers, F.W.H. 1889j. Multiplex personality [a letter]. *Journal of the Society for Psychical Research* 4: 148-149.

Myers, F.W.H. and Barrett, W.F. 1889. Review of *D.D.Home, his Life and Mission* by Mme. Home. *Journal of the Society for Psychical Research* 4: 101-136.

Myers, F.W.H. *et al.* (Lodge, Leaf,James). 1890. A record of observations of certain phenomena of trance. *Proceedings of the Society for Psychical Research* 6: 436-659.

Myers, F.W.H. 1890a. A defence of phantasms of the dead. *Proceedings of the Society for Psychical Research* 6: 314-357.

Myers, F.W.H. 1890b. Review of A.Aksakof's animismus and spiritismus. *Proceedings of the Society for Psychical Research* 6: 665-674.

Myers, F.W.H. 1890c. Review of *The Gift of D.D. Home* by Mme Home. *Journal of the Society for Psychical Research* 4: 249-252.

Myers, F.W.H. 1890d. Are apparitions objective or subjective? *Journal of the Society for Psychical Research* 4: 244-248.

Myers, F.W.H. 1891a. Review of *The Principles of Psychology* by William James. *Proceedings of the Society for Psychical Research* 7: 111-131.

Myers, F.W.H. 1891b. Science and a future life. *Nineteenth Century* 29: 628-647.

Myers, F.W.H. 1891c. Abstract of 'The mechanism of suggestion.' *Journal of the Society for Psychical Research* 5: 170-172.

Myers, F.W.H. 1891d. Two new cases of spontaneous change of personality. *Journal of the Society for Psychical Research* 5: 93-96.

Myers, F.W.H. 1891e. Mr Hensleigh Wedgwood. *Journal of the Society for Psychical Research* 5: 96.

Myers, F.W.H. 1891f. The case of 'Edina.' *Journal of the Society for Psychical Research* 5: 100-105.

Myers, F.W.H. 1891-1892. On alleged movements of objects, without contact, occurring not in the presence of a paid medium. *Proceedings of the Society for Psychical Research* 7: 146-198,383-394.

Myers, F.W.H. and Sidgwick, H. 1892. The second international congress of experimental psychology. *Proceedings of the Society for Psychical Research* 8: 601-611.

Myers, F.W.H. 1892a. Note on a visit to Kalmar. *Proceedings of the Society for Psychical Research* 7: 370-373.

Myers, F.W.H. 1892b. On indications of continued terrene knowledge on the part of phantasms of the dead. *Proceedings of the Society for Psychical Research* 8: 170-252.

Myers, F.W.H. 1892c. William Stainton-Moses. *Proceedings of the Society for Psychical Research* 8: 597-600.

Myers, F.W.H. 1892d. [A letter on prayer.] *Journal of the Society for Psychical Research* 5: 231-322.

Myers, F.W.H. 1892e. An appeal to non-informants. *Journal of the Society for Psychical Research* 5: 235-236.

Myers, F.W.H. 1892f. The subliminal consciousness. Chapter 1: General characteristics and subliminal messages. *Proceedings of the Society for Psychical Research* 7: 298-327.

Myers, F.W.H. 1892g. The subliminal consciousness. Chapter 2: The mechanism of suggestion. *Proceedings of the Society for Psychical Research* 7: 327-355.

Myers, F.W.H. 1892h. The subliminal consciousness. Chapter 3: The mechanism of genius. *Proceedings of the Society for Psychical Research* 8: 333-361.

Myers, F.W.H. 1892i. The subliminal consciousness. Chapter 4: Hypermnesic dreams. *Proceedings of the Society for Psychical Research* 8: 362-404.

Myers, F.W.H. 1892j. The subliminal consciousness. Chapter 5: Sensory automatisms and induced hallucinations. *Proceedings of the Society for Psychical Research* 8: 436-535.

Myers, F.W.H. 1893/1961. *Fragments of Inner Life*. Privately printed then S.P.R. published.

Myers, F.W.H. 1893a. The subliminal consciousness. Chapter 6: The mechanism of hysteria. *Proceedings of the Society for Psychical Research* 9: 3-25.

Myers, F.W.H. 1893b. The subliminal consciousness. Chapter 7: Motor automatism. *Proceedings of the Society for Psychical Research* 9: 26-128.

Myers, F.W.H. 1893c. Modern poets and the meaning of life. *Nineteenth Century* 33: 93-111.

Myers, F.W.H. 1893d. *Science and a Future Life with Other Essays*. London: Macmillan.

Myers, F.W.H. 1893e. The Congress of psychical science at Chicago. *Journal of the Society for Psychical Research* 6: 126-129.

Myers, F.W.H. 1893f. Professor Wundt on hypnotism and suggestion. *Mind* 2: 95-101.

Myers, F.W.H. 1894a. Report on the census of hallucinations. Appendix G. A proposed scheme of apparitions. *Proceedings of the Society for Psychical Research* 10: 415-422.

Myers, F.W.H. 1894b. Psychical research. *National Review-II* 24: 190-209.

Myers, F.W.H. 1894c. [Comments on character of D.D. Home.] *Journal of the Society for Psychical Research* 6: 176-179.

Myers, F.W.H. 1894d. The Anglo-French Psychological Society. *Journal of the Society for Psychical Research* 6: 263-264.

Myers, F.W.H. 1894e. [Comments on Eusapia Paladino.] *Journal of the Society for Psychical Research* 6: 336-339.

Myers, F.W.H. 1894-1895. The experiences of W.Stainton-Moses. *Proceedings of the Society for Psychical Research* 9: 245-352, 11: 24-113.

Myers, F.W.H. 1895a. Resolute credulity. *Proceedings of the Society for Psychical Research* 9: 213-234.

Myers, F.W.H. 1895b. Robert Louis Stevenson. *Journal of the Society for Psychical Research* 7: 6-7.

Myers, F.W.H. 1895c. The subliminal self.Chapter 8: The relation of supernormal phenomena to time;-Retrocognition. *Proceedings of the Society for Psychical Research* 11: 334-407.

Myers, F.W.H. 1895d. The subliminal self. Chapter 9: The relation of supernormal phenomena to time;-Precognition. *Proceedings of the Society for Psychical Research* 11: 408-593.

Myers, F.W.H. 1895e. The need for experiments in automatism. *Journal of the Society for Psychical Research* 8: 30-31.

Myers, F.W.H. 1895f. Reply to Dr Hodgson. *Journal of the Society for Psychical Research* 8: 55-64.

Myers, F.W.H. 1895g. Reply to Mr Page Hopps, concerning Eusapia Paladino. *Journal of the Society for Psychical Research* 7: 164.

Myers, F.W.H. 1896a. Glossary of terms used in psychical research. *Proceedings of the Society for Psychical Research* 12: 166-174.

Myers, F.W.H. 1896b [A.Le Baron's Automatism]. *Proceedings of the Society for Psychical Research* 12: 295-297.

Myers, F.W.H. 1896c. Lord Leighton. *Journal of the Society for Psychical Research* 7: 208.

Myers, F.W.H. 1896d. Experimental dreams. *Journal of the Society for Psychical Research* 7: 218-220.

Myers, F.W.H. 1896e. Professor Delboeuf. *Journal of the Society for Psychical Research* 7: 294.

Myers, F.W.H. 1897a. Recent experiments in normal motor automatism. *Proceedings of the Society for Psychical Research* 12: 316-318.

Myers, F.W.H. 1897b. Hysteria and genius. *Journal of the Society for Psychical Research* 8: 51-58, 69-70.

Myers, F.W.H. 1897c.The moral and intellectual limits of suggestion. *Journal of the Society for Psychical Research* 8: 83-87,95-96.

Myers, F.W.H. 1897d. Richard Holt Hutton. *Journal of the Society for Psychical Research* 8: 132.

Myers, F.W.H. 1897e. [Review of *Guesses at the Riddle of Existence* by Goldwin Smith.] *Journal of the Society for Psychical Research* 8: 163-164.

Myers, F.W.H. 1898a. On the possibility of a scientific approach to problems generally classed as religious: 187-197. In *Papers read before the Synthetic Society 1896-1908: and written comments thereon circulated among members of the Society.* Ed.Balfour, A.J.London: Spottiswoode.

Myers, F.W.H. 1898b. One door will open: 212-216. In *Papers read before the Synthetic Society 1896-1908: and written comments thereon circulated among members of the Society.* See above.

Myers, F.W.H. 1898c. [Review of *Letters from Julia.* Ed. W.T. Stead.] *Proceedings of the Society for Psychical Research* 13: 612-614.

Myers, F.W.H. 1898d. The psychology of hypnotism. *Proceedings of the Society for Psychical Research* 14: 100-108.

Myers, F.W.H. 1898e. [Review of *L'année psychologique.*] *Proceedings of the Society for Psychical Research* 14: 146-147.

Myers, F.W.H. 1898f. Discussion of reciprocal and other cases received. *Journal of the Society for Psychical Research* 8: 318-325.

Myers, F.W.H. 1898g. Man's survival of death. *National Review-II* 32: 230-242.

Myers, F.W.H. 1898h. Dr. G.B. Ermacora. *Journal of the Society for Psychical Research* 8: 244.

Myers, F.W.H. 1898i. W.E. Gladstone. *Journal of the Society for Psychical Research* 8: 260.

Myers, F.W.H. 1899a. Provisional sketch of a religious synthesis: 264-274. In *Papers read before the Synthetic Society 1896-1908: and written comments thereon circulated among members of the Society.* See above.

Myers, F.W.H. 1899b. [Review of *Experimental Study of Visions* by Morton Prince.] *Proceedings of the Society for Psychical Research* 14: 366-372.

Myers, F.W.H. 1899c. [Review of *Some Peculiarities of the Secondary Personality* by G.T.W. Patrick.] *Proceedings of the Society for Psychical Research* 14: 382-386.

Myers, F.W.H. 1899d. [Remarks on Eusapia Paladino in Paris in 1898.] *Journal of the Society for Psychical Research*. 9: 4.

Myers, F.W.H. 1899e. The Society for Psychical Research and Eusapia Paladino. *Journal of the Society for Psychical Research* 9: 35.

Myers, F.W.H. 1900a. [Review of *L'annéee psychologique*, 5th année.] *Proceedings of the Society for Psychical Research* 15: 105-107.

Myers, F.W.H. 1900b. Presidential address. *Proceedings of the Society for Psychical Research* 15: 110-127.

Myers, F.W.H. 1900c. John Ruskin. *Journal of the Society for Psychical Research* 9: 208-210.

Myers, F.W.H. 1900d. Mary H. Kingsley. *Journal of the Society for Psychical Research* 9: 279-280.

Myers, F.W.H. 1900e. The Marquis of Bute, K.T. (Vice-President S.P.R.). *Journal of the Society for Psychical Research* 9: 310-311.

Myers, F.W.H. 1901a. Pseudo-possession. *Proceedings of the Society for Psychical Research* 15: 384-415.

Myers, F.W.H. 1901b. Addendum to report on 4th international congress of experimental psychology. *Proceedings of the Society for Psychical Research* 15: 447-448.

Myers, F.W.H. 1901c. In memory of Henry Sidgwick. *Proceedings of the Society for Psychical Research* 15: 452-462.

Myers, F.W.H. 1903/1904. *Human Personality and Its Survival of Bodily Death*. London and New York: Longmans.

Myers, F.W.H. 1904a. [Lines on] G.F.Watts, R.A. *Journal of the Society for Psychical Research* 11: 268-269.

Myers, F.W.H. 1904b. *Fragments of Prose and Poetry Edited By His Wife Eveleen Myers*. London: Longmans.

Myers, F.W.H. 1921. *Collected Poems with Autobiographical and Critical Fragments Edited By His Wife Eveleen Myers*. London: Macmillan.

Myers, F.W.H. 1919/1992. Introduction Myers, L. *Human Personality and Its Survival of Bodily Death*. Norwich: Pilgrim Books.

Myers, F.W.H. 1960/2001. Ed. Smith, S., Foreword Huxley, A., Introduction Mishlove, J. *Human Personality and Its Survival of Bodily Death*. Virginia: Hampton Roads.

Nevill, Ralph. 1906. Ed. *The Reminiscences of Lady Dorothy Neville*. London: Thomas Nelson.

Newsome, David. 1961. *Godliness and Good Learning. Four Studies on a Victorian Ideal*. London: John Murray.

Newsome, David. 1997. *The Victorian World Picture*. London: John Murray.

Newsome, David. 1980. *On the Edge of Paradise. A.C.Benson: The Diarist*. London: John Murray.

Nicol, Fraser. 1966. The silences of Mr Trevor Hall. *International Journal of Parapsychology*. 8: 5-59.

Nicol, Fraser. 1968. Classic experiments in telepathy under hypnosis. A historical survey: 8-16. In *Psi and altered states of consciousness: Hypnosis, drugs,dreams & psi*. Eds. Cavanna, Roberto & Ullman, Montague. New York: Parapsychology Foundation.

Nicol, Fraser. 1972. The founders of the SPR. *Proceedings of the Society for Psychical Research* 55: 341-367.

Noakes, Richard J. 1998. *Cranks and Visionaries. Science, Spiritualism and Transgression in Victorian Britain.* Ph.D. University of Cambridge.

Noakes, Richard. 2004. Spiritualism, science and the supernatural in mid-Victorian Britain: 23-43. In *The Victorian Supernatural.* Eds. Bown, Nicola, Burdett, Carolyn & Thurschwell, Pamela. Cambridge: Cambridge University Press.

Noakes, Richard. 2008. The historiography of psychical research: lessons from histories of the sciences. *Journal of the Society for Psychical Research* 72: 65-85.

Noseda, M.& Mclean,G.R. 2008. [letter.] Where did the scientific method go? *Nature Biotechnology* 26: 26-28.

Noyes, Ralph. 1999. The other side of Plato's wall: 244-262. In *Ghosts, Deconstruction, Psychoanalysis, History.* Eds. Buse, Peter and Stott, Andrew. London: Macmillan.

Oppenheim, Janet. 1985. *The Other World. Spiritualism and Psychical Research in England 1850-1914.* Cambridge: Cambridge University Press.

Oppenheim, Janet. 1991. *'Shattered Nerves' Doctors, Patients and Depression in Victorian England.* Oxford: Oxford University Press.

Oram, Arthur. 1998. *The System In Which We live.* Surrey: Talbot.

Osis, Karlis. 1980. Apparitions: a new model. Abstracts and papers from the twenty-third annual convention of the Parapsychological Association. *Research in Parapsychology*: 1-2.

Ostrander, Sheila & Schroeder, Lynn. 1999. *Psychic Discoveries. The Iron Curtain Lifted.* London: Souvenir Press.

Owen, Alex. 1989. *The Darkened Room. Women, Power and Spiritualism in Late Victorian England.* London: Virago Press.

Owen, Alex. 2001. Occultism and the 'Modern' self in fin-de-siècle Britain: 71-96. In *Meanings of Modernity. Britain from the Late Victorian Era to World War II.* Eds.Daunton, Martin and Rieger, Bernhard. Oxford: Berg.

Owen, Alex. 2004. *The Place of Enchantment. British Occultism and the Culture of the Modern.* Chicago: University of Chicago Press.

Palfreman, Jon. 1979. Between skepticism and credulity: a study of Victorian scientific attitudes to modern spiritualism: 201-236. In *On the Margins of Science. The Social Construction of Rejected Knowledge.* Ed. Wallis, R. Staffordshire: University of Keele Press.

Parsons, Gerald. 1988. Ed. *Religion in Victorian Britain. Volume IV. Interpretations.* Manchester: Manchester University Press In Association with the Open University Press.

Parry, R. St. John. 1926. *Henry Jackson O.M. A Memoir.* Cambridge: Cambridge University Press.

Peirce, C.S. 1887a. Criticism on 'Phantasms of the Living.' An examination of an argument of Messrs.Gurney, Myers, and Podmore. *Proceedings of the American Society for Psychical Research* 1: 150-157.

Peirce, C.S. 1887b. Mr Peirce's rejoinder. *Proceedings of the American Society for Psychical Research* 1: 180-215.

Perkin, Harold. 2002. *The Rise of Professional Society. England since 1880.* London: Routledge.

Perry, Ralph Barton. 1948. *The Thought and Character of William James. Briefer Version.* Cambridge, Mass.: Harvard University Press.

Pick, Daniel. 1989/1996. *Faces of Degeneration. A European Disorder c1848-c1918.* Cambridge: Cambridge University Press.

Pick, Daniel. 2000. *Svengali's Web. The Alien Enchanter in Modern Culture.* Newhaven and London: Yale University Press.

Piddington, J.G. 1903-1904a. The trance phenomena of Mrs Thompson. *Journal of the Society for Psychical Research* 11: 74-76.

Piddington, J.G. 1903-1904b. On the types of phenomena displayed in Mrs Thompson's trance. *Proceedings of the Society for Psychical Research* 18: 104-307.

Piddington, J.G. 1908. A series of concordant automatisms. *Proceedings of the Society for Psychical Research* 22: 19-416.

Pierce, Arthur H. & Podmore, F. 1895-1897. Subliminal self or unconscious cerebration? *Proceedings of the Society for Psychical Research* 11: 317-322.

Piper, Alta L. 1929. *The Life and Works of Mrs Piper.* London: Kegan Paul, Trench, and Trubner.

Playfair, Guy Lyon. 1985. *If This Be Magic.* London: Jonathan Cape.

Podmore, Frank. 1889-1890. Phantasms of the dead from another point of view. *Proceedings of the Society for Psychical Research* 6: 229-313.

Podmore, Frank. 1898-1899. Discussion of the trance phenomena of Mrs Piper 1. *Proceedings of the Society for Psychical Research* 14: 50-78.

Podmore, Frank. 1900-1901. [Review of *The Alleged Haunting of B-House* by Lord Bute and A. Goodrich Freer.] *Proceedings of the Society for Psychical Research* 15: 98-100.

Podmore, Frank. 1902. *Modern Spiritualism. A History and A Criticism.*London: Methuen.

Podmore, Frank. 1907. [Review of *Henry Sidgwick: a Memoir* by A.S. and E.S.] *Proceedings of the Society for Psychical Research* 19: 432-450.

Polidaro, M. and Rinaldi,G.M. 1998. Eusapia's sapient foot: a new consideration of the Feilding report. *Journal of the Society for Psychical Research* 62: 242-256.

Porter, Katherine H. 1958. *Through a Glass Darkly. Spiritualism in the Browning Circle.* Kansas: University of Kansas Press.

Prel, Carl du. 1889/2008. Trans. Massey,C.C. *The Philosophy of Mysticism V.1 & V.2.* London: George Redway.

Price, Leslie. 1985. Astral Bells in Notting Hill. *Theosophical History* 1: 25-35.

Price, Leslie. 1986. *Madame Blavatsky Unveiled? A new discussion of the most famous investigation of The Society for Psychical Research.* London: Theosophical History Centre.

Price, Leslie. 1999. *The Mystery of Stainton Moses. An address given in 1992 on the centenary of his death.* London: Psychic Pioneer Publications.

Price, Leslie. 2006. *Preface to the Online Edition of the First S.P.R. Report on Madame Blavatsky.* Blavatsky Study Centre: www.blavatskyarchives.com.

Radin, Dean. 1997. *The Conscious Universe. The Scientific Truth of Psychic Phenomena.* New York: HarperCollins.

Raia, Courtenay Green. 2005. *The Substance of Things Hoped For: Faith, Science and Psychical Research in the Victorian Fin de Siècle.* University of California. Ph.D.

Raia, Courtenay Green. 2007. From ether theory to ether theology: Oliver Lodge and the physics of immortality. *Journal of the History of the Behavioural Sciences* 431: 19-43.

Rao, K. Ramakrishna. 2002. *Consciousness Studies. Cross-Cultural Perspectives.* North Carolina: McFarland.

Raverat, Gwen. 1953. *Period Piece. A Cambridge Childhood*. London: Faber and Faber.

Rayleigh, Lord. 1919. Presidential address. *Proceedings of the Society for Psychical Research* 30: 275-290.

Richet, Charles. 1923. Trans. de Brath, Stanley. *Thirty Years of Psychical Research*. New York: Macmillan.

Rimmer, W.G. 1960. *Marshalls of Leeds. Flax Spinners 1788-1886*. Cambridge: Cambridge University Press.

Rive, Richard. 1988. *Olive Schreiner Letters. Volume I 1871-1899*. Oxford: Oxford University Press.

Robson, Colin. 2002. *Real World Research*. Oxford: Blackwell.

Rockall, Annette. 2007 (26.11.2007). Personal communication re F.W.H. Myers' Athenaeum membership.

Rothblatt, Sheldon. 1968. *The Revolution of the Dons. Cambridge and Society in Victorian England*. London: Faber and Faber.

Rose, Jonathan. 1986. *The Edwardian Temperament 1895-1919*. Ohio: Ohio University Press.

Roy, Archie. E. 1996. *The Archives of the Mind*. Essex: SNU Publications.

Roy, Archie. 2008. *The Eager Dead. A Study in Haunting*.Brighton: The Book Guild.

Rozenzweig, Mark R. *et al*. 2000. *History of the International Union of Psychological Science*. Hove: Psychology Press.

Rylance, Rick. 2000. *Victorian Psychology and British Culture 1850-1880*. Oxford: Oxford University Press.

Salter, Helen & Newton, Isabel. 1940. Alice Johnson. *Proceedings of the Society for Psychical Research* 46: 16-22.

Salter, Helen. 1950a. Impressions of some early workers in the SPR. *Journal of Parapsychology* 14: 29-41.

Salter, Helen. 1950b. Mrs Leonora Piper. *Journal of the Society for Psychical Research* 35: 341-344.

Salter, W.H. Papers. Trinity College Library, Cambridge: A/1, B/1 etc.

Salter, W.H. 1928. An experiment in pseudo-scripts.*Proceedings of the Society for Psychical Research* 36: 525-554.

Salter, W.H. 1948. *An Introduction to the Study of Scripts*. Privately printed.

Salter, WH. 1950. *Trance Mediumship. An Introductory Study of Mrs Piper and Mrs Leonard*. Glasgow: Society for Psychical Research.

Salter, W.H. 1955a. *Memoirs*. Unpublished. Trinity College Library, Cambridge.

Salter, W.H. 1955b. The S.P.R. and the Myers' 'Sealed Packet'. *Journal of the Society for Psychical Research* 38: 18-20.

Salter, W.H. 1958a. F.W.H. Myers' posthumous message. *Proceedings of the Society for Psychical Research* 52: 1-32.

Salter, W.H. 1958b. Frederic W.H.Myers. *Journal of the Society for Psychical Research* 39: 261-266.

Salter, W.H. 1960. Historical background to 1959 report on enquiry into spontaneous cases. *Proceedings of the Society for Psychical Research* 53: 83-93.

Salter, W.H. 1961a. G.A.Smith. *Journal of the Society for Psychical Research* 41: 219-221.

Salter, W.H. 1961b. *Zoar. The evidence of psychical research concerning survival*. London: Sidgwick and Jackson.

Saltmarsh, H.F. 1938/1975. *Evidence of Personal Survival From Cross Correspondences*. New York: Arno Press.

Sarbin, Theodore R. and Juhasz, Joseph B. 1967. The historical background of the concept of hallucination. *Journal of the History of the Behavioural Sciences* 3: 339-356.

Schneer, Jonathan. 1999. *London 1900. The Imperial Metropolis*. New Haven and London: Yale University Press.

Schueller, H.M. and Peters, R.L. 1967-1969. 3 Vols. *The Letters of John Addington Symonds*. Detroit: Wayne University Press.

Schultz, Bart. 2004. *Henry Sidgwick. Eye of the Universe. An Intellectual Biography*. Cambridge: Cambridge University Press.

Searle, G.R. 2004. *A New England. Peace and War 1886-1918*. Oxford: Clarendon Press.

Seiler, R.M. 1987. Ed. *Walter Pater. A Life Remembered*. Calgary: Calgary University Press.

Shamdasani, Sonu. 1993. Automatic writing and the discovery of the unconscious. *Spring: A Journal of Archetype and Culture* 54: 100-131.

Shamdasani, Sonu. 2003/2004. *Jung and the Making of Modern Psychology. The Dream of a Science*. Cambridge: Cambridge University Press.

Sheldrake, Rupert. 1981/1987. *A New Science Of Life. The Hypothesis of Formative Causation*. London: Paladin.

Sheldrake, Rupert. 1995/2002. *Seven Experiments That Could Change The World*. Vermont: Park Street Press.

Sheldrake, Rupert. 2003. *The Sense Of Being Stared At and other aspects of The Extended Mind*. London: Hutchinson.

Sheppard, E.A. 1974. *Henry James and The Turn of the Screw*. Oxford: Oxford University Press.

Shermer, Michael. 2002. *In Darwin's Shadow. The Life and Science of Alfred Russel Wallace. A Biographical Study on the Psychology of History*. New York: Oxford University Press.

A.S. and E.M.S. (Arthur and Eleanor Sidgwick). 1906. *Henry Sidgwick. A Memoir*. London: Macmillan.

Sidgwick, Eleanor (Mrs Henry). 1885. Notes on the evidence, collected by the Society,for phantasms of the dead. *Proceedings of the Society for Psychical Research* 3: 69-150.

Sidgwick, Eleanor (Mrs Henry). 1886. Results of a personal investigation into the physical phenomena of spiritualism, with some critical remarks on the evidence for the genuineness of such phenomena. *Proceedings of the Society for Psychical Research* 4: 45-74.

Sidgwick, Eleanor (Mrs Henry). 1900-1901. Discussion of the trance phenomena of Mrs Piper 2. *Proceedings of the Society for Psychical Research* 15: 16-38.

Sidgwick, Eleanor. 1911. 'Confessions' of a telepathist. *Journal of the Society for Psychical Research*: 115-132.

Sidgwick, Eleanor *et al.* (Verrall, Johnson, Piddington). 1912-1913. A reply to Joseph Maxwell's paper on cross-correspondences and the experimental method. *Proceedings of the Society for Psychical Research* 26: 375-418.

Sidgwick, Eleanor. 1915. A contribution to the study of the psychology of Mrs Piper's trance phenomena. *Proceedings of the Society for Psychical Research* 28: 1-652.

Sidgwick, Eleanor. 1916. Mrs A.W.Verrall. *Proceedings of the Society for Psychical Research* 29: 170-176.

Sidgwick, Eleanor. 1923. On hindrances and complications in telepathic communication. *Proceedings of the Society for Psychical Research* 34: 28-69.

Sidgwick, Eleanor. 1925. In memory of Sir William Fletcher Barrett. *Proceedings of the Society for Psychical Research* 35: 413-418.

Sidgwick, Eleanor. 1929. [Reply to E.J. Dingwall's attack on the cross-correspondences.] *Journal of the Society for Psychical Research* 25: 69-72

Sidgwick, Eleanor. 1932. The SPR: A short account of its history and work on the occasion of the Society's jubilee in 1932. *Proceedings of the Society for Psychical Research* 41: 1-26.

Sidgwick, Ethel. 1938. *Mrs Henry Sidgwick. A Memoir.* London: Sidgwick and Jackson.

Sidgwick, Henry. Papers. Trinity College Library, Cambridge: Add.Ms.c.100 etc.

Sidgwick, Henry. 1882a. Address by president at the first general meeting. *Proceedings of the Society for Psychical Research* 1: 7-12.

Sidgwick, Henry. 1882b. Address by president at the second general meeting. *Proceedings of the Society for Psychical Research* 1: 65-69.

Sidgwick, Henry. 1883. Address by president at the fourth general meeting. *Proceedings of the Society for Psychical Research* 1: 245-50.

Sidgwick, Henry. 1884a. Address by president at the fourth general meeting. *Proceedings of the Society for Psychical Research* 2: 152-156.

Sidgwick, Henry. 1884b. Address by president at the eleventh general meeting. *Proceedings of the Society for Psychical Research* 2: 238.

Sidgwick, Henry. 1888. Address by president at the twenty-eight general meeting. *Proceedings of the Society for Psychical Research* 5: 271-278.

Sidgwick, Henry. 1889. Address by the president at the thirty-second general meeting. *Proceedings of the Society for Psychical Research* 6: 1-6.

Sidgwick, Henry. 1892. The international congress of experimental psychology. *Journal of the Society for Psychical Research* 5: 283-293.

Sidgwick, Henry and Myers, F.W.H. 1892. The second international congress of experimental psychology. *Proceedings of the Society for Psychical Research* 8: 601-611.

Sidgwick, Henry. 1894. Disinterested deception. *Journal of the Society for Psychical Research* 6: 274-278.

Sidgwick, Henry, Sidgwick, Eleanor and Johnson, Alice. 1894. Census of hallucinations. *Proceedings of the Society for Psychical Research* 10.

Sidgwick, Henry. 1895. Eusapia Paladino. *Journal of the Society for Psychical Research* 7: 148-159.

Sidgwick, Henry. 1896. The third international congress of psychology. *Journal of the Society for Psychical Research* 7: 295-299.

Simon, Linda. 1998. *Genuine Reality. A Life of William James.* New York: Harcourt Brace.

Sinnett, A.P. 1881/1969. *The Occult World.* London: Theosophical Publishing House.

Sinnett, A.P. 1883/1972. *Esoteric Buddhism.* London: Theosophical Publishing House.

Sinnett, A.P. 1922. *The Early Days of Theosophy in Europe.* London: Theosophical Publishing House.

Skrupskelis, Ignas K. and Berkeley, Elizabeth M.. *et al*. 1992-2004. Eds.12 Vols. *The Correspondence of William James*. Charlottesville: University Press of Virginia.

Skultans, Vieda. 1983. Mediums, controls and eminent men: 15-26. In *Women's Religious Experience*.Ed. Holden, Pat. London and Canberra: Croom Helm.

Sladen, Douglas. 1915. *Twenty Years of My Life*. London: Constable.

Sladen, Douglas. 1939. *The Story of My Life*. London: Hutchinson.

Sneyd-Kynnersley, E.M. 1908. *H.M.I. Some Passages in the Life of One of H.M. Inspectors of Schools*. London: Macmillan.

Society for Psychical Research archive. Cambridge University Library, Cambridge: SPR 1/1, 2/1 etc.

Solomon, Grant & Jane. 1999. *The Scole Experiment. Scientific Evidence for Life after Death*. London: Piatkus.

Sommer, Andreas. 2008. *The influence of Carl du Prel on Frederic W.H. Myers*: research proposal.

Sommer, Andreas. 2009a. 'From astronomy to transcendental Darwinism.' Carl du Prel (1839-1899). *Journal of Scientific Exploration* 23: 1-10.

Sommer, Andreas. 2009b. (13.2.2009). Personal communication re Myers and Wundt.

Stanley, H.M. Papers. Royal Museum for Central Africa, Brussels: RMCA correspondence section 2.6., 432 onwards. And also 5970 and 6861.

Spalding, Francis. 2001. *Gwen Raverat. Friends, Family & Affections. A Biography*. London: The Harvill Press.

Spencer, F.H. 1928. *An Inspector's Testament*. London: English Universities Press.

Stack, J.H. 1884. On contemporary evidence as to 'Phantasms of the Living in India'.*Journal of the Society for Psychical Research* 1: 72-76.

Stead, W.T. 1970. *A Casebook of True Supernatural Stories*. New York: University Books.

Stein, Robert D. 1968. *The Impact of the Psychical Research Movement on the Literary Criticism of Frederic WH Myers*. Ph.D. Northwestern University.

Steinmeyer, Jim. 2005. *Hiding the Elephant. How Magicians Invented the Impossible*. London: Arrow Books.

Stephen, J.K. 1891/1898. *Lapsus Calami And Other Verses*. Cambridge: Macmillan and Bowes.

Stevenson, Ian. 1990. Thoughts on the decline of major paranormal phenomena. *Proceedings of the Society for Psychical Research* 57: 149-162.

Stevenson, Ian. 1998. [Letter on Munves and Mrs Piper.] *Journal of the Society for Psychical Research* 62: 282-283.

Stout, G.F. 1903. Mr F.W.H. Myers on 'Human Personality and Its Survival of Bodily Death.' *Hibbert Journal* 2: 44-64.

Stray, Christopher. 1998. *Classics Transformed. Schools, Universities and Society in England, 1830-1960*. Oxford: Oxford University Press.

Stray, Chrisopher. 2006 (23.07.2006). Personal communication re R.C. Jebb papers.

Stray, Christopher. 2007 (7.5.2007). Personal communication re J.K.Stephen reference: Trinity Add.Ms.c.185.442.

Stuart, James. 1911. *Reminiscences*. London: Chiswick Press.

Sutherland, Gillian. 1972. Ed. *Studies in the growth of nineteenth-century government*. London: Routledge and Kegan Paul.

Sutherland, Gillian. 1973. *Policy-Making in Elementary Education 1870-1895*. Oxford: Oxford University Press.

Sutherland, Gillian. 2006. *Faith, Duty and the Power of Mind. The Cloughs and their Circle*. Cambridge: Cambridge University Press.

Sweet, Matthew. 2001. *Inventing the Victorians*. London: Faber and Faber.

Tabori, Paul. 1972. *Pioneers of the Unseen*. London: Souvenir Press.

Taine, Hippolyte. 1957. Trans. Hyams, E. *Notes on England*. London: Thames and Hudson.

Targ, Russell. 2004. Foreword Huston, Jean. *Limitless Mind. A guide to remote viewing and transformation of consciousness*. California: New World Library.

Taylor, Eugene. 1996. *William James on Consciousness beyond the Margin*. Princeton: Princeton University Press.

Taylor, Jenny Bourne & Shuttleworth, Sally. 1998/2003. Eds. *Embodied Selves. An Anthology of Psychological Texts 1830-1890*. Oxford: Clarendon Press.

Taylor, Jenny Bourne. 2007. Psychology at the fin de siècle: 13-30. In *The Cambridge Companion to the Fin de Siècle*. Ed.Marshall, Gail. Cambridge: Cambridge University Press.

Taylor, Miles and Wolff, Michael. 2004. *The Victorians since 1901. Histories, Representations and Revisions*. Manchester: Manchester University Press.

Taylor, Una. 1924. *Guests and Memories. Annals of a Seaside Villa*. Oxford: Humphrey Milford, Oxford University Press.

Tennant family papers. West Glamorgan Archive Service, Swansea: D/DT.Vol 3: 2532 onwards.

Thalbourne, Michael A.and Storm, Lance. 2005. *Parapsychology in the Twenty-First Century. Essays on the Future of Psychical Research*. North Carolina and London: McFarland.

Thompson, F.M.L. 1988. *The Rise of Respectable Society. A Social History of Victorian Britain*. Cambridge, Mass.: Harvard University Press.

Thomson, J.J. 1936. *Recollections and Reflections*. London: Bell.

Thomson, Patricia. 1977. *George Sand and the Victorians. Her Influence and Reputation in Nineteenth Century England*. London: Macmillan.

Thouless, R.H. 1968. Review of *Obituary –The Hodgson Report on Madame Blavatsky* by Adlai E.Waterman.*Journal of the Society for Psychical Research* 44: 341-349.

Thouless, R.H. 1972. *From Anecdote to Experiment in Psychical Research*. London: Routledge.

Thurschwell, Pamela. 2001. *Literature, Technology and Magical Thinking 1880-1920*. Cambridge: Cambridge University Press.

Thurschwell, Pamela. 2004. [Review of *The Invention of Telepathy 1870-1901* by Roger Luckhurst.] *Victorian Studies* 46: 503-505.

Treffert, Darold A. 1989. *Extraordinary People*. London. Bantam Press.

Treitel, Corinna. 2004. *A Science for the Soul. Occultism and the Genesis of the German Modern*. Baltimore and London: John Hopkins University Press.

Tromp, Marlene. 2006. *Altered States. Sex, Nation, Drugs, and Self-Transformation in Victorian Spiritualism*. Albany: State University of New York Press.

Tucker, Keith. 1994. *Chronicle of Cadoxton*. Neath: Historical Projects.

Tullberg, Rita McWilliams. 1975/1998. Introduction Sutherland, Gillian.*Women at Cambridge*. Cambridge: Cambridge University Press.

Turner, Frank Miller. 1974. *Between Science and Religion. The Reaction to Scientific Naturalism in Late Victorian England.* Newhaven and London: Yale University Press.

Turner, Frank M. 1981. *The Greek Heritage in Victorian Britain.* New Haven and London: Yale University Press.

Turner, Frank M. 1993. *Contesting Cultural Authority. Essays in Victorian Intellectual Life.* Cambridge: Cambridge University Press.

Tyrrell, G.N.M. 1946. *The Personality of Man.* London: Penguin Books.

Tyrrell, G.N.M. 1954. *The Nature of Human Personality.* London: George Allen and Unwin .

Tyrrell, G.N.M. 1953/1961. *Science and Psychical Phenomena & Apparitions in one volume.* New York: University Books.

Underwood, Peter. 1988. [Re Mackenzie's 'Continuation Of A Haunted House'.] *Journal of the Society for Psychical Research* 55: 170-171.

Verrall, Mrs A.W. 1906. On a series of automatic writings. *Proceedings of the Society for Psychical Research* 20: 1-432.

Verrall, Mrs A.W. 1910. Classical and literary allusions in Mrs Piper's trance. *Proceedings of the Society for Psychical Research* 24: 39-85.

Victorian Travellers Guide to 19th Century England & Wales. 1864/1985. London: Bracken Books.

Walker, Mary. 1990. Between fiction and madness: the relationship of women to the supernatural in late Victorian Britain: 230-258. In *That Gentle Strength. Historical Perspectives on Women in Christianity.*Ed. with introduction by Coon, Lynda L., Haldane, Katherine J. and Sommer, Elizabeth E.

Walkowitz, Judith R. 1992. *City of Dreadful Delight. Narratives of Sexual Danger in Late-Victorian London.* London: University of Chicago Press.

Wallace, Alfred Russel. 1874. A Defence of Modern Spiritualism. *Fortnightly Review* 15: 630-657, 785-807.

Wallace, Alfred Russel. 1905. *A Record of Events and Opinions Vol II.* London: Chapman and Hall.

Waller, David. 2009. *The Magnificent Mrs Tennant.* Newhaven & London: Yale University Press (in press).

Warcollier, R. 1959-1960. Charles Richet. *Journal of the Society for Psychical Research* 40: 157-162.

Ward, Maisie. 1934. *The Wilfred Wards and the Transition.* London: Sheed and Ward.

Ward, Wilfrid. Papers. University of St Andrews Library, St.Andrews: Ward VII /217 onwards.

Warner, Marina. 2006. *Phantasmagoria. Spirit Visions, Metaphors, and Media into the Twenty-first Century.* Oxford: Oxford University Press.

Waterman, Adlai E. 1963. *Obituary-The Hodgson Report on Madame Blavatsky.* Madras: Theosophical Publishing House.

Waterman, Adlai E. 1969-1970. The 'Hodgson Report' on Madame Blavatsky. *Journal of the Society for Psychical Research*: 188-197.

West, D.J. 1948. A mass observation questionnaire on hallucinations. *Journal of the Society for Psychical Research* 34: 187-196.

Wiener, Martin. 1981. *English Culture and the Decline of the Industrial Spirit, 1850-1980.* Cambridge: Cambridge University Press.

Wiley, Barry H. 2005. *The Indescribable Phenomenon. The Life and Mysteries of Anna Eva Fay*. Seattle: Hermetic Press.

Williams, John Peregrine. 1984. *The Making of Victorian Psychical Research. An Intellectual Elite's Approach to the Spiritual World*. Ph.D. Thesis.University of Cambridge.

Williams, J.P. 1985. Psychical research and psychiatry in late Victorian Britain: trance as ecstasy or trance as insanity: 233-254. In *The Anatomy of Madness. Essays in the History of Psychiatry. Vol 1 People and ideas*. Eds. Bynum,W.F., Porter, Roy and Shepherd, Michael. London and New York: Tavistock Publications.

Wilson, A.N. 1999. *God's Funeral*. John Murray: London.

Wilson, A.N. 2002. *The Victorians*. London: Hutchinson.

Windschaffel, Ruth Clayton. 2006. Politics, religion and text: W.E.Gladstone and spiritualism. *Journal of Victorian Culture* 11: 1-29.

Winter, Alison. 1998. *Mesmerized. Powers of Mind in Victorian Britain*. Chicago: University of Chicago Press.

Wiseman, Richard. 1991-1992. The Feilding report: a reconsideration. *Journal of the Society for Psychical Research* 58: 129-152.

Wiseman, Richard and Morris, Robert L. 1995. *Guidelines for Testing Psychic Claimants*.New York: Prometheus Books.

Wynne, Catherine. 2006. Arthur Conan Doyle's domestic desires: mesmerism, mediumship and *Femmes Fatales*: 223-243. In *Victorian Literary Mesmerism*.Eds. Willis, Martin and Wynne, Catherine. Amsterdam: Rodopi.

X, Miss. 1889. Recent experiments in crystal vision. *Proceedings of the Society for Psychical Research* 5: 486-521.

X, Miss. 1895. A provisional account of an enquiry into second sight in the Highlands. *Journal of the Society for Psychical Research* 7: 2-5.

X, Miss. 1897. A passing note on a haunted house. *Journal of the Society for Psychical Research* 8: 20-25.

Yeazell, Ruth Bernard. 1997. *The Death and Letters of Alice James*. Boston: Exact Change.

Young, Robert M. 1985. *Darwin's Metaphor. Nature's place in Victorian culture*. Cambridge: Cambridge University Press.

Zeldin, Theodore. 1977. *France 1848-1945 Vol. II*. Oxford: Clarendon Press.

Zeepvat, Charlotte. 1998. *Prince Leopold. The Untold Story of Queen Victoria's Youngest Son*. Stroud: Sutton Publishing.

Ziman, John. 2000/2002. *Real Science. What it is, and what it means*. Cambridge: Cambridge University Press.

Zöllner, Johann. 1882. Trans. Massey, C.C. *Transcendental Physics*. London: W.H. Harrison.

Zorab, G. 1976. Parapsychological developments in the Netherlands. *European Journal of Parapsychology* 1: 57-82.

Index